Gateway to American Government

The Bridge to Success on Florida's EOC Civics Test

Revised Color Edition

Lea Ann Burnside Commemorative Edition

Mark Jarrett, Ph.D. ▪ **Robert Yahng, J.D.**

With illustrations by Jerianne Van Dijk

Florida Transformative Education

Copyright © 2020 by Florida Transformative Education

All rights reserved. Copying or projecting this book without permission of the publisher is a violation of federal copyright law. An exception is granted to teachers who wish to project pages of this book if an entire class set of these books is present and in use by students at the time of such projection. All other unauthorized copying or projecting of this material will be prosecuted by the publisher to the fullest extent permitted by law. For permission requests, write to the publisher, addressed "Attention: Permissions Coordinator," at the address below.

Florida Transformative Education
10 Folin Lane
Lafayette, CA 94549
Tel: (925) 906-9742 Fax: (925) 939-6557   www.floridasocialstudies.com

Florida Transformative Education and its logo are registered trademarks.

Printed in the United States of America

Our books are printed on long-lasting acid-free paper. When it is available, we choose paper that has been manufactured by environmentally responsible processes. These may include using trees grown in sustainable forests, incorporating recycled paper, minimizing chlorine in bleaching, or recycling the energy produced at the paper mill.

ISBN 978-0-9976835-5-4

Revised Color Edition

25 24 23 22 21 20   10 9 8 7 6 5 4 3 2 1

About the Authors

Mark Jarrett studied at Columbia University (B.A.), the London School of Economics (M.A. in international history), Stanford University (Ph.D. in history), and the University of California at Berkeley, where he received a law degree with honors (Order of the Coif). He was an editor of the school's law review and received the American Jurisprudence Award for Comparative Legal History. He studied constitutional law with Robert Post, past dean of the Yale Law School. Mark has taught at Hofstra University, at the Mander Portman School in London, and in the New York City Public Schools. He has served as a test writer for the New York State Board of Regents, and practiced law at Baker & McKenzie, the world's largest law firm. He is the co-author of more than 30 test preparation books and textbooks. James Sheehan, past President of the American Historical Association, describes Mark's recent book, *The Congress of Vienna and its Legacy* (London: I.B. Tauris, 2013), as "beautifully written" and providing "a fine sense of political structures without losing the human element," while Robert Jervis, past President of the American Political Science Association, calls his book a "model treatment." It was a *Choice* "Outstanding Title" for 2014.

Robert Yahng has taught Honors U.S. Government and Honors Micro and Macroeconomics at Salesian High School in Richmond, California, for the past 16 years. He has been the school's Chairman of the Board of Directors from 2003 to 2013. Robert earned a B.A. in History at Berea College in Kentucky, the South's first interracial college, where his grandfather, father and mother were professors. He received his Juris Doctor degree from the University of Kentucky School of Law. Robert was a partner in the law firm of Baker & McKenzie for 21 years. He was the Managing Partner of its San Francisco and Palo Alto offices in the 1990's, and also founded its Taipei office. From 1999 to 2002, he served as a Public Governor on the Board of Governors of the Pacific Stock Exchange. He has been a member of the Board of Trustees of Berea College since 2003, of which he is currently Chairman. From 1997 to 2014, he was the Chairman of American Bridge Company, which constructed the Bob Graham Sunshine Skyway Bridge, and the new Bay Bridge in San Francisco, as well as many other national landmarks, including the Chrysler Building in New York City. From 1967 to 1972, Robert served in the USAF and was honorably discharged with the rank of captain.

The Cover

The cover shows the Arlington Memorial Bridge, Washington Monument, and Lincoln Memorial in Washington, D.C.

Contents

	Preface	i
Chapter 1	The Origins of American Government	1
Chapter 2	Americans Declare Their Independence	25
Chapter 3	The Story of Our Constitution	55
Chapter 4	A Quick Tour of the Constitution	77
Chapter 5	Congress: Our Legislative Branch	105
Chapter 6	The Presidency: Our Executive Branch	131
Chapter 7	The Federal Courts: Our Judicial Branch	149
Chapter 8	The Rule of Law	167
Chapter 9	The Bill of Rights and Later Amendments	199
Chapter 10	"May It Please the Court": The Supreme Court in Action	225
Chapter 11	Federalism: Federal, State and Local Governments Acting Together	263
Chapter 12	The Obligations, Responsibilities and Rights of Citizens	291
Chapter 13	Political Parties and Elections	319
Chapter 14	Interest Groups and the Media	345
Chapter 15	Public Policy	373
Chapter 16	Types of Governments	389
Chapter 17	American Foreign Policy	421
Chapter 18	A Practice End-of-Course Assessment in Civics	465
	The U.S Constitution and the Bill of Rights	479
	Index	488

Dedication

This printing of *Gateway to American Government Revised Color Edition* is dedicated to the memory of a very special educator: Mrs. Lea Ann Burnside of LaBelle Middle School in Hendry County, in south central Florida. A graduate of LaBelle High School herself, Lea started teaching in 1999. She was instrumental in the adoption of our book by her district, and she gave us essential advice when we revised it. Lea was always willing to give of her time in order to help others. She spent hours in telephone conversations with us discussing such matters as whether we should include the Electoral College in this revised edition, even though the Electoral College does not appear in the Content Focus terms. Lea also helped organize a popular Facebook group for civics teachers across the state, "FL Civics Teachers." Her life was tragically cut short when she was just 52 years old.

One of her middle school students remembers her best: "Hi, my name is Andrea. I'm one of Mrs. Burnside students. To be honest, I loved her as if she were my Mom. I cared for her. I loved her as a friend. She was like a Mom to me. She always had time to listen to my stories. In fact, she gave me an award and the day that she gave it to me I cried because I loved her as a teacher." Lea combined intelligence, an understanding of her students, a dedication to hard work, and a love for her students and community in equal measure. She is greatly missed.

Acknowledgments

The authors wish to thank the following individuals for their generous help and advice:

Ms. Jackie Viana, District Social Studies Supervisor of Miami-Dade County Public Schools and 2010 American Civic Education Teacher Award (ACETA) Teacher of the Year, for her encouragement, suggestions and her devotion to the needs of the teachers and students of her district. In addition we wish to thank Ms. Annette Boyd Pitts of the Florida Law Related Education Association, Inc.; Dr. Benjamin Ginsberg, David Bernstein Professor of Political Science and Chair of the Center for Advanced Governmental Studies at Johns Hopkins University; Dr. Alison McLafferty, formerly of the History Department of the University of California at Berkeley; Dr. Lynne W. Holt, Policy Analyst at the University of Florida, Warrington College of Business Administration; Ms. Cherie Arnette, Social Studies Specialist for the Escambia County School District; Mr. Michael DiPierro, formerly at Broward County Public Schools and currently Social Studies Education Specialist at the Florida Department of Education; Dr. Mark Pearcy, formerly at Manatee School District and now teaching Social Studies methods at Rider University in Pennsylvania; Ms. Mary Smith, former Social Studies coordinator for the Cypress-Fairbanks Independent School District, the third largest public school district in Texas; and Ms. Teri Lusk, Middle School Social Studies Teacher at Stanley Middle School in Lafayette, California, for their suggestions, recommendations and criticisms of sections of this book. The authors would also like to thank Mr. Alex Jarrett, Ms. Julia Jarrett, Ms. Małgorzata Jarrett, Ms. Monica de la Rosa, and Ms. Liz Wong for a multitude of services in the preparation of this book, from finding images and typing to writing initial drafts of some study cards. Thank you also to artist Jerianne Van Dijk for her wonderful illustrations. Finally, we would like to thank Jonathan Peck and Joan Keyes of Dovetail Publishing Services for their creativity in the design and layout of this book.

This is not to be taken as an endorsement of this product by any of the individuals or their organizations listed above. In fact, in some cases we were not able to follow all of their recommendations. Any remaining errors are therefore our own. Nevetheless we have endeavored to remain as doggedly close as possible to the content requirements of the Item Specifications guide for Florida's Middle School EOC Test in Civics. Everything mentioned in that guide is, we truly believe, clearly and comprehensively explained in this book. We hope you enjoy reading and using this book as much as we enjoyed writing it.

Preface

"We Want You!" America's Future and Your Citizenship Skills

Welcome to civics! Civics is the study of government and citizenship.

Why is it so important for you to study civics?

The answer lies in the fact that you are either an American citizen or may someday become one. For the future prosperity and success of our nation, we depend on you to perform your obligations and responsibilities as a citizen—to vote, to obey laws, to pay taxes, and to serve on a jury if summoned. Perhaps you may even run for political office or serve in the armed forces in our nation's defense. Look around your classroom. Maybe you or one of your classmates will be a future mayor, district court judge, U.S. Senator, or even President of the United States.

You will also want to receive the rights and benefits of citizenship, including freedom of speech, freedom of religion, security of property, the right to expect others to follow the law, and the right to help choose our leaders and to shape our nation's policies.

All this lies within your grasp! That is because the United States has a democratic government and we live under the rule of law.

In fact, the United States was the first large nation in modern history to adopt the democratic system of government. In a democratic government, people are the ultimate source of governmental power. Instead of being ruled by all-powerful kings or dictators, we elect our leaders to fixed terms in office. We give them only limited powers, carefully defined in our Constitution and other laws.

What is Government?

Much of this book describes the American system of government. You may be wondering: what, exactly, is government?

Government is the organization that makes up rules for the community, settles disputes, and protects the community from outsiders. It not only makes these rules, but also has the power to enforce them.

The word *govern* comes from a Greek word, *kubernan*, which means to steer a ship. Just as sailors steer a ship, our government steers our society in the right direction.

What is Citizenship?

Not everyone living in the United States can participate in government by voting, holding political office or serving on juries. To fully participate in our democratic system of government, one must be an American citizen. A **citizen** is a legally recognized member of a community.

The ancient Greeks were the first to develop the concept of citizenship, just as they were the first to develop the system of democracy. In fact, the two concepts often go hand in hand. However, for Greeks the concept of citizenship was very limited. It did not include foreigners, women, children or slaves.

The ancient Romans expanded the concept of citizenship into a legal category. Citizens of the Roman Empire were entitled to certain rights. The Romans strengthened their empire by granting the rights and benefits of Roman citizenship to conquered peoples who promised to obey their laws. In fact, our word "citizen" comes from *civis*, the ancient Roman word for citizen, and from *civitas*, the Roman word for city. A Roman citizen was, in effect, a member of the imperial city of Rome.

Today, the world is divided into almost 200 independent countries. Each country has its own rules for citizenship. Citizenship—legal recognition of being the member of a country—gives a person the right to live in that country and to carry its passport when traveling to other countries.

In the United States, citizens are entitled to special rights but also bear special obligations and responsibilities. Our system of democratic government relies on the active participation of its citizens to succeed. As you know, American citizens are expected to vote, to obey laws, to pay taxes, and to serve on juries. Young men must also register for possible future military service. Americans also have the right to express their opinions, to complain to their government leaders, and to run for public office.

To fulfill their obligations and responsibilities, and to enjoy their rights, our citizens should be informed, be active, and respect the rights of others. Voting becomes a meaningless exercise if we don't know the major issues, listen to the chief arguments on each side, check what we are told against known facts, and come to our own conclusions. Active participation in the political process is just as important as being informed. Democratic government would quickly collapse if everyone left volunteer efforts, the support of candidates, and running for public office to someone else.

The lessons of history teach us, again and again, that terrible things can happen to a society when its citizens are uninformed, misinformed, or not actively engaged in their government.

So, as you read this book, keep this message in mind: we are all depending on **you**!

How Does One Become an American Citizen?

Everyone born in the United States, or born from American parents (even when abroad), is automatically an American citizen. This is known as **birthright citizenship**.

Not everyone living in the United States today, however, is a citizen. Some people are visitors or **lawful permanent residents** (*foreign nationals who are authorized to live and work in the United States permanently*).

A foreign national can become an American citizen by being "**naturalized**." To be naturalized, a person must: (1) be at least 18 years old, (2) be a lawful permanent resident, and (3) have lived in the United States for five years before applying. Applicants must also (4) be of "good character," (5) have a working knowledge of English, and (6) pass a brief test on American history and government. Finally, the applicant must (7) swear an oath of loyalty to the United States. You will learn more about the naturalization process later in this book.

What You Will Learn in this Book

Gateway to American Government explains everything you need to know to become an informed and active citizen.

This book begins by examining the roots of our system of democratic government in England and colonial times. You will learn how English traditions and new ideas in Europe in the 17th and 18th centuries led people to develop more democratic forms of government. The English colonies, far from European rulers, provided fertile ground for these new ideas to take shape.

Then you will learn about the American Revolution, the Declaration of Independence, and the U.S. Constitution. American colonists first struggled with the question of whether to become independent. Afterwards, they had the problem of designing a new system of government that would be effective but that would still respect individual rights. To make sure our national government was strong enough but not oppressive, the authors of the U.S. Constitution introduced the separation of powers, checks and balances, limited powers and federalism. The result was the system of government we still have today—with its separate legislative, executive and judicial branches, and its division of power between our federal (*national*) government and the state governments.

After learning how our system of government came into being, you will then explore how it works today. First, you will look at Congress, our national law-making body. Who sits in Congress? How are its members selected? How is Congress organized? How does it make our laws? Next, you will look at the Presidency. How is the President of the United States elected? What are the President's powers under the Constitution? What roles does the President play today?

After that, you will consider the judicial branch—the U.S. Supreme Court and other federal courts. You will learn how the Supreme Court established its power of "judicial review"—the ability to declare a state or federal law "unconstitutional" if the Court determines it conflicts with the U.S. Constitution. You will also learn what laws are, what courts do, and the differences between state and federal laws, civil and criminal laws, and statutory and common law (*laws passed by legislatures and those based on prior court decisions*).

Next, you will look at the Bill of Rights and later amendments to the U.S. Constitution that expanded the rights of individuals. You will also review several important Supreme Court decisions that interpreted and expanded individual rights.

From here, you will move to state governments—especially the government of Florida—and examine the complex relationship between our federal and state governments known as "federalism."

After this, you will look at the nature of citizenship, and how citizens participate in politics and government to determine public policy—the decisions that our government actually makes. You will review what citizenship is and how foreign nationals can become American citizens. You will also look more closely at the obligations, responsibilities and rights of citizenship. Then you will see how citizens can participate in political decision-making by joining political parties, by participating in election campaigns, and by voting in elections. You will also see how public opinion is shaped by political advertisements, paid lobbyists and the "media"—newspapers, magazines, television, radio and the Internet. And you will see how people can influence local decision-making.

Finally, you will look at the different types of governments around the world, and consider how the United States relates to the rest of the international community through its foreign policy.

Through the study of civics, you will learn how government affects your life now and in the future, and how you can influence government through the exercise of informed, active and responsible citizenship.

Florida's Civics End-Of-Course Assessment

This year you will be studying civics. You will also be taking Florida's Civics End-of-Course Assessment. The assessment will have 52 to 56 multiple-choice questions, testing your knowledge of 40 Benchmarks.

Florida's 40 Civics Benchmarks

SS.7.C.1.1 Recognize how Enlightenment ideas including Montesquieu's view of separation of powers and John Locke's theories related to natural law and how Locke's social contract influenced the Founding Fathers.

SS.7.C.1.2 Trace the impact that the Magna Carta, English Bill of Rights, Mayflower Compact, and Thomas Paine's *Common Sense* had on colonists' views of government.

SS.7.C.1.3 Describe how English policies and responses to colonial concerns led to the writing of the Declaration of Independence.

SS.7.C.1.4 Analyze the ideas (natural rights, role of the government) and complaints set forth in the Declaration of Independence.

SS.7.C.1.5 Identify how the weaknesses of the Articles of Confederation led to the writing of the Constitution.

SS.7.C.1.6 Interpret the intentions of the Preamble of the Constitution.

SS.7.C.1.7 Describe how the Constitution limits the powers of government through separation of powers and checks and balances.

SS.7.C.1.8 Explain the viewpoints of the Federalists and the Anti-Federalists regarding the ratification of the Constitution and inclusion of a bill of rights.

SS.7.C.1.9 Define the rule of law and recognize its influence on the development of the American legal, political, and governmental systems.

SS.7.C.2.1 Define the term "citizen," and identify legal means of becoming a U.S. citizen.

SS.7.C.2.2 Evaluate the obligations citizens have to obey laws, pay taxes, defend the nation, and serve on juries.

SS.7.C.2.3 Experience the responsibilities of citizens at the local, state, or federal levels.

SS.7.C.2.4 Evaluate rights contained in the Bill of Rights and other amendments to the Constitution.

SS.7.C.2.5 Distinguish how the Constitution safeguards and limits individual rights.

SS.7.C.2.6 Simulate the trial process and the role of juries in the administration of justice.

SS.7.C.2.7 Conduct a mock election to demonstrate the voting process and its impact on a school, community, or local level.

SS.7.C.2.8 Identify America's current political parties, and illustrate their ideas about government.

SS.7.C.2.9 Evaluate candidates for political office by analyzing their qualifications, experience, issue-based platforms, debates, and political ads.

SS.7.C.2.10 Examine the impact of media, individuals, and interest groups on monitoring and influencing government.

SS.7.C.2.11 Analyze media and political communications (bias, symbolism, propaganda).

SS.7.C.2.12 Develop a plan to resolve a state or local problem by researching public policy alternatives, identifying appropriate government agencies to address the issue, and determining a course of action.

SS.7.C.2.13 Examine multiple perspectives on public and current issues.

SS.7.C.2.14 Conduct a service project to further the public good.

SS.7.C.3.1 Compare different forms of government (direct democracy, representative democracy, socialism, communism, monarchy, oligarchy, autocracy).

SS.7.C.3.2 Compare parliamentary, federal, confederal, and unitary systems of government.

SS.7.C.3.3 Illustrate the structure and function (three branches of government established in Articles I, II, and III with corresponding powers) of government in the United States as established in the Constitution.

SS.7.C.3.4 Identify the relationship and division of powers between the federal government and state governments.

SS.7.C.3.5 Explain the constitutional amendment process.

SS.7.C.3.6 Evaluate constitutional rights and their impact on individuals and society.

SS.7.C.3.7 Analyze the impact of the 13th, 14th, 15th, 19th, 24th, and 26th amendments on participation of minority groups in the American political process.

SS.7.C.3.8 Analyze the structure, functions, and processes of the legislative, executive, and judicial branches.

SS.7.C.3.9 Illustrate the lawmaking process at the local, state, and federal levels.

SS.7.C.3.10 Identify sources and types (civil, criminal, constitutional, military) of law.

SS.7.C.3.11 Diagram the levels, functions, and powers of courts at the state and federal levels.

SS.7.C.3.12 Analyze the significance and outcomes of landmark Supreme Court cases including, but not limited to, *Marbury v. Madison, Plessy v. Ferguson, Brown v. Board of Education, Gideon v. Wainwright, Miranda v. Arizona, In re Gault, Tinker v. Des Moines, Hazelwood v. Kuhlmeier, United States v. Nixon,* and *Bush v. Gore.*

SS.7.C.3.13 Compare the constitutions of the United States and Florida.

SS.7.C.3.14 Differentiate between local, state, and federal governments' obligations and services.

SS.7.C.4.1 Differentiate concepts related to U.S. domestic and foreign policy.

SS.7.C.4.2 Recognize government and citizen participation in international organizations.

SS.7.C.4.3 Describe examples of how the United States has dealt with international conflicts.

The questions on the Civics End-of-Course Assessment will be distributed as follows:

Theme	Benchmarks	Chapters in this Book	Percentage
Origins and Purposes of Law and Government	SS.7.C.1.1–1.9; SS.7.C.3.10.	Chapters 1–4 and 8.	25%
Roles, Rights and Responsibilities of Citizens	SS.7.C.2.1–2.2, 2.4–2.5; SS.7.C.3.6–3.7, 3.12.	Introduction and Chapters 9–10 and 12.	25%
Government Policies and Political Processes	SS.7.C.2.8–2.13; SS.7.C.4.1–4.3.	Chapters 13–15 and 17.	25%
Organization and Function of Government	SS.7.C. 3.1–3.5, 3.8, 3.11, 3.13–3.14.	Chapters 4–7, 11 and 16.	25%

This book can help you to learn more about American government and citizenship. It can also help you to perform your very best on the End-of-Course Assessment. *Gateway to American Government* can be used either by itself or alongside another textbook. It contains everything you need to learn about American government and citizenship to do well on the test.

Special Features of *Gateway to American Government*

▶ We usually learn best when we have a general idea of what we are about to learn in advance. Every chapter in this book begins with information that tells you what the chapter is about. First, there is the **title** of the chapter, which describes its topic. This is followed by a **list of Florida Social Studies Standards** that are covered in the chapter. These cover all of the Benchmarks listed above.

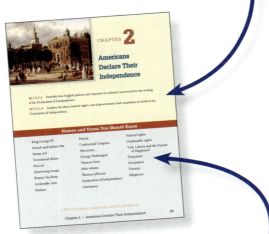

▶ At the bottom of the first page of each chapter is a list of **Names and Terms You Should Know.** You can use this list to guide your way through the chapter. Most of these terms are either listed in the Benchmarks or in the "Item Specifications" guide provided to those teachers who are writing your test.

▶ This is followed by **Florida "Keys" to Learning**. No, these aren't the real Florida Keys at the south-

ern end of the state! They are the keys to what you should know for the test. This section provides a summary of the most important ideas and facts, forming the backbone to the chapter. You should look at these before you read the chapter for an overview. Once you have finished the chapter, you can read through the "Keys" again as a form of review. Finally, you may want to review all 17 **Florida "Keys" to Learning** sections (one for each chapter) just before you take the Civics End-of-Course Assessment.

▶ The **"Keys"** are followed by the main text of the chapter. Each chapter is divided into sections. The text is accompanied by illustrations, diagrams, graphs and maps. Information in each chapter is organized around core concepts to make it easier to learn.

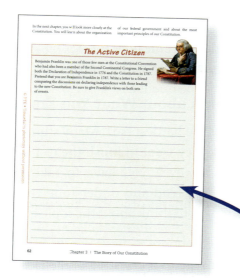

▶ Throughout the text, you will find **The Active Citizen**. In these activities, you may be asked to conduct research, to interpret a historical document, to role-play, or to participate in government and politics.

▶ A special **Enrichment** icon indicates information that will not be on the EOC Test but that helps in understanding civics. Many of these enrichment sections have a blue background.

▶ At the end of each chapter, there are several additional features to reinforce your understanding, and check your knowledge. First, there is a series of **Review Cards**. These cards summarize the most important information in the chapter, which may appear on Florida's End-of-Course Assessment. You can use these **Review Cards** in a variety of ways. You might cover part of a **Review Card** and check if you can recall the information you have covered. You might make your own pictures to illustrate a **Review Card** or add further information. You can also use **Review Cards** to test your friends, or to make sample test questions. As you read through the book, you can assemble your own personal collection of **Review Cards**. Scramble them up to see if you can recall their contents when they are not in order.

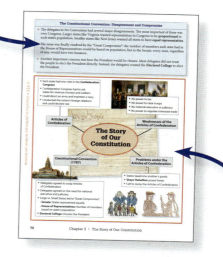

▶ The **Review Cards** are followed by a **Concept Map**. This map provides an overview showing how all the developments in the chapter are related.

▶ Each content chapter concludes with **What Do You Know?** This is a series of practice multiple-choice questions, similar in format to the assessment items on Florida's End-of-Course Assessment.

The last chapter of the book provides **a final practice test** covering all of the Benchmarks in the book. The questions on this test follow the same test specifications and the same distribution as the actual Florida Civics End-of-Course Assessment. By taking this test and reviewing any errors you make, you can be sure you have prepared your very best for the test!

Preface | "We Want You!": America's Future and Your Citizenship Skills

There are many ways to use this book. You may want to use it as your main resource. It covers everything you need to know for the test. Or you may wish to use it with another textbook. After you complete each unit in your other book, you can review what you have learned by reading related chapters in *Gateway to American Government*.

You may also want to use this book for a final review in the weeks just before the test. With its many special learning features, reading through this book should be a great way for you to recall everything you have studied to prepare for the test.

How to Answer a Multiple-Choice Question

Besides knowing what is being tested, you also have to be a good test-taker to do your best on this or any test. Here are three steps we recommend for answering multiple-choice questions on Florida's Civics End-of-Course Assessment. These same steps can be used, in fact, to answer multiple-choice questions on almost any test:

1. Understand the Question

Make sure you read the question carefully. Take special care to examine any graph, picture, document or other information that appears as part of the question itself.

Make sure you understand what the question asks for. Questions on the Civics End-of-Course Assessment will most likely ask you one of the following:

- to identify the **cause** of something: *what made it happen?*
- to identify the **effect** or **impact** of something: *how did it change things?*
- to **explain** or **describe** an event or development: *how did it happen? what is it like?*
- to **identify** or **define** something: *what is it?*
- to **compare** two or more things: *what are their* **similarities** *and* **differences?**
- to **sequence** events: *in what order did they occur? which was first or last?*
- to **interpret** a document, an illustration, a cartoon, a map, a table, or a graph
- to make a **generalization** or to draw a **conclusion**

- to provide an **example** of something: *which best illustrates this principle?*
- to make a **prediction**: *what is most likely to happen next?*

2. Think about What You Know

Here comes the hardest part. Many students wish to rush ahead: they want to finish the test early. To do your best, however, you have to take your time. Once you have read and understood the question, take a moment to think about the topic it asks about.

For example, suppose a question asks you how colonial concerns led to the writing of the Declaration of Independence. You should think about what you can remember about the causes of the American Revolution and how those events led the colonists to declare independence. You might recall the Stamp Act, "taxation without representation," the Boston Tea Party, the Intolerable Acts, the violence at Lexington and Concord, and the meeting of the Second Continental Congress. You might also remember how the members of the Continental Congress debated whether to seek independence, and how Thomas Jefferson wrote the first draft of the Declaration.

Then you might try to answer the question in your mind *without looking at the answer choices*.

3. Answer the Question

Now you are actually ready to answer the question. Look carefully again at the question itself. Then look at all four answer choices. Eliminate any answer choices that are obviously wrong or irrelevant (*not related to the question or its topic*). Then choose the *best* of the remaining answer choices, based on your knowledge and understanding.

If you have extra time after you have finished the test, be sure to check your work again to eliminate any careless mistakes.

Special Types of Questions

Many questions on Florida's End-of-Course Assessment will ask about a "graphic" that is a part of the question. It is important for you to be able to interpret these different types of graphics, including maps, graphs, charts, tables, political cartoons, illustrations, photographs, and timelines. Each of these is simply another way of presenting or displaying information.

Questions may ask what the graphic shows, or they may ask you to make an inference or draw a conclusion about the graphic. You might also be asked to identify the causes or effects of a situation or event described by the picture, timeline, photograph or other graphic. Often you will have to apply your knowledge of civics to answer the question.

The rest of this chapter looks at six of the most important types of graphics that may appear on the test.

Maps

A map shows geographical information. It may show the boundaries between states, the locations of cities, or election districts. A *key* or *legend* will often explain any symbols on the map. Maps may also have a *scale* to show what their dimensions represent in real life, and a *compass* (or *direction indicator*).

- What does this map show?
- Based on the map, how many states gave their electoral votes to Donald Trump in the 2016 presidential election?
- Based on the map, how many electoral votes did Florida have in the 2016 election?
- What conclusions can you draw from this map?

Graphs

Graphs are used to display quantitative information. A *bar graph* has bars representing different amounts. Often it is used to compare things, such as the number of Representatives different states have in the House of Representatives, or the number of federal judges.

- Based on the graph, which group of federal judges is the largest? Why?

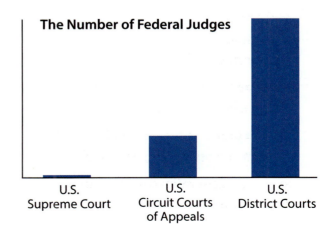

Line graphs show how the number or size of something has changed over time. For example, a line graph might show the number of federal employees from 1865 to today. Or it could show annual federal government revenues from 1900 to 2000. To interpret a line graph, be sure to understand both the "Y-axis" on its left side and the "X-axis" on its bottom. Usually the Y-axis is a "yard stick," providing the numbers for measuring, while the X-axis indicates the passage of time.

▶ Based on the graph, which five-year period saw the least increase in salary for a U.S. District Court Judge?

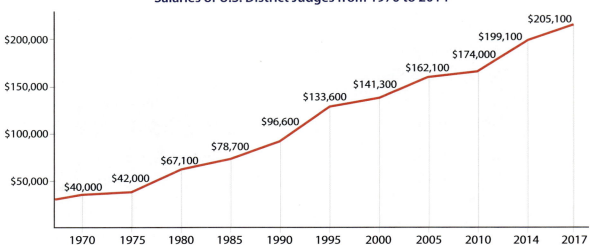

Charts and Tables

Charts and tables often present information in rows and columns. This format makes it easy to locate particular facts or numbers. The top row usually provides headings, telling the reader what each column stands for. The left column lists the individual items the chart or table describes.

Year	Florida Circuit Court Judge Salary	U.S. District Court Judge Salary
2001	$130,000	$145,100
2002	$133,250	$150,000
2003	$134,650	$154,700
2004	$134,650	$158,100
2005	$139,497	$162,100
2006	$145,080	$165,200
2007	$146,080	$165,200
2008	$145,080	$169,300
2009	$142,178	$174,000
2010	$142,178	$174,000

Sources: Office of State Courts Administrator and Administrative Office of the U.S. Courts

▶ Which judicial officer was more highly paid in 2010: a U.S. District Court Judge or a Florida Circuit Court Judge?

▶ In which years was the difference in salary between federal and Florida trial judges the greatest? The least?

▶ Have salaries for judges always increased with the passage of time? Explain your answer.

▶ What conclusions can you draw from this table?

Political Cartoons

A political cartoon is a drawing by an artist commenting on current affairs, social conditions or events. Political cartoons often challenge authority or expose corruption. Cartoonists may use satire, exaggerated features, or comparisons to make their point.

When looking at a political cartoon, be sure to understand what it shows. What is the time period of the cartoon? Who is represented? What are the

xiv Preface | "We Want You!": America's Future and Your Citizenship Skills people in the cartoon doing? Are there any special symbols or references? Think about the key issues of the time period if it is a political cartoon from the past. Finally, what is the cartoonist's message?

This cartoon makes a statement about what politicians were expecting from Wall Street and corporate interests ("trust interests") in 1904. Thomas Taggart, on the left, was born in Ireland but immigrated to the United States as a young boy. He was Chairman of the Democratic National Committee from 1904 to 1908. George B. Cortelyou, on the right, was born in New York City. He was with President McKinley when the latter was shot in 1901. He was a close friend of President Theodore Roosevelt's. He was Secretary of Commerce as well as Chairman of the Republican National Committee in 1904, when this cartoon was made.

▶ Describe what the cartoon shows.
▶ Which features are exaggerated or distorted in this cartoon?
▶ What is the cartoonist's view of the relationship between the two major political parties and the corporations on Wall Street?
▶ Explain your interpretation using evidence from the cartoon.

Photographs and Illustrations

A photograph or an artist's illustration (a drawing or painting) can show us what a place is like, how a person looks, or what happened at an event. To interpret a photograph or illustration, you have to be a good detective. What details does the picture show? Consider the faces and clothing of any people in the photograph or picture. Also, consider the setting or background. What can you learn from it?

Think of the photograph or illustration as a piece of evidence. A photograph might be used, for example, to show the activities of a congressional committee. From the photograph, you can see where the committee meets, how many members are on the committee, and how energetic or tired the members seem. You can also see the members' ages, their gender, and their cultural diversity. You can further get a sense of the attitudes and relationships between members of the committee and the public. Questions on a photograph or illustration may ask you what the picture shows or to draw conclusions from it. The photograph above is from a special Senate Committee investigating a break-in into Democratic headquarters at the Watergate hotel and office complex in June 1972. The committee hearings took place almost a year later and were nationally televised.

▶ Based on the photograph, what was the atmosphere during the committee hearings?
▶ How diverse was the committee's membership? Would you expect to see greater diversity today? Explain your answer.
▶ What conclusions can you draw from this photograph?

Preface | "We Want You!": America's Future and Your Citizenship Skills

Timelines

A timeline shows a series of events arranged along a line in the order, or sequence, in which they occurred. Usually, the left side of the timeline marks the beginning of the time period it shows, and the right side marks the end. As dates move from left to right, they move closer to the present. A timeline usually shows a series of related events. It is useful because we can see exactly when they occurred and how they relate to each other. Questions on timelines may ask about how the events on the timeline are related, or they may ask you to make an inference or draw a conclusion about the events that are shown.

▶ What other events might be placed on this timeline?

▶ What were some of the consequences of the events shown on the timeline?

▶ Make your own timeline showing how you spent today.

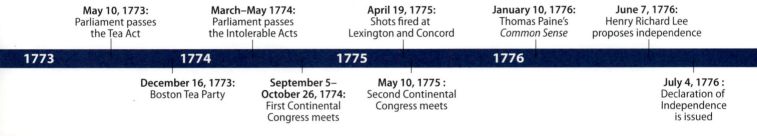

Question Complexity

Florida's Civics End-of-Course Assessment has questions with different levels of complexity. Some questions will test your ability to recall information. They may simply ask you to recognize the definition of a concept like democracy or the separation of powers.

Other questions will require you to go through one or more steps to answer the question. These questions test your thinking skills as well as your knowledge of civics. You might be asked to explain an issue, to determine the relationship between an event and a concept, to identify the cause or effect of something, or to identify why something is important. For example, you could be asked to identify how ideas in the Declaration of Independence influenced the Constitution.

The most complex questions will require you to reason through a series of multiple steps to reach an answer. These questions may ask you to:

▶ analyze similarities and differences
▶ solve or predict the outcome of a problem
▶ draw conclusions from historical information
▶ provide a justification (*reason*) for a policy or action
▶ predict the long-term result or change from something
▶ analyze how changes have influenced people or institutions (you might, for example, be asked to explain how our modern political system has been affected by an event or change)
▶ take a principle or concept from a historical excerpt in the question, and apply that same principle or concept to something else, such as to our system of government today.

To answer these more challenging questions, follow the same three steps you learned earlier in this preface. *Understand the Question:* Be sure to read any primary sources or other data in the question carefully. Also make sure you understand what the question is asking for. *Think about What You Know:* Think about what you can recall about the topic of the question. If the question asks for connections to our modern political system, be sure to think about the world today. Try to draw connections in your mind. *Answer the Question:* Select the best answer choice.

CHAPTER 1

The Origins of American Government

SS.7.C.1.1 Recognize how Enlightenment ideas including Montesquieu's view of separation of powers and John Locke's theories related to natural law, and how Locke's social contract influenced the Founding Fathers. (See also Chapters 2 and 4.)

SS.7.C.1.2 Trace the impact that the Magna Carta, English Bill of Rights, Mayflower Compact and Thomas Paine's *Common Sense* had on colonists' views of government. (See also Chapters 2, 3, and 4.)

> Every chapter of this book has a section called "Names and Terms You Should Know." In these sections, circle or highlight any names or terms that are unfamiliar to you.

Names and Terms You Should Know

Enlightenment	Separation of powers	Mayflower Compact
Enlightenment ideas	Legislative power	Thomas Paine
John Locke	Executive power	*Common Sense*
Social contract	Judicial power	Limited monarchy
Government	Magna Carta	Self-government
Natural law	Trial by jury	Individual rights
Montesquieu	English Bill of Rights	Founding Fathers

© FTE • Unlawful to photocopy without permission

Florida "Keys" to Learning

1. The Enlightenment was a movement of ideas that took place in Europe and America in the late 17th and 18th centuries. European thinkers used science to better understand the world. They also tried to apply scientific thinking to human society and relations.

2. John Locke believed in natural law—that there were rules, or "laws," in nature. He believed that one of these laws was that all people should enjoy the basic rights of life, liberty, and property. Locke further wrote that people entered into a social contract, or agreement, with one another when they formed a community. As part of this social contract, members of the community agreed to obey their ruler. The ruler, in turn, promised to protect the individual rights of his subjects. If a ruler broke his promises, Locke argued, the people had the right to rebel and overthrow him.

3. A French nobleman, Baron de Montesquieu, felt that societies work best when the powers of government are divided among separate legislative, executive, and judicial branches. The legislative branch has the power to make laws. The executive branch has the power to carry out or enforce the laws. Finally, the judicial branch has the power to interpret how the laws are applied to specific cases. Montesquieu's ideas had a great influence on the American colonists.

4. The colonists who founded the United States also looked to English traditions for their ideas on government.

5. Centuries earlier, King John of England had been forced by his barons to sign Magna Carta in 1215. The barons were the leading nobles. In this Great Charter, King John promised that no free man could be imprisoned or have his property taken away except after a trial by jury by his peers (*social equals*), following the laws of the land. King John also promised not to raise new taxes without the consent of his barons. England became a limited monarchy—one in which the ruler's rights were limited by law.

6. In 1620, the Pilgrims signed the Mayflower Compact. They agreed to create their own government for their colony and to obey its rules. This was the birth of self-government in the colonies—the idea that people could, to some extent, govern themselves.

7. Later English kings did not always respect their subjects' rights. In the 17th century, the king and Parliament entered into a series of conflicts. In 1688, King James II was overthrown in the Glorious Revolution. England's new rulers promised to respect their subjects' rights in the English Bill of Rights in 1689. They promised that members of Parliament would enjoy freedom of speech, that no armies would be raised in peacetime or taxes collected without the approval of Parliament, that citizens could petition (*make written requests*) the government and bear arms, and that no excessive (*too much*) bail would be demanded or cruel and unusual punishments imposed.

8. In the 1770s, American colonists came into conflict with the British government. Early in 1776, Thomas Paine published *Common Sense*. In this pamphlet, Paine argued that it made no sense for the colonies to be governed by a distant island and that they should seek independence.

9. The principles of Magna Carta, the Mayflower Compact and the English Bill of Rights, as well as Paine's writings, greatly influenced America's "Founding Fathers."

To understand the American system of government today, we must actually travel back in time. We have to return to the colonial period, more than 200 years ago, when the thirteen colonies in North America were still ruled by England.

What was the Enlightenment?

In those days, the people of Europe and America were very impressed by the discoveries of science. For example, the Englishman Sir Isaac Newton had discovered the "laws" of gravity. With these laws, Newton was able to predict the speed at which a ball fell to the ground. He could also predict the movements of the planets in space.

People were amazed by these discoveries. European thinkers began to apply this same scientific approach in order to understand human society and make it better. They believed that there were **natural laws** that explained how people behaved, just as the laws of gravity could explain how objects moved. Some saw these laws as the work of God.

Because these thinkers brought the light of reason to everything they studied, their movement became known as the **Enlightenment.** Enlightened thinkers applied human reason to understand the world. They refused to blindly follow tradition, authority, or superstition. In their place, they proposed the use of reason to make the world a better place.

Sir Isaac Newton

John Locke and the Social Contract

One of the earliest Enlightenment thinkers was another Englishman, **John Locke**. Locke believed that we are all like blank sheets of paper at birth. Later experiences and education then shape each of us as a person. Differences develop from differences in our experiences and education, and not because one of us is better or nobler than another at birth.

Enlightened thinkers like Locke began to question social relationships. They questioned the special position that nobles and the Church held in most European countries at the time. (Nobles were landowners with special privileges.) These thinkers also questioned the power of kings. Most kings claimed to hold their power directly from God, but was this claim reasonable?

John Locke didn't think so. He rejected the idea that rulers receive their powers from God. Instead, **Locke said that rulers receive their powers from the people whom they govern. A group of people makes an agreement, known as the social contract**, to form a community. This community then makes an agreement with a ruler. The members of the community promise to obey the ruler. The ruler, in turn, promises to protect their **individual rights**. The whole purpose of this **social contract**, Locke wrote, was to protect these **individual rights**.

The ruler forms a **government**—a body that protects the community, provides laws and settles disputes between members.

Like most Enlightened thinkers, Locke believed in **natural law**. These were not laws passed by governments, but rules that all societies must follow, just as nature followed the laws of gravity. They were based on common sense, such as the belief that killing or stealing is wrong. These laws applied to all societies at all times. **Locke believed that natural law guaranteed each of us the right to life, liberty, and the use of our own property.** He saw these as natural rights, and believed that no government should be able to take them away.

John Locke

Chapter 1 | The Origins of American Government

If a king or government made a law that went against natural law, Locke said this law was unjust. Locke thought that people should not obey such unjust laws. If a ruler repeatedly went against natural law, then his subjects even had the right to overthrow him. This in fact happened at the very time that Locke was writing. King James II of England was very unpopular. He threatened many traditional rights. In 1688, leading members of the English Parliament overthrew him. The following year, Locke wrote a book to justify their actions. Locke explained that the government was established by a **social contract** between a ruler and his people. If a ruler, like King James II, repeatedly violated (*broke*) this contract, then the people had the right to rebel and overthrow him.

Divine Right Theory

Many kings claimed that their powers came from God. Therefore, their powers were unlimited.

Locke's Theory of Social Contract

> Locke claimed that rulers received their power from the people. The people therefore had the right to overthrow an unjust King.

The Active Citizen

Imagine you are an American colonist in 1689. You have just read some of Locke's writings. Write a short letter to a friend explaining why you agree or disagree with his views.

Your letter should have these parts:

(1) A greeting:

Dear _____ ,

(2) A statement of your point of view: I agree/disagree with Locke's views on the social contract.

Continues ▶

Chapter 1 | The Origins of American Government

(3) A short summary of Locke's views:

Locke says that rulers do not get their powers from God. Instead, their powers come from the people they rule. People promise to obey their ruler. The ruler, in turn, promises to protect and help his/her people. Locke calls this the "social contract." If the ruler breaks his/her promise, then the people have the right to change the ruler.

(4) A brief statement of why you agree or disagree with Locke:

I think Locke must be right/wrong because . . .

(5) a closing:

Your friend, _____

Baron de Montesquieu and the Separation of Powers

Baron de Montesquieu

Another Enlightenment thinker who wrote about government was a French nobleman, Charles de Secondat, **Baron de Montesquieu**. Montesquieu studied governments in several countries and drew comparisons. He thought, for example, that different systems of government worked better in different countries because of their size. Switzerland was so small it could be a democracy in which every citizen helped make decisions. Russia was so large that all power had to be placed in the hands of a single absolute ruler.

Montesquieu also came up with the idea of the **separation of powers**. He thought the government of England was especially successful because one body, the Parliament, made the laws. A second "branch" of government, the king, enforced those laws. A third "branch," the English courts, interpreted and applied the laws.

Montesquieu concluded that it was best to separate the powers of government into three parts:

▶ The **legislative branch** makes the laws.

▶ The **executive branch** executes (*carries out*) the laws.

▶ The **judicial branch** interprets the laws and rules on their application to specific cases. For example, a court may have to decide if a person did a crime. The court not only looks at the actions of the accused but also what the law means in that situation.

Montesquieu thought that this **separation of powers** was good. It kept government leaders from becoming too powerful or trying to boss everyone else around. Having a **separation of powers** made it harder for government leaders to abuse their power. Each branch needed the cooperation of the other branches to do its work.

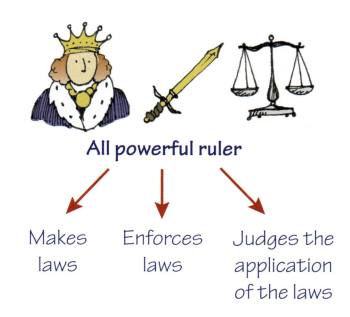

Makes laws | Enforces laws | Judges the application of the laws

Unitary Power

In this system, a single ruler holds all power.

Legislative branch | Executive branch | Judicial branch

Makes laws | Enforces laws | Judges the application of the laws

Montesquieu's Separation of Powers

In this system, the powers of government are divided among three separate branches.

Chapter 1 | The Origins of American Government

The English Heritage and the Impact of Historic Documents

The people living in the thirteen colonies were also very influenced by English tradition. Because England has a protected island location, the English developed several traditions different from the rest of Europe.

> For the EOC test, you do not need to know the origins of the ideas in the Magna Carta, the English Bill of Rights or the Mayflower Compact. But it helps to know this background to understand their main ideas and impact.

Magna Carta

Back in the early 1200s, King John of England wanted to increase his powers so that he could fight his wars in France. John introduced new taxes and forced some of his subjects to give him loans that he never planned to pay back. He also made demands on the Church. The King's leading nobles—known as the barons—joined with Church leaders and England's largest towns in an armed rebellion against the King. To end the rebellion, John met with his unhappy barons on the field of Runnymede in 1215. John signed a charter of rights that he granted to his subjects, which became known as Magna Carta, or the "Great Charter."

Although his main enemies were the barons, King John granted these rights to all free Englishmen. Two of the most important rights were these:

1. The king would not imprison or take away the property of his subjects without a **trial by a jury** of peers (*equals*) based on the laws of the land. In a trial by jury, a group of ordinary citizens sit together to hear the evidence and decide the case.

2. The king would not impose new taxes without the approval of a committee of 25 barons.

The Magna Carta

Later English kings agreed to respect the rights granted by King John in Magna Carta. These rights belonged to all free Englishmen and became an

---

The Active Citizen

Clause 12. No [special taxes] shall be imposed on our kingdom, unless by common counsel (*consent*) of our kingdom . . .

Clause 14. For obtaining the common counsel of the kingdom . . . we will cause to be summoned (*called*) the archbishops, bishops, abbots, earls, and greater barons, severally by our letters . . .

Clause 39. No freemen shall be taken or imprisoned or [have his property taken] or exiled (*sent away*) or in any way destroyed, nor will we go upon him nor send upon him, except by the lawful judgment of his peers (*equals*) or by the law of the land.

Clause 40. To no one . . . will we refuse or delay right or justice.

—King John of England, Magna Carta (1215)

▶ Which of these rights do you think was most important? Why?
▶ How did Magna Carta turn England into a "limited monarchy"?
▶ Which of the rights above do American citizens enjoy today?

King John signing Magna Carta

8 Chapter 1 | The Origins of American Government

important part of English law. England became a **limited monarchy**—one in which its ruler's powers were limited by law (also known as a "constitutional monarchy").

Parliament

Because of Magna Carta, English kings began calling together assemblies of nobles whenever they needed more money. They also began inviting representatives from counties and towns to participate. These assemblies became known as **Parliaments**. To *parley* means "to talk."

Parliament developed into two houses. English nobles sat in the **House of Lords**. Elected representatives from the towns and counties sat in the **House of Commons**.

The Mayflower Compact

In 1607, England established its first permanent colony in North America at Jamestown. Thirteen years later, a group of Pilgrims sailed across the Atlantic to establish a colony where they could worship God in their own way. The Pilgrims landed at Plymouth Rock, Massachusetts. Before leaving their ship, the *Mayflower*, all the men on board agreed to a set of rules to govern themselves.

The agreement the Pilgrims signed is known as the **Mayflower Compact**.

Sometimes the language of the past can be difficult to understand. In this document, the colonists agreed to "combine" themselves into "a body politic"—or a political body—in order to pass their own laws. The signers of the Mayflower Compact further promised to submit to and obey all such laws of the community.

With this document, we can see the beginnings of a strong tradition of colonial self-government. The basic idea of **self-government** is that people can govern themselves. This tradition of self-government was further reinforced by the establishment of colonial legislatures, like the House of Burgesses in Virginia, and by the town meetings of New England.

> *IN THE NAME OF GOD. We whose names are underwritten, the loyal subjects of King James, of Great Britain, France and Ireland having undertaken for the glory of God, and advancement of the Christian faith, and honor of our country, a voyage to plant the first colony in the Northern parts of Virginia, do [agree] and combine ourselves together into a body politic (a government made by the community), for our better order and preservation and … to enact and frame just and equal laws, ordinances, acts, and constitutions from time to time, as shall be thought most convenient for the general good of the colony, unto which we promise all due submission and obedience.*
>
> *—In witness whereof we sign our names at Cape Cod, 11th of November [1620]*

The Active Citizen

▶ Imagine you were about to land in a new place in an unfamiliar land. What rules do you think you and your companions would make?

▶ How do your rules compare to those of the Mayflower Compact?

Chapter 1 | The Origins of American Government

The English Bill of Rights

Back in England, King Charles I attempted to increase his royal power. He began collecting new taxes and forced loans, and he tried to rule England without calling for a meeting of Parliament. Some people felt these actions violated (*went against*) Magna Carta. In 1642, a civil war broke out between Parliament and the King. Parliament won the contest and executed King Charles I in 1649. A military leader took control of the English government. When this leader died, Charles II (the son of Charles I) was restored to the throne. Charles II was a very popular ruler. But after his death the next king, his younger brother James, did not cooperate with Parliament. James II was overthrown by Parliamentary leaders in the Glorious Revolution of 1688. James II fled to France.

To safeguard their rights from royal interference, Parliament passed the English Bill of Rights in December 1689. This important document limited the powers of the king. It firmly established the supreme power of Parliament and showed that England was a limited monarchy. The Bill of Rights also introduced many specific safeguards for individual liberty. A century later, many of the same safeguards were placed in the U.S. Constitution and the Bill of Rights.

The English Bill of Rights stated that:

- Members of Parliament had freedom of speech.
- The king could not collect new taxes without the approval of Parliament.
- The king could not have a standing army without the approval of Parliament.
- The king had to hold Parliament every year.
- People had the right to bear arms to defend themselves.
- Any subject could petition the government. (To petition is to write to the government for a redress of grievances.)
- An accused person could not be held for excessive bail, nor be subjected to any "cruel and unusual" punishment. (Bail is an amount of money paid as a guarantee to permit an accused person to remain out of jail while waiting for trial. If the person fails to show up at trial, the bail is forfeited.)

The American Revolution and Thomas Paine's *Common Sense*

Almost a century later, the British Parliament decided to place new taxes on the American colonists to help pay for their defense. The colonists felt that these new taxes were being placed on them without their consent (*agreement*). The cry was heard throughout the colonies that "taxation without representation is tyranny!" The colonists had clearly been influenced by English traditions and by John Locke's social contract theory.

Parliament, however, felt the colonists were too far away to ask their permission. They tried several different types of taxes, but each one led to even greater protests from the American colonists. By 1775, fighting broke out between the colonists and Britain. Fighting quickly spread from New England to the other colonies. The American Revolution had begun!

In January 1776, **Thomas Paine**, an English visitor to the colonies, published an influential pamphlet. Paine called his pamphlet *Common Sense*. Paine argued that it was "common sense" that the thirteen colonies should not be governed by the tiny island of Great Britain, many thousands of miles away.

Based on Enlightenment ideas, Paine argued that the time had come for colonists to become independent and govern themselves. Paine wrote that the cost of the colonists' connection to Britain far outweighed any benefits the colonists received. Finally, Paine attacked the system of monarchy. He recommended that the colonists adopt a democratic system of government without a king or queen.

Thomas Paine

> *I have heard it stated by some that America has prospered from her connection with Great Britain, and that this connection is necessary for her future happiness. We may as well say that because a child has had milk, that it is never to have meat. I challenge the warmest supporter of Britain to show a single advantage that this Continent can gain by being connected with Great Britain. . . .*
>
> —Thomas Paine, *Common Sense* (1776)

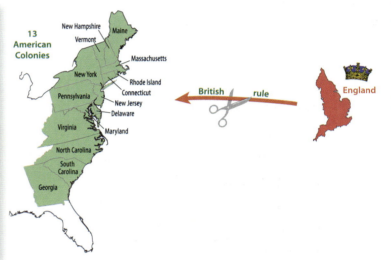

The Active Citizen

▶ How were Paine's ideas influenced by John Locke and the Enlightenment?

The Impact of these Historic Documents on Colonial America

Each of the documents and beliefs described in this chapter influenced the colonists' views on government and the later **"Founding Fathers"** (the men who established the American system of government).

▶ Because of **Magna Carta**, the English colonists enjoyed a system of trial by jury. They were also protected against new taxation by the king without the approval of Parliament.

▶ The **Mayflower Compact** established a strong tradition of colonial self-government. While some issues, such as defense of the colonies from France or Spain, were decided in Great Britain, many local issues were left to the colonists themselves to decide.

▶ Each of the 13 colonies eventually established its own colonial legislature. In most of the colonies,

Chapter 1 | The Origins of American Government

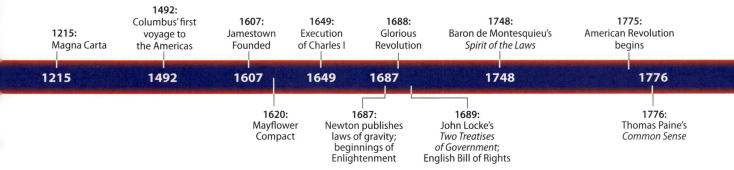

the king appointed a royal governor and the landowners of the colony elected the members of the colonial legislature.

- Because of the **English Bill of Rights**, the English colonists felt they should have all the rights of freeborn Englishmen. This meant they could not be taxed without the approval of Parliament, they were permitted to carry arms to protect themselves, and they could not be subjected to cruel and unusual punishments or excessive bail.

- John Locke's theory of the **social contract** gave the colonists the idea that the powers of government were based on their own consent (*approval*). This theory especially influenced the American Revolution and the "Founding Fathers" who wrote the Declaration of Independence and the Constitution. You will learn more about these later documents in the next chapter.

- Montesquieu's ideas on the **separation of powers** were based on English methods of government. In England, power was divided between the king, Parliament, and the courts of law. In the colonies, power was divided between the royal governor, the colonial legislature and the courts of law. Montesquieu believed that this separation of powers was beneficial. His ideas on the separation of powers greatly influenced the authors of the U.S. Constitution. They created a government with three separate branches, just as Montesquieu had proposed. You will learn more about the Constitution in later chapters.

- **Thomas Paine's** *Common Sense* encouraged the colonists to declare their independence during the American Revolution.

When learning about historic documents, it is important to remember:

- Who wrote the document
- When and where it was written
- Why it was written
- The main ideas of the document
- Its impact (*effects*)

Name _____

Fill in the last two columns in the chart below.

Document	Date	Author	Main Ideas	Importance
Magna Carta	1215	King John		
Mayflower Compact	1620	Pilgrims		
Writings on the social contract	1689	John Locke		
English Bill of Rights	1689	English Parliament		
Writings on the separation of powers	1748	Baron Charles de Montesquieu		
Common Sense	1776	Thomas Paine		

Explain the following concepts in your own words.

Concept	Explanation
Natural Law	
Limited Monarchy	
Self-government	
Separation of Powers	

Chapter 1 | The Origins of American Government

Name _____

Fill in the charts below.

Magna Carta (1215)

What rights did the Magna Carta give to free Englishmen?	How did this document influence the colonists?

How did rights given by Magna Carta differ from rights based on natural law?

Mayflower Compact (1620)

Describe this document.	How did this document influence the colonists?

How were the ideas in this document similar to John Locke's later idea of a social contract?

Name _____

Fill in the charts below.

Natural Law	
How does "natural law" differ from the laws created by governments?	What rights did John Locke believe each citizen had based on "natural law"?

John Locke's *Social Contract* (1689)	
Describe John Locke's "Social Contract."	How did this theory differ from the "divine right of kings"?
How did Locke's ideas influence the colonists?	

Chapter 1 | The Origins of American Government

Name _____

1. Imagine it is 1215 and you are King John of England. Write a short declaration to your subjects explaining the new rights you have granted (*given*) them in Magna Carta.

....
....
....
....
....
....
....
....
....

2. Imagine you are a Pilgrim colonist in 1620. Write a paragraph to a friend in England describing the Mayflower Compact and why you decided to sign it.

....
....
....
....
....
....
....
....
....
....
....
....

Name _____

3. Complete the paragraph frame below.

The Enlightenment

The Enlightenment took place in Europe in the 17th and 18th centuries. People were very impressed by the achievements of science. Sir Isaac Newton, for example, had discovered the "laws" of gravity. From these discoveries, many people concluded that natural laws also controlled how people as well as nature behaved. A natural law is _____ _____.

Two influential Enlightenment thinkers were John Locke and the Baron de Montesquieu. John Locke rejected the idea that kings received their powers from God. Instead, he argued that each person had certain natural rights. These natural rights included _____.

Locke wrote that each group of people living together made an agreement known as a social contract. In each social contract, people agreed to form a community and to give all of their power to a monarch (a king or queen). In this contract, the job of the monarch was to _____ _____. The job of the people was to _____ _____.

Locke said that if the monarch didn't carry out his or her job, then the people had the right to _____.

Locke wrote just after the Glorious Revolution in England (1688). He justified Parliament's actions in overthrowing King James II. Locke's ideas had a great influence on the American colonists. They would later help inspire the American Revolution.

A second important Enlightenment thinker was the Baron de Montesquieu. He was a French nobleman. Montesquieu wrote in favor of the separation of _____. In this system, the powers of government are separated. An assembly, like the English Parliament, has the _____ power. This is the power to _____. An individual, like the king or queen, has the _____ power. This is the power to _____. A court system, like the English courts, has the _____ power. This is the power to _____ _____.

Montesquieu realized that when power is separated into three different branches, no one individual or group _____. Montesquieu's ideas also greatly influenced the "Founding Fathers"—the men who established the American government.

Chapter 1 | The Origins of American Government

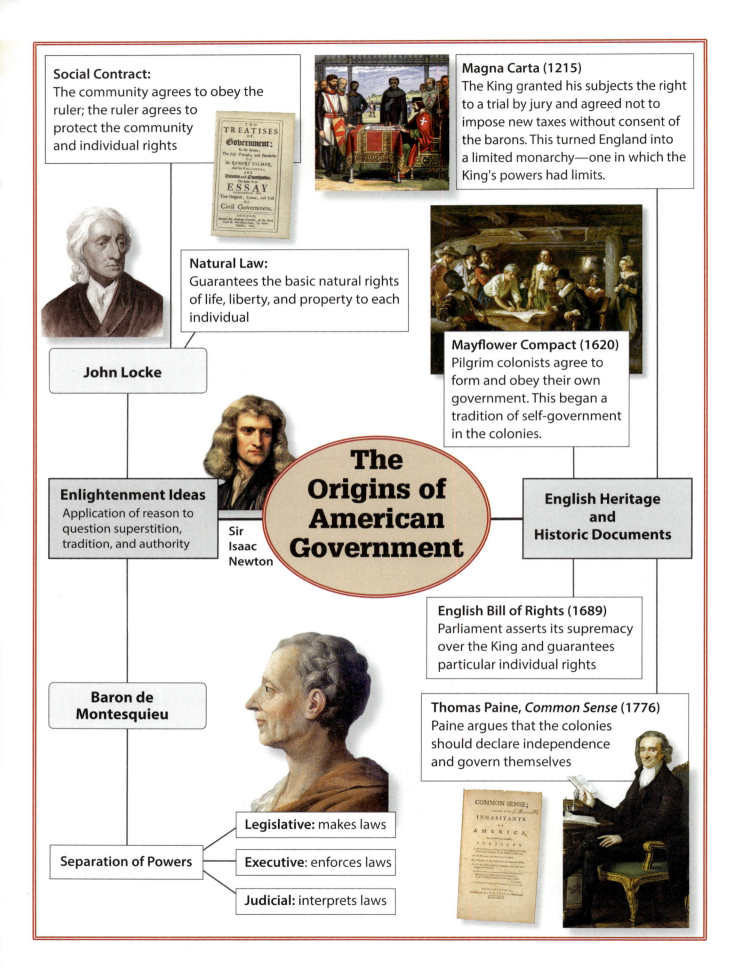

Review Cards: The Origins of American Government

The Enlightenment

- The **Enlightenment** was a movement of ideas in Europe and America in the late 17th and 18th centuries.
- Enlightenment thinkers tried to apply human reason to understand and improve society and government.
- Two important Enlightenment thinkers were John Locke and Montesquieu.

John Locke on Natural Law and the Social Contract

- Locke believed that people enjoyed certain basic rights under **natural law**. These "**natural rights**" included the right to life, liberty, and property. No government had the right to take away those natural rights.
- Locke wrote that people joined together under a **social contract** to form a community to protect themselves and their individual rights.
- As part of this social contract, the community gives its power to a ruler, whom it promises to obey.
- If the king (or queen) breaks their promise to respect the rights of his individual subjects, then the people have the right to rebel against their authority.

Baron de Montesquieu's Separation of Powers

A French nobleman, Montesquieu believed that the powers of government should be divided among three branches:

- **Legislative** branch has the power to make laws
- **Executive** branch has the power to carry out and enforce the laws; and
- **Judicial** branch has the power to interpret and apply the law to particular cases.

Montesquieu's idea of dividing up legislative, executive and judicial powers is known as the **separation of powers**. He believed that this separation of powers would prevent government leaders from becoming too strong or abusing their power.

Magna Carta (1215)

- An agreement forced on King John of England by his barons (*nobles*). It established important rights that were later enjoyed by all free Englishmen.
- The King promised not to impose new taxes or loans without the consent of a committee of barons.
- The King also promised that no freeman would be imprisoned or lose his property or be otherwise punished except after a **trial by jury** based on the law of the land.
- Magna Carta limited the king's power. It turned England into a **limited monarchy.** Under Magna Carta, the King could not impose new taxes without the consent of his subjects. Every freeborn Englishman was also entitled to a trial by jury when accused of a crime, as well as for the right to a trial by jury.

Mayflower Compact (1620)

- The Pilgrims sailed to North America to start their own colony where they could worship God in their own way.
- Before leaving the ship, they signed an agreement to form their own community and to obey its rules. The **Mayflower Compact** established the principle of **self-government** in the colonies. This was the idea that on many matters, the colonists could govern themselves.

The English Bill of Rights (1689)

- King James II tried to increase his royal powers. He was overthrown in the Glorious Revolution in 1688.
- Parliament passed the **English Bill of Rights** in 1689, shortly after James II was overthrown.
- The English Bill of Rights stated that members of Parliament would enjoy freedom of speech, that no armies would be raised in peacetime nor taxes imposed (*placed on citizens*) without the approval of Parliament, that citizens could petition (*make requests to*) the government, and that no excessive bail or cruel and unusual punishments would be imposed.

Thomas Paine's *Common Sense*

- In the 1770s, American colonists came into conflict with the British government. Fighting broke out in 1775.
- Early in 1776, Thomas Paine published *Common Sense*.
- Paine argued that it made no sense for the colonies to be governed by a distant island and that the colonists should seek independence. Paine also recommended that the colonists establish a democracy in America.

What Do You Know?

SS.7.C.1.1

1. According to John Locke, which agreement did individuals enter into when forming their own society?
   - A. constitution
   - B. social contract
   - C. Mayflower Compact
   - D. English Bill of Rights

SS.7.C.1.1

2. According to John Locke, which rights were guaranteed by natural law?
   - A. freedom of worship and the right to petition
   - B. trial by jury and no cruel punishments
   - C. freedom of speech and of the press
   - D. life, liberty and property

SS.7.C.1.2

3. The statement below is an excerpt from Magna Carta (1215).

> No freeman shall be taken or imprisoned or disseised or oulawed or exiled or any way destroyed, nor will we go upon him nor send upon him, except by the lawful judgment of his peers or by the law of the land.

Which right was guaranteed in this excerpt from Magna Carta?

A. no taxation without representation
B. freedom of the press
C. freedom of religion
D. trial by jury

SS.7.C.1.1

4. Which example illustrates Montesquieu's idea of the separation of powers?

A. Citizens of the United States choose many of their public officials in elections.
B. The state government of Florida has a governor, state legislature and state court system.
C. Individual rights to life, liberty and property are guaranteed by natural law.
D. People have the right to overthrow an unjust government.

SS.7.C.1.1

5. How was Locke's social contract theory related to his belief in natural law?

A. He argued subjects had the right to rebel against a ruler who acted against natural law.
B. He argued that whatever the king did was good according to natural law.
C. He argued that natural law required the colonists to be given their independence.
D. He argued that God had especially chosen kings to rule over their subjects as part of natural law.

SS.7.C.1.2

6. Which describes an impact of Magna Carta on the American colonists in the 1770s?

A. They believed they could not be taxed without their consent.
B. They believed they could not be governed by a far-away island.
C. They thought they had the right to overthrow a king who did not protect their rights.
D. They favored a separation of the powers of government into different branches.

Chapter 1 | The Origins of American Government

SS.7.C.1.1

7. What most attracted the Founding Fathers to Montesquieu's idea of the separation of powers?
   A. It could prevent the central government from becoming tyrannical and oppressive.
   B. It could protect the rights of the nobility from the actions of the king.
   C. It could preserve the privileges of the monarch and nobles from popular attack.
   D. It could raise judicial power to a level of equality with legislative and executive power.

SS.7.C.1.2

8. Which right was established by Magna Carta in 1215?
   A. the right to vote in elections
   B. the right to choose the monarch
   C. the right to freedom of speech
   D. the right to a trial by jury

SS.7.C.1.2

9. Which document confirmed the rights of English subjects after the overthrow of James II in the Glorious Revolution?
   A. Magna Carta
   B. Mayflower Compact
   C. English Bill of Rights
   D. Montesquieu's *Spirit of the Laws*

SS.7.C.1.1 & 1.2

10. Which of the following were most similar?
    A. the Mayflower Compact and John Locke's social contract theory
    B. the English Bill of Rights and Thomas Paine's *Common Sense*
    C. Magna Carta and Montesquieu's separation of powers
    D. the Mayflower Compact and Montesquieu's separation of powers

SS.7.C.1.2

11. The diagram below indicates that the colonists based some of their political views on historic documents.

    | Mayflower Compact | → | Self-government |
    | English Bill of Rights | → | ? |

    Which phrase completes the diagram?
    A. Natural law
    B. Separation of powers
    C. Divine Right of Kings
    D. Guarantees of individual rights

SS.7.C.1.2

12. The statements below are from the 1776 Virginia Declaration of Rights.

> 1) That in all capital or criminal prosecutions a man hath a right to demand . . . evidence in his favor, and to a speedy trial by an impartial jury . . .
> 2) That the legislative, executive, and judiciary department shall be separate and distinct . . .
> 3) That the freedom of the press is one of the great bulwarks of liberty, and can never be restrained . . .
> 4) That a well-regulated militia, composed of the body of the people, trained to arms, is the proper, natural, and safe defense of a free state . . .

Which statement guarantees a right first granted by Magna Carta?

A. 1   C. 3
B. 2   D. 4

SS.7.C.1.2

13. The statements below are from three of the first amendments to the U.S. Constitution.

> *"Congress shall make no law . . . prohibiting . . . the right of the people . . . to petition the government for a redress of grievances."*
> —First Amendment
>
> *"[T]he right of the people to keep and bear arms shall not be infringed"*
> —Second Amendment
>
> *"[No] cruel and unusual punishments [shall be] inflicted"*
> —Eighth Amendment

Which earlier document contained similar rights?

A. Magna Carta (1215)
B. The Mayflower Compact (1620)
C. The English Bill of Rights (1689)
D. Montesquieu's *Spirit of the Laws* (1784)

SS.7.C.1.1

14. Which statement describes the influence of natural-law beliefs on John Locke and other Enlightenment thinkers?

A. They argued it was natural for subjects to obey established governments.
B. They questioned any practices that seemed to go against reason and natural law.
C. They believed that royal power was natural because it was based on divine right.
D. They claimed church teachings should not be challenged since they rested on natural law.

Chapter 1 | The Origins of American Government

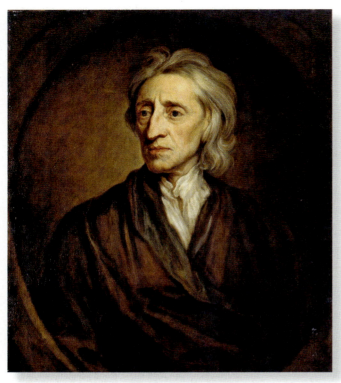
John Locke (1632–1704)

Charles de Secondat, Baron de Montesquieu (1689–1755)

The ideas of Locke and Montesquieu were read and discussed in Europe and the colonies during the Enlightenment.

24   Chapter 1 | The Origins of American Government

CHAPTER 2

Americans Declare Their Independence

SS.7.C.1.3   Describe how English policies and responses to colonial concerns led to the writing of the Declaration of Independence.

SS.7.C.1.4   Analyze the ideas (natural rights, role of government) and complaints set forth in the Declaration of Independence. (See also Chapter 1.)

Names and Terms You Should Know

- Policies
- Taxation
- Representation
- Natural rights
- Quartering soldiers
- Second Continental Congress
- Thomas Paine

- Declaration of Independence
- Colonial grievances
- Self-evident
- Endowed
- Unalienable rights
- "Life, Liberty and the Pursuit of Happiness"
- Institute

- Derive
- Consent of the governed
- Assent
- Abolish
- Trial by jury
- Suspend
- Dissolve legislatures
- Oppression
- Tyranny

Florida "Keys" to Learning

1. British policies after the French and Indian War and colonial responses led to the American Revolution and Declaration of Independence.

2. After the French and Indian War, the British government was deeply in debt. It had borrowed large sums of money to pay for the war. Parliament passed a series of laws to tax the colonists. However, it made no attempt to obtain the colonists' consent (*agreement*). The British passed the Stamp Act, but repealed it after colonial protests. Then it passed the Townshend duties, taxing glass and other goods. When the colonists again protested, it repealed those. Finally, Parliament passed the Tea Act.

3. Colonists objected that these taxes were all forms of "taxation without representation." Colonial assemblies sent petitions to Parliament to change these laws, and colonists boycotted (*refused to buy*) British goods in protest.

4. To prevent colonial unrest, the British government sent more troops to North America. The government quartered (*sheltered*) some of these troops in colonists' barns and homes.

5. The "Boston Tea Party" was a protest against the Tea Act. A group of colonists boarded British ships at night and threw their chests of tea into Boston Harbor. The British government was greatly angered by this destruction of property. It passed the "Intolerable Acts," closing Boston Harbor and suspending the colonial legislature.

6. British troops and armed colonists fired on each other at Lexington and Concord in April 1775. The American Revolution had begun.

7. Delegates from the colonies met in two Continental Congresses. At first, the Continental Congress did not seek independence but wanted the British to change their policies. King George III refused to compromise with the colonists.

8. In January 1776, Thomas Paine published his pamphlet, *Common Sense*, urging the colonists to seek independence and to create a democracy.

9. In June 1776, a majority of the Second Continental Congress finally agreed to support a resolution in favor of independence.

10. A special committee of five members was formed to write a declaration that would explain this decision to the other colonists and to the rest of the world. The main author of the Declaration was Thomas Jefferson.

11. The Declaration of Independence announced the American theory of government: (1) that people have certain "unalienable rights"—rights to "life, liberty, and the pursuit of happiness"—which cannot be taken away; (2) that governments are created to protect these rights; (3) that when a government tries to destroy these rights, its people have the right to change that government—even by force if necessary; and (4) that people should not change their government lightly.

12. Much of the Declaration is taken up by its list of colonial grievances—or complaints—against King George III. These justified the colonists' decision to declare independence. These grievances included the fact that the King had taxed the colonists without their consent, quartered his troops in their homes, suspended their legislatures, cut their trade, and waged war on the colonists.

13. The colonists therefore declared their independence. They also announced their right as a new nation to declare war and make alliances. This cleared the way for the Americans to conclude alliances with France and Spain to help them in the war against the British.

14. The Declaration of Independence has had a global impact. It has influenced other peoples who wanted to free themselves from foreign rule. Its promise of equality for all peoples, while not realized at the time, helped inspire later reform movements, including abolitionism, women's fight for the right to vote, and the Civil Rights Movement of the 1950s and 1960s.

In the last chapter, you learned how England established thirteen colonies in North America. These colonists enjoyed the same rights as people in Great Britain. They had all the rights given by Magna Carta and the English Bill of Rights. The colonists also enjoyed some unique powers of **self-government**. Each colony had its own legislature, which resolved many local problems. The colonies were simply too far from England for many important decisions to be made there.

The French and Indian War

In 1754, Britain went to war with France. This conflict became known in America as the **French and Indian War.** France eventually lost the war and was forced to surrender its colonies in North America. Canada and the Ohio River Valley came under British rule.

The American colonists were pleased with this outcome. They no longer had to worry about defending themselves against the French and their Indian allies. On the other hand, the British government found itself deeply in debt. It had borrowed large sums of money to pay for the war.

> You don't need to know the names of specific acts, like the Stamp Act, for the EOC. But you should have a general idea of the British policies and American concerns that led to the American Revolution.

British Policies and Colonial Reactions: Taxation without Representation

People living in Britain were already paying more in taxes than the colonists in North America. The British government therefore decided that the colonists should pay more towards their own defense. It adopted a new **policy** (*a course of action or series of steps taken by a government*). Parliament passed a series of laws to tax the colonists. Since the colonies were so far from London, no attempt was made to obtain their **consent** (*agreement*).

The first of these laws was the Stamp Act. It passed in 1765. This act required every official document, newspaper or pamphlet in the colonies to have an expensive government stamp.

The colonists were greatly angered by the Stamp Act. They objected (*complained*) that this was "taxation without representation." Colonists held marches and rallies against the Stamp Act. Colonial assemblies sent petitions (*formal requests*) to Parliament to change the law. Colonists boycotted (*refused to buy*) British goods. Protestors held a special "Stamp Act Congress" in New York City. Some angry colonists even captured government tax collectors and poured hot tar and placed feathers on them.

The British government was taken by surprise by the number of protests against the Stamp Act. Parliament acted quickly to repeal (*cancel; withdraw*) the Stamp Act. But the British government still needed to collect money from the colonists. It kept to its policy of trying to tax the colonists. Parliament therefore passed a series of new taxes, known as the Townshend duties. These placed new taxes on paper, paint, glass, lead and tea. These common goods were shipped to the colonies from Britain.

Colonists harrassing a British tax collector

Chapter 2 | Americans Declare Their Independence

Once again, Parliament passed these taxes without the consent of the colonists. Members of Parliament still felt that the colonists were too far away to consult (*discuss or check*) with them.

Could the colonists have sent their own representatives to Parliament? At a time when crossing the Atlantic was slow, any colonial representatives in London would soon have been out of touch with the colonists in America. Most colonial leaders did not want to be represented in Parliament. Instead, they wanted to make their own laws in their own colonial assemblies. Such laws would include any new taxes.

The colonists formed special committees to protest against the Townshend duties. To prevent unrest, the British government sent more troops to North America. More than 4,000 soldiers were sent to Boston alone. The government **quartered** some of these troops in colonists' barns and homes. To "**quarter**" means to send soldiers to live on private citizens' properties. The homeowner was expected to provide food and lodging (*a place to stay*) to each soldier.

Parliament finally repealed (*canceled or withdrew*) the hated Townshend duties. However, it kept to its general policy and passed a new tax on tea in their place. British ships carrying tea arrived in Boston

Colonists dressed as Indians throw tea into Boston Harbor

Harbor in December 1773. A group of colonists, dressed as American Indians, boarded the ships at night and threw their chests of tea into the harbor in protest. This event became known as the "Boston Tea Party."

The British government was greatly angered by this destruction of property. Parliament passed the Intolerable Acts. Boston Harbor was closed. The Massachusetts legislature was **suspended** (*temporarily closed*). The British government also said it would appoint all officials in Massachusetts until the tea was paid for. Finally, royal officials would no longer be put on trial for crimes in the colonies, but would be tried in Great Britain.

The Active Citizen

In your own words, summarize the British policies that annoyed colonists in the years after the French and Indian War. Then describe colonial responses to those policies.

British Policies	Colonial Responses

28 Chapter 2 | Americans Declare Their Independence

The Outbreak of the Revolution

In response to British policies, twelve of the thirteen colonies sent representatives to Philadelphia to meet as a "Continental Congress" in September 1774. The Congress assembled, sent protests to Britain, and agreed to a boycott (*refusal to buy*) of British goods. Its members also decided that a second Continental Congress should be held in May 1775. Then they went home.

Meanwhile, American "Patriots" organized in Boston. They collected guns and ammunition (*bullets and gunpowder*). The Royal Governor of Massachusetts sent soldiers to seize colonial leaders and arms just outside Boston. British troops and armed colonists fired on one another at Lexington and Concord in April 1775, starting the American Revolution.

The Second Continental Congress was about to meet. Many of the delegates to the Second Continental Congress were already on their way to Philadelphia. The Second Continental Congress began its meetings in May 1775. Most of the delegates from the other colonies strongly supported the decision of Massachusetts to resist the British. They encouraged the other colonies to join in the struggle.

The Continental Congress formed its own army, known as the "Continental Army." Next it chose George Washington, a Virginian, to command it. Washington was an experienced commander from the French and Indian War.

George Washington, age 40

The Question of American Independence

Even after the outbreak of fighting, most colonists still wanted to remain under British rule. Many colonists had relatives in Great Britain. Others were merchants who traded goods with Britain. Most saw themselves as loyal subjects of the King, who were resisting the unfair policies of his ministers.

In July 1775, the Continental Congress issued a declaration (*public statement*) explaining why the colonists were resisting the British government. The declaration contained a long list of colonial grievances. But it also emphasized that the colonists were not seeking independence: "We have not raised armies with ambitious designs of separating from Great Britain and establishing Independent States." Two days later, the Continental Congress sent a petition to George III, the King of Great Britian. The colonists asked the King for peace and reconciliation.

King George III refused to receive the colonists' petition. Instead, he told Parliament that the colonies were in open rebellion. The King accused the colonists of planning to separate from Britain. Parliament passed an act forbidding all trade with the colonists until the rebellion was crushed. The King declared the rebellious colonists to be outside of the scope of his protection. All American ships, ports and sailors became subject to capture.

The King also sent more troops to America to fight the colonists. His forces included foreign mercenaries (*hired soldiers*) from Germany. These steps greatly angered the colonists.

In January 1776, Thomas Paine published his pamphlet, *Common Sense*. As you learned in the last chapter, Paine argued that the colonists received little benefit from their connection with Great Britain. Paine urged the colonists to seek independence.

Chapter 2 | Americans Declare Their Independence

John Adams

In March 1776, General Washington and his troops drove the British out of Boston. Washington then moved his army to New York City. However, with the help of their fleet of ships, the British were able to land troops on nearby Long Island. Washington lost battles on Long Island and in New York City that summer and fall. Washington retreated across the Delaware River.

Most colonists now felt that Britain had treated them badly. They disliked British taxes, placed on them without their consent. Even more, they resented the use of armed force. More and more colonists agreed with Thomas Paine that they should end their connection with Great Britain. They wanted to free themselves from British rule.

Many colonists also believed that they could not obtain allies (*friendly countries that would act with them*) so long as they remained subjects of the British King. Only by becoming independent could they ever hope to conclude alliances with foreign powers, like France and Spain. They needed the help of these foreign powers to win the Revolutionary War.

The Second Continental Congress began debating the question of American independence early in 1776.

John Adams, a lawyer from Massachusetts, was one of the strongest voices for independence. Adams persuaded many of the other delegates to vote in favor of separating from England.

In June 1776, Richard Henry Lee, a Virginian, introduced a resolution proposing independence:

> *Resolved, That these United Colonies are, and of right ought to be, free and independent States, that they are absolved from all allegiance to the British Crown, and that all political connection between them and the State of Great Britain is, and ought to be, totally dissolved.*

Word Helper
absolve = to release or set free
allegiance = loyalty to a superior
British Crown = the King
connection = a link or formal association
dissolved = ended or eliminated

A special committee of five members was formed to write a declaration explaining this decision to other colonists and to the rest of the world. A young Virginian, Thomas Jefferson, was the main author of the Declaration. Two other important members of the committee were John Adams and Benjamin Franklin. Jefferson wrote the first draft (*written version*) of the Declaration. The Declaration was later revised by the committee and then by the Continental Congress itself.

The Active Citizen

Imagine it is early in 1776. Your class should divide into different groups, representing the different colonies at the Second Continental Congress. Hold a discussion on whether or not the colonies should declare their independence from Great Britain. Groups representing different colonies should present the most important arguments either for or against independence. For example, "We, the representatives of the Colony of Virginia, favor independence because . . ." After your discussion, take a class vote.

The Declaration of Independence

For the EOC test, you should be sure to know the main ideas of the Declaration of Independence.

You probably have already heard of the Declaration of Independence. It was signed on July 4th—still our national holiday. Every year we celebrate the signing of the Declaration with parades, speeches and fireworks. But what makes this document so very special to Americans?

The Declaration of Independence actually accomplished five things:

1. It declared American independence. It boldly stated that the colonies were no longer part of the British Empire. The former colonists were no longer subjects of King George III.
2. It announced a theory of government based on natural law and the protection of individual rights.
3. It listed the grievances (*complaints*) of the colonists against King George III and the British government.
4. It justified the conduct of the colonists, both to their fellow countrymen and to the rest of the world.
5. It announced the arrival of the United States as an independent and equal member of the international community, able to wage war and to make alliances. This cleared the way for the former colonies to conclude alliances with France and Spain.

It can be difficult to understand a document that was written more than 200 years ago. But the Declaration of Independence has been so influential, both in the United States and other countries, that it is important to read some of this original document for yourself.

1. You will see that the first paragraph of the Declaration states that it sometimes becomes necessary for a people to end the ties that once joined them to others. When they do, they should explain their reasons for doing so to the rest of the world.

2. The next section is the most famous part of the Declaration. It states the American theory of government. This theory is based on a belief in natural rights and John Locke's social contract. It begins by stating that all people enjoy certain "**unalienable rights**" under natural law. These are God-given rights that cannot be taken away. Among these rights are "**life, liberty and the pursuit of happiness.**"

3. The Declaration next explains that people institute (*create, establish*) governments to protect these rights. It is the **role**, or purpose, of government to protect these rights. When a government acts to destroy these rights, its citizens have the right to abolish (*end*) that government and to create a new one.

   The Declaration recognizes that people should not change their government lightly. Disagreement with a few government decisions does not justify changing an entire system of government. But when there has been a long pattern of abuses (*harmful actions*), showing that the government has become **oppressive** (*harsh and unfair*) and **tyrannical** (*dictatorial and cruel*), then the people clearly have the right to change their government.

4. Such has been the case, the Declaration argues, for the American colonists. The British government has made repeated injuries against them. The Declaration lists many of these specific abuses. This list of **grievances**, or **complaints**, is actually the longest section of the Declaration. These include:

   ▶ refusing to approve necessary laws
   ▶ placing taxes on the colonists without their consent

For the EOC test, you should know the main colonial grievances.

Chapter 2 | Americans Declare Their Independence

- quartering troops in colonists' homes
- suspending trial by jury in many cases
- making judges dependent on the King's will
- sending royal officials and colonists for trial in Britain instead of in the colonies
- suspending or dissolving colonial legislatures

> To **dissolve** a legislature is to end its meetings, dismiss its members, and send its members home. To **suspend** a legislature is to stop its meetings temporarily.

The Declaration works up to the most serious grievances at the very end of the list:

- The King has cut off their trade.
- He has made war on the colonists.
- He has hired foreign mercenaries against them.
- He has ordered the burning down of towns.
- He has even stirred up neighboring American Indians to attack them.

5. The final paragraphs of the Declaration explain that the colonists have tried to settle their disagreements with Britain peacefully, but that all of their attempts have failed. The time has therefore come for the colonists to declare their independence.

The last paragraph of the Declaration actually contains the same wording as the resolution for independence already proposed in the Continental Congress: the former colonies are and of right should be free and independent states. The colonists therefore no longer consider themselves to be subjects of the King. They further claim the right to wage war and to make alliances on their own behalf.

> Can you find the phrase "Declaration of Independence" in the document? Curiously, it does not appear there, although people began referring to it as the "Declaration of Independence" almost as soon as it was signed.

Benjamin Franklin, John Adams, and Thomas Jefferson

32 Chapter 2 | Americans Declare Their Independence

Now try reading the Declaration of Independence for yourself. Some of its more difficult words are defined to the right of each section. Then rewrite each section of the Declaration in your own words below.

In CONGRESS, July 4, 1776.
The unanimous Declaration of the thirteen United States of America.

Introduction: The Purpose of the Declaration

When in the course of human events, it becomes necessary for one people to dissolve the political bands which have connected them with another, and to assume among the Powers of the Earth the separate and equal station to which the Laws of Nature . . . entitle them, a decent respect to the opinions of mankind requires that they should declare the causes which impel them to the separation.

dissolve = to make disappear; to end
political bands = ties that bind together
connect = to join together
Powers = independent countries or states with military strength
separate and equal station = independent and equal position
entitle = to give a right to something
impel = to force
separation = a division of something into separate parts

▶ Explain what this section says in your own words: _____

▶ What was the purpose of this introduction?

Chapter 2 | Americans Declare Their Independence

> The next two sections are the most important part of the Declaration. Be sure to know these sections for the EOC test.

A Theory of Government Based on Natural Law and Individual Rights

*We hold these truths to be **self-evident**, that all men are created equal, that they are **endowed** by their **Creator** with certain **unalienable** Rights, that among these are Life, Liberty and the pursuit of Happiness.*

self-evident = obvious, clear
endowed = given
Creator = God
unalienable = not capable of being taken away (usually spelled "inalienable")

▶ Explain what this section says in your own words: _____

▶ What is meant by "unalienable rights" in this paragraph?

▶ How was this paragraph from the Declaration influenced by the earlier writings of John Locke?

34 Chapter 2 | Americans Declare Their Independence

> *That to secure these rights, Governments are **instituted** among Men, **deriving** their just powers from the **consent** of the governed[.] That whenever any Form of Government becomes destructive of these ends, it is the Right of the People to alter or to **abolish** it, and to **institute** new Government . . . organizing its powers in such form, as to them shall seem most likely to effect their Safety and Happiness.*

secure = to obtain
instituted = created
derive = to obtain from; to come from
consent = agreement
alter = to change
abolish = to end; to get rid of
institute = to start; to create
organize = arrange in order
effect = to bring about

▶ Explain what this section says in your own words: _____

_____

_____

_____

_____

_____

_____

▶ According to the Declaration, when do people have the right to abolish (*end*) their government and create a new one?

_____

_____

_____

_____

_____

_____

_____

Chapter 2 | Americans Declare Their Independence

Prudence, indeed, will dictate that Governments long established should not be changed for light and transient causes . . . But when a long train of abuses and usurpations, pursuing invariably the same object evinces a design to reduce them under absolute Despotism, it is their right, it is their duty, to throw off such Government, and to provide new Guards for their future security.

prudence = cautious and careful judgment
dictate = to demand; to determine
transient = temporary; not important
long train = long chain or series of events
usurpation = a wrongful taking of someone else's rights
pursue = to chase after something in order to obtain it
invariably = always, without change
object = goal
evince = to provide evidence of
design = a plan; a purpose
absolute = total; complete
despotism = an oppressive and arbitrary power

▶ Explain what this section says in your own words: _____

▶ Why do you think the Declaration says that governments should not be changed for "light and transient causes"?

▶ Do you agree that citizens should overthrow a government whose actions reveal a plan to establish an "absolute Despotism"? Why or why not?

Such has been the patient sufferance of these Colonies; and such is now the necessity which constrains them to alter their former Systems of Government. The history of the present King of Great Britain is a history of repeated injuries and usurpations, all having in direct object the establishment of an absolute Tyranny over these States. To prove this, let Facts be submitted to a candid world.

patient = willing to accept delays without becoming annoyed
sufferance = suffering
constrain = to force; to restrict or limit
alter = to change
usurpation = a wrongful taking of someone's rights
tyranny = a cruel and oppressive government; a power exercised without legal right
submit = to present or give to another
candid = truthful; straightforward; frank

▶ Explain what this section says in your own words: _____

_____

_____

_____

_____

▶ Why did the colonists believe they needed to explain their theory of government to justify their decision to declare independence?

_____

_____

_____

_____

▶ How did this section of the Declaration reflect the views of Thomas Paine?

_____

_____

_____

_____

Chapter 2 | Americans Declare Their Independence

▶ Would the Declaration of Independence have been just as effective without these sections explaining the colonists' theory of government? Give one or more reasons in support of your answer.

IN CONGRESS, JULY 4, 1776.

The unanimous Declaration of the thirteen united States of America.

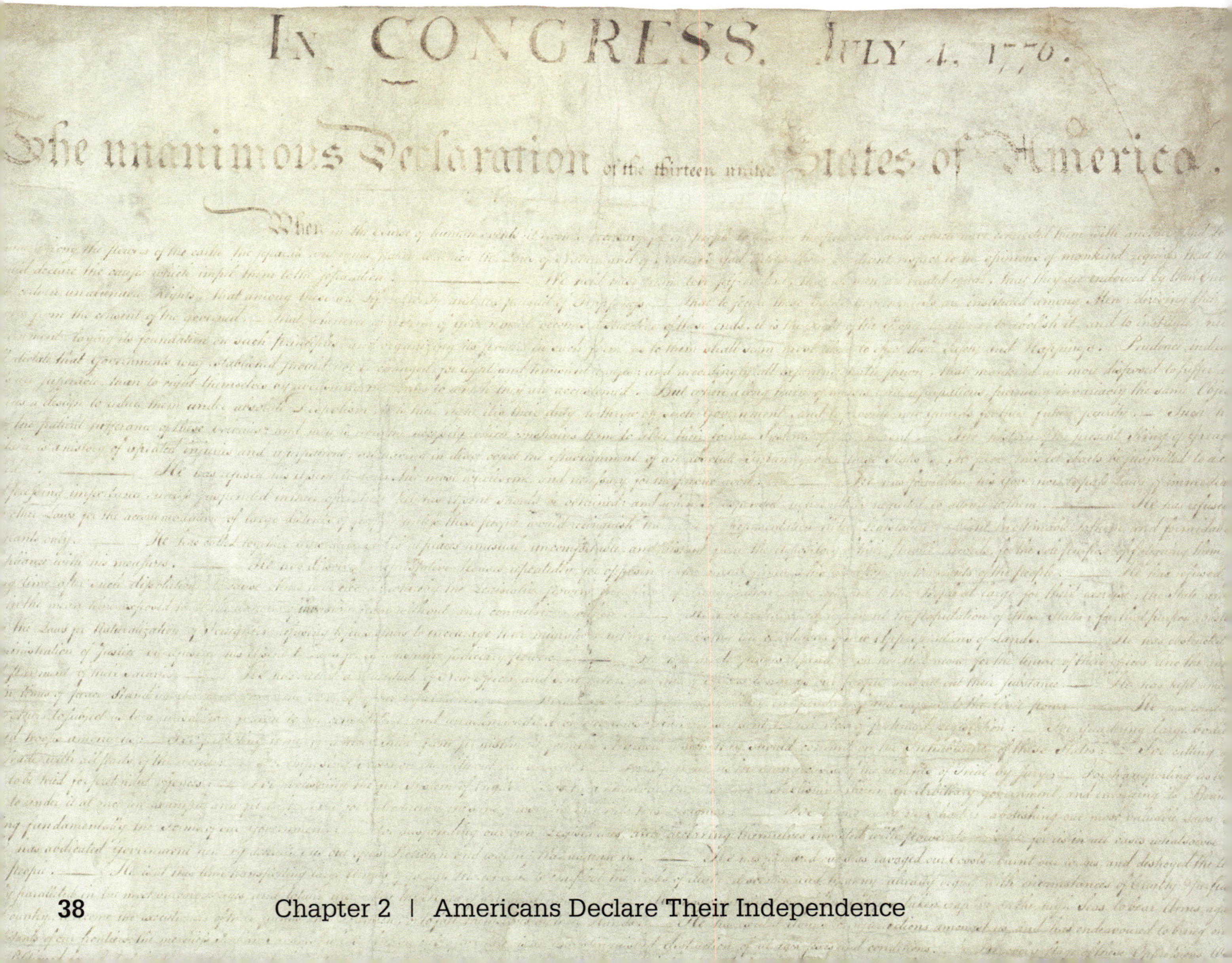

The List of Colonists' Grievances (*Complaints*)

In this next section, the Declaration lists the grievances that the colonists had against King George III and the British government.

*He has refused his **Assent** to Laws, the most wholesome and necessary for the public good. . . .*

*He has **dissolved** Representative Houses repeatedly . . . .*

He has made Judges dependent on his Will alone for the tenure of their offices, and the amount and payment of their salaries . . .

He has kept among us, in times of peace, Standing Armies without the Consent of our legislatures . . .

*For **quartering** large bodies of armed troops among us . . .*

For cutting off our Trade with all parts of the world:

For imposing Taxes on us without our Consent:

For depriving us in many cases, of the benefit of Trial by Jury. . .

*For **suspending** our own Legislatures . . . .*

He has plundered our seas, ravaged our coasts, burnt our towns, and destroyed the lives of our people.

*He is at this time transporting large Armies of foreign Mercenaries to complete the works of death, desolation, and **tyranny**, already begun. . . .*

assent = approval; agreement
wholesome = beneficial
public good = what is good for the community
dissolve = to dismiss; to close; to end
dependent = to depend upon; to be based upon
will = the part of the mind that determines what a person wants or desires
tenure = period in which they hold their offices
standing army = an army of soldiers ready to fight
consent = agreement; approval
quarter = to shelter troops in private homes
impose = to force on someone
deprive = to take away
transport = to carry from one place to another
suspend = to temporarily stop
plunder = to steal; to rob
transport = take or carry from one place to another
mercenary = a soldier who fights for money; a hired troop
desolation = complete destruction
tyranny = a cruel and oppressive government; a power exercised without legal right

▶ Explain what this section says in your own words: _____

_____

_____

_____

_____

_____

Chapter 2 | Americans Declare Their Independence

▶ Which of these grievances do you think were the most important ones? Justify your answer with evidence.

▶ Do you think that these grievances made it impossible for the colonists to remain in the British Empire? Or was it still possible to find a peaceful solution?

King George III has Refused the Colonists' Attempts at Compromise

*In every stage of these **Oppressions** We have Petitioned for Redress in the most humble terms: Our repeated Petitions have been answered only by repeated injury. A Prince, whose character is thus marked by every act which may define a **Tyrant**, is unfit to be the ruler of a free people. . . .*

oppression = harsh and unjust treatment

petition = (*verb*) to send a formal written request to an official or government body; (*noun*) a formal written request to a government or legislature

redress = a remedy; something to correct or make right a problem or an injustice

tyrant = despot; a dictator; someone who seizes or uses power unjustly

▶ Explain what this section says in your own words: _____

_____

_____

_____

▶ Why did the colonists feel it was important to show that they had attempted to obtain a peaceful "redress" of their grievances?

_____

_____

_____

▶ Do you believe King George III was a tyrant? What evidence did the Declaration provide to show that the British were planning to establish a "tyranny" over the colonists?

_____

_____

_____

English King George III

Colonists Therefore Declare Their Independence

We, therefore, the Representatives of the United States of America, in General Congress, Assembled, . . . do, in the Name, and by Authority of the good People of these Colonies, solemnly publish and declare, That these united Colonies are, and of Right ought to be Free and Independent States; that they are Absolved from all Allegiance to the British Crown, and that all political connection between them and the State of Great Britain, is and ought to be totally dissolved; and that as Free and Independent States, they have full Power to levy War, conclude Peace, contract Alliances, establish Commerce, and to do all other Acts and Things which Independent States may of right do. . . .

solemn = formal; sincere; serious
publish = make publicly known
absolve = to release or set free
allegiance = loyalty to a superior
British Crown = the King
connection = a link or formal association
dissolved = ended or eliminated
commerce = trade
levy war = make war
contract Alliances = sign treaties of alliance with other countries

▶ Explain what this section says in your own words: _____

_____

_____

_____

_____

_____

▶ What was the importance of this phrase at the end of the Declaration of Independence: "that as Free and Independent States, they have full Power to levy War, conclude Peace, contract Alliances . . ."

_____

_____

_____

_____

_____

Chapter 2 | Americans Declare Their Independence

▶ If you had been a colonist in 1776, would the Declaration of Independence have persuaded you to support the independence of the colonies? Why or why not?

_____
_____
_____
_____
_____
_____
_____
_____
_____
_____
_____

Enrichment

The Impact of the Declaration of Independence

The Declaration had an immediate effect on the colonists. It allowed them to open talks with France and Spain to conclude military alliances. It also helped them to win support from other Americans for the Revolutionary War.

The Declaration was actually the first time that a group of colonists made a public announcement while breaking away from imperial rule. This example was soon followed by other countries. It helped lead to the outbreak of a revolution in France in 1789 and to later revolutions throughout Latin America. According to Harvard historian David Armitage, more than a hundred countries later copied the example of the American Declaration of Independence. Many of these countries actually borrowed some of the wording of the American Declaration.

The Declaration had other effects, even within the United States itself. The colonists did more than declare their independence from Britain. The Declaration of Independence proclaimed (*announced publicly*) a new theory of government based on equality and individual rights. It announced that all men were created equal and enjoyed certain unalienable rights that could not be taken away. While American society was far from equal at the time, the Declaration laid the seeds for further change and later demands for equality. President Lincoln was thus able to breathe new life into the Declaration 86 years later when he abolished slavery. Since then, the Declaration has been used in support of voting rights for women, the Civil Rights Movement, and movements for equality for women, minority groups, and Americans with disabilities.

The Active Citizen

1. Did you know that Thomas Jefferson originally had a paragraph in the Declaration condemning George III for promoting the slave trade? This paragraph was taken out of the Declaration to win the support of South Carolina and other slave-holding states. Was it wrong for slave-holding states to support a declaration in the name of freedom and equality? Can we hold earlier Americans to the same standards we have today? How might American history have been different if Jefferson's paragraph against the slave trade had been left in the Declaration?

2. In 1848, women reformers met in Seneca Falls, New York. They adopted the following Declaration of Sentiments:

> "We hold these truths to be self-evident: that all men and women are created equal; that they are endowed by their Creator with certain inalienable rights; that among these are life, liberty, and the pursuit of happiness; that to secure these rights governments are instituted, deriving their just powers from the consent of the governed. . . . The history of mankind is a history of repeated injuries and usurpations on the part of man toward woman, having in direct object the establishment of an absolute tyranny over her."

▸ What did this statement owe to the Declaration of Independence of 1776?

▸ Why do you think the American Declaration of Independence has been so influential?

Name _____

Define each word or phrase and then make up a sentence using that word or phrase.

Word/Phrase	Definition	Sentence
British policies		
taxation without representation		
to quarter troops		
to derive their powers		
governments are instituted		
unalienable rights		
to suspend or dissolve legislatures		
tyrannical		
self-evident		
assent		
oppression		

Name _____

The Story of the Declaration of Independence

After several years of disagreement over taxation and representation, fighting finally broke out between the colonists and Great Britain in April of 1775. The colonies sent representatives to Philadelphia, where they formed the Second Continental Congress. The Second Continental Congress established a colonial army to oppose the British.

In January 1776, Thomas Paine published a popular pamphlet, *Common Sense*. Paine argued that it made no sense for a large area like the American colonies to be governed by a small and distant island. Paine therefore argued that the colonies should _____.

Paine's arguments persuaded many colonists.

After a year of fighting, the members of the Continental Congress finally decided to declare _____.

They appointed Thomas Jefferson and others to write a declaration explaining their decision to the rest of the world.

Jefferson was the main author of the Declaration of Independence. He began this famous document by explaining the colonists' theory of government. This part of the Declaration was based on John Locke's _____ theory.

The Declaration states that all men are created_____. The Declaration further states that all men have certain *unalienable*, or natural, rights. Among these natural rights are the rights to
_____
_____.

The Declaration then explains that governments are actually created by people to *protect* these rights. When a government continually attacks these rights instead of protecting them, the people therefore have the right to _____.

Such has been the case, the Declaration argues, for the colonists.

The next part of the Declaration lists the grievances that the colonists have against King George III of Great Britain and his government. (A grievance is a _____.) Some of the grievances that the Declaration mentions are the following:

The King has _____.

He has _____.

He has _____.

He has _____.

Because of these grievances, the Declaration concludes that the colonists no longer owe the King their allegiance (*loyalty and obedience*).

Instead, the colonies now declare themselves to be free and _____ states.

They further claim the right to form their own alliances, to engage in trade, to make war, and to conclude peace, just as any other nation would do.

The signing of the Declaration of Independence on July 4, 1776, marked the birth of our nation—the United States of America. The event is still celebrated by Americans each year on the holiday known as the Fourth of July, or Independence Day.

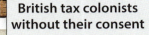
- Stamp Act
- Townshend Duties
- Tea Duty

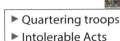
- Boycotts
- Petitions to Parliament
- Boston Tea Party
- Continental Congress

- Quartering troops
- Intolerable Acts
- Firing on colonists at Lexington and Concord

British tax colonists without their consent

"Taxation without representation is tyranny!"

British Policies **Colonial Concerns** **British Responses**

Causes of the American Revolution

Americans Declare Their Independence

Declaration of Independence

- Paine's *Common Sense* calls for the colonies to become independent.
- King George III refuses to compromise
- Second Continental Congress approves independence
- Thomas Jefferson is main author of the Declaration

Main Ideas
- People have unalienable rights (life, liberty, and the pursuit of happiness)
- Governments are instituted (*created*) to protect these rights
- Governments derive (*obtain; get*) their just powers from the consent of the governed.
- Governments that are destructive of individual rights can be overturned
- List of colonial grievances (*complaints*): the King imposed taxes without the people's consent, suspended trial by jury, dissolved legislatures, etc.
- Colonists therefore declare their independence.

Chapter 2 | Americans Declare Their Independence

Review Cards: Americans Declare Their Independence

The Road to Revolution

- From 1754 to 1763, Britain was at war with France in the French and Indian War. The French lost their North American colonies, but the costs of the war put the British in debt.
- After the war, the British government adopted **policies** placing new taxes on the American colonists.
- Their first attempt to tax the colonists was the Stamp Act, a tax on every official document. British policies led to **colonial concerns**. Colonists argued that because they did not have representatives in the British Parliament, they had not agreed to this tax: "Taxation without representation is tyranny!"
- The colonists' marches, rallies, petitions, boycotts, and even tar-and-feathering of officials led the British Parliament to repeal (*cancel; take back*) the Stamp Act.
- Parliament kept, however, to the same policy of taxing the colonists. It next passed the Townshend duties (*taxes*) on various imports, like paper and glass. British troops were sent to control the colonists, and these troops were sometimes **quartered** (*sheltered*) in colonists' homes.
- Because of continuing colonial unrest, Parliament also repealed the Townshend duties. However, it passed a new tax on tea. Colonists protested against the tea duty in December 1773 with the Boston Tea Party. Colonists boarded a ship and threw its tea into the harbor.
- Parliament passed the Intolerable Acts to punish Boston for destroying the chests of tea. These acts closed Boston Harbor and **suspended** the Massachusetts legislature until the tea was paid for.

Outbreak of the Revolution

- Twelve colonies sent representatives to a "Continental Congress" to discuss their responses to British policies. The delegates sent protests to London, organized boycotts, and agreed to meet again.
- American Patriots and British troops fired at each other at Lexington and Concord, beginning the **American Revolution** in April 1775.
- The Second Continental Congress met and formed the Continental Army to fight the British.
- At first, most American colonists did not want independence. But when the British refused to give in to their reasonable demands and the fighting continued, many colonists changed their minds.

The Declaration of Independence

- By 1776, many colonists came to agree with Thomas Paine's pamphlet **Common Sense**, which urged the colonies to seek independence and create a democratic form of government without a king or queen.
- In June 1776, a resolution was introduced in the Second Continental Congress, proposing independence.
- A special committee wrote the **Declaration of Independence**. Thomas Jefferson was the main author. The document was approved by the Second Continental Congress on July 4, 1776. The colonies became independent states.

Main Ideas of the Declaration

- The Declaration announced American independence and explained this decision to the rest of the world. It presented a new theory of government, listed the colonists' grievances against the British, and established the United States as a new and independent nation able to make alliances and treaties.
- The Declaration explained that all people had certain "**unalienable rights**." These were God-given, **natural rights** to which everyone was entitled. Among these rights were "life, liberty, and the pursuit of happiness." Governments were "instituted" (*formed*) to protect those rights.
- The Declaration was based on the ideas of John Locke. It stated that governments "derive (*obtain; get*) their just powers from the consent (*agreement*) of the governed." This meant that governments receive their power from the people.
- People therefore had a right to overthrow any government that did not protect their natural rights.
- The Declaration claimed that Britain's government had become tyrannical. A tyrannical government is one that oppresses the people. The Declaration included a list of **colonial grievances** to prove it. The King had placed taxes on the colonists without their consent. He had quartered troops in their houses, cut off their trade, denied them trial by jury, suspended their legislatures, and sent troops to burn their towns and destroy their lives. Because of these actions, the colonists were declaring independence.
- The Declaration introduced a new theory of government based on liberty and equality. Its language has been used by many social movements in the United States, especially those on behalf of women and minorities.

What Do You Know?

SS.7.C.1.3

1. Which grievance contributed to the American colonists' desire for independence?
   A. British policies had made frontier lands too expensive.
   B. The King had denied the colonists their freedom of religion.
   C. The British government had been too generous to the Indian tribes.
   D. The British government had taxed the colonists without their consent.

SS.7.C.1.3

2. What was the main purpose of the tar-and-feathering shown in this British caricature of the colonists?
   A. to protest their being taxed without their consent
   B. to protest the high cost of British manufactured goods
   C. to protest British involvement in the French and Indian War
   D. to protest the quartering of troops in colonists' own homes

SS.7.C.1.3

3. The diagram below describes events leading to the Declaration of Independence.

   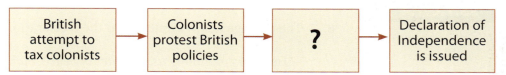

   Which event completes the diagram?
   A. British give up the attempt to tax the colonists.
   B. British apply armed force against the colonists.
   C. British agree to give the colonists their independence.
   D. British grant the colonists representation in Parliament.

SS.7.C.1.3

4. In the 1760s and 1770s, the British Parliament passed the Stamp Act, Townshend duties, Tea Act, and Intolerable Acts. What was the impact of these British policies?
   A. Indian tribes were able to keep their lands.
   B. Colonists began to think of becoming independent.
   C. The British government was able to pay off its debts.
   D. The French were defeated in the French and Indian War.

Chapter 2 | Americans Declare Their Independence

SS.7.C.1.4

5. Which complaint against King George III is stated in the Declaration of Independence?

   A. He had quartered his troops among the colonists.

   B. He had forced the colonists to accept the practice of slavery.

   C. He had required the colonists to trade with French merchants.

   D. He had failed to defend the colonists in the French and Indian War.

SS.7.C.1.4

6. Which document publicized the concept of "natural rights," later found in the Declaration of Independence?

   A. *Magna Carta*

   B. the English Bill of Rights

   C. the Mayflower Compact

   D. John Locke's explanation of the *Social Contract*

SS.7.C.1.4

7. According to the Declaration of Independence, what was an "unalienable right" that all governments should protect?

   A. the right to social equality

   B. the right to personal liberty

   C. the right to religious equality

   D. the right to elect government officials

SS.7.C.1.4

8. The passage below comes from the Declaration of Independence (1776).

   > "He has kept among us, in times of peace, Standing Armies without the Consent of our legislatures . . ."

   Which section of the Declaration contained this passage?

   A. its list of colonial grievances

   B. its justification of the conduct of the colonists

   C. its theory of government based on a social contract

   D. its announcement of American independence from Britain

SS.7.C.1.4

9. Which statement best describes the role of government according to the Declaration of Independence?

   A. "The main purpose of government is to expand and glorify the state."

   B. "The main purpose of government is to protect the unalienable rights of individuals."

   C. "The main purpose of government is to protect the rights and privileges of His Majesty, the King."

   D. "The main purpose of government is to promote the general welfare of the community by taking steps toward social equality."

Chapter 2 | Americans Declare Their Independence

SS.7.C.1.4

10. The passage below comes from the Declaration of Independence.

    "We hold these truths to be self-evident, that all men are created equal, that they are endowed by their Creator with certain unalienable Rights, that among these are Life, Liberty and the pursuit of Happiness. That to secure these rights, Governments are instituted among Men, deriving their just powers from the consent of the governed."

    According to this passage, what is the principal role of government?
    A. To promote greater social equality
    B. To protect the natural rights of citizens
    C. To glorify the ruler in the eyes of the Creator
    D. To help individuals cooperate against the forces of nature

SS.7.C.1.4

11. The diagram below summarizes ideas from the Declaration of Independence.

    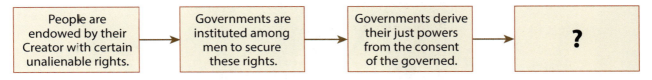

    Which statement completes the diagram?
    A. Because governments derive their just powers from the consent of the governed, they are incapable of acting against the people.
    B. Whenever any form of government becomes destructive of these ends, it is the right of the people to take peaceful measures to alter those policies.
    C. Whenever any form of government becomes destructive of these ends, it is the right of the people to alter or abolish it, and to institute new government.
    D. Because governments derive their powers from the consent of the governed, it is the obligation of the people to obey their government whatever it commands.

SS.7.C.1.4

12. Based on the Declaration of Independence, which is a natural right?
    A. the right to vote
    B. the right to bear arms
    C. the right to pursue happiness
    D. the right to equal protection of the laws

Chapter 2 | Americans Declare Their Independence

George Washington entering Philadelphia at the end of the Revolutionary War.

CHAPTER 3

The Story of Our Constitution

SS.7.C.1.5 Identify how the weaknesses of the Articles of Confederation led to the writing of the Constitution.

SS.7.C.1.7 Describe how the Constitution limits the powers of government through separation of powers and checks and balances. (See also Chapter 4.)

SS.7.C.3.3 Illustrate the structure and function (three branches of government established in Articles I, II, and III with corresponding powers) of government in the United States as established in the Constitution. (See also Chapters 4, 5, 6 and 7.)

Names and Terms You Should Know

State	To enforce laws	Congress
Confederation	National court system	House of Representatives
Articles of Confederation	Unanimous consent	Senate
Confederation Congress	Debt	President
Sovereign	Shays' Rebellion	Veto
To regulate trade	Constitutional Convention	

Florida "Keys" to Learning

1. After independence was declared, each former colony became a new state. Members of the Second Continental Congress agreed to the Articles of Confederation as a form of association between the states.

2. The Articles created a very weak central government. The new central government consisted of a "Congress" made up of representatives from the states. The state governments remained "sovereign" except for those powers they gave to Congress.

3. The new central government created by the Articles had the power to declare war, to exchange ambassadors with foreign nations, to enter into treaties and alliances, to resolve disputes between states, to regulate (*set rules for; control*) relations with certain Indian tribes, to borrow money, to build a navy, and to direct an army.

4. The government under the Articles had no national executive and no national court system (*judicial branch*). It could not raise its own troops or tax citizens. Any new law needed to be approved by nine states, and all thirteen states had to agree to any changes in the terms of the Articles of Confederation ("unanimous consent").

5. The Confederation Congress successfully negotiated a peace treaty with Britain and established a system for admitting new states into the United States.

6. Because the national government was weak, foreign nations could threaten American property and interests. American trade between states suffered, not enough money was printed, and the government threatened not to pay off its debts.

7. In Massachusetts, the state government raised taxes and foreclosed on farms to collect debts. Daniel Shays helped lead a rebellion in protest. The state militia eventually ended the rebellion. Events like Shays' Rebellion made many Americans desire a stronger central government.

8. In Philadelphia in May 1787, fifty-five delegates gathered at the state house to revise the Articles of Confederation. Instead, the delegates decided to write a whole new constitution—a plan of basic rules for government. Their assembly became known as the Constitutional Convention.

9. The members of the Constitutional Convention agreed that the country needed a stronger national government with separate legislative, executive and judicial branches.

10. The delegates disagreed about the future Congress. Larger states like Virginia wanted representation in Congress to be proportional to each state's population. Smaller states like New Jersey wanted all states to have equal representation.

11. The issue was finally resolved by the "Great Compromise": the number of members each state had in the House of Representatives would be based on population, but in the Senate, every state would have two Senators.

12. Many of the delegates did not trust the people to elect the President directly. Instead, the delegates created the Electoral College to elect the President.

The Articles of Confederation

After independence was declared, each colony became a separate and independent state.

> A **state** is a territory with its own government.

When the Second Continental Congress appointed a committee to write the Declaration of Independence, it also appointed a second committee to decide how the thirteen new states should cooperate. This committee drafted the **Articles of Confederation**. The Articles were debated for almost an entire year in the Continental Congress. Then they were sent to the state legislatures. The Articles of Confederation were finally approved by all thirteen states in 1781.

> A **confederation** is an association—an organization of separate states that cooperate together.

The Articles of Confederation created a "league of friendship," to which all thirteen states belonged.

After their experiences with Great Britain, most Americans feared giving too much power to the central government. They did not want a remote authority taxing them or threatening their rights, as the British government had done.

The Articles of Confederation therefore left most governmental powers in the hands of the states. The Articles set up a loose association in which the thirteen states could cooperate, especially in dealing with **foreign affairs** (*relations with other countries*). This association had a "Congress," which was the only branch of the national government. There was no national executive or national court system.

The **Confederation Congress**, the new body created by the Articles, was actually a council made up of the representatives of thirteen powerful, independent states. Each state had **one vote** in Congress.

Page 1 from the Articles of Confederation

> For the EOC test, you should know the main provisions of the Articles of Confederation and the weaknesses of the government it created.

Provisions of the Articles of Confederation

1. The new Confederation was to be known as the "United States of America."
2. Each state was to remain generally **sovereign** (*to have final authority*). The states kept all governing powers except those few given exclusively (*only*) to the Confederation Congress.
3. The **Congress** of the Confederation was to meet every year. Each state was to send from two to seven delegates to the Congress. Each state had one vote in Congress. All states, whatever their size, thus had equal representation.
4. Congress was given the **exclusive** power to declare war, to exchange ambassadors with foreign states, to enter into treaties and alliances, to set weights and measurements, to resolve disputes between states, to establish post offices, and to regulate (*set rules for; control*) relations with Indian tribes not found within one state. These powers could only be exercised by Congress and not by the states.
5. Congress could also borrow money, and build and equip a navy.
6. Congress had the power to direct its own army. However, it could not raise its own troops: these were contributed by the states.
7. All the expenses of the Confederation were to be paid from a general fund. State legislatures

Chapter 3 | The Story of Our Constitution

contributed to this fund. Congress could not directly tax citizens on its own.

8. The approval of nine states was needed to pass any new law in Congress.

9. All thirteen states had to agree to any changes in the Articles of Confederation. Changes to the Articles required **unanimous consent** (*complete agreement by everyone*).

Under the Articles, individual state governments remained more powerful than the central government. For example, states could print their own money. They could tax goods brought from other states. Only the state governments could collect taxes and raise troops. The Congress of the Confederation relied on contributions from the states to pay its expenses, yet had no power to force states to contribute. Each state government had its own executive and courts, while the Confederation lacked both of these. Could such a government work?

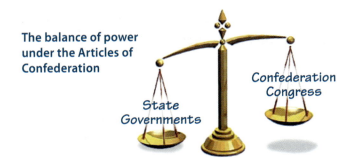

The balance of power under the Articles of Confederation

Main Weaknesses of the National Government under the Articles of Confederation

1. Congress had no power to tax.
2. Congress had no power to raise its own troops.
3. Congress had no power to regulate trade.
4. Congress had no power to enforce its laws.
5. There was no national court system.
6. There was no national executive to provide central leadership.
7. Changes to the Articles required unanimous consent (*complete agreement by everyone*).

The Active Citizen

▶ Imagine a family with two children. One child is given allowance money to spend each week. The second child is told to ask the first child for money. Which child is likely to become more powerful in this relationship? How is this situation similar to the relationship between the central government and the states under the Articles of Confederation?

▶ How did the experience of British rule affect the authors of the Articles of Confederation?

▶ What in your opinion was the greatest weakness of the Articles of Confederation? Explain your answer in a well-written paragraph.

America under the Articles of Confederation

Once the Articles of Confederation were approved in 1781, the Continental Congress was replaced by the Confederation Congress. These were critical years when it was unclear whether the former colonies would survive as independent, democratic states.

The Confederation Congress had several major accomplishments. It sent delegates to negotiate the peace treaty with Great Britain that ended the American Revolution. (To "negotiate" is to discuss issues and settle on terms.) The Congress also created an orderly procedure for new territories to be admitted into the United States as states.

Nevertheless, serious problems soon arose. First, there were problems with foreign nations. The British refused to abandon several of their forts in the Northwest despite the terms of the peace treaty ending the Revolutionary War. Spain challenged the borders of the new United States to the southwest. In far away North Africa, pirates attacked American ships once protected by the British navy. Without a strong national government, there was no one to watch over American interests.

Then there were growing economic difficulties at home. Despite winning the Revolution, many Americans faced hard times. To raise revenues, states taxed one another's goods. This hurt trade. There was a general shortage of money. Some state governments refused to honor their debts or to pay overseas lenders. The Confederation Congress lacked money, even though it owed back pay to veterans who had fought in the American Revolution.

A growing number of Americans believed that the state governments were becoming tyrannical and

Congress under the Articles of Confederation

State Governments

corrupt. Some state governments threatened freedom of religion; others failed to respect private property rights. George Washington feared that the jealousies and divisions of the states would prevent the development of a genuine national spirit. James Madison feared the "tyranny of the majority"—that state governments would not respect the rights of minorities, including property-owners.

Shays' Rebellion

In Massachusetts, an economic crisis led the state government to raise taxes and increase its efforts to collect its debts (*amounts of money owed to others*). It foreclosed on farms (*took ownership*) and sent debtors (*those who owed money*) to prison. Many of these struggling farmers had fought as soldiers in the Revolution. Poor farmers protested. Demonstrators shut down courts trying to collect taxes and debts. They demanded that Massachusetts print cheap paper money, as nearby Rhode Island had done. This would have raised prices and made the farmers' debts easier to repay.

Daniel Shays, a Massachusetts farmer, had served as a captain during the American Revolution. Shays led a group of angry farmers and debtors who attacked one of the state's courthouses. They demanded freedom for debtors, cheap paper money, and lower taxes. Shays' Rebellion created a wave of fear among wealthy landowners and merchants across the country. There was no national army to put down the rebellion if Massachusetts was unable to stop its spread.

Daniel Shays with fellow protestor

For the EOC test, you should know that the weaknesses of the Articles of Confederation and the fears excited by Shays' Rebellion led to the meeting of the Constitutional Convention.

A Call to Revise the Articles

In the end, the Massachusetts militia (*citizens' military force*) was able to crush Shays' Rebellion. But with all the other problems facing the country under the Articles of Confederation, many Americans began to think that it was time for a change. Merchants feared the loss of trade; army officers feared the loss of their

Chapter 3 | The Story of Our Constitution   59

back pay; lenders feared the loss of their loans to the government.

In 1786, a meeting was held in Annapolis, Maryland, to discuss trade between the states. Five states sent representatives. The members called for a meeting to be held in Philadelphia the following year. Its purpose would be to revise the Articles of Confederation. All thirteen states were invited to send representatives.

The Maryland State House, where the Annapolis meeting took place

"Miracle at Philadelphia"— The Constitutional Convention

Fifty-five delegates gathered at the state house in Philadelphia in May 1787. It was the same building where eight of them had signed the Declaration of Independence 11 years earlier.

Back in 1776, the colonists had cut their ties to Britain in the name of liberty. The challenge now was to construct a central authority strong enough to defend the nation and promote its well-being, yet not so strong that it would threaten individual liberties.

Every state except Rhode Island sent representatives to Philadelphia to revise the Articles. All of the delegates were men who owned property. More than half of them had trained as lawyers. One third of these men had fought in the Revolution.

The delegates immediately elected George Washington to preside over their proceedings. Just as quickly, they voted to keep their discussions secret from the public, in order to encourage a freer exchange of ideas.

Next, the delegates took a surprising step. They decided to replace the Articles of Confederation rather than just to revise them. The delegates set about writing a new **constitution**—a plan of basic rules for government. Their assembly became known as the **Constitutional Convention**.

The Active Citizen

Imagine that your class is about to form its own government. You must answer a series of questions to do so:

▶ Who should make the class rules?

▶ Who should make sure those rules are obeyed?

▶ Who should settle disputes between class members?

▶ Who should pay for class expenses?

▶ Who should be in charge of communicating with other classes?

Make a chart or outline showing your ideas for a plan of government for your class.

A **constitution** generally provides a framework for government. It limits government authority and protects the rights of the people. A government created by a written constitution is known as a **constitutional government**. Because we have a written constitution, we live under a constitutional government.

What the Delegates Agreed on

The delegates who met in Philadelphia in 1787 generally agreed that the government created by the Articles of Confederation was too weak. But how would they remedy (*fix*) this?

George Washington presiding over the Constitutional Convention

> This speech identified some of the weaknesses of the Articles of Confederation.

The Active Citizen

In his opening address, Governor Edmund Randolph of Virginia pointed to these weaknesses in the present system of government:

"(1) the Confederation produced no security against foreign invasion . . .

(2) the [Confederate] government could not check the quarrels between states nor a rebellion in any . . .

(3) there were many advantages which the United States might acquire (*get*), which were not attainable under the Confederation, such as a productive impost (*a tax on goods coming from other countries*)—counteraction of the commercial regulations of other nations—pushing of commerce . . .

(4) the [Confederate] government could not defend itself against the encroachments (*improper advances*) from the states . . ."

—James Madison's *Notes of the Constitutional Convention*, for May 29, 1787

Continues ▶

Chapter 3 | The Story of Our Constitution

▶ Which of the weaknesses identified by Governor Randolph do you feel was most important? Explain your answer.

_____
_____
_____
_____
_____
_____
_____
_____
_____
_____

▶ Imagine that you are a delegate at the Constitutional Convention. Complete this letter to your family from Philadelphia by explaining how the weaknesses of the Articles of Confederation have led the delegates to decide to write a whole new constitution.

Philadelphia, May 1787

Dear _____

We are meeting here in Philadelphia. We are sworn to secrecy, but I will tell you a little about what is going on if you promise not to tell anyone else. All of the delegates agree that the government created by the Articles of Confederation is too weak. Some of its major weaknesses are _____
_____
_____
_____
_____
_____

No one can see any good way to save the Articles of Confederation, so we have agreed to write a whole new constitution in their place.

Your loving _____

Only a few days after Governor Randolph's speech, the delegates passed the following resolution:

"That a national government ought to be established consisting of a supreme legislative, executive and judiciary."

The new national government would therefore have a separation of powers between three independent branches. This was just what Montesquieu had recommended, and what most of the state constitutions already had.

The members of the Constitutional Convention further agreed that the new legislature should have two houses, similar to the British Parliament:

- The first house, to be known as the **House of Representatives**, would represent the people. Its members would be elected directly by the people.
- The second house, to be known as the **Senate**, would represent the wisdom, wealth and property of America. As one delegate put it, the Senate should have "the most distinguished characters by rank and property." Senators would serve for longer terms than members of the House of Representatives. This way they would not be subject to the same popular pressures.

The delegates equally recognized the need for a national executive to provide leadership and to carry out the laws. But should this national executive be a single person or a small group?

After some debate, the members of the Constitutional Convention decided that the national executive should be one individual, known as the **President**. They further decided that the President should be given the power to **veto** (*deny or refuse*) new laws passed by Congress. However, to make sure the President was not too powerful, the delegates decided that two-thirds of both houses of Congress should be able to override the President's veto. Finally, they decided on the need for a national judiciary—the Supreme Court.

> You do not need to know about this disagreement for the EOC test, but it explains why the two houses of Congress are organized differently.

Enrichment

Large against Small

Of course, the delegates did not agree on everything. Their most important disagreement was over representation in the new houses of Congress.

Here, the larger states opposed the smaller ones. The larger states felt it was unfair for smaller states to have an equal voice in Congress when they had fewer people. The smaller states feared that the larger states would abuse their power if they were given more representatives because of their larger populations.

Virginia—then the most populous state in the nation—proposed that the representation of each state in Congress should be in proportion to its population. That is, the number of each state's representatives should be based on the size of its population.

The delegates from Virginia wished to apply this principle to *both* houses of Congress. Since Virginia, Massachusetts and Pennsylvania had the largest populations, they would therefore hold the most seats in both the House of Representatives and the Senate.

Chapter 3 | The Story of Our Constitution

New Jersey, one of the smallest states, suggested just the opposite. Its delegates even changed their minds about having two houses. They argued that representation in the legislature should remain as it had been under the Articles of Confederation. Each state should have an **equal** number of representatives in just one house. At the heart of this disagreement were conflicting views on the role of states in the future national government.

The Active Citizen

William Paterson

Mr. William Paterson (*New Jersey*): "Give the large states an influence in proportion to their [size], and what will be the consequence? Their ambition will be proportionally increased, and the small states will have everything to fear. New Jersey will never [agree]. She would be swallowed up. He had rather submit to a monarch, to a despot, than submit to such a fate. . . ."

Mr. James Wilson (*Pennsylvania*): "[A]s all authority was derived from the people, equal numbers of people ought to have an equal number of representatives, and different numbers of people different numbers of representatives. This principle had been improperly violated in the Confederation, owing to the urgent circumstances of the time . . . If small states will not [agree] to this plan, Pennsylvania . . . would not [agree] to any other . . ."

James Wilson

—James Madison's *Notes of the Constitutional Convention*, for June 9, 1787

▸ Explain in your own words why Paterson opposes letting the larger states have more representatives in Congress.

_____

_____

▸ Explain in your own words why Wilson argues larger states should be permitted to have more representatives in Congress.

_____

_____

▸ Which speaker would you have supported—Paterson or Wilson? Explain your answer.

_____

_____

▸ Imagine that you are a delegate to the Constitutional Convention in 1787. Using a separate sheet of paper, prepare a short speech (1–2 paragraphs) to the other delegates at the Constitutional Convention in which you address the disagreement between the large and small states.

The "Great Compromise"

Have you ever had a disagreement and settled it with a compromise? A **compromise** occurs when each side in a dispute gives up something in order to reach a solution that both sides can accept. The delegates from Connecticut proposed just such a compromise in 1787:

▶ States should enjoy proportional representation in the **House of Representatives**. States with larger populations would have more representatives there. This would benefit the larger states.

▶ Each state should have an equal number of Senators in the **Senate**. This would benefit the smaller states.

After two months of debate, a revised version of the Connecticut plan was finally adopted. The delegates agreed that each state would have **two Senators** in the Senate, and a number of representatives **proportional** to its population size in the House of Representatives. This solution became known as the "Great Compromise." It explains the organization of the two houses of Congress that we still have today.

You do not need to know about the Electoral College for the EOC test.

Enrichment

The Electoral College

The delegates also disagreed over how to choose the President. Many of the delegates did not trust the people quite enough to permit them to elect the President directly. James Madison of Virginia, for example, thought that Congress should select the President.

The delegates eventually decided that the President should be chosen by a group of special "electors," known together as the Electoral College. Each state would have a number of electors equal to the total number of its representatives in both houses of Congress.

To become President, a candidate would need the support of a majority of these electors. If no candidate won a majority, then the election would be decided by the House of Representatives.

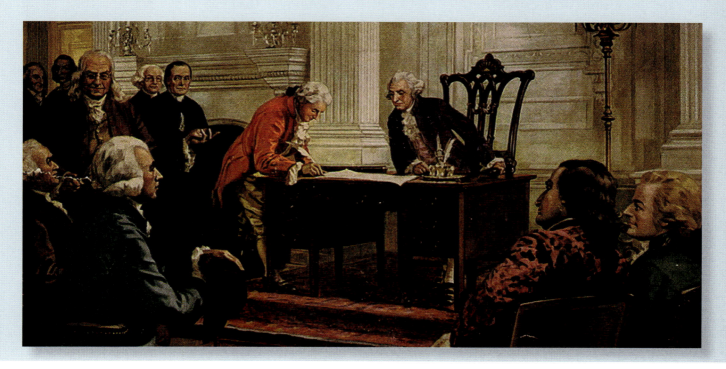

Chapter 3 | The Story of Our Constitution

In the next chapter, you will look more closely at the Constitution. You will learn about the organization of our federal government and about the most important principles of our Constitution.

The Active Citizen

1. How did the structure of Congress under the Constitution differ from that of Congress under the Articles of Confederation?

2. Benjamin Franklin was one of those few men at the Constitutional Convention who had also been a member of the Second Continental Congress. He signed both the Declaration of Independence in 1776 and the Constitution in 1787. Pretend that you are Benjamin Franklin in 1787. Write a letter to a friend comparing the discussions on declaring independence with those leading to the new Constitution. Be sure to give Franklin's views on both sets of events.

Comparing Two Structures of National Government

Articles of Confederation

One Branch

Congress of the Confederation

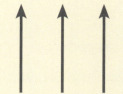

States

Each state sends several delegates but has only one vote in the Congress.

U.S. Constitution

Three Separate Branches

Article I. Legislative Branch
(makes the laws)

Congress

House of Representatives	Senate
Representatives elected by the people; states represented according to population	Two Senators from each state

Article II. Executive Branch
(enforces the laws; heads the government; controls the armed forces; directs foreign policy)

President
Vice-President
• Chosen by the Electoral College

Article III. Judicial Branch
(interprets and applies the laws)

Supreme Court
• Justices appointed by the President
• Lifetime tenure (term in office)

Changing (amending) the Articles or the Constitution

Unanimous consent (agreement by all the states)	2/3 of each house of Congress + 3/4 of the states

Powers

• No power to tax	• Congress has power to tax
• No power to raise its own army	• Congress has power to raise an army
• No power to regulate trade	• Congress has power to regulate trade
• No power to enforce its own laws	• President has power to enforce laws

Chapter 3 | The Story of Our Constitution

Name _____

Complete the concept ladder below by adding your own descriptions and explanations.

The Articles of Confederation (1781)

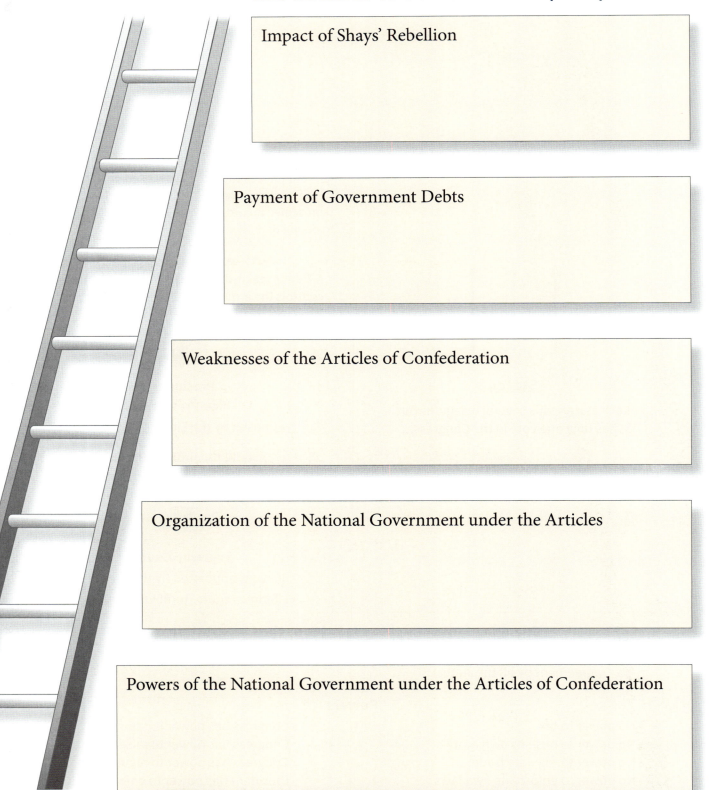

Impact of Shays' Rebellion

Payment of Government Debts

Weaknesses of the Articles of Confederation

Organization of the National Government under the Articles

Powers of the National Government under the Articles of Confederation

Chapter 3 | The Story of Our Constitution

Name _____

Complete the concept ladder below by adding your own descriptions and explanations.

The Constitutional Convention (1787)

Creation of a National Executive

"Great Compromise" and the Structure of Congress

Disagreement over Representation in Congress

Separation of Powers into Three Branches

Who Attended

Why It Was Held

Chapter 3 | The Story of Our Constitution

Name _____

Pretend you are a member of the Constitutional Convention. Write a note to another member of the Convention giving your views on the most important issues facing the Convention.

To Mr. _____, representative from the State of _____

My dear Sir,

In my humble view, the main weaknesses of our Articles of the Confederation are _____

_____

_____

_____

Therefore, I think we should forget about trying to revise the Articles. Instead, we should write a whole new Constitution.

It is very clear to me that our national government needs to have its own separate executive, legislative, and judicial branches.

Some people wonder whether the head of our new national executive should be one person or a small group. I believe _____

_____

_____

_____ .

I do not believe that the common people can know our leaders well enough or watch them closely enough to actually decide directly which ones should be chosen as President. Therefore, I believe the President should be chosen by _____

_____

_____

_____ .

Chapter 3 | The Story of Our Constitution

As you know, we have had plenty of debate over our new legislature, known as Congress. Should each state have the same number of representatives, or should larger states have more representatives?

I believe _____

_____

_____

_____.

This is because _____

_____

_____

_____

_____.

We have agreed on creating a national court system. Article III of the Constitution creates the Supreme Court, but we cannot agree on whether to create other, lower federal courts. To avoid any more disagreements, this issue has been left to our future Congress. I hope they decide to _____

_____

_____

_____.

There are those who fear that our new government will be too strong. They say it might abuse and oppress ordinary citizens. But I say that we need a stronger government to protect us from foreign countries and unrest at home.

I believe the Constitution can establish a strong and stable government while also protecting our individual liberties.

Yours sincerely with utmost respect,

Your very humble servant,

_____

Chapter 3 | The Story of Our Constitution

Name _____

Using as many of the names and terms from this chapter as you can, write two paragraphs explaining how the weaknesses of the Articles of Confederation led to the writing of the Constitution.

_____
_____
_____
_____
_____
_____
_____
_____
_____
_____
_____
_____
_____
_____

Review Cards: The Story of Our Constitution

The Articles of Confederation: Relationship to the States

After independence was declared, members of the Second Continental Congress drafted the **Articles of Confederation**.

- The Articles established a "league of friendship" between the 13 states.
- After their experiences under British rule, the members of the Second Continental Congress did not want to make a central government that was too strong. The Articles created a very weak central government, consisting of a "Congress" made up of representatives from the states.
- Most power remained with the states themselves, which had adopted their own state constitutions. The state governments remained sovereign (*supreme; the highest authority*) except for those powers given to Congress.

The Articles of Confederation and the Powers of the Confederation Congress

Each state had only **one vote** in the Confederation Congress.

The **Confederation Congress**—the only body of national government created by the Articles of Confederation—had these powers:

- Its main power was over foreign affairs: it could declare war, exchange ambassadors with foreign nations, and enter into treaties and alliances.
- It could also resolve disputes between states and regulate relations with certain Indian tribes.
- The Confederation Congress could borrow money, build a navy, and "direct" an army.

The national government created by the Articles of Confederation had several important **weaknesses**:

- **It could not raise its own troops**.
- **It could not tax citizens**; instead, it relied on the states to contribute money.
- Nine states were needed to approve any new law, and all thirteen states had to agree to any changes in the Articles (**unanimous consent**).
- There was **no national executive or judicial branch**.

Weaknesses of the Articles of Confederation Bring Problems

Under the Articles of Confederation, the nation had many problems, in both foreign and economic affairs.

- Because their national government was so weak, many Americans feared that foreign nations might take advantage of them.
- American trade suffered when states began to tax each other's goods, did not print enough money, and refused to pay their debts.
- During **Shays' Rebellion**, Massachusetts farmers rebelled when the state began to foreclose on their farms to collect debts. **Daniel Shays**, a former captain in the Revolution, led these protestors in attacking courthouses. There was no national army to put down the rebellion if it spread. The state militia eventually ended the rebellion.
- Events like Shays' Rebellion made many Americans desire a stronger central government. In 1786, representatives from several states called for the Articles to be revised.

The Constitutional Convention

- In 1787, fifty-five delegates, headed by George Washington, met in Philadelphia to revise the Articles of Confederation. They ended up scrapping the Articles altogether and writing a whole new **constitution** (*plan of government*). Their meeting became known as the **Constitutional Convention**.
- The members of the **Constitutional Convention** agreed that the country needed a stronger national government with separate legislative, executive, and judicial branches.
  - The new legislature would have two houses: the **House of Representatives**, representing the general population, and the **Senate**, representing those of wealth, property, and political experience.
  - The new executive would be the **President**. The President would have the power to veto laws passed by Congress, but such vetoes could be overridden by a two-thirds majority of each house of Congress.
  - The new judiciary would be the **Supreme Court**.

The Constitutional Convention: Disagreement and Compromise

▶ The delegates to the Convention had several major disagreements. The most important of these was over Congress. Larger states like Virginia wanted representation in Congress to be **proportional** to each state's population. Smaller states like New Jersey wanted all states to have **equal representation**.

▶ The issue was finally resolved by the "Great Compromise": the number of members each state had in the House of Representatives would be based on population, but in the Senate, every state, regardless of size, would have two Senators.

▶ Another important concern was how the President would be chosen. Most delegates did not trust the people to elect the President directly. Instead, the delegates created the Electoral College to elect the President.

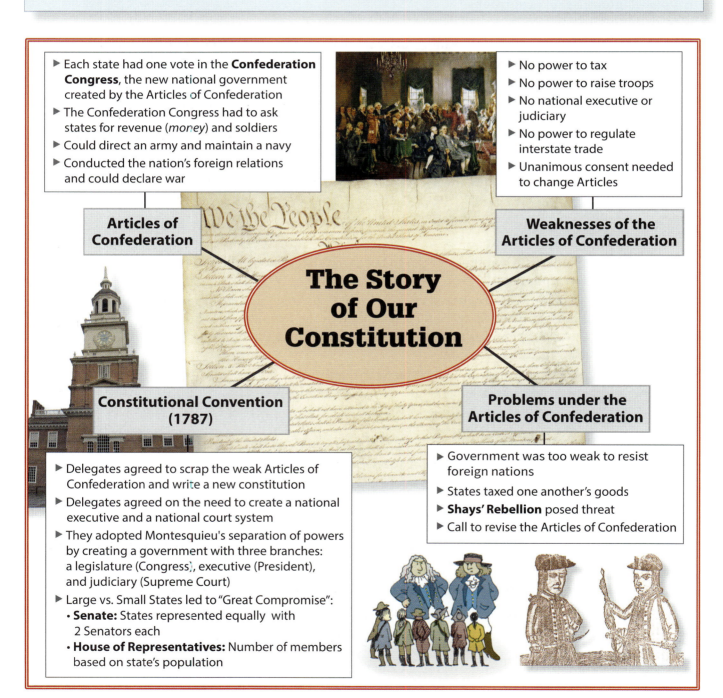

Articles of Confederation
- Each state had one vote in the **Confederation Congress**, the new national government created by the Articles of Confederation
- The Confederation Congress had to ask states for revenue (*money*) and soldiers
- Could direct an army and maintain a navy
- Conducted the nation's foreign relations and could declare war

Weaknesses of the Articles of Confederation
- No power to tax
- No power to raise troops
- No national executive or judiciary
- No power to regulate interstate trade
- Unanimous consent needed to change Articles

Problems under the Articles of Confederation
- Government was too weak to resist foreign nations
- States taxed one another's goods
- **Shays' Rebellion** posed threat
- Call to revise the Articles of Confederation

Constitutional Convention (1787)
- Delegates agreed to scrap the weak Articles of Confederation and write a new constitution
- Delegates agreed on the need to create a national executive and a national court system
- They adopted Montesquieu's separation of powers by creating a government with three branches: a legislature (Congress), executive (President), and judiciary (Supreme Court)
- Large vs. Small States led to "Great Compromise":
  • **Senate:** States represented equally with 2 Senators each
  • **House of Representatives:** Number of members based on state's population

The Story of Our Constitution

Chapter 3 | The Story of Our Constitution

What Do You Know?

SS.7.C.1.5

1. The postage stamp on the left shows a committee of the Second Continental Congress drafting the Articles of Confederation.

   Why did this committee create a weak central government?

   A. to encourage more trade between states

   B. to preserve the powers of the individual states

   C. to promote national security against foreign invasion

   D. to permit the taxation of citizens to pay the nation's debts

SS.7.C.1.5

2. How did Americans' experience under British rule influence the form of government they established under the Articles of Confederation?

   A. The new legislature had two houses, just like the British Parliament.

   B. The states were sovereign, just as the colonies had been under British rule.

   C. The new central government was not given any power to direct the military.

   D. The new central government was not able to tax citizens as the British government had tried to do.

SS.7.C.1.5

3. Which steps would the Confederation Congress have taken in the event of another war?

A.	B.	C.	D.
Declare war	Declare war	Ask states for permission to declare war	Declare war with the states
↓	↓	↓	↓
Raise its own troops to defend the nation	Ask states to contribute troops and funds	Borrow money	Pass a tax law to fund the army and build the navy
↓	↓	↓	↓
Pass a tax to raise money	Direct the army and navy	Raise an army and a navy	Direct the army and navy

SS.7.C.1.5

4. By 1786, why did many merchants want the Articles of Confederation to be replaced?

   A. Several states were taxing the activities of the Confederation.

   B. States were discouraging trade by taxing one another's goods.

   C. Congress was forcing the states to contribute to its general fund.

   D. The national government had printed so much money that it lost its value.

Chapter 3 | The Story of Our Constitution   75

SS.7.C.1.5

5. How did the U.S. Constitution solve a problem created by the Articles of Confederation?

    A. It stopped the national government from imposing taxes.

    B. It gave the national government the power to raise an army.

    C. It required unanimous consent of the states to pass amendments

    D. It prevented acts of piracy against American ships off the coast of Africa.

SS.7.C.1.5

6. The illustration on the left, from a popular almanac in 1787, shows Captain Daniel Shays.

    Why did his rebellion send a wave of fear among wealthy merchants and landowners?

    A. Officers worried about losing their back pay.

    B. Shays planned to take money from the rich and give it to the poor.

    C. There was no national army to put down domestic unrest if it spread.

    D. Bankers and other lenders feared the loss of loans to their national government.

SS.7.C.1.5

7. Which weakness of the Articles of Confederation was addressed by the Constitution?

    A. the continuation of slavery

    B. the lack of a national court system

    C. the absence of a balanced budget

    D. the need to strengthen the power of the states

SS.7.C.3.3

8. Below are two opposing views expressed at the Constitutional Convention.

1	2
As delegates from small states, we insist on a national legislature in which each state receives equal representation.	As delegates from large states, we believe that representation should be based on population. States with more people should have more representatives.

    Which feature of American government today was the outcome of this disagreement at the Constitutional Convention?

    A. A Bill of Rights was added to the Constitution to protect individual rights.

    B. Each state can decide how its own representation in Congress is determined.

    C. Representation in both our federal and state legislatures is now based on population.

    D. States have equal representation in one house of Congress and representation based on their population in the other.

Chapter 3 | The Story of Our Constitution

CHAPTER 4

A Quick Tour of the Constitution

SS.7.C.1.6 Interpret the intentions of the Preamble of the Constitution.

SS.7.C.1.7 Describe how the Constitution limits the powers of government through separation of powers and checks and balances.

SS.7.C.1.8 Explain the viewpoints of the Federalists and the Anti-Federalists regarding the ratification of the Constitution and inclusion of a bill of rights.

SS.7.C.3.3 Illustrate the structure and function (three branches of government established in Articles I, II, and III with corresponding powers) of government in the United States as established in the Constitution. (See also Chapters 5, 6 and 7.)

SS.7.C.3.4 Identify the relationship and division of powers between the federal government and state governments. (See also Chapter 11.)

Names and Terms You Should Know

U.S. Constitution	Common defense	Federalism
Preamble	General welfare	Ratification
"We the People"	Ordain	Federalists
"More perfect Union"	Limited government	Anti-Federalists
Establish justice	Constitutional government	*The Federalist Papers*
Domestic tranquility	Separation of powers	*Anti-Federalist Papers*
Posterity	Checks and balances	Bill of Rights

Florida "Keys" to Learning

1. The U.S. Constitution was finally approved by the delegates to the Constitutional Convention on September 17, 1787. The same document still governs the United States, more than two hundred years later.

2. The new Constitution consisted of a preamble (*introduction*) and seven articles.

3. The Preamble provided six purposes for establishing the Constitution: to "form a more perfect Union," to "establish justice," to "insure domestic tranquility" (*peace at home*), to "provide for the common defense," to "promote the general welfare," and to "secure the blessings of liberty."

4. Article I established the legislative branch, known as Congress. Congress has two "houses": the Senate and the House of Representatives. In the Senate, each state is represented by two Senators. In the House of Representatives, each state is represented in proportion to its population. Congress has special "enumerated powers" listed in the Constitution, such as to coin money and declare war. In addition, Congress has the power to pass any law "necessary and proper" for carrying out its enumerated powers. A bill must pass both houses of Congress and be approved by the President to become a law. Two-thirds of each house of Congress can override the President's veto.

5. Article II established the executive branch: the President and Vice President. The President must be a natural-born citizen who is at least 35 years old. The President is chosen by the Electoral College and serves for a four-year term. The President enforces federal law, serves as Commander in Chief of the armed forces, makes appointments, and delivers a "State of the Union" Address. The President can be impeached and removed by Congress for misconduct.

6. Article III established the judicial branch. The Supreme Court was established as the highest court in the land. The Constitution gave Congress the power to create any lower federal courts.

7. Article IV concerned state governments and the admission of new states to the United States.

8. Article V established procedures for amending the Constitution.

9. Article VI is known as the "Supremacy Clause," because it states that the Constitution and federal laws are the "supreme law" of the land.

10. Article VII set up procedures for ratifying (*approving*) the Constitution by state conventions.

11. The Constitutional Convention wanted to create a central government strong enough to protect the nation and to promote greater cooperation, while not so strong that it would oppress (*mistreat, abuse*) the people.

12. The system of government they introduced rested on several key principles: popular sovereignty, limited government, federalism, separation of powers, and checks and balances.

13. Based on Article VII, the proposed Constitution had to be ratified (*approved*) by special state conventions. At least nine states had to ratify it for adoption.

14. The Anti-Federalists opposed ratification. They felt the new federal government would be too strong and would threaten individual rights and liberties. They also demanded that a "bill of rights" be included in the Constitution.

15. The Federalists supported ratification (*approval*). They believed the country needed a stronger government. They argued that the federal government would not grow too powerful because its power would be divided between the states and the federal government. Power would be further separated among the three branches of the federal government, as Montesquieu had recommended.

16. Three leading Federalists published essays, known as *The Federalist Papers*, in favor of ratification. The "Anti-Federalist Papers" were various writings against ratification.

A Quick Tour of the Constitution

In the last chapter, you learned about the Articles of Confederation and the Constitutional Convention. By August 1787, the delegates in Philadelphia had completed the first draft (*written version*) of the new constitution. The final document was approved by the Convention just over one month later. It consisted of a preamble and seven articles. The same document still governs us, more than two centuries later. This chapter will give you an overview of the main provisions of the Constitution.

The Preamble

> Be sure to know the purposes of government stated in the Preamble for the EOC test.

The first part of the Constitution is the Preamble. A **preamble** is an introductory statement. The Preamble to the U.S. Constitution states the intentions (*aims*) of its authors. The Preamble explains the goals of the Constitution, which remain the goals of our federal government today:

> *We the People of the United States, in order to form a more perfect Union, establish justice, insure domestic tranquility, provide for the common defense, promote the general welfare, and secure the blessings of liberty to ourselves and our posterity, do ordain and establish this Constitution for the United States of America.*

- **"We the People"** = the citizens of the United States
- **More perfect** = more complete; better than before
- **Union** = a group of states united under one government
- **Establish justice** = to enforce laws fairly
- **Tranquility** = calm and peacefulness
- **Domestic tranquility** = peaceful and calm inside the country
- **Common defense** = defense of the entire community
- **General welfare** = well-being (happiness, health and good fortune) of the entire community
- **Posterity** = all future generations; those who will live after us
- **Ordain** = order or decree

Explain what each phrase of the Preamble means in your own words:

"We the People" _____

_____

_____

"in order to form a more perfect Union," _____

_____

_____

Chapter 4 | A Quick Tour of the Constitution

"establish justice," _____
_____
_____

"insure domestic tranquility," _____
_____
_____

"provide for the common defense," _____
_____
_____

"promote the general welfare," _____
_____
_____

"and secure the blessings of liberty to ourselves and our posterity," _____
_____
_____

"do ordain and establish this Constitution for the United States of America." _____
_____
_____

The Active Citizen

▶ Why did the Preamble begin with the words, "We the People"?

▶ What does this say about the source of power in American government?

Comparing the First and Final Drafts of the Preamble

Enrichment

The first draft of the Constitution was submitted to the Constitutional Convention on August 6, 1787. It began:

"We the people of the States of New Hampshire, Massachusetts, Rhode Island and Providence Plantations, Connecticut, New York, New Jersey, Pennsylvania, Delaware, Maryland, Virginia, North Carolina, South Carolina and Georgia do ordain, declare, and establish the following Constitution for the Government of Ourselves and our Posterity."

The Constitution was finally approved by the Constitutional Convention on September 17, 1787. It began:

"We the People of the United States, in order to form a more perfect Union, establish justice, insure domestic tranquility, provide for the common defense, promote the general welfare, and secure the blessings of liberty to ourselves and our posterity, do ordain and establish this Constitution for the United States of America."

Look at the two columns in the box above. Compare the first draft of the Preamble to the Constitution with the final version.

▶ What changes do you see? _____

_____

▶ What was the significance (*importance*) of those changes? _____

_____

▶ Did the Constitution "form a more perfect Union" than the Articles of Confederation? Discuss this question with a partner and then share your views with the class.

▶ The Preamble to the Constitution is generally viewed as a statement of the goals and purposes of our national government. Which **two** goals do you think are the most important ones?

☐ form a more perfect Union   ☐ provide for the common defense

☐ establish justice   ☐ promote the general welfare

☐ insure domestic tranquility   ☐ secure the blessings of liberty

Explain your selections (*choices*): _____

_____

_____

_____

Chapter 4 | A Quick Tour of the Constitution

▶ Which of these goals do you think can best be met by our national government? Mark these with "**N**." Which of these goals can best be met by state governments? Mark these with "**S**."

____ form a more perfect Union   ____ provide for the common defense

____ establish justice   ____ promote the general welfare

____ insure domestic tranquility   ____ secure the blessings of liberty

Explain your selections: _____

_____

_____

_____

The Organization of our Federal Government

The first three articles (*an article is a separate paragraph or section of a legal document*) of the Constitution established the basic structure of our national government—known as the "**federal government**." These articles created three separate branches of government with different powers and responsibilities:

Article I. The Legislative Branch: Congress

▶ This first article established the legislative branch, known as **Congress**.

▶ Congress has two "houses": the **Senate** and the **House of Representatives**.

▶ In the Senate, each state is represented by **two Senators**.

▶ In the House of Representatives, each state is represented by a number of members **in proportion to its population**.

▶ Members of the House of Representatives are elected for two-year terms.

▶ Senators are elected for six-year terms. (In the original Constitution, they were chosen by their state legislatures, but since 1913, Senators have been elected.)

▶ Article I gives Congress very specific powers (sometimes known as the "**enumerated powers**"). These include the power to declare war, to lay and collect taxes, to raise and support an army and navy, to coin money, to borrow money, to regulate trade between states, to establish post offices, to grant patents and copyrights, and to

- create lower courts. Patents and copyrights give inventors and authors sole ownership rights over their works for a limited period.
- Congress was also given the power to pass any law "**necessary and proper**" for carrying out the powers listed above. The clause granting this power has become known as the Elastic Clause.
- A **bill** must pass both houses of Congress and must be signed by the President in order to become a law. The President can **veto** (*reject*) a bill by refusing to sign it. A two-thirds majority in each house can pass a bill without the President's signature. This is known as "**overriding a veto**."

> You will learn more about Congress and the law making process in Chapter 5.

The Active Citizen

- List two important rules about Congress found in Article I of the Constitution.

Article II. The Executive Branch: the Presidency

- This second article established the offices of President and Vice President.
- The President must be a natural-born citizen who is at least 35 years old. The President is chosen by the Electoral College. After being elected, the President serves for a four-year term.
- The President enforces our federal laws, serves as the Commander in Chief of our armed forces, appoints and receives ambassadors, negotiates treaties, gives a "State of the Union" Address, and appoints judges and other federal officials.
- Congress can remove the President from office for misconduct by **impeachment**.

> You will learn more about the Presidency in Chapter 6.

The Active Citizen

- List two important rules about the President found in Article II of the Constitution.

Article III. The Judicial Branch: the Supreme Court

- This third article established the **Supreme Court** as the highest court in the land.
- The Supreme Court decides all disputes between states or concerning foreign ambassadors. The Supreme Court can also hear appeals of other cases.
- Federal judges hold office for life, during "good behavior." They can be impeached for misconduct.
- The Constitution did not create any lower federal courts. However, it gave Congress the power to create lower federal courts in the future.

> You will learn more about the Supreme Court and other federal courts in Chapter 7.

Chapter 4 | A Quick Tour of the Constitution   83

The Active Citizen

▶ List two important rules about the judicial branch found in Article III of the Constitution.

The Constitution also has a number of other important provisions.

Article IV. The States
▶ The citizens of every state enjoy the same rights and privileges in all other states.
▶ Congress can admit new states into the "Union" (*our nation*).
▶ Every state is guaranteed the **republican** form of government (*a government of representatives elected by the people*).
▶ Further prohibitions on state governments are found in Article I. For example, states cannot enter treaties, make alliances, or coin money. A **prohibition** is something prohibited or forbidden.

Article V. The Amending Process
▶ The Constitution can be **amended** (*added to or changed*).
▶ An **amendment** to the Constitution is harder to pass than an ordinary law. It must be approved by two-thirds (2/3) of each house of Congress and then be ratified by three-fourths (3/4) of the states.

You will learn more about amending the Constitution in Chapter 9.

Article VI. The Supreme Law of the Land
▶ The Supremacy Clause states that the Constitution and all federal laws are the "supreme law of the land."

Article VII. Ratification
▶ This last article established a procedure for deciding if the new Constitution should be adopted. Each state was to hold a special convention. The new Constitution would go into effect once nine of the thirteen states **ratified** (*approved*) it.

The Active Citizen

▶ How did the new Constitution remedy the major weaknesses of our national government under the Articles of Confederation? Use information from Chapters 3 and 4 to complete the chart below.

Weaknesses under the Articles of Confederation	How the Constitution Remedied this Weakness
Congress had no power to tax.	Article I gave Congress the power to lay and collect taxes.
Congress had no power to raise its own troops.	
Congress had no power to regulate trade.	
Congress had no power to enforce its laws.	
There was no national court system.	
There was no national executive to provide central leadership.	

▶ Review the chart on page 67 in the previous chapter and make your own Venn diagram comparing the Articles of Confederation and the Constitution.

Principles of the Constitution

The delegates to the Constitutional Convention struggled with one central issue. They wanted to create a central government strong enough to protect them and to promote greater cooperation, while not so strong that it would oppress (*mistreat or abuse*) them.

The system of government they introduced to solve this problem rested on several key principles:

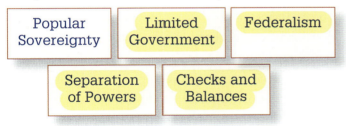

Popular Sovereignty

Popular Sovereignty
The People are Sovereign

The very first words of the Constitution are "We the People." This expresses the fact that under our system of government, the people are the source of all political power.

John Locke had written that people choose their own government through a social contract. The Declaration of Independence likewise announced that governments "deriv[e] their just powers from the consent of the governed."

A **sovereign** is the supreme—or highest—authority in any government. It is the authority that everyone else must obey. British subjects often referred to their king as their "Sovereign." In the United States, **the people are sovereign**—they are the final, supreme political authority.

The American people expressed their will by ratifying the Constitution. They continue to express their will by electing their representatives. These representatives, in turn, appoint other officials and make the decisions of government.

Limited Government

Chapter 4 | A Quick Tour of the Constitution   85

The second principle of the Constitution is that of **limited government.** One of the main reasons for having a **constitutional government** (a government based on a written constitution) is that the constitution defines and limits the power of the government over its citizens. The U.S. Constitution established a much stronger national government. But this government was still only given **limited powers**. It had only those powers specifically listed in the Constitution (especially in Article I). These powers were granted to it by the people.

All other powers, not listed in the Constitution, were left to the state governments and the people. These limits on the powers of our national government thus guaranteed (*made sure of*) the continuing importance of the state governments.

This should be compared to conditions in many other countries at the time. Many rulers enjoyed absolute power. There were no limits to what these rulers could do. The Tsar of Russia, for instance, could imprison his subjects and take away their property at will. Every person owed the Tsar absolute obedience. In the United States, neither Congress nor any state government has the power to take away someone's property or liberty without just cause and fair procedures.

Federalism

National (federal) government has some responsibilities

State governments have other responsibilities

A family may decide to divide its household tasks. The mother may cook the dinner; the father may wash the dishes; the children may clear the table and dry the dishes.

The Constitution created a similar division of responsibilities between our national government, known as the **federal government**, and the state governments.

The federal government is responsible for affairs affecting the nation as a whole, such as national defense. It has the sole (*exclusive*) power to appoint ambassadors, negotiate treaties, and declare war. Local matters, such as maintaining local roads and educating young people, are left to the states. Congress has no power to dictate what children learn in school, or what speed people drive their cars on local roads. This division of power and responsibility between our national and state governments is known as **federalism**.

The authors of the Constitution believed that the division of powers between the federal and state governments would ensure that the federal government did not become overpowering. They also believed this division of authority would provide the best way of governing an area as large as the United States.

> You will learn more about federalism and state government in Chapter 11.

Separation of Powers

Within the federal government itself, power is further divided by the **separation of powers**. The Constitutional Convention created a federal government with three separate branches: legislative, executive and judicial. Each branch exercises its own separate power:

- ▶ **Legislative Power**—the power to make federal laws—is exercised by Congress.

- ▶ **Executive Power**—the power to carry out and enforce federal laws—is exercised by the President.

- ▶ **Judicial Power**—the power to hear and decide cases applying federal law to specific situations—is exercised by the Supreme Court.

This separation of powers was based on the ideas of **Baron de Montesquieu**, whom you read about in Chapter 1. In fact, by 1787 each state already had a separation of powers in its own state constitution.

The authors of the Constitution saw the separation of powers as yet another way of making sure that the federal government did not become too strong.

In an **absolute monarchy**, a king or queen holds all of the powers of government. The monarch makes the laws, enforces the laws, and decides if the laws have been correctly applied. It is impossible for ordinary citizens to challenge anything that the king or queen has done. (You will learn more about absolute monarchies in Chapter 16.)

With the separation of powers, it becomes more difficult for the government to commit arbitrary (*unreasonable*) and unfair acts. Once the legislature makes a law, it is left to an independent executive to enforce that law in a fair and reasonable manner. A separate judiciary then decides if the application of the law was fair and just.

Each branch further acts as a "watchdog" over the others. Each branch makes sure that the other branches do not grow too strong. "Ambition," James Madison explained, thus curbs (limits) "ambition."

The separation of powers and system of checks and balances (about which you will read below) thus limit the power of our federal government so that it does not threaten our individual liberties.

Checks and Balances

Closely related to the separation of powers was the creation of a system of **checks and balances**. Each branch was given several specific powers to "**check**"—or *stop*—the other two. The overall aim of these checks and balances was to prevent any one branch of the federal government from becoming too strong.

The system of checks and balances also created an incentive for the different branches to cooperate.

Checks on Congress

- Each house of Congress checks the other house: the approval of both houses is needed to pass any new law.
- To pass a bill into law, Congress requires the signature of the President. The President can check Congress by **vetoing** its proposed legislation (refusing to sign the bill), although two-thirds of each house can override the veto.

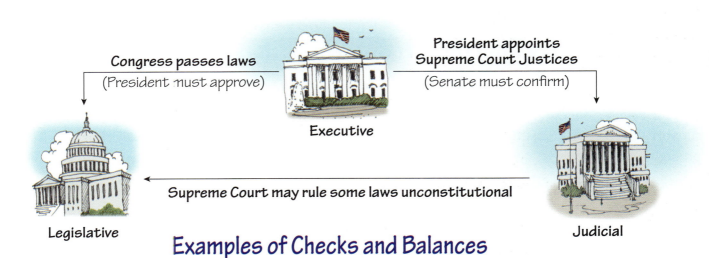

Examples of Checks and Balances

Chapter 4 | A Quick Tour of the Constitution

- The Supreme Court can check Congress by ruling that a federal law is **unconstitutional** (*violates some aspect of the Constitution*).

Checks on the President

- The President appoints Justices to the Supreme Court, ambassadors and other officials, but these appointments must be **approved by a majority of the Senate**.
- The President negotiates treaties with foreign nations, but these treaties must be **approved by two-thirds of the Senate**.
- The President controls foreign policy and acts as the Commander in Chief of the armed forces, but **only Congress can declare war**.
- The President establishes programs, but Congress can refuse to provide money for these programs.
- Congress can **impeach** the President.

- The Supreme Court can check the President by ruling that an executive order or Presidential action is **unconstitutional**.

Checks on the Supreme Court

- Congress can override decisions of the Supreme Court on federal law by passing a new law.
- Congress and the states can override the Supreme Court's interpretation of the Constitution by amending the Constitution.
- The President can influence the composition of the Supreme Court through judicial appointments.
- Congress can impeach federal judges, as civil officers, for treason, bribery or other crimes.
- The President can grant a pardon to someone convicted of a federal crime.

The Active Citizen

- Which of these checks do you think are the most effective ones? Why?
- Make a Venn diagram or chart comparing the principles of separation of powers and checks and balances. How are these principles alike? How are they different?
- How were the separation of powers and the system of checks and balances designed to limit the new federal government and prevent it from growing too strong?
- Do the separation of powers and the system of checks and balances make our government too slow?

The Debate over Ratification

Our Constitution begins with these stirring words: "We the People." But did the American people truly support the new Constitution when it was proposed?

Patrick Henry, a popular patriotic leader, loudly questioned the claim: "What right had they to say, 'We, the people?' . . . Who authorized (*gave permission to*) them to speak the language of, 'We, the people,' instead of, 'We, the states?' . . . The people gave them no power to use their name. That they exceeded (*went beyond*) their power is perfectly clear."

Article VII of the new Constitution set forth a procedure for its official adoption. The Constitution would come into force once it was **ratified** (*officially approved*) by nine states. To decide on ratification, each state held a special ratifying convention.

Federalists against Anti-Federalists

Debates now sprang up in all thirteen states to decide whether the Constitution should be ratified. Those who favored the new constitution called themselves **Federalists**. Opponents of the new constitution became known as **Anti-Federalists**.

Many of the Anti-Federalists, such as Samuel Adams, Patrick Henry and Richard Henry Lee, had been leading patriots during the American Revolution. They feared that the proposed Constitution would establish a central government just as oppressive as the British government had been. The Anti-Federalists were convinced that the new government would threaten personal liberties.

The Federalists warned that if a stronger central government were not soon adopted, the country might split apart or be invaded by foreign powers. They further argued that the new central government would never become despotic or oppressive. This was because of several safeguards built into the Constitution itself.

Constitutional Safeguards

- The division of power between the federal government and the states
- The separation of powers within the federal government
- The system of checks and balances

The most important Federalist arguments were published by Alexander Hamilton, James Madison and John Jay in a series of articles known as *The Federalist Papers*.

The purpose of *The Federalist Papers* was to persuade the ratifying convention in New York to approve the Constitution. *The Federalist Papers* argued that a stronger government was badly needed, while the principles of federalism, the separation of powers, and checks and balances would protect the liberty of every citizen.

The Active Citizen

"Ambition must be made to counteract ambition.... It may be a reflection on human nature, that such devices should be necessary to control the abuses of government. But what is government itself, but the greatest of all reflections on human nature? If men were angels, no government would be necessary. If angels were to govern men, [no] controls on government would be necessary. In framing a government which is to be administered by men over men, the great difficulty lies in this: you must first enable the government to control the governed; and in the next place oblige it to control itself...."

—James Madison, *Federalist No. 51*, February 6, 1788

▶ Why does Madison believe that different "devices" are needed to prevent the potential abuses of government?
_____
_____

▶ How did the new Constitution use "ambition" to counteract "ambition"? What steps did it take to make the government control itself?
_____
_____

Word Helper
ambition = strong desire to do something
counteract = act against
reflection = a thought; also something that bounces back
framing = making; designing
administered = managed or run by
oblige = require

Chapter 4 | A Quick Tour of the Constitution

Because the Federalists published *The Federalist Papers*, many historians refer to the writings of the Anti-Federalists as the "Anti-Federalist Papers". This name simply refers to the best essays and pamphlets written by those who opposed ratification of the Constitution.

Clashing Viewpoints on a Bill of Rights

A **bill of rights** is a list of rights guaranteed to individuals, such as freedom of religion or freedom of speech. In Chapter 1, you learned how King John had granted his subjects certain rights in 1215, and how Parliament had issued the English Bill of Rights in 1689.

After the American colonies achieved their independence, most states included a bill of rights in their state constitutions. However, the idea of a bill of rights was hardly discussed at all at the Constitutional Convention, where it was quickly dismissed.

The **Anti-Federalists** strongly criticized the absence (*lack*) of a bill of rights in the new Constitution. They felt that this revealed that the true aim of the authors of the Constitution was actually to rob the people of their liberties.

In *The Federalist Papers*, Alexander Hamilton argued that, while a bill of rights might be very helpful in a monarchy, it was quite unnecessary in a government formed by the people themselves:

> "[B]ills of rights are, in their origin, [agreements] between kings and their subjects . . . [T]hey have no application to constitutions [based on] the power of the people, and executed by their immediate representatives and servants. Here, in strictness, the people surrender nothing, and as they retain (*keep*) everything, they have no need of particular reservations."

Even so, to win support for the Constitution in the state ratifying conventions, the Federalists promised to add a bill of rights.

After the Constitution was adopted, the first Congress did indeed propose a bill of rights in the form of twelve amendments in 1789. James Madison, a leading Federalist, was actually the one to introduce these in Congress.

Ten of the twelve proposed amendments were quickly ratified by the states and became part of the Constitution by 1791. These first ten amendments became known as the **"Bill of Rights."** The First Amendment may be the most famous one. It guarantees freedom of speech, freedom of the press, the right to assemble, the right to petition the government, and freedom of religion. You will learn more about this and the other amendments in the Bill of Rights in Chapter 9.

Pretend you are a Federalist who supports ratification of the Constitution. Write a letter to a friend giving your views.

It is clear that we need a stronger national government. But many fear that the new federal government under the proposed Constitution will oppress us. I disagree. We will be protected by several important constitutional principles.

Federalism will protect us by _____.

The separation of powers will protect us by _____.

Finally, the system of checks and balances will protect us by_____.

For these reasons, I believe you should support ratification of the Constitution.

The Active Citizen

▶ Imagine that your class is a state convention in 1788, deciding whether or not to ratify the new Constitution. Some members of the class should pretend to be Federalists. Others should pretend to be Anti-Federalists. Your "convention" should then debate the question of ratification. Be sure to consider the absence of a bill of rights as part of the debate. After the debate is over, your class should take a vote on whether the Constitution should be ratified.

▶ Imagine it is 1788. Write your own newspaper article for or against ratification of the Constitution. Also make your own political cartoon to accompany your article.

Add your cartoon below.

Chapter 4 | A Quick Tour of the Constitution

Name _____

Make a question relating to each box of words and phrases. Then exchange questions with a classrooom partner and answer them.

- Constitution
- Preamble
- "We the People"
- Posterity
- Ordain

- More perfect Union
- Justice
- Domestic tranquility
- Common defense
- General welfare
- Blessings of liberty

- Congress
- House of Representatives
- Senate
- Senator
- Elastic Clause
- Veto

- President
- Vice President
- Electoral College
- Commander in Chief
- "State of the Union" Address
- Impeachment

- Judicial Branch
- Supreme Court
- Supreme Court Justice
- "Good behavior"
- Lifetime appointment

Name _____

Fill in the charts below.

Limited Government	
Define this constitutional principle:	How does limited government differ from other constitutional principles?
Give an example of something in the Constitution illustrating limited government:	Give an example *not* illustrating limited government:

Federalism	
Define this constitutional principle:	How does federalism differ from other constitutional principles?
Give an example of something in the Constitution illustrating federalism:	Give an example *not* illustrating federalism:

Chapter 4 | A Quick Tour of the Constitution

Name _____

Fill in the chart below.

Separation of Powers	
Define this constitutional principle:	How does the separation of powers differ from other constitutional principles?
Give an example of something in the Constitution illustrating the separation of powers:	Give an example *not* illustrating the separation of powers:

Checks and Balances	
Define this constitutional principle:	How do checks and balances differ from other constitutional principles?
Give an example of something in the Constitution illustrating checks and balances:	Give an example *not* illustrating checks and balances:

Chapter 4 | A Quick Tour of the Constitution

Checks and Balances

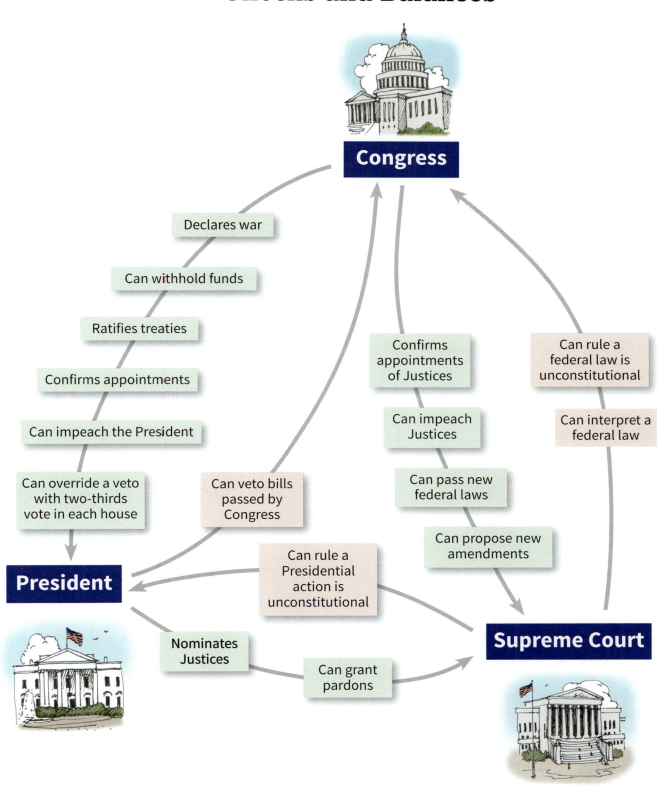

▶ Why did the authors of the Constitution create this system of checks and balances?
▶ Does the Constitution have too many checks?

Chapter 4 | A Quick Tour of the Constitution

Name _____

Fill in the chart below.

Our Federal Government

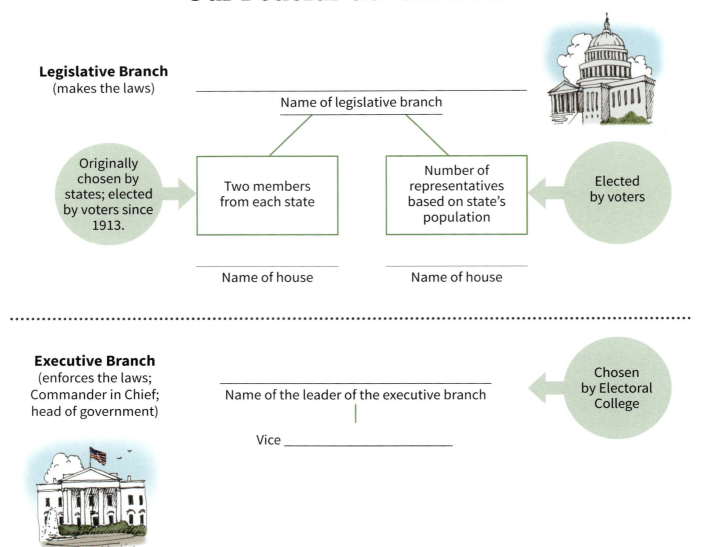

Legislative Branch
(makes the laws)

Name of legislative branch

Originally chosen by states; elected by voters since 1913.

Two members from each state

Number of representatives based on state's population

Elected by voters

Name of house

Name of house

Executive Branch
(enforces the laws; Commander in Chief; head of government)

Name of the leader of the executive branch

Vice _____

Chosen by Electoral College

Judicial Branch
(interprets the laws and applies them to specific cases)

Name of highest court

Lower federal courts (created in 1789)

Appointed for life terms

96   Chapter 4 | A Quick Tour of the Constitution

Review Cards: A Quick Tour of the Constitution

The Preamble

The **Preamble** (*introduction*) states six purposes for establishing the Constitution. In fact, the Preamble describes the six purposes of our federal government in general:

(1) To "**form a more perfect Union**": The new national government would be stronger and more unified than the government under the Articles of Confederation. Under the Articles of Confederation, for example, states had taxed one another's goods, hurting the national economy. Under the new government, which would unite the country, Americans would act together.

(2) To "**establish justice**": This is one of the roles of governments generally. Unlike the Articles of Confederation, this new government would have a national court system.

(3) To "**insure domestic tranquility**" (*peace at home*): Shays' Rebellion had demonstrated that the national government needed greater resources to insure peace and to maintain order.

(4) To "**provide for the common defense**": Several potential threats had shown the need for a stronger national government to defend American interests against foreign powers.

(5) To "**promote the general welfare**": The new national government would promote the "general welfare"—the general well-being of all its citizens.

(6) To "**secure the blessings of liberty**": "Liberty" (individual freedom) was one of the "unalienable" rights mentioned in the Declaration of Independence. Only by being strong, however, could the new national government protect liberty and other individual rights.

The Structure of Our Constitution: Article I

Article I: Congress: the legislative branch—makes the laws.
- Two houses: Senate and House of Representatives.
- Every state has two Senators.
- Each state is represented in the House of Representatives in proportion to its population.
- **"Enumerated" Powers:** the specific powers of Congress listed in the Constitution, such as to coin money and declare war.
- **Necessary and Proper Clause**, also known as the Elastic Clause: Congress has whatever other powers it needs to carry out its enumerated powers.
- A bill must pass both houses of Congress and be approved by the President to become a law. Two-thirds of each house of Congress can override the President's veto.

The Structure of Our Constitution: Article II

Article II. The President: the executive branch—carries out the laws.
- The President enforces our federal laws.
- The President also acts as Commander in Chief of our armed forces.
- The President must be a natural-born citizen and be at least 35 years old.
- The President is elected by the Electoral College.
- The President can be impeached and removed by Congress for misconduct.

Chapter 4 | A Quick Tour of the Constitution

The Structure of Our Constitution: Article III

Article III. The Supreme Court: the judicial branch—interprets and applies the laws.
- The Supreme Court is the highest court in the land.
- Federal judges hold their offices for life during "good behavior" (until retirement or removal for misconduct).
- Congress was given the power to create lower federal courts.

The Structure of Our Constitution: Other Articles

Article IV—On state governments and the admission of new states into the United States.

Article V—**Amendment process**—establishes procedures for amending (*adding or changing*) the Constitution.

Article VI—The "**Supremacy Clause**"—The Constitution and federal laws are the "supreme law" of the land.

Article VII—Process for **ratifying** (adopting) the Constitution by state conventions.

The Ratification Debate

Based on Article VII, the proposed Constitution had to be **ratified** (*approved*) by special state conventions. At least 9 states had to ratify it for adoption. A lively debate took place in each state over whether the new Constitution should be adopted.

- **Anti-Federalists:** The **Anti-Federalists** opposed ratification. They felt the new federal government, proposed by the Constitution, would be too strong and would threaten individual rights and liberties. They also demanded that a "bill of rights" be included in the Constitution.
- *The Anti-Federalist Papers:* The various writings of the Anti-Federalists.
- **The Federalists:** The **Federalists** supported ratification of the new Constitution. They believed the country needed a stronger government for defense against foreign powers and to ensure tranquility (*calm*) at home. They argued that the federal government created by the Constitution would not become too powerful or oppressive because power would be divided between the states and the federal government. Power would be further divided among the three separate branches of the federal government, which would check and balance each other.
- *The Federalist Papers:* Three leading Federalists—Alexander Hamilton, James Madison, and John Jay—published essays to persuade members of the New York Convention to ratify the Constitution. Afterwards, these essays were published in a single book as *The Federalist Papers*.

Constitutional Principles

Popular Sovereignty: The people are the final, supreme authority; the source of all political power.

Limited Government: The federal government has only those powers granted to it in the Constitution.

Federalism: Governmental responsibilities are divided between the **federal** (national) government and the **state** governments.

Separation of Powers: The powers of the federal government are divided among three branches: the legislative, executive, and judicial.

Checks and Balances: Each branch of the federal government has specific powers to check the other branches; for example, the President can **veto** legislation; the Senate can refuse to **confirm** a nomination or to **ratify** a treaty.

Illustrate Constitutional Principles with Quotations

Your teacher will divide your class into five groups. Each group will be assigned one of the constitutional principles on the chart on the next page. Your group should (1) identify the articles where your assigned principle is found in the Constitution, and (2) illustrate that principle with a quotation from one of the delegates to the Constitutional Convention. Your group should look online for a copy of the Constitution to identify the articles where the principle is found. They can find quotations by the delegates in Chapters 3 and 4 of this book, or also on the Internet. The members of your group should place their answers in the chart on the next page. Then they should fill in the rest of the chart using the information and examples found by other groups.

For example, for checks and balances a group might use this quotation, which can be found in Madison's writings online:

> *"Place three individuals in a situation [in which] the interest of each depends on the voice of the others, and give to two of them an interest opposed to the rights of the third. Will the latter be secure?"*
>
> —James Madison, 1821

▶ What is Madison saying in this quotation about the power of two branches of government to check the actions of a third branch?

The quotation in *The Active Citizen* on page 89 might also be used to illustrate the concept of checks and balances.

Chapter 4 | A Quick Tour of the Constitution

Name ________________________________

Fill in the chart below.

Constitutional Principles		
	Article(s)	Quotation
Limited Government		
Checks and Balances		
Federalism		
Separation of Powers		
Popular Sovereignty		

Name _____

Complete the following text.

The Story of Our Constitution

The 57 members of the Constitutional Convention assembled in Philadelphia on May 25, 1787. They continued their meetings until late September. They met in the same building where the members of the Second Continental Congress had signed the _____ eleven years earlier.

In 1787, the delegates were sent to Philadelphia to revise the _____. They quickly decided to replace them with a whole new constitution and a stronger national government. They generally agreed that the new national government should have three separate branches, including an _____ branch and a _____ branch, as well as a legislative branch.

The new legislature was to be known as Congress. Most of the delegates believed that Congress should have two houses, like the British Parliament. Delegates from larger states, such as Virginia, proposed that the number of representatives each state had in Congress should be based on _____ _____. Members from smaller states, such as New Jersey, disagreed. Many of them even decided that Congress should have only one house. They argued that in Congress, the number of representatives that each state had should be _____.

This dispute over representation in Congress was only finally resolved when the representatives from Connecticut proposed a skillful compromise. They proposed that the two houses of Congress should be organized differently. In the Senate, each state would have _____. In the House of Representatives, each state would have _____.

This "Great Compromise" explains the way in which our Congress is still organized today.

The members of the Constitutional Congress also discussed how the President, the head of the new executive branch, should be chosen. Many delegates feared that ordinary citizens did not know individual leaders well enough to choose the President themselves. So they decided that the President would be selected by the _____. Each state would have a number of electors equal to the number of that state's Senators and _____ in Congress.

The members of the Constitutional Convention further set up a process for approval of the Constitution by the people. Before it could be adopted, the new Constitution had to be _____ by at least nine of the thirteen states. Those who favored adopting the new Constitution became known as the _____. Those who opposed the new Constitution became known as the _____. One of their strongest criticisms was that the proposed Constitution lacked a _____. By June 1788, enough states had approved the Constitution for it to go into effect. Some of the largest states, like Virginia and New York, actually approved the Constitution after this date. George Washington became our first President in 1789. We are still governed by the same Constitution more than 200 years later.

Chapter 4 | A Quick Tour of the Constitution

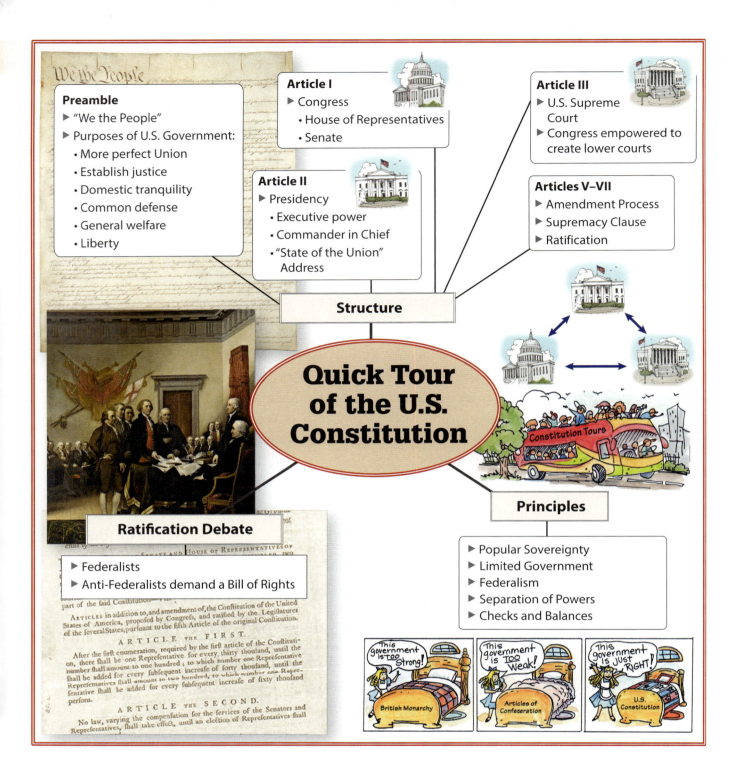

Chapter 4 | A Quick Tour of the Constitution

What Do You Know?

SS.7.C.1.6

1. Why did the *Preamble* to the Constitution begin with the phrase, "We the People"?
   - A. to indicate that the national government had limited powers
   - B. to indicate that the states had been associated in a confederation
   - C. to indicate that federal power was separated among three branches
   - D. to indicate that the American people were the ultimate source of its authority

SS.7.C.1.6

2. Which identifies one of the goals of government listed in the Preamble?
   - A. to guarantee employment to all citizens
   - B. to expand the nation's frontiers westward
   - C. to establish independence from Great Britain
   - D. to protect the rights and freedom of all citizens

SS.7.C.1.7

3. The chart below shows the organization of the government of the United States, based on the Constitution.

The Legislative Branch: makes laws	The Executive Branch: enforces laws	The Judicial Branch: applies laws and settles disputes
Article I: Congress	Article II: Presidency	Article III: Supreme Court

   Which constitutional principle is illustrated by the chart?
   - A. federalism
   - B. separation of powers
   - C. checks and balances
   - D. popular sovereignty

SS.7.C.1.7

4. When the President nominates an individual to serve as Secretary of State, the Senate must confirm the appointment. Which constitutional principle does this illustrate?
   - A. limited government
   - B. popular sovereignty
   - C. separation of powers
   - D. checks and balances

Chapter 4 | A Quick Tour of the Constitution

SS.7.C.1.7

5. The list below provides three examples of actions by the U.S. government.

   > ▸ The President meets with the Prime Minister of the United Kingdom.
   > ▸ The Supreme Court declares a law unconstitutional.
   > ▸ Congress passes a new environmental law.

   Which constitutional principle do these examples illustrate?
   A. limited government
   B. popular sovereignty
   C. separation of powers
   D. checks and balances

SS.7.C.1.7

6. Which example illustrates the principle of checks and balances?
   A. The Supreme Court interprets a federal law.
   B. The President vetoes legislation proposed by Congress.
   C. The President confers with the members of the Cabinet.
   D. A case between citizens from different states is tried in a federal court.

SS.7.C.1.8

7. Why did Anti-Federalists believe that it was critically important for a democratic society to provide constitutional guarantees for free speech and a free press?
   A. They encouraged citizens to vote.
   B. They encouraged an open exchange of ideas.
   C. They supported the growth of political parties.
   D. They helped government leaders to control the people.

SS.7.C.1.8

8. What was one of the Anti-Federalists' strongest arguments against the Constitution?
   A. It did not create a national executive.
   B. It did not include a list of protected rights for individuals.
   C. The new central government would be too dependent on the states.
   D. The new central government would be too weak to protect American interests abroad.

SS.7.C.1.8

9. What was one outcome of the debate between Federalists and Anti-Federalists over the ratification of the Constitution?
   A. the later addition of the Bill of Rights
   B. the acquisition of Florida from Spain
   C. the spread of slavery into Western territories
   D. the acquisition of the Louisiana Purchase from France

CHAPTER 5

Congress: Our Legislative Branch

SS.7.C.2.9 Evaluate candidates for political office by analyzing their qualifications . . . (See also Chapter 13.)

SS.7.C.3.3 Illustrate the structure and function (three branches of government established in Articles I, II, and III with corresponding powers) of government in the United States as established in the Constitution. (See also Chapters 4, 6 and 7.)

SS.7.C.3.8 Analyze the structure, functions, and processes of the legislative, executive, and judicial branches. (See also Chapters 4, 6 and 7.)

SS.7.C.3.9 Illustrate the lawmaking process at the local, state, and federal levels. (See also Chapter 12.)

Names and Terms You Should Know

- Article I
- House of Representatives
- Senate
- Delegated powers
- Enumerated powers
- Coin and print money
- Declare war
- Naturalization laws
- Regulation of immigration
- Regulation of trade
- "Necessary and proper"
- Implied powers
- Elastic Clause
- Impeachment
- Treaty
- Presidential appointments
- Confirmation
- Caucus
- Speaker of the House
- President pro tempore of the Senate
- Majority leader
- Minority leader
- "State of the Union" Address
- Bill
- Committee
- Conference committee
- Veto

Florida "Keys" to Learning

1. Congress is the legislative, or law-making, branch of the federal government.

2. Congress has two chambers or "houses": the House of Representatives and the Senate. The House has 435 members. The number of representatives each state has in the House is proportional to the size of its population. In the Senate, there are 100 members. Each state has 2 Senators.

3. Congress has "enumerated" powers. Its "enumerated" powers are those specifically listed in Article I, Section 8. These include the power to tax and spend, to borrow, to coin and print money, to declare war, to raise and support armies, to maintain a navy, to regulate interstate commerce, to make rules for immigration and naturalization (*becoming a U.S. citizen*), and to establish lower federal courts.

4. Congress also has "implied" powers. These powers are not specifically listed in the Constitution, but are based on the Elastic Clause. This clause gives Congress the power to make "all laws which shall be necessary and proper for carrying into execution" the enumerated powers. This clause permits Congress to do anything it reasonably needs to do to perform its enumerated powers.

5. Congress also has special powers to oversee and check the other branches. For example, Congress has the power to impeach and remove the President and other federal officers. The Senate must confirm Presidential nominations and ratify treaties.

6. Based on the system of checks and balances, Congress can be checked in several ways. The President can veto (*turn down; refuse*) legislation passed by Congress. Congress can only override the President's veto with a vote of two-thirds of each house. The Supreme Court can declare Congressional laws to be unconstitutional.

7. To be a Representative, a person must be at least 25 years old, be a U.S. citizen for 7 years, and live in the state represented. To be a Senator, a person must be at least 30 years old, be a U.S. citizen for 9 years, and live in the state represented.

8. The key leaders of Congress are the Speaker of the House (the leading member of the majority party in the House), the Vice President of the United States (who serves as President of the Senate), and the President pro tempore of the Senate (who presides over the Senate when the Vice President is absent). There is also a majority leader and a minority leader for each house.

9. Congress does most of its work in committees. These consist of three types. Standing committees are permanent committees that deal with all bills on particular subjects. Special (or select) committees are created for specific and temporary purposes. Conference committees are formed by members of both houses to eliminate inconsistencies between the different versions of a bill passed in each house.

10. To become a law, a bill must pass through several steps. First, it is introduced by a Representative or Senator in one of the houses. Then it is sent to committee, where it can be "pigeonholed," disapproved or approved. If approved, it is reintroduced to the house for debate and vote on the floor of the house. If the bill is approved in one house, it goes through the same stages in the other house. Then it goes to a conference committee to iron out differences between the two versions of the bill. Lastly, it goes to the President for final approval. The President can sign, veto or "pocket veto" the bill. Congress can override the President's veto with a two-thirds majority in each house.

The delegates to the Constitutional Convention energetically debated which powers should be given to the new federal government. Following the suggestions of the Baron de Montesquieu, they separated the new government's powers among three branches. They hoped that each branch would act as a watchdog, making sure that the other two branches did not grow too powerful or oppressive (*abusive*).

Congress was viewed at the time as the most powerful branch of government. Under the "Great Compromise," Congress was given two houses. The division of Congress into two houses was seen as another way to limit its power. For a bill (*a proposed law*) to become law, a majority (*more than half*) of both houses of Congress would be needed to approve it.

In this chapter, you will learn more about Congress, our legislative branch.

The Structure of Congress

> "All legislative powers . . . shall be vested in a Congress of the United States . . ."
> —U.S. Constitution, Article I, Section 1

The Constitution created Congress as the branch to make all federal laws. The new Congress consisted of two separate houses or chambers: the **Senate** and the **House of Representatives**.

The Senate 100 members

The House of Representatives 435 members

Be sure to know the enumerated and implied powers of Congress for the EOC test.

The Powers of Congress

The Constitution gave Congress both legislative (*law-making*) and non-legislative powers.

The "Enumerated" Powers

The specific powers of Congress are listed in Article I, Section 8 of the Constitution. These are sometimes known as the "**delegated**" or "**enumerated**" (*listed*) powers. These powers include:

1. The power to tax and to spend

Congress has the power to "lay (*raise*) and collect taxes, duties, imposts and excises, to pay the debts and provide for the common defense and general welfare of the United States."

Congress thus has the power to raise money through taxes and to spend it for defense and the public welfare.

Originally, Congress' power to tax was limited to duties on imports (*foreign goods entering the U.S.*) and to taxes on the sale of particular goods. The Sixteenth Amendment, passed in 1913, also gave Congress the power to tax individual and corporate incomes. Since that time, income taxes have become the government's chief source of revenue (*income*). Since states also have the power to tax, this is known as a **concurrent power**—a power shared by the federal and the state governments.

Chapter 5 | Congress: Our Legislative Branch

2. The power to borrow money

Congress is able to borrow money. It does so by selling government bonds (*certificates*). These bonds entitle their owners to interest payments (*payments for the use of money*). This is also a concurrent power.

3. The power to regulate trade between states

Under the Articles of Confederation, economic rivalries between the states became intense. States restricted the flow of goods across state lines. Under the Articles of Confederation, Congress had no power to remedy this situation. The Constitution gave the new Congress the power "to regulate commerce with other nations, among the states, and with the Indian tribes." Commerce is the buying, selling and trading of goods and services. Commerce between parties in different states of the United States is known as "interstate commerce." Congress thus has the power to regulate (*make rules for*) trade between states and with foreign countries. This is one of the most important powers of the federal government.

4. The power to regulate immigration and naturalization (*granting immigrants citizenship*)

The Constitution gave Congress the power to make laws regulating how immigrants can enter the United States and how they can become U.S. citizens. These powers are held by the federal government alone and are not shared with the states.

5. The power to establish standard weights, coin money, and punish counterfeiters

Congress was given the power to print and coin money and to "fix the standards of weights and measures." This provision allowed Congress to establish a common currency, ending the confusion that had existed when each state had issued its own money. Congress was also given the power to punish counterfeiting (*making false money*), which became a federal crime.

6. The power to establish post offices

Communication by mail was essential in the days before the telegraph, telephone, radio and Internet. The Second Continental Congress had appointed Benjamin Franklin as Postmaster General as early as 1775. The Articles of Confederation had given the Confederation Congress "the sole and exclusive right and power of … establishing or regulating post offices from one State to another, throughout all the United States." The Constitution followed this example and gave Congress the power "to establish post offices and post roads," so that the mail might be delivered. Congress continues to regulate the U.S. Postal Service today.

7. The power to establish patents and copyrights

Copyrights provide authors with an exclusive right to their writings for a limited period of time. Patents give inventors similar exclusive rights to use, lease or sell their inventions for a limited period of time. These exclusive rights provide incentives to authors and inventors to develop new products and to share the fruits of their labors. Congress has the power to regulate both patents and copyrights.

8. The power to declare war

Only Congress can declare war. Although this power belongs solely to Congress, the President is able to send troops overseas for a short period of time in an emergency. This is part of the President's power as Commander in Chief. To prevent the President from sending troops overseas for longer periods of time without a declaration of war or the approval of Congress, Congress passed the War Powers Act in 1973. Based on this law, the President can send troops overseas in an emergency for 60 days, but must withdraw them if the approval of Congress is not obtained within that time period.

9. The power to establish a system of lower federal courts

The delegates to the Constitutional Convention could not agree on whether or not to create additional federal courts below the U.S. Supreme Court. As a compromise, it was left to the future Congress to decide. Congress was given the power to create lower federal courts but was not required to do so.

When it met, the very first Congress decided to create "inferior" (*lower*) federal courts in the Judiciary Act of 1789. You will learn more about these courts in Chapter 7. Congress also has the power to determine what kinds of matters these courts can decide.

10. The power to raise and support armies

The Confederation Congress had lacked the power to raise its own army. It was therefore dependent on the states. The new Constitution gave the power to raise and support armies to the federal government. Because of its powers to tax and spend money, Congress was given the power to decide on the **budget** (*spending allowance*) of the nation's armed forces (today, the U.S. Army, Navy, Marines and Air Force).

11. The power to maintain a navy

Congress was given the power to build and maintain a navy, just as it is able to raise and support armies on land.

The Active Citizen

▶ Select one of the "delegated" or "enumerated" powers above. Then explain to another member of your class why that power is still important today. Consider the impact of the exercise of this power on the public, as well as its expense.

▶ Write a short letter to a friend explaining why you feel it was a good or bad idea to give the power you selected above to Congress.

The Implied Powers: The Elastic Clause

In addition to its enumerated powers, Congress also has "**implied**" powers. These are powers that are not directly stated in the Constitution, but that are implied (*strongly suggested*).

The basis for the implied powers is the Necessary and Proper Clause, found at the end of Article I, Section 8. (A **clause** is a short section.) This clause gave Congress the power—

> "To make all Laws which shall be necessary and proper for carrying into Execution the foregoing (*previous*) Powers, and all other Powers vested (*placed; put*) by this Constitution in the Government of the United States . . ."

The meaning of "necessary and proper" is not entirely clear. "Necessary" usually means needed, while "proper" means what is right or appropriate. Alexander Hamilton argued that the Necessary and Proper Clause gave Congress the power to create a national bank. He said that having a bank was necessary because it would help Congress to carry out its enumerated powers. Others felt that the creation of a national bank, while helpful, was not actually "necessary." They concluded that Congress had no power to create it.

In a famous case in 1819, the U.S. Supreme Court faced the same issue: did Congress have the power to establish a national bank? The creation of such a national bank was not one of the enumerated powers of Congress.

Those who interpreted the Constitution strictly made the following argument to the Court:

1. The power to create a national bank was not expressly granted to Congress by the Constitution. It was not one of the enumerated powers.

2. Congress did not need to create a national bank in order to exercise its enumerated powers. Congress could carry them out without the bank.

3. Therefore, Congress had no implied power to create a national bank.

Chapter 5 | Congress: Our Legislative Branch

The Supreme Court rejected this strict interpretation. Instead, it argued that it was "necessary and proper" for Congress to create a national bank in order to exercise many of its enumerated powers. The Constitution gave Congress specific powers to collect taxes and to borrow money. It also gave Congress the power to raise armies and to pay for them. Having a bank would give Congress a place to keep the money it collected from taxes. It would also create a place from which Congress could borrow money in an emergency. The Court concluded that having a bank would help Congress to carry out its enumerated powers. It was therefore "necessary and proper" for Congress to create a national bank.

> "*To its enumeration of powers* [the Constitution adds] *that of making 'all laws which shall be necessary and proper for carrying into execution the foregoing powers.*"
>
> *If the end be legitimate* (lawful and reasonable), *and within the scope* (range or limits) *of the Constitution, all the means* (ways) *which are appropriate* (proper or suitable; fitting), *which are plainly adapted to that end, and which are not prohibited, may constitutionally be employed to carry it into effect.*"
>
> —U.S. Supreme Court, *McCulloch v. Maryland*, 1819

The Court's interpretation gave Congress wide **implied powers**. Congress could do almost anything that was not prohibited (*forbidden*), so long as it was undertaken in order to help it in the exercise of its enumerated powers.

Because the Necessary and Proper Clause stretched the powers of Congress, it has also come to be known as the **Elastic Clause**.

The Active Citizen — Enrichment

▶ Can you restate the famous ruling of the Supreme Court in 1819 in the box above in your own words? What powers did the Court believe were given to Congress by the Elastic Clause?

▶ Do you think "Elastic Clause" is a good name for this clause? Why or why not?

▶ Hold a class debate on the following resolution.

Resolved: The Elastic Clause was a mistake because it gave the federal government too much power.

Other Powers of Congress

Some of the powers of Congress have nothing to do with making laws. Instead, they are powers that Congress has to check the other branches. These powers include the following:

1. Impeachment.
Congress has the "sole power of impeachment." This is the power to accuse members of the executive and judicial branches of abuses of power or unlawful activities, and to remove them from office.

In impeachment proceedings, the House of Representatives acts first. It has the power to "**impeach**" or accuse. Once a government official is successfully impeached in the House of Representatives, the Senate conducts an impeachment trial. Convicting the official requires a vote of two-thirds of the Senate. If the accused official is convicted, he or she is removed from office.

2. Choosing a President in Some Cases.
Congress can sometimes play a role in the election of the President. The President is actually chosen by the

electors of the Electoral College. The Constitution says that each state must choose a number of electors equal to the number of its Senators and Representatives combined. These electors vote for the President. If a candidate wins a majority of the electoral vote then he or she becomes the next President. However, if no candidate receives a majority, then the House of Representatives chooses the President. In this case, each state is given one vote.

3. Advice and Consent.

Treaties. The Constitution requires the President to obtain the "advice and consent" of the Senate for the ratification of a **treaty**—a solemn agreement between two or more countries. The Senate must approve (or "ratify") every treaty by a two-thirds vote.

Confirmation (*approval*) **of Presidential Appointments.** The President also **nominates** (*proposes*) and appoints ambassadors, Justices of the Supreme Court, other federal judges, and all other federal officers of the United States, including Cabinet members and military officers. In all these cases, the "advice and consent" of the Senate is required. The Senate must **confirm** (*approve*) such appointments by a simple majority vote.

For important nominations (such as a Supreme Court Justice or Cabinet member), a Senate committee usually conducts an investigation, holds hearings, and makes recommendations. Then the nomination is taken to the floor of the Senate, where it is debated and the entire Senate votes on the confirmation.

4. Propose Constitutional Amendments.

Congress can propose **amendments** (*additions; changes*) to the Constitution. Amendments to the Constitution are usually proposed by a vote of two-thirds of each house of Congress. They then have to be ratified by three-fourths of the states. You will learn more about amendments in Chapter 9.

5. Investigative Powers.

Congress has implied powers of **investigation**. These are needed for Congress to perform its tasks. To write good laws, Congress needs to investigate social, economic, and political conditions. Congressional committees have the power to issue **requests** for documents and other evidence, and to require individuals to appear before them to answer questions and provide expert testimony.

The 435 members of the U.S. House of Representatives in full session

Chapter 5 | Congress: Our Legislative Branch

Structure and Powers of Congress

Structure

The Senate:
100 members. Each state has two Senators.

The House of Representatives:
435 members. Each state has a number of representatives in proportion to its population.

Powers

Enumerated Powers (also known as the **"Delegated Powers"**): These powers are specifically listed in Article I of the Constitution:

▶ The power to raise taxes and borrow money
▶ The power to coin and print money
▶ The power to raise and support the armed forces
▶ The power to declare war
▶ The power to regulate trade between states or with foreign countries
▶ The power to regulate immigration
▶ The power to make rules for naturalization

Implied Powers: These powers are based on the Elastic Clause:

▶ The power to pass any law "necessary and proper" for carrying out the enumerated powers

Other Powers: Additional powers were given to Congress to check the other branches:

▶ The power to confirm Presidential appointments, including Supreme Court Justices
▶ The power to ratify (*approve/confirm*) treaties (*agreements with other nations*)
▶ The power to impeach and remove the President, federal judges and other federal officials for misconduct

1. Which of the enumerated powers do you think are the most important? Why?
2. What limits are there to the "implied powers" of Congress?

Limits on Congressional Power

These are several important limits on the powers of Congress:

1. Some of these limits are based on the system of checks and balances. Congress can be "checked" by the other two branches. The President, for example, can veto proposed laws even though they have passed both houses of Congress.
2. The Supreme Court can rule that laws enacted by Congress are unconstitutional and therefore invalid.
3. Congress can only exercise those enumerated and implied powers granted to it by the Constitution.
4. The Constitution and the Bill of Rights prohibit Congress from passing laws denying certain individual rights. For example, Congress cannot pass a law that takes away freedom of religion. It also cannot pass a law that denies individuals the right to petition the courts for a writ of *habeas corpus*. You will learn more about some of these specific prohibitions in Chapters 9 and 12.

Be sure to know the qualifications for serving in Congress for the EOC test.

Who Can Become a Member of Congress?

As you know, there are 435 Representatives in the House of Representatives. The number of seats in the House is fixed. The distribution of these seats is readjusted among the 50 states every ten years, based on their population size according to the U.S. Census.

To qualify to become a member of the House of Representatives, an individual must:

1. Be a U.S. citizen for at least seven years;
2. Be at least 25 years old; and
3. Be a resident of the state in which he or she is elected.

Each member of the House is elected by the voters of a single Congressional district.

You also already know that there are 100 U.S. Senators in the Senate—two for each state. The qualifications for becoming a Senator are stricter than those for becoming a Representative.

To become a U.S. Senator, an individual must:

1. Be a U.S. citizen for at least nine years;
2. Be at least 30 years old; and
3. Be a resident of the state in which he or she is elected.

Senators are elected by the voters of an entire state. There are no other constitutional requirements to serve in Congress. Most members of Congress today have backgrounds in business, law, or education.

The Active Citizen

- Why do you think the requirements for entering the Senate are stricter than for the House?
- Search on the Internet for information about the member in the House of Representatives from your Congressional district. What is his or her background? Why did he or she enter politics? Then write a letter asking your representative these same questions. Ask if your representative feels satisfied with what he or she has achieved by being a member of Congress. Finally, send your letter to the local office of your member of Congress and see what reply you receive.

Chapter 5 | Congress: Our Legislative Branch

> Be sure to know the leaders of Congress and the three types of committees for the EOC test.

Congress at Work

Each Congressional term begins in January of an odd-numbered year, such as 2015, and lasts two years. Before the new term begins, the major political parties (the Democrats and Republicans) hold private meetings, known as "**caucuses**," to reach agreements on issues, and to choose leaders.

The House of Representatives on Opening Day. The term of a member of the House is two years. All members are elected to serve their two-year terms at the same time, so they all go through the process of re-election at the end of each term.

When Congress assembles for the new term, the members of the House elect the **Speaker of the House**, who presides over their proceedings. The Speaker is actually determined in advance by the **majority party** (*the party with the larger number of members*).

Next the House elects its other officers. It also appoints its members to Congressional committees and committee chairs. Once these tasks are completed, the House sends a message to the Senate that it is ready for the President's "State of the Union" Address.

The Senate on Opening Day. The term of each Senator is six years. One third of all Senators face election every two years. Thus only one third of the Senators are serving new terms when the Senate opens. This method of electing its members provides continuity to the Senate. The Vice President of the United States serves as the President of the Senate. The Senate also elects a "**President pro tempore**," who presides over the Senate when the Vice President is absent. The President pro tempore is the leading member of the majority party in the Senate. Senators are then assigned to fill vacancies on committees and other positions in the Senate.

In both the Senate and the House, the majority party chooses a **majority leader**—a member of their party who will manage their interests. The minority party in each house similarly chooses a **minority leader**. The Senate is then also ready to hear the President's "State of the Union" Address.

The President's "State of the Union" Address. The President is required by the Constitution to inform Congress of the "State of the Union." Since 1913, Presidents have personally appeared before Congress to give their "State of the Union" Address. Shortly after Congress notifies the President that it is ready, the President delivers the address before Congress, other officials, and live television. The address covers both domestic and foreign affairs. It provides an agenda for the coming term, and recommends the legislation that the President believes is needed by the nation.

Congressional Committees

Imagine that your class is about to plan a party. It has to arrange music, food, decorations and invitations. It would be more efficient to divide students into several smaller groups, or "committees," to perform this work, rather than to have the whole class arrange all aspects of the party.

For greater efficiency, Congress is similarly organized into committees. Most of the work of Congress is actually performed in these committees. The three most important types of committees are:

Standing Committees. Each house currently has about 20 standing committees. These are by far the most important committees in Congress. Each standing committee is a permanent committee that deals with all bills on a particular subject. Standing committees continue from session to session of Congress. Each standing committee represents the entire House or Senate in miniature. Political party ratios on committees reflect the strength of that party in the house at large. Thus, if there were 40 Democrats and 60 Republicans in the Senate, the Democrats would have 4 and

114　　Chapter 5　|　Congress: Our Legislative Branch

Standing Committees: decide on bills on particular subjects

Special Committees: are temporary and formed for special purposes, such as to conduct an investigation

Conference Committees: make sure the same bill is passed by both houses

Republicans would have 6 members on a standing committee of 10 in the Senate.

The chairperson of each standing committee and subcommittee belongs to the majority party. The chairperson holds important powers, such as the power to decide which of the many bills the committee will consider.

Special Committees. Special committees (also known as select committees) are created for a specific and temporary purpose. For example, a special committee might be formed to investigate the continuing effects of pollution in the Gulf of Mexico from the Deepwater Horizon oil spill in 2010.

Conference Committees. No bill can be sent to the White House to be signed into law unless it passes both houses in the exact same form. Members of both houses therefore act together in a conference committee to eliminate inconsistencies between the Senate and the House versions of the bill. You will learn more about the role of the conference committee in the law-making process in the next section of this chapter.

Examples of Standing Committees

House of Representatives
House Committee on Foreign Affairs
House Committee on Ways and Means
House Committee on Appropriations

Senate
Senate Committee on Foreign Relations
Senate Committee on the Judiciary
Senate Committee on Finance

The U.S. House of Representatives Finance Committee

The Active Citizen

▶ Research one of the standing committees from the Senate or House of Representatives on the Internet. You might also telephone or email the office of one of the members of this committee for additional information. Then give an oral presentation, PowerPoint or Prezi presentation to your class, or make a video, on the work of this committee.

Chapter 5 | Congress: Our Legislative Branch

How Congress is Organized

Qualifications of Members

Senate: A Senator must be at least 30 years of age, a U.S. citizen for 9 years and live in the state represented. Senators are elected to a 6-year term. Each Senator is elected by the voters of an entire state.

House of Representatives: A Representative must be at least 25 years of age, a U.S. citizen for 7 years and live in the state represented. Representatives are elected to a 2-year term. Each Representative is elected by the voters of a single Congressional district.

Key Leaders

- **Speaker of the House:** Presides over House proceedings; elected by House members.
- **President pro tempore of the Senate:** Presides over Senate proceedings when the Vice President of the United States, who usually presides over the Senate, is absent.
- **Majority leader:** Manages the interests of the majority party in either the Senate or House of Representatives.
- **Minority leader:** Manages the interests of the minority party in either the Senate or House of Representatives.

Committees

Committees are working groups of members from both parties, reflecting party strength in the house as a whole. Most of the work of Congress is done in committee.

- **Standing committees:** Permanent committees that deal with all bills on a particular topic, such as the House Committee on Foreign Affairs.
- **Special committees:** Special committees created for temporary purposes such as to conduct an investigation.
- **Conference committee:** A committee with members from both houses that eliminates inconsistencies between House and Senate versions of the same bill.

1. How do the terms for a Senator and member of the House of Representatives differ?
2. Why do the members of the House and Senate organize themselves into committees?
3. If there are 55 Republicans and 45 Democrats in the Senate, how many Republican members would there be in a standing committee of 20?

How a Bill Becomes a Law

Be sure to know how a bill becomes a law for the EOC test.

A **bill** is a proposed law. A bill for a federal law can only be introduced by a member Congress.

A Bill is Introduced

In the House of Representatives, a member of the House introduces the bill by placing it in the "hopper," a wooden box monitored by the House clerk. In the Senate, a Senator introduces a bill by submitting the bill to the Senate clerk. Once the bill is introduced, it is numbered (preceded by H.R. for the House of Representatives or S. for Senate) and entered into the *House Journal* or *Senate Journal,* and the *Congressional Record,* which records all the proceedings (*activities*) of Congress.

The Committee Stage

Bills in the House are then sent to the Speaker of the House. The Speaker assigns them to the appropriate standing committee. The presiding officer of the Senate, usually the President pro tempore, decides which committee should receive bills in the Senate. The standing committee is the one that focuses on the subject of the bill.

The chairperson of the committee has the power to decide which of the many submitted bills are actively considered by the committee. If the chairperson decides that the bill is not of great importance, the bill is pushed aside (*"pigeonholed"*) and is not considered any further. Most bills, in fact, die in committee.

If the bill is not pushed aside, it is placed on the list of items for the committee to discuss when it meets. Using its investigative powers, the committee then conducts research on the bill. It may hold public hearings, and it may even visit locations affected by the bill. Special interest groups give their opinions. Experts and government officials may be required to appear before the committee to give testimony. The committee may make some changes to the bill. Once it has approved the bill, it sends it back to the full house.

Action on the House and Senate Floors

Both houses of Congress require some discussion and debate before the final vote on any bill is taken. Members give speeches in favor of or against the bill.

Debate and Vote in the House. Due to the sheer number of Representatives in the House, strict rules limit its debate. The Speaker of the House can limit debate by selecting those members who are permitted to speak. The Speaker can also force those who are straying from the subject of the bill to stop speaking. Once a bill has been debated, the House is finally ready to vote. If a **majority**—more than half—of the House approves the bill, the bill is sent to the Senate for consideration.

Debate and Vote in the Senate. With fewer members, rules for debate are looser in the Senate than in the House. Senators are permitted to speak freely and without any limit. They are not even required to stick to the subject of the bill. This freedom gives any Senator who opposes a bill and knows it is likely to pass the opportunity to speak endlessly for as long as he or she can remain standing. While the Senator speaks, the business of the Senate comes to a halt. This tactic of delay is called a filibuster. To end a filibuster, three-fifths of all Senators (60 Senators) must vote in favor of a motion to limit further debate. Once the debate is finished, the bill is put to a vote. If a majority of the Senate votes for the bill, it is sent to the House of Representatives for consideration, or if it came from there, it goes to a conference committee.

Conference Committee

A bill cannot become a law unless the House and Senate have both approved the bill in the *same* form. The exact same bill must pass each house. Yet by the time a bill has passed through each house of Congress, it has usually been amended, changing it in some way. To deal with the problems this creates,

Chapter 5 | Congress: Our Legislative Branch

members of the House and Senate form a joint committee known as a "conference committee." This committee allows members of the two houses to confer (*talk to one another*). The conference committee reviews the different versions of the bill and then creates an acceptable compromise. This compromise bill is then sent back to both the House and Senate, where members can either vote for or against the bill. No further changes or amendments to the bill are permitted at this stage. If a majority in each house of Congress votes for the bill, then it is ready to go to the President for approval.

The President's Options

A bill that has successfully passed through both houses of Congress still requires the President's signature to become a law. This is part of our constitutional system of checks and balances.

After receiving a bill passed by Congress, the President has three options:

1. **Sign it:** The President can approve the bill by signing it. The bill then becomes a new law.

2. **Veto it :** The President can **veto** (*reject or disapprove*) the bill. The bill is then returned to Congress. If two-thirds of the members present in each house of Congress vote to override the President's veto, then the bill becomes law. However, overriding a President's veto is usually difficult.

3. **Do nothing:** The President can refuse to either sign or veto a bill. Then what happens depends on whether Congress is still in session.

   ▶ If Congress is in session at the end of the ten days (not counting Sundays), the bill becomes a law.

   ▶ If Congress adjourns (*goes on a break*) within ten days of sending the bill to the President, the bill goes "into the President's pocket" and does *not* become a law. This method of killing a bill is known as a "pocket veto."

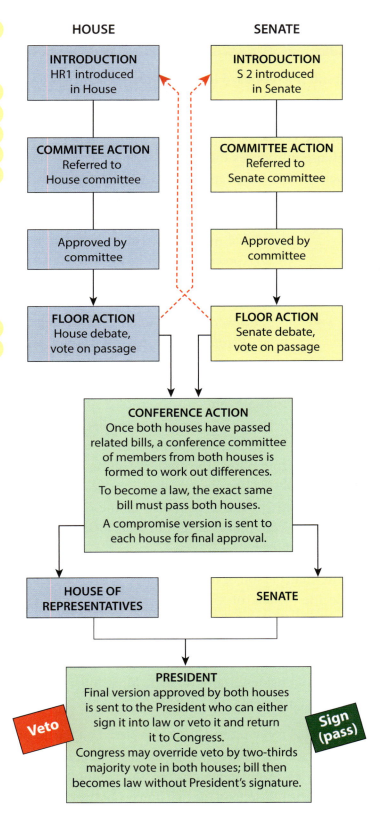

118   Chapter 5 | Congress: Our Legislative Branch

The Active Citizen

▶ Why did the authors of the Constitution require the approval of the President, the head of the executive branch, before a bill could become a law?

_____

_____

_____

_____

_____

▶ Why did the authors of the Constitution permit a two-thirds majority in each house to override the President's veto of proposed legislation?

_____

_____

_____

_____

_____

▶ Imagine you are a member of the House of Representatives. Describe a typical day. (Hint: You might visit congress.gov or the website of the Center on Representative Government at Indiana University for more details.)

_____

_____

_____

_____

_____

_____

_____

A "Facebook" Page for Your Representative

Look up information on one of your U.S. Senators or your local member of Congress (House of Representatives). Then create a mock "Facebook" page for that Senator or House Member.

Name: ______________________________

Position: (circle one) U.S. Senator Member of the U.S. House of Representatives for the ______________ District

About: ______________________________

____

____

Political Views: ______________________________

____

____

Worked at: ______________________________

____

____

Friends: ______________________________

____

____

Studied at: ______________________________

____

____

Political Views: ______________________________

____

____

Details: ______________________________

____

____

Friends: ______________________________

____

____

Life Events: ______________________________

____

____

Likes: ______________________________

____

____

Photos:

Add Friend ···

Add Friend ···

Add Friend ···

Add Friend ···

Add Friend ···

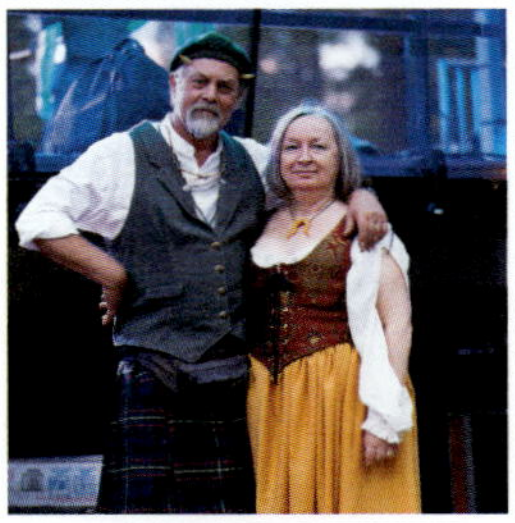

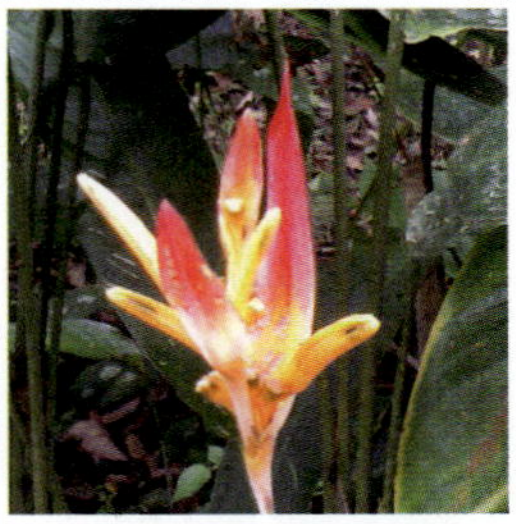

Name _____

Review the following list of Congressional powers.

Power to tax	Power to approve Presidential appointments of federal officers (Senate)
Power to coin and print money	Power to do whatever is "necessary and proper" to carry out the other powers
Power to regulate interstate trade	
Power to maintain a navy	Power to oversee and investigate
Power to charter a national bank	Power to raise and support armies
Power to borrow	Power to ratify treaties (Senate)
Power to impeach federal officers	

Now group these powers into the following two categories:

Enumerated Powers	Implied Powers

Answer these questions about the Elastic Clause:

The Elastic Clause	
What is the meaning of the Elastic Clause?	How has this clause been interpreted by the U.S. Supreme Court?
What are examples of actions taken by Congress that were based on the Elastic Clause?	What are examples of actions taken by Congress that were **not** based on the Elastic Clause?

Name _____

Describe each step in the chart below, which shows how a bill becomes a law.

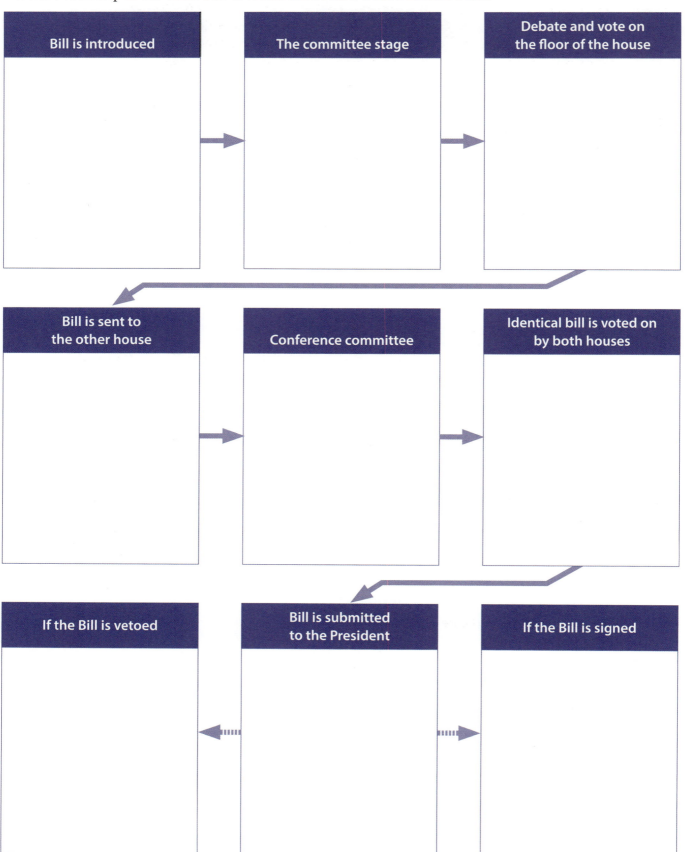

Chapter 5 | Congress: Our Legislative Branch

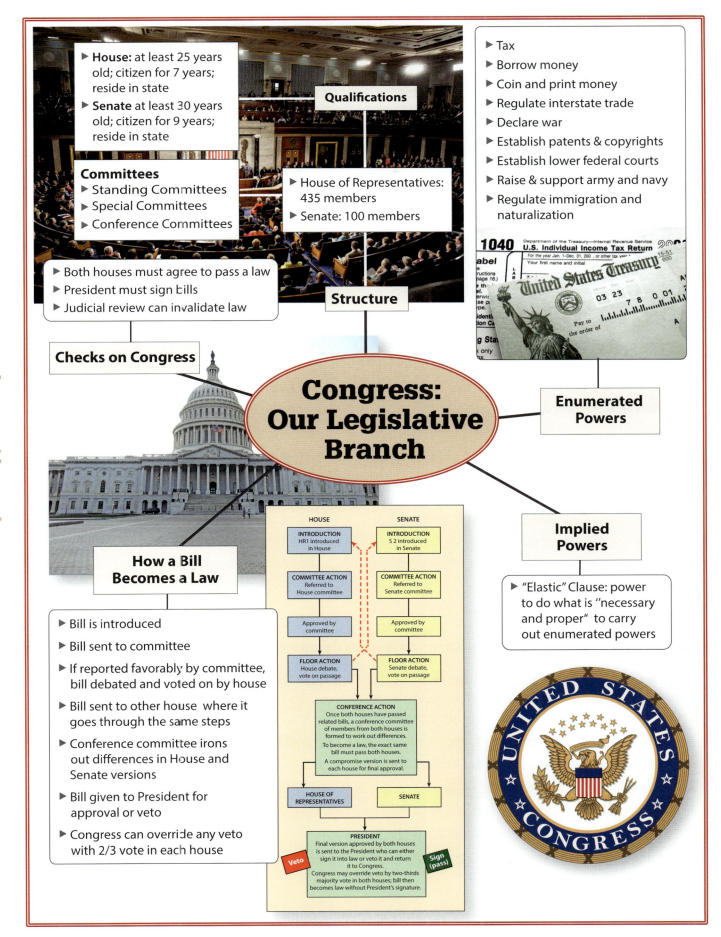

Chapter 5 | Congress: Our Legislative Branch

Review Cards: Congress—Our Legislative Branch

The Structure of Congress

- Congress is the **legislative**, or law-making, branch of the federal government.
- Congress has two houses: the **House of Representatives** and the **Senate**.
- **The House has 435 members.** Each state's number of representatives is proportional to the size of its population. **In the Senate, there are 100 members. Each state has two Senators.**

The Enumerated Powers of Congress

The **"enumerated" powers** of Congress are specifically listed in Article I, Section 8. These describe the powers of the federal government. Many of these powers had not belonged to the Confederation Congress. To "**regulate**" something is to control it by making rules for it.

- Power to **tax** and **spend**
- Power to **borrow** money
- Power to **coin** and **print money**
- Power to **declare war**
- Power to **raise** and **support armies**
- Power to maintain a navy
- Power to **regulate interstate trade**
- Power to establish standard weights
- Power to punish counterfeiters
- Power to establish post offices
- Power to establish patent system
- Power to establish copyrights
- Power to regulate **immigration**
- Power to regulate **naturalization**
- Power to establish lower federal courts

Other Powers of Congress

The Constitution gives Congress several non-legislative powers (*powers other than law-making*). This is mainly because of the system of **checks and balances**. These non-legislative powers allow Congress to oversee and check the other branches.

- Power to **impeach** the President, Vice President and other federal officers
- Power to impeach Supreme Court Justices and other federal judges
- Power to **approve appointments**—Senate confirms Presidential nominations by a majority vote
- Power to **ratify** treaties—Senate ratifies treaties by a two-thirds vote
- Power to propose constitutional amendments
- Power to choose the President if no candidate wins in the Electoral College—this is decided by the House of Representatives
- Power to investigate

The Implied Powers of Congress

- "**Implied**" means strongly suggested but not directly stated.
- The "**implied**" **powers** are not specifically listed in the Constitution but they are based on the **Elastic Clause**.
- This clause gives Congress the power "[t]o make all laws which shall be necessary and proper for carrying out the enumerated powers."
- Did this clause give Congress only those additional powers absolutely necessary to perform its "enumerated" powers? Or did this clause permit Congress to do anything that reasonably assisted it in performing its "enumerated" powers?
- The Supreme Court has ruled that anything reasonably related to Congress's duties and not otherwise prohibited is permitted: "If the end be legitimate, and within the scope of the Constitution, all the means which are appropriate may constitutionally be employed to carry it into effect." On the basis of its implied powers, the Congress created a national bank. The power to create a bank was not one of the enumerated powers, but this step helped Congress to carry out its other powers.

Limits on Congressional Power

- The President can **veto** legislation passed by Congress. Congress can **override** the President's veto with a vote of two-thirds of each house.
- Powers not given to Congress are reserved for the states and the people (see Chapter 9, for the 10th Amendment).
- Congress is prohibited from passing *ex post facto* laws, or suspending writ of *habeas corpus* (see Chapter 12).

Officers of Congress

- **Speaker of the House**: The leading member of the majority party, who is elected as Speaker by a vote in the House. The Speaker chairs the proceedings of the House and decides which committees bills are sent to.
- **Vice President** of the United States: Serves as **President of the Senate** and chairs proceedings of the Senate. The Vice President votes in the case of a tie in the Senate.
- **President pro tempore of the Senate**: The leading member of the majority party, who presides over the Senate when the U.S. Vice President is absent.
- **Majority leader**: Both the Senate and the House choose a majority leader—a member of the **majority party** who manages the interests of the party in that house of Congress.
- **Minority leader**: The **minority party** in each house similarly chooses a minority leader.

Chapter 5 | Congress: Our Legislative Branch

Congressional Committees

- **Standing committee**: A permanent committee in Congress that deals with all bills on a particular subject. Each standing committee represents the entire house (Senate or House of Representatives) in miniature. Each political party has a number of seats on the committee proportional to its representation in the house as a whole.
- **Special (or select) committee**: Committees created for a specific and temporary purpose such as to conduct an investigation.
- **Conference committee**: Members of both houses form a conference committee to eliminate differences between the versions of a bill passed in each house.

How a Bill Becomes a Law

- **Introduction of the bill**: Only a member of Congress can introduce a bill. Once the bill is introduced, it is numbered and submitted to the appropriate standing committee.
- **Committee stage**: The chairperson of the committee decides if the committee will consider the bill or if it should be left to die in committee. If it is considered, the committee will investigate the bill, hold public hearings, examine experts and so on.
- **Debate and vote**: If the bill is approved by the committee, it will be sent back, often with changes, for discussion and a vote on the floor of the House or Senate. Often the bill will be amended in some way before it is passed. Bills need a simple **majority** vote (*more than half*) to pass.
- **Bill sent to other house**: Once the bill is passed in one house of Congress, it is sent to the other house, where it goes through the same stages.
- **Conference committee**: If a bill passes both houses of Congress, it is usually changed in some way in each house by amendments. To become a law, a bill must pass both houses of Congress in the same form. Members from each house join together in a conference committee, where they iron out the differences in the two versions of the bill. The same bill then goes back to both houses, which can either approve or deny the bill without amendments. If the exact same bill passes both houses, it is ready to be sent to the President for signature.
- **Submitted to the President**: The President can approve the bill, **veto** the bill with a message to Congress, or do nothing at all. If the bill is vetoed, a two-thirds (2/3) vote in each house can override the veto.

Who can be a Member of Congress?

	House of Representatives	Senate
Minimum Age	25 years old	30 years old
Length of US Citizenship	7 years	9 years
Residence	Resident of state where elected	Resident of state where elected
Number of Members	435	100

Chapter 5 | Congress: Our Legislative Branch

What Do You Know?

SS.7.C.2.9

1. The four individuals below are thinking of running for the office of U.S. Senator from Florida.

1.	2.	3.	4.
Joe Black was born in Canada and is 26 years old. He moved to Miami, Florida, when he was six and became a US citizen in 2009.	Marisol Sanchez was born in Miami, Florida to two Cuban parents. She is now 35 years old and is a law student.	Roberto Mendez is a new arrival to Florida. He was born in New York City but has only lived in Florida two years. He is 29 years old.	Juan Fuentes was born in Cuba and has only lived in the United States for four years. He feels very strongly about immigration problems. He is 36 years old.

Which of these candidates is qualified to become a U.S. Senator?

A. Joe Black

B. Juan Fuentes

C. Roberto Mendez

D. Marisol Sanchez

SS.7.C.3.3

2. Which is an example of an "enumerated" power of Congress?

A. the power to tax exports

B. the power to declare war

C. the power to issue hunting licenses

D. the power to operate public school districts

SS.7.C.3.3

3. The diagram on the right shows details about the U.S. government.

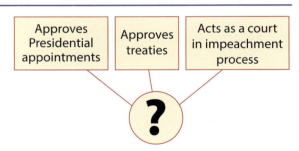

Which branch of government completes the diagram?

A. The Senate

B. The Cabinet

C. The Supreme Court

D. The House of Representatives

Chapter 5 | Congress: Our Legislative Branch

SS.7.C.3.9

4. Why do most of the bills introduced in Congress never become law?
   A. They are defeated in floor votes.
   B. They never get out of committee.
   C. They are vetoed by the President.
   D. They are overruled by the U.S. Supreme Court.

SS.7.C.3.9

5. In Congress, where does most of the work on bills take place?
   A. special committees
   B. standing committees
   C. conference committees
   D. floor of the House or Senate

SS.7.C.3.9

6. What happens when the House and the Senate pass different versions of the same bill?
   A. The House bill is changed to conform to the Senate bill.
   B. The Senate bill is changed to conform to the House bill.
   C. A conference committee is appointed to resolve the differences.
   D. A standing committee from one house is chosen to resolve the differences.

SS.7.C.3.3

7. What steps does the Constitution provide if there is persuasive evidence that the President of the United States has committed treason?
   A. The President can be arrested and forced to resign.
   B. The President can be impeached by the Supreme Court.
   C. The President cannot be removed until convicted in a court of law.
   D. The President can be impeached by the House and removed by the Senate.

SS.7.C.3.3

8. Which action is an example of an "implied" power?
   A. Congress votes to raise income taxes.
   B. Congress holds an investigation on women in the military.
   C. Congress declares war on a country for sponsoring terrorism.
   D. Congress decides to close post offices in rural areas on Saturdays.

SS.7.C.3.8

9. A bill is passed by both the House and the Senate. The bill is then submitted to the President. Which is **not** an option for the President?

    A. let the bill die in committee

    B. sign the bill and it becomes law

    C. veto the bill and inform Congress of the reasons for the veto

    D. not sign the bill and after 10 days, if Congress is not in session, the bill dies

SS.7.C.3.9

10. The diagram below shows some of the steps involved in passing a federal law.

    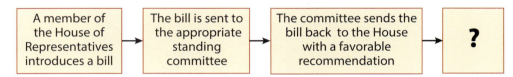

    What is the next step in the lawmaking process?

    A. The President signs the bill.

    B. The bill is sent to the Senate.

    C. The bill is sent to a conference committee.

    D. The bill is debated on the floor of the House.

SS.7.C.3.3

11. Which is an example of a check on congressional power?

    A. the power of Congress to declare war

    B. the power of the President to veto a bill

    C. the power of the states to collect their own taxes

    D. the power of the Supreme Court to try cases between states

SS.7.C.3.8

12. Which official chairs the proceedings of the U.S. House of Representatives?

    A. Sergeant-at-Arms
    C. President pro tempore

    B. Speaker of the House
    D. Vice President of the United States

SS.7.C.3.9

13. The President and Congress have different views on climate change. Congress sent the President a bill requiring all cars made in the United States to run on electricity. The President vetoed the bill. Which step is required to pass the bill over the President's veto?

    A. approval of the bill by a majority of each house of Congress

    B. approval of the bill by a majority of Supreme Court Justices

    C. approval of the bill by two-thirds of each house of Congress

    D. approval of the bill by three-quarters of the state legislatures

Chapter 5 | Congress: Our Legislative Branch

SS.7.C.3.3

14. The Venn diagram below compares two types of powers under the U.S. Constitution.

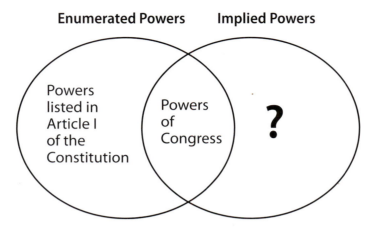

Which description completes the Venn diagram?

A. Powers required to interpret laws
B. Powers reserved for the Congress and the people
C. Powers needed to carry out the enumerated powers
D. Powers used to check the executive and legislative branches

SS.7.C.3.8

15. What is the role of the President pro tempore of the Senate?

A. vote in the Senate in case of a tie vote
B. make sure fellow party members vote on important bills
C. preside over Senate proceedings if the Vice President is absent
D. become the next President of the United States if the President dies

CHAPTER 6

The Presidency: Our Executive Branch

SS.7.C.2.9 Evaluate candidates for political office by analyzing their qualifications, experience, issue-based platforms, debates, and political ads. (See also Chapter 13.)

SS.7.C.3.3 Illustrate the structure and function (three branches of government established in Articles I, II, and III with corresponding powers) of government in the United States as established in the Constitution. (See also Chapters 3, 4, 5 and 7.)

SS.7.C.3.8 Analyze the structure, functions, and processes of the legislative, executive, and judicial branches. (See also Chapters 5 and 7.)

SS.7.C.3.9 Illustrate the lawmaking process at the local, state, and federal levels. (See also Chapters 5 and 11.)

SS.7.C.4.1 Differentiate concepts related to U.S. domestic and foreign policy. (See also Chapter 17.)

Names and Terms You Should Know

President	Veto	Commander in Chief
Vice President	Appointment	Foreign relations
Presidential appointment	Pardon	Ambassador
Executive order	Impeachment	Cabinet
	"State of the Union" Address	

Florida "Keys" to Learning

1. Article II of the Constitution gives several important powers to the President. The President has the "executive power" to enforce the laws. The President is also Commander in Chief of the armed forces. The President has the power to negotiate treaties. The President has the power to nominate ambassadors, chiefs of executive departments and Supreme Court Justices. The President delivers an annual (yearly) "State of the Union" Address to Congress. The President can veto laws passed by Congress and has the power to give pardons for federal crimes.

2. The President also has other powers. These are implied, given by Congress, or based on the need to defend the nation. Such powers include consulting with the Cabinet, exercising general control over foreign policy, and assuming emergency powers in wartime. The President makes executive orders and can send troops to foreign countries for a limited period without declaring war.

3. There are several checks on Presidential power. These are part of our Constitution's system of checks and balances. Congress can override a Presidential veto, choose not to fund the President's programs, refuse to approve Presidential appointments or treaties, or impeach the President. Congress has also passed the War Powers Act, limiting the President's ability to send troops abroad. The Supreme Court can declare Presidential acts to be unconstitutional.

4. The President plays many roles: Head of State, Commander in Chief, Chief Executive, Chief Legislator, Chief Diplomat, Chief Economist, Chief of Security, party leader, and the moral leader of America. The President can appeal to the nation through television, newspapers, radio, the Internet, and public appearances.

5. To become President, a person must be a U.S. citizen from birth, be at least 35 years old, and have been a U.S. resident for at least 14 years before taking office. A naturalized citizen cannot become President.

6. Each term in office is 4 years. The President is limited to two elected terms.

7. If the President is assassinated or unable to serve, the Vice President is next in line for the office.

8. The President and Vice President are chosen in a national election. Candidates for President first compete for their party's nomination. The nominees from each party then campaign against one another for election in November. The President is actually chosen by the Electoral College. Electors from each state generally vote for the candidate winning the most votes in their state in the November election.

9. The President can be impeached and removed from office for treason or other high crimes. The impeachment process has two stages. First, the House impeaches the President (here, "impeach" means to accuse or charge). Then the Senate can remove the President by a two-thirds vote after a trial presided over by the Chief Justice of the Supreme Court.

132 Chapter 6 | The Presidency: Our Executive Branch

The second branch of our federal government is the Presidency. Many consider this to be the most dynamic of the three branches: the President today is vastly more powerful than the members of the Constitutional Convention could have ever imagined. In this chapter, you will study the Presidency.

You should know the powers of the President for the EOC test.

The President's "Expressed" Powers

From their experiences under British rule, the delegates in Philadelphia in 1787 were afraid of a chief executive with too much power. Yet they knew from their experience under the Articles of Confederation that without a chief executive, the national government could not manage the problems of a young democracy. The powers given to the President in Article II reflected these concerns.

The President's "Expressed" (or listed) powers are summarized below.

▶ **First and foremost, the President was granted the "executive power":**

> "The executive power shall be vested (*placed*) in a President of the United States of America."

The phrase **"executive power" ordinarily refers to the power to carry out or enforce the laws.** The President is also to "take care that the laws be faithfully executed," and takes an oath to "faithfully execute" the office of President and to "preserve, protect and defend" the Constitution.

▶ **The President is also the "Commander in Chief" of the armed forces of the United States:**

> "The President shall be Commander in Chief of the Army and Navy of the United States, and of the militia of the several States, when called into the actual service of the United States."

The Constitution thus placed a civilian (*non-soldier*) at the head of the military. As a single individual, the President was better able than Congress to direct the nation's armed forces and to take decisive action in the event of an emergency.

Presidents have used their power to call state militia into national service many times. The most famous example was on April 15, 1861, when President Abraham Lincoln summoned the militia of several states at the beginning of the Civil War.

▶ **The President has the power to appoint members of the executive departments.**

Particular departments are not specified in the Constitution, but from the beginning they have included the Secretary of State and the Secretary of the Treasury. Appointments must meet with the approval of a majority of the Senate. This is another example of the system of checks and balances in the Constitution.

> The President "shall nominate, and by and with the advice and consent of the Senate, shall appoint . . . all other officers of the United States."

The President can also request the advice of these officers in writing:

> The President "may require the opinion in writing of the principal officer in each of the executive departments, upon any subject relating to the duties of their respective offices."

▶ **The President has the power to make treaties** (*solemn agreements between foreign nations*), **with approval of the Senate:**

> The President "shall have Power, by and with the advice and consent of the Senate, to make Treaties."

While the President can negotiate treaties, approval by two-thirds of the Senate is required to "ratify" (*approve*) each treaty, putting it into force.

Chapter 6 | The Presidency: Our Executive Branch

- The President has the power to appoint ambassadors—official representatives of the United States to other countries—and to receive the ambassadors and other diplomatic representatives of other nations:

> The President "shall nominate, and by and with the advice and consent of the Senate, shall appoint Ambassadors, other public Ministers and Consuls..."
>
> The President "shall receive Ambassadors and other public Ministers..."

- The President appoints the "Justices" (*judges*) of the U.S. Supreme Court. These must be approved by the Senate:

> The President "shall nominate, and by and with the advice and consent of the Senate, shall appoint... Justices of the Supreme Court..."

- The President has several specific powers with respect to Congress. The President delivers the "State of the Union" Address:

> The President "shall from time to time give to the Congress Information of the State of the Union, and recommend to their Consideration such Measures as he shall judge necessary and expedient..."

This responsibility gives the President the opportunity to share views with Congress and the American people and to make recommendations for the security and welfare of the country, which Congress can include in its annual budget.

- The President has the power to **veto** (*turn down*) legislation submitted by Congress. The President's veto can be overridden by a two-thirds vote of the members present in each house of Congress (see Chapter 5). However, the President's veto power is so formidable that of the more than 2,500 Presidential vetoes, only about a hundred of them have been successfully overridden by Congress.
- The President has the power to call Congress into special session, or to adjourn the two houses of Congress if they cannot agree on the time of adjournment (*temporary recess or break*).
- Finally, the President has the power to grant pardons for federal crimes:

> The President "shall have the power to grant reprieves and pardons for offences against the United States, except in cases of impeachment."

A **pardon** forgives an individual for having committed a crime. It releases the person from prison, waives all penalties, and restores the person's civil rights. The power to grant pardons is often associated with executive power, and Governors in every state can pardon those accused of state crimes.

Enrichment

In an article published in *The New York Times*, President Bill Clinton discussed the history of Presidential pardons. He justified the 140 pardons that he granted on the last day of his Presidency:

> "A President may conclude a pardon or commutation is [justified] for several reasons: the desire to restore full citizenship rights, including voting, to people who have served their sentences and lived within the law since; a belief that a sentence was excessive or unjust; personal circumstances that [justify] compassion; or other unique circumstances. The exercise of executive [mercy has been] controversial. The reason the framers of our Constitution vested (*put*) this broad power in the Executive Branch was to assure that the President would have the freedom to do what he deemed (*thought*) to be the right thing, regardless of how unpopular a decision might be."

Bill Clinton

Chapter 6 | The Presidency: Our Executive Branch

Some uses of the pardoning power have been especially controversial. President Washington pardoned the leaders of the Whiskey Rebellion, President Ford pardoned President Nixon for his involvement in the Watergate Scandal, President Carter pardoned Vietnam War draft resisters, and President George H.W. Bush pardoned former U.S. Defense Secretary Weinberger and five other defendants for their involvement in the Iran-Contra affair.

You should know the President's implied powers for the EOC test.

The President's Implied and Other Powers

Like Congress, the President also exercises "implied" and other powers, such as those delegated by Congress or necessary to defend our nation in an emergency.

Meeting with the Cabinet

The heads of the fifteen executive departments in the executive branch meet together as the President's "Cabinet." The Cabinet is not mentioned in the Constitution. However, the Constitution gives the President the right to appoint heads of departments and to request their written opinions.

President George Washington began the first Cabinet in 1789 with four members: the Secretary of State (Thomas Jefferson), the Secretary of the Treasury (Alexander Hamilton), the Secretary of War, and the Attorney General. Today, there are fifteen heads of executive departments in the Cabinet, as well as the Vice President of the United States and seven other Cabinet officers.

The President not only appoints Cabinet members but also has the power to dismiss them. This is another implied power.

The Conduct of our Nation's Foreign Relations

President Washington was also the first to assert Presidential control of foreign policy. The basis of this power is to be found in the President's powers to make treaties, to receive and appoint ambassadors, and to act as Commander in Chief. On these grounds, the President takes charge of America's relations with other countries. You will learn more about American foreign policy in Chapter 17.

Emergency Powers in Wartime

Presidents typically exercise emergency powers in wartime, with or without the approval of Congress.

During the Civil War, Abraham Lincoln suspended several civil liberties guaranteed by the Constitution, including the right to a writ of *habeas corpus*. Lincoln also issued the Emancipation Proclamation, freeing the slaves in Southern states in rebellion, as an exercise of his emergency wartime powers. The Supreme Court later ruled that Lincoln did not have the authority to suspend *habeas corpus*.

During World War I, Congress gave President Wilson power to limit the exercise of free speech. During World War II, President Franklin D. Roosevelt ordered the internment of Japanese Americans on the West Coast on the basis of his emergency wartime powers.

Executive Orders

Since the time of George Washington, Presidents have issued executive orders. These orders have the force of laws, although they have not been

Chapter 6 | The Presidency: Our Executive Branch

passed by Congress. This practice is based on the responsibility of the President to execute laws passed by Congress. Executive orders are thus meant to implement (*put into effect*) the legislation of Congress. Past Presidents have issued executive orders to ration consumer goods, to control wages and prices, and to carry out laws affecting civil rights. One of the most famous of President Roosevelt's executive orders permitted the forced internment (*confinement; imprisonment*) of Japanese Americans during World War II. Another of his executive orders ended racial discrimination in the award of defense contracts. In 1948, President Truman issued an executive order ending racial discrimination in the armed services. On average, Presidents issue about a hundred executive orders a year. Over time, Presidents have issued more than 14,000 executive orders.

War-Making Powers/Military Interventions

According to our Constitution, only Congress can declare war. However, of the hundreds of armed conflicts in which the United States has engaged, only five have actually been declared wars. The most important armed conflicts of the past seventy years—the Korean War, the Vietnam War, and the two Gulf Wars—have been fought by American troops without any declaration of war at all.

When responding to an attack or planning an action against a foreign threat, it may not always be a good strategy to obtain a public declaration of war. Acting as Commander in Chief, the President is able to take immediate steps in defense of the nation.

Know these checks for the EOC test.

Checks on Presidential Power

As with the other branches, there are important checks on the President's powers. This is part of our Constitution's system of checks and balances:

- Congress can override a Presidential veto.
- All spending by the federal government is made by Congress. Without the support of Congress, the President is unable to fund (*pay for*) any government activities.
- The President must obtain Senate confirmation (*approval*) of appointments and treaties.
- The War Powers Act, passed by Congress in 1973, limits the President's ability to send troops overseas for longer than 60 days without the approval of Congress.
- The Supreme Court can declare acts of the President unconstitutional.
- Congress can impeach and remove the President for misconduct.

The Many Roles of the President

As the leader of the nation, the President plays many roles. Some say the President wears many hats.

Head of State

As the Head of State, the President represents the United States, both in dealing with foreign nations and on ceremonial occasions, such as national holidays.

Commander in Chief of the Armed Forces

The President is advised by the Joint Chiefs of Staff, but the President alone has final authority over

U.S. military operations. President George W. Bush, for example, launched invasions of Afghanistan and Iraq, while President Barack Obama approved the raid into Pakistan that captured and killed the terrorist Osama Bin Laden. The President also has final responsibility for the use of nuclear weapons.

Chief Executive

The President holds "executive power." As Chief Executive, the President is in charge of the entire federal government.

Chief Legislator

The President acts as the nation's Chief Legislator. The President recommends legislation in the "State of the Union" Address. The President communicates with Congress, pressures members of Congress to support recommended legislation, and vetoes legislation that he or she opposes.

Chief Diplomat

The President conducts American foreign policy in cooperation with Congress. The President's personal interaction with world leaders, such as President Putin of Russia or President Xi Jinping of China, heightens the belief among Americans and foreigners that the President bears the chief responsibility for the handling of American foreign policy and diplomacy.

Chief Economist

During the Great Depression (a severe economic downturn from 1930 to 1939 when many Americans lost their jobs), President Franklin D. Roosevelt took active steps to restore the American economy with legislation. He introduced measures like social security, for disabled, unemployed and retired workers—which we still have today. The Employment Act of 1946 stated that it was the "continuing policy and responsibility" of the federal government "to promote maximum employment, production and purchasing power."

Ever since, American voters have looked to the President for solutions when the economy is performing badly and unemployment is high. If the President fails to revive the economy, the President will often lose in the next election.

The President generally discusses the economy in the "State of the Union" Address. The President's proposed legislative programs and budget also affect the economy. Once a year, the President further issues an annual *Economic Report of the President*.

Chief of Security

The President is responsible for the security of the United States. The President sits atop a vast intelligence network, which includes information from the Central Intelligence Agency (CIA), the FBI, the armed services, the Department of Homeland Security, and the National Security Agency (NSA). The NSA eavesdrops, monitors and analyzes data and protects electronic systems.

Party Leader

The President is the leader of one of the two major political parties. The President has always been elected to the White House with the help of that party and continues to work closely with party leaders and members to pass proposed legislation. The President may pressure fellow party members to vote with their party in Congress. The President may also speak in support of fellow party members in re-election campaigns.

Moral Leader

The President serves as the nation's moral voice. President Theodore Roosevelt referred to the Presidency as the "bully pulpit" because the President could so easily attract public attention. The President can then use this opportunity to address those moral issues of greatest concern.

Chapter 6 | The Presidency: Our Executive Branch

The President wears many different "hats." Choose one of the many roles that the President has that is described in this chapter. Identify the role you have selected on the brim of the hat and then describe the role on the tall crown (or "stove pipe" section) of the hat.

> You should know the requirements for becoming President for the EOC test.

Who Can Become President?

The constitutional requirements for becoming President of the United States, like those for becoming a member of the House of Representatives or the Senate, are few in number:

To be eligible to become President of the United States, an individual must:

1. Be born in the United States. "Naturalized" citizens (who became citizens after migrating here) cannot serve as President;
2. Be at least 35 years of age; and
3. Be a resident of the United States for at least 14 years before taking office.

There are no other constitutional requirements. Most recent Presidents have worked in law or business before entering politics.

Term in Office. The President is elected for a "term" of four years. President George Washington served for two terms in office before he stepped down. All later Presidents followed his example, until President Franklin D. Roosevelt ran for a third term while World War II was raging in Europe. Roosevelt was elected for a fourth term and died in office from a heart attack. **The Twenty-second Amendment now limits the President to a maximum of two elected terms.**

The Vice President. The Vice President must meet the same requirements and serves the same term as the President. If the President dies or leaves office for any reason, the Vice President becomes the next President.

> You do **not** need to know how the President is selected for the EOC test.

How the President is Chosen

Enrichment

Have you ever dreamt of becoming President of the United States? You would get to live in the White House for free, and have your own cook, private movie theater and swimming pool. You could hold press conferences or go on television whenever you wanted, and telephone other world leaders.

So, you may be wondering, how does one actually go about becoming President? Meeting the minimal constitutional requirements is, of course, just the beginning.

138   Chapter 6 | The Presidency: Our Executive Branch

The Nomination

The first step in running for President is winning the nomination of one of the two major political parties. A **political party** is an organization of citizens who share similar views and who work together to get some of their members elected to public office. Each of the major national political parties—the **Democrats** and **Republicans**—will nominate only one candidate for President.

Each party holds a series of primary elections in different states. Citizens vote on their party's candidates to determine which one of them should represent the party as its nominee. The nominees are chosen at each party's national convention, held in the summer before the Presidential election.

At the convention, delegates also adopt a party platform stating the party's positions on important issues. Finally, the nominee for President also selects and announces the nominee for Vice President. The two candidates run together on a single "ticket."

The Election Campaign

Once the national conventions are over, the nominees of the two major parties have three months to campaign against one another. They conduct energetic campaigns advertising on television, delivering speeches, attending meetings, and raising campaign funds—all to gain the support of voters. They also debate each other on national television. Campaign costs, especially for television advertising, are tremendous.

The Electoral College

The election for the President and Vice President occurs on the first Tuesday after November 1st. The final process of selecting the President and Vice President does not actually happen in the election itself, but in the **Electoral College**. Each state is given the same number of electoral votes as it has Senators and Representatives in Congress. In most states, the electors are required to vote for the candidate who wins the most votes in their state in the general election.

There are 538 electoral votes in all in the Electoral College (including three electoral votes for Washington, D.C.). To win the Presidential election, the candidate must receive more than half of these, or 270 electoral votes.

The Active Citizen

▶ Sometimes the winner of the most votes in the popular election does not win in the Electoral College. This happened in both 2000 and 2016. Should the Electoral College be eliminated? Hold a class debate on the following: *"Resolved: The Electoral College should be eliminated and the President should be elected by popular vote."*

> You should know about impeachment for the EOC test.

The Impeachment Process

The Constitution establishes procedures in case there is a need to remove the President from office for "treason, bribery, or other high crimes and misdemeanors." This process is known as *impeachment*. The impeachment of a government official does not impose any kind of penalties, fines or imprisonment at all. It simply removes the official from office. Once removed, the official may also face proceedings in a criminal or civil court.

Chapter 6 | THE PRESIDENCY: Our Executive Branch

In the case of the President, the impeachment process occurs in two stages. In the first, the President is **impeached** (*accused*) in the House of Representatives. If a majority of the House votes to impeach the President, then the process moves into the second stage, where the President is **tried** in the Senate. The Chief Justice of the Supreme Court presides at the trial. A vote of two-thirds of the Senate is needed to convict and remove the President from office. If the President is removed, then the Vice President becomes the new President.

House of Representatives
Impeaches (*charges*) the President

Senate
Tries and removes the President

The Active Citizen

Enrichment

There are frequent surveys of historians, political scientists and other experts rating the past Presidents of the United States. Here are two such surveys:

The Ten "Best" Presidents

Ranking	Siena College Research Institute[1]	Nate Silver, *New York Times*[2]
1 (Best)	Abraham Lincoln	Abraham Lincoln
2	Franklin D. Roosevelt	Franklin D. Roosevelt
3	Theodore Roosevelt	George Washington
4	George Washington	Theodore Roosevelt
5	Thomas Jefferson	Thomas Jefferson
6	James Madison	Harry Truman
7	James Monroe	Woodrow Wilson
8	Woodrow Wilson	Dwight Eisenhower
9	Harry Truman	John F. Kennedy
10	Dwight Eisenhower	Ronald Reagan

[1] Siena College Research Institute Survey's poll of historians and political scientists (2010)
[2] "Contemplating Obama's Place in History, Statistically," *New York Times* (January 23, 2013)

The Ten "Worst" Presidents

Ranking	Siena College Research Institute[1]	Nate Silver, *New York Times*[2]
35	Benjamin Harrison	Benjamin Harrison
36	William H. Harrison	Herbert Hoover
37	Herbert Hoover	John Tyler
38	John Tyler	Millard Fillmore
39	Millard Fillmore	George W. Bush
40	George W. Bush	Andrew Johnson
41	Franklin Pierce	William H. Harrison
42	Warren G. Harding	Warren G. Harding
43	James Buchanan	Franklin Pierce
44 (Worst)	Andrew Johnson	James Buchanan

[1] Siena College Research Institute Survey's poll of historians and political scientists (2010)
[2] "Contemplating Obama's Place in History, Statistically," *New York Times* (January 23, 2013)

▶ Your teacher should divide your class into groups. Each group should use the Internet to research one President from the list of best Presidents and one President from the list of worst Presidents. Consider: (1) the background and experience of each individual; (2) the problems the country faced when he became President; (3) how well he coped with those problems; and (4) which Presidential powers and roles he used to implement his policies.

▶ After completing your research, compare the two Presidents you have studied. Why is one considered to be one of our best Presidents and the other one of our worst?

▶ Groups should report their findings to the class, and then class members should discuss if they agree with the classification of Presidents on the lists above. Which changes, if any, would you make if your class had to rank the ten best and ten worst Presidents for yourselves?

A Summary of the Presidency

Qualifications to be President

- Must be a "natural born" citizen (*not* a "naturalized" citizen)
- Must have lived in the United States for at least 14 years
- Must be at least 35 years old

Powers of the President

Expressed Powers (Powers found in Article II of the Constitution)

- **Executive Power:** The Constitution places the federal government's executive power in the President. The President has a duty to "execute" the laws and "to preserve, protect and defend the Constitution." As the nation's chief executive, the President has control over all federal departments and agencies.
- **Commander in Chief:** The President is the Commander in Chief of the nation's armed forces.
- **Appointment Power:** With the advice and consent of the Senate, the President appoints (*chooses*) all U.S. ambassadors, all Justices of the U.S. Supreme Court, and all federal officers.
- **Treaty-Making Power:** With the consent of a two-thirds majority of the Senate, the President can make treaties with other countries.
- **Receive ambassadors:** The President receives ambassadors from foreign nations.
- **Veto Power:** The President can sign or veto a bill passed by Congress; Congress can override a Presidential veto with a two-thirds majority in each house.
- **Other Powers relating to Congress:** The President informs Congress of the "**State of the Union**"; recommends measures to Congress; and can convene (*call together*) and **adjourn** (*suspend or temporarily break off*) sessions of Congress.
- **Pardoning Power:** The President can **pardon** (*forgive; let free*) those accused of federal crimes.

Implied and Other Powers

- **Foreign Relations:** The President conducts our nation's **foreign relations** (*relations with other countries*).
- **Cabinet:** The President often meets with the heads of **executive departments,** known as the **Cabinet**, which gives the President advice. The President has the power to remove Cabinet officers as well as to appoint them.
- **Executive orders:** The President issues **executive orders**.
- **Emergency Powers:** The President has an implied power to take immediate steps to defend our nation if it is attacked or if there is any kind of national emergency.

Impeachment

Congress has the power to **impeach** (*charge*) and remove the President for "Treason, Bribery, or other High Crimes and Misdemeanors."

Impeachment is a two-step process:

- **Impeachment**: A majority of the House of Representatives must vote to impeach the President.
- **Removal:** Once impeached by the House, the President is tried in the Senate. The Chief Justice of the Supreme Court presides over the trial. To remove the President from office requires a vote of two-thirds of the Senate.

Name _____

Read the names and terms below. Then decide in which column each name or term belongs and place it in the proper column below.

- Executive power
- Commander in Chief
- State militia
- National Guard
- Treaty
- Executive departments
- Cabinet
- Appoints ambassadors
- Receives ambassadors
- "State of the Union" Address
- Veto
- Calls a special session of Congress
- Adjournment of Congress
- Suspension of *habeas corpus* in wartime
- Economic Report of the President
- Central Intelligence Agency (CIA)
- National Security Agency (NSA)
- Holds press conferences
- Grants pardons

Chief Executive	Chief Legislator

Military Leader	Chief Diplomat	Chief Economist

Chief of Security	Moral Leader

Use several of the terms and phrases above to write a paragraph describing some of the roles that the President plays in American life.

_____
_____
_____
_____

Chapter 6 | The Presidency: Our Executive Branch

Name _____

Fill in the chart below.

The Presidency
The President's expressed powers
The President's implied and other powers
The responsibilities of the President
How the President may be removed

Chapter 6 | The Presidency: Our Executive Branch

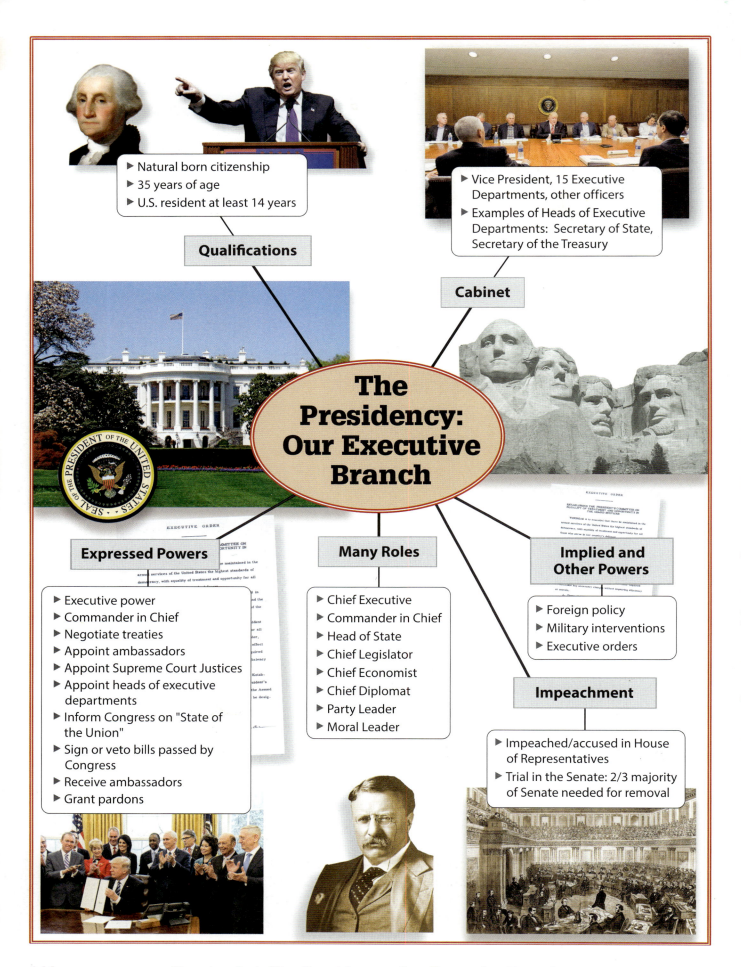

Review Cards: The Executive Branch

The President

The delegates to the Constitutional Convention feared creating a national executive with too much power, similar to the English King. On the other hand, their experiences under the Articles of Confederation showed that a national executive was necessary to provide leadership.

Expressed Powers

The President has a number of expressed powers under Article II of the Constitution. These include the **"executive power"** (the power to enforce the laws), powers over military and foreign affairs, powers to make government appointments, and powers to check the actions of Congress:

- The President can consult with the Cabinet.
- The President is **Commander in Chief** of the armed forces.
- The President has the power to negotiate treaties (with approval of two-thirds of the Senate), to appoint ambassadors, and to receive foreign ambassadors and other diplomats.
- The President has the power to appoint the heads of executive departments, as well as Supreme Court Justices. These appointments require confirmation by a majority of the Senate.
- The President delivers the **"State of the Union"** Address to Congress to share views and make recommendations. The President can veto legislation passed by Congress, and can summon Congress into a special session.
- The President has the power to grant **pardons** for federal crimes.

Implied and Other Powers

Like Congress, the President has implied powers:

- The President has general control over foreign policy and can assert emergency powers in wartime (even without Congressional approval), based on Presidential powers as Commander in Chief.
- The President can issue **executive orders**—these have the force of law but do not require the approval of Congress.
- As Commander in Chief, the President can send troops to foreign countries without declaring war. However, the **War Powers Act of 1973** limits this power: the President must inform Congress of military actions abroad and withdraw the troops after 60 days if Congress refuses to authorize the action.

The President's Many Roles

- The President plays many roles: Head of State, Commander in Chief of the armed forces, Chief Executive, Chief Legislator, Chief Diplomat, Chief Economist, Chief of Security, party leader, and the moral leader of America. The President has the ability to appeal to the nation through television, Twitter, and other modern methods of communication.

Chapter 6 | The Presidency: Our Executive Branch

Checks on Presidential Power

- There are several checks on Presidential power: Congress can override a Presidential veto, choose not to fund the President's suggested programs, refuse to approve Presidential appointments or treaties, apply the War Powers Act, and impeach the President.
- The Supreme Court can declare Presidential acts, including executive orders, unconstitutional.

Qualifications and Terms of the Presidency

- **Qualifications:** The President must be a U.S. citizen from birth, be at least 35 years of age, and be a U.S. resident for at least 14 years before taking office.
- **Terms in Office:** Presidential terms are for four years. The Twenty-Second Amendment limits the President to two elected terms. If the President dies or leaves office for any reason, the **Vice President** becomes the next President.

Executive Departments and the Cabinet

- The President is assisted by 15 executive departments.
- Each executive department is headed by a "Secretary" (except the Department of Justice, which is headed by the Attorney General). For example, the State Department—which handles foreign relations—is headed by the Secretary of State. The Treasury Department—which handles economic policies—is headed by the Secretary of the Treasury.
- The Vice President, the heads of the 15 executive departments, and a few other officers form the **Cabinet**. The Cabinet meets regularly and gives advice to the President. Although the Cabinet is not mentioned in the Constitution, every President has been advised by the Cabinet.

The Impeachment Process

- The President can be impeached for treason or other high crimes. **Impeachment** is simply removal from office and includes no other punishment. It has two stages:
  - First, a majority of House of Representatives votes whether to **impeach**.
  - Second, if the House votes to impeach, then the President is **tried** in the Senate. The Chief Justice of the Supreme Court presides over the trial. Two-thirds of the Senate must vote to convict the President in order to remove the President from office.

The Impeachment Process

House of Representatives  **Senate**

- Impeaches (charges) the President
- Majority vote needed to impeach the President

- Tries the President
- Chief Justice of the Supreme Court conducts the trial
- Two-thirds majority needed to remove the President

What Do You Know?

SS.7.C.2.9

1. Which individual could qualify as a candidate for President of the United States?
   A. Max is 67 years old; he has lived in Ontario, Canada for all of his life; he was born in Detroit.
   B. Martha is 45 years old; she has lived in Chicago for the last 18 years; she was born in Tampa.
   C. Samuel is 27 years old; he has lived in New York City for the past 3 years; he was born in Israel of American parents.
   D. Karen is 42 years old; she has lived in Boston for the last 26 years; she was born in Ireland of Irish parents.

SS.7.C.3.3

2. Which constitutional power provides the basis for the President's day-to-day control of U.S. foreign relations?
   A. the power to appoint and receive ambassadors
   B. the power to appoint Justices of the Supreme Court
   C. the power to inform Congress of the "State of the Union"
   D. the power to summon Congress in times of national emergency

SS.7.C.1.7

3. The War Powers Act of 1973 limited the powers of the President as Commander in Chief. Which principle of constitutional government did passage of this law illustrate?
   A. Federalism
   B. Limited government
   C. Checks and balances
   D. Separation of powers

SS.7.C.3.3

4. Which power does the Constitution give to the President to check Congress?
   A. the power to appoint heads of departments
   B. the power to veto proposed federal legislation
   C. the power to pardon offenders for federal crimes
   D. the power to inform Congress of the "State of the Union"

SS.7.C.3.3

5. When the President of the United States hosts the President of France at a dinner at the White House, what role is the President performing?
   A. Chief Diplomat
   B. Chief Legislator
   C. Chief Executive
   D. Commander in Chief

Chapter 6 | The Presidency: Our Executive Branch

SS.7.C.3.3

6. During the 1976 Presidential campaign, Jimmy Carter promised to pardon draft evaders from the Vietnam War to help heal the wounds of the war. Shortly after he was elected, President Carter pardoned about 100,000 of them. How was he able to pardon so many at once?
   A. By exercising an implied power
   B. By exercising a customary power
   C. By exercising an emergency power
   D. By exercising a power found in the Constitution

SS.7.C.3.3

7. The diagram below shows details about the United States government.

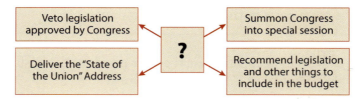

   Which phrase completes the diagram?
   A. Presidential powers as Head of State
   B. Presidential powers in relation to Congress
   C. Presidential powers as Commander in Chief
   D. Presidential powers as Chief Executive Officer

SS.7.C.3.8

8. Which role does the President perform when speaking at a political rally in support of a candidate running for Congress?
   A. Party Leader   C. Chief Diplomat
   B. Head of State   D. Chief Executive

SS.7.C.3.3

9. The headline shown on the left appeared in newspapers on December 20, 1998.

   Which step is next in the impeachment process?
   A. The President is tried in the Supreme Court.
   B. The President is tried before the U.S. Senate.
   C. The President can appeal to the Supreme Court.
   D. Three-fourths of the states must agree to the impeachment.

SS.7.C.3.8

10. How does an executive order differ from a federal law?
    A. Executive orders are not subject to judicial review.
    B. Executive orders are not limited by the Constitution.
    C. Executive orders do not need to be approved by Congress.
    D. Executive orders are limited to military and foreign affairs.

CHAPTER 7

The Federal Courts: Our Judicial Branch

SS.7.C.3.3 Illustrate the structure and function (three branches of government established in Articles I, II, and III with corresponding powers) of government in the United States as established in the Constitution. (See also Chapters 4, 5, and 6.)

SS.7.C.3.8 Analyze the structure, functions, and processes of the legislative, executive, and judicial branches. (See also Chapters 4, 5, and 6.)

SS.7.C.3.11 Diagram the levels, functions, and powers of courts at the state and federal levels. (See also Chapter 8.)

Names and Terms You Should Know

U.S. Supreme Court	Jurisdiction	Writ of certiorari
Judge	Trial Court	U.S. District Court
Justice	Jury	U.S. Court of Appeals
Chief Justice	Appeal	Judicial Review
Impeachment	Appellate Court	

© FTE ▪ Unlawful to photocopy without permission

Florida "Keys" to Learning

1. The role of the judicial branch is to resolve disputes, interpret the law and apply laws to specific cases.

2. The U.S. Supreme Court is superior to all other courts in the United States. The Supreme Court is composed of one Chief Justice and eight Associate Justices. These Justices are not elected but appointed by the President to serve for "good behavior"—that is, for life. The authors of the Constitution gave them lifetime appointments to protect the independence of the judiciary.

3. In the United States, there are many different kinds of courts. The territory and type of cases over which a court exercises its legal authority is known as its jurisdiction. A case can only be brought in a court that has jurisdiction over it. Federal courts have limited jurisdiction, since the Constitution only gives the federal government limited powers.

4. The U.S. Supreme Court has "original jurisdiction" in all cases affecting foreign ambassadors, foreign diplomats or states of the United States as parties to the dispute. It acts as a trial court in these cases. In all other cases, the U.S. Supreme Court exercises appellate jurisdiction. That is, it only reviews decisions from lower courts that losing parties bring to it. The losing party must appeal the decision by the lower court.

5. A party seeking review by the Supreme Court must file a petition for a writ of certiorari (*an order by an appellate court granting a request for judicial review*). The Supreme Court is not required to hear all appeals and only a small number of these petitions are granted.

6. The Supreme Court generally makes its decisions after hearing an "oral argument." Sometime after oral argument, the Justices discuss the case and take a vote to reach a decision. One Justice from the majority will be chosen to write an opinion on the decision. Other Justices are free to write their own dissenting opinions.

7. Article III of the Constitution created the Supreme Court but no other federal courts. However, the article gave Congress the power to create "inferior" (lower level) federal courts if it chose to do so.

8. The very first Congress decided to make lower federal courts. These federal courts now consist of the 94 U.S. District Courts and 13 U.S. Courts of Appeals.

9. Each state has at least one U.S. District Court. Florida has three U.S. District Courts. These are trial courts that hear cases on federal issues or between citizens of different states. These courts can have juries.

10. The 13 U.S. Courts of Appeals review cases on appeal. They are not trial courts. They are appellate courts. They hear appeals from the U.S. District Courts in their "Circuit" (the region over which they have jurisdiction).

11. One of the most important powers of the U.S. Supreme Court and other federal courts is the power of judicial review. The U.S. Supreme Court and other federal courts can declare that a law is unconstitutional.

Chapter 7 | The Federal Courts: Our Judicial Branch

In the last two chapters, you learned about Congress and the Presidency. In this chapter, you will study the third branch of our federal government, the **judicial branch**. The role of this branch is to resolve disputes, interpret laws and apply laws to specific cases.

The Supreme Court

The Articles of Confederation had lacked a national court system. The Constitution took care of this weakness by creating a national court. Article III of the Constitution established the U.S. Supreme Court. "Supreme" means the highest or most powerful—superior to all others. The Constitution also gave Congress the power to create "inferior" (*lower-level*) federal courts.

Composition of the Supreme Court

A **judge** is the public official who oversees a court of law. A judge on the U.S. Supreme Court is known as a "**Justice**." The Constitution did not establish the number of Supreme Court Justices. Instead, it left this decision up to Congress. As the new nation grew, Congress added new Justices to the Court.

Since 1869, there have been nine Justices: one **Chief Justice** and eight **Associate Justices**.

The Chief Justice presides over the Court's proceedings. The Chief Justice also acts as the spokesperson for the Court, serves as the nation's highest judicial officer, gives the oath of office to the President of the United States, and presides over any impeachment trial of the President in the Senate.

Selection Process for U.S. Supreme Court Justices

Supreme Court Justices are not elected officials. Instead, they are nominated (*proposed; named*) by the President and confirmed by a majority vote in the U.S. Senate. The President nominates individuals with distinguished legal careers who often share the President's own general outlook. At one time, Senate confirmation was routine. However, in more recent years, the examination of nominees by the Senate Judiciary Committee has become more challenging. This is an important example of the Constitution's system of checks and balances.

Lifetime Appointments

Supreme Court Justices—and, in fact, all federal judges—hold their office for "**good behavior**." This means that they are appointed for life. The average length of time that Justices have served on the Supreme Court has been about 16 years.

Why do federal judges enjoy their appointments for life? The authors of the Constitution wanted to make sure that judges were truly independent and would base their decisions on an impartial interpretation of the law. They especially resented the pressure that King George III had placed on judges in the years leading to the American Revolution. By appointing judges for life, the authors of the Constitution made them less subject to popular and political pressures. Federal judges don't have to worry about being re-

Chapter 7 | The Federal Courts: Our Judicial Branch

elected or re-appointed. Their lifetime positions support the independence of the judiciary. This maintains the separation of powers.

Federal judges remain in office unless they die, resign, or are impeached and removed by Congress for bribery, treason or other "high crimes." Impeachment of federal judges has been rare. Samuel Chase is the only U.S. Supreme Court Justice ever to have been impeached. No Supreme Court Justice has ever been removed from office.

Justice Samuel Chase

The Active Citizen

▸ Should federal judges be appointed or elected? Write a short "letter to the editor" giving your view on this issue. State your position and write one paragraph giving your reasons.

▸ In small groups, discuss whether it is better for federal judges to be appointed for limited terms, such as six years, or to be appointed for life. Each group should report its conclusions to the whole class.

Jurisdiction

Be sure to know what jurisdiction is for the EOC test.

A court of law is a public place where decisions are taken affecting the enforcement of laws or the settling of disputes. As you know, a judge presides over the proceedings of the court. Court decisions have the force of law. Courts can issue court orders, judgments, summary judgments and opinions. (You will learn more about some of these in Chapter 8.)

In the United States, there are many different kinds of courts—from traffic courts and municipal courts to federal courts. When a person is accused of a crime, when a person is injured by the carelessness of another, or when two businesses have a dispute, to which court should they look for help?

The territory and type of cases over which a court has legal authority is known as its jurisdiction. The word "jurisdiction" comes from *juris*, the Roman word for "law," and *dictio*, the word for "saying." A court's jurisdiction is the territory over which it "says the law."

One of the first jobs of a lawyer in taking any case is deciding *which* court has jurisdiction. Is this a case for state or federal court? And at which location should the case be filed?

The Active Citizen

▸ Imagine that you are a delegate at the Constitutional Convention in 1787. The Convention is discussing the possibility of a federal court system. Over which types of cases would you give jurisdiction to the new federal courts? Explain your answer.

Federal Jurisdiction

The principle of **limited government** extends to the judicial branch. Just as Congress has limited powers, federal courts have limited jurisdiction. They cannot decide all cases. Their jurisdiction is limited because federal power itself is limited.

Federal courts can only decide the following types of cases:

- Cases involving federal law, including the U.S. Constitution itself
- Cases involving the United States, individual states or foreign powers as parties
- Cases between citizens of different states—even if the dispute is under state law

---

The Active Citizen

How well can you interpret the actual language of the Constitution? Article III of the Constitution defines the jurisdiction of the federal courts. It states that the jurisdiction of federal courts includes:

1. "all Cases . . . arising under this Constitution, the Laws of the United States, and Treaties made, or which shall be made, under their Authority;" *These are cases involving federal law, including the Constitution.*

2. "all Cases affecting Ambassadors, other public Ministers and Consuls; . . . [all cases] to which the United States shall be a Party; [all cases] between two or more States; [or] between a State and Citizens of another State;" *These are cases involving foreign diplomats, the United States, or one of the 50 states as a party.*

3. [all Cases] "between Citizens of different States; . . . and between a State, or the Citizens thereof, and foreign States, Citizens or Subjects" *These are cases between citizens from different states. Federal courts judge these cases because a state court might favor its own citizens.*

▶ Why do federal courts have jurisdiction over only some kinds of cases? How does this demonstrate the constitutional principle of limited government?

▶ If you had been writing the Constitution, would you have given federal courts jurisdiction over any other types of cases? If so, which ones? Explain your answer.

The Jurisdiction of the Supreme Court

Original Jurisdiction

The U.S. Supreme Court has "original jurisdiction" in all cases affecting foreign ambassadors and other diplomats, or where one of the states, such as Florida, is a party. "Original jurisdiction" means that the case begins—or originates—with this court. In other words, the U.S. Supreme Court is the first court to hear all cases involving these parties.

In these circumstances, the Supreme Court effectively acts as a "trial court." There have only been about thirty cases where the U.S. Supreme Court acted as a trial court. Most have involved disputes between states. For example, in *Florida v. Georgia* (1854), the U.S. Supreme Court resolved a border dispute between Florida and Georgia. In this case, the Court eventually ruled in favor of Florida,

Chapter 7 | The Federal Courts: Our Judicial Branch

setting the boundary between the two states that still exists today.

The original jurisdiction of the U.S. Supreme Court was the subject of one of the most famous Supreme Court cases—*Marbury v. Madison*. You will learn more about this case later in this chapter and again in Chapter 10.

Appellate Jurisdiction

In all other cases, the U.S. Supreme Court exercises appellate jurisdiction. In these cases, the court acts as an **appellate court**. This means the Supreme Court cannot try these cases. It can only **review** decisions by lower courts sent to it on appeal. The party that loses the case in the lower court asks the appellate court to look over the decision and determine if it was decided correctly.

When the Constitution was first adopted, the Supreme Court was required to review all appeals sent to it. The number of such appeals soon became overwhelming. The U.S. Courts of Appeals were created in 1891. Since that time, parties in federal court must first appeal their cases to one of the U.S. Courts of Appeals. If a party loses its case in the U.S. Court of Appeals, it then has the right to appeal to the Supreme Court. Parties in state courts can also appeal to the U.S. Supreme Court if their case involves issues of federal law.

Be sure to know what a writ of certiorari is for the EOC test.

A party seeking review by the Supreme Court must file a petition for a **writ of certiorari**. About 10,000 such petitions are filed with the Supreme Court each year. The Supreme Court is not required to review all of these cases. If the Supreme Court decides to review a particular case, it issues a writ of certiorari. A writ of certiorari is an order by an appellate court granting a request for review of a lower court decision.

The Supreme Court carefully selects which cases to hear. It generally chooses those cases it believes to be of genuine national importance. These cases typically involve the interpretation of an important federal law or the U.S. Constitution.

Fewer than one out of every 100 petitions to the Supreme Court are granted a writ of certiorari each year. The Court generally hears "oral argument" and issues written opinions on only 75 to 80 of these cases. It also usually resolves another 50 cases without oral argument.

A Day in the Life of the Supreme Court — Enrichment

The Court's term begins each year on the first Monday of October and usually lasts until the following July. When the Court is sitting, the Justices first meet privately in the morning to discuss cases. The Justices have already read "briefs"—written legal arguments—from both sides of the case. Law clerks or staff attorneys may have also written memoranda summarizing the key issues and the law. The Chief Justice may even ask for a preliminary vote by the Justices on a case.

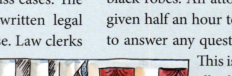

Oral Argument

Public sessions begin promptly at 10:00 in the morning. The Justices enter the courtroom wearing their black robes. An attorney for each side of the case is given half an hour to make an oral presentation and to answer any questions that the Justices might ask. This is known as "oral argument." Usually the Court hears oral argument on two cases a day.

During oral argument, the Justices will usually interrupt the speaker with questions many times throughout the presentation.

154 Chapter 7 | The Federal Courts: Our Judicial Branch

Reaching a Decision

Sometime after oral argument, the Justices discuss the case among themselves in a private conference. After the case is fully discussed—which may take more than one meeting—a vote is taken.

Writing the Opinion

One of the Justices is assigned to write the decision for the majority. Justices who do not agree with part or all of the majority opinion may write their own **dissenting opinions**. A draft of the majority opinion is printed and given to all of the Justices. They reply with comments, which the author of the majority opinion often has to take into account. At this point, some of the Justices may have even changed their minds. In Chapter 10, you will read several excerpts from actual Supreme Court opinions. Here is how one Supreme Court Justice described the process:

Each Justice studies each case in sufficient detail to resolve the question for himself. In a very real sense, each decision is an individual decision of every Justice. The process can be a lonely, troubling experience....

I would particularly emphasize that, unlike the case of a Congressional or White House decision, Americans demand of their Supreme Court judges that they produce a written opinion, the collective expression of the judges subscribing [agreeing] to it, setting forth the reason which led them to the decision.

These opinions are the exposition [explanation], not just to lawyers, legal scholars and other judges, but to our whole society, of the bases upon which a particular result rests...

—Justice William J. Brennan, Jr., "How the Supreme Court Arrives at Decisions"

The Active Citizen

- How did Justice Brennan see Supreme Court decisions as different from Presidential and Congressional decisions?
- Why did Justice Brennan believe that the practice of publishing Supreme Court opinions was so important?
- Is the practice of publishing dissenting opinions too divisive? Explain your answer.
- Imagine that you are a Justice of the U.S. Supreme Court. Write a letter to a friend in which you describe a typical day when the Court is in session.

> Be sure to know the two types of lower federal courts for the EOC test.

The "Lower" Federal Courts

At the Constitutional Convention, the possibility of creating federal courts below the Supreme Court was hotly debated. The delegates could not agree. Many felt these courts were unnecessary. Others feared the Supreme Court would be flooded with petitions if lower federal courts were not created. As a skillful compromise, the members of the Constitutional Convention finally agreed to let the future Congress decide the issue. Article III created the Supreme Court but no other federal courts. However, the same article gave Congress the power to create "inferior" (*lower-level*) federal courts if it wished to do so. The very first Congress did so in the Judiciary Act of 1789.

U.S. District Courts

Today, there are 94 U.S. District Courts. Each state has at least one U.S. District Court. Florida has three U.S. District Courts: one for the Florida Northern District, one for the Florida Middle District, and one for the Florida Southern District.

Except for the U.S. Supreme Court in rare instances, the U.S. District Courts are the only federal trial courts. Therefore the U.S. District Courts are also the only federal courts to have juries. A **jury** is a group of local citizens who hear the evidence at trial and decide the case. If a dispute involves federal law or if it involves citizens from different states, the parties have the right to have their case tried in U.S. District Court. There they will receive a trial, similar in many ways to one that might take place in a state court. In Chapter 8, you will learn more about how cases are tried in state courts.

U.S. Courts of Appeals

There are also now 13 **U.S. Courts of Appeals**. Twelve of these cover district courts from a specific region, forming a judicial "**Circuit**." A circuit is a circular route. The term comes from a time when judges traveled around their districts and held court sessions at various locations along their route. Sometimes a U.S. Court of Appeals is even referred to as a "Circuit Court." Florida, for example, belongs to the **U.S. Court of Appeals for the Eleventh Circuit**, which also includes Alabama and Georgia. The Eleventh Circuit covers nine U.S. District Courts.

The U.S. Courts of Appeals are not trial courts. Their judges do not try cases. They are **appellate courts**. When a party loses in U.S. District Court, it has the right to appeal the decision to the U.S. Court of Appeals in its Circuit. The U.S. Court of Appeals then reviews the record of the trial to see whether the law was interpreted correctly and applied fairly. Three judges ordinarily review each case. If two of the three believe the trial court made an important error, they can send the case back to the trial court with instructions for a retrial. The party that loses on appeal has the right to look even

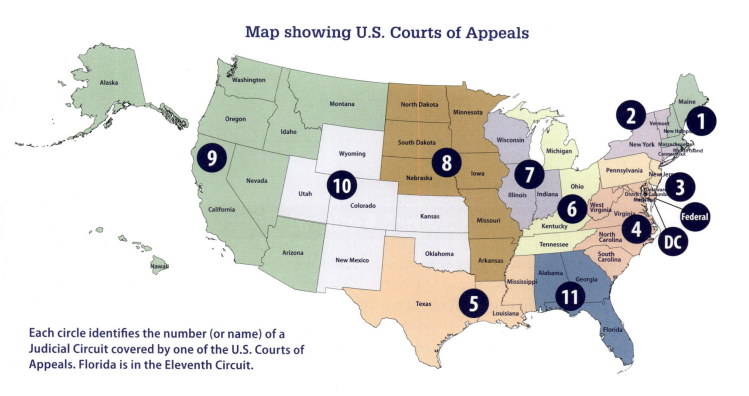

Map showing U.S. Courts of Appeals

Each circle identifies the number (or name) of a Judicial Circuit covered by one of the U.S. Courts of Appeals. Florida is in the Eleventh Circuit.

farther to obtain justice. If a party believes the law has been misinterpreted or misapplied by the U.S. Court of Appeals, it can petition for a writ of certiorari from the U.S. Supreme Court. There is no guarantee, however, that the Supreme Court will accept its petition and hear its case.

In the next chapter, you will learn more about the differences between trial and appellate courts.

Judicial Review

One of the most important powers of the Supreme Court and other federal courts is the power of **judicial review**. Federal courts can rule that either a law passed by Congress or an executive order issued by the President is unconstitutional. This means that the law or order is not permitted under the U.S. Constitution and cannot be enforced. The power of judicial review is one of the most important checks on actions by Congress or the President.

Chief Justice John Marshall

The phrase "judicial review" is not to be found in the Constitution itself. Chief Justice John Marshall introduced the practice in the case of *Marbury v. Madison* in 1803. In this landmark decision, Marshall declared that part of the Judiciary Act of 1789 was, in fact, **unconstitutional**. Congress had exceeded its powers under the Constitution. This meant that this section of the Judiciary Act could not be enforced. Marshall argued that it was the Supreme Court's role to decide on the constitutionality of laws because it is the job of courts to interpret the law and to explain what the law is. You will study the case of *Marbury v. Madison* in more detail in Chapter 10.

"Judicial review" is not a separate process in addition to the Court's other activities. Congress does not send bills or new laws over to the Court for advice on whether they are constitutional. The Supreme Court and other federal courts cannot issue "advisory opinions." They do not make recommendations to the legislature or the executive. They can only declare that a law is unconstitutional if that law comes before them as part of an actual dispute between two or more parties.

Chapter 7 | The Federal Courts: Our Judicial Branch

Name _____

Review the following list of terms and phrases.

Supreme Court	Trial court	U.S. District Court
Supreme Court Justice	Jury	U.S. Court of Appeals
Chief Justice	Appeal	Judicial review
Impeachment	Appellate court	
Jurisdiction	Writ of certiorari	

Now group these names and terms into the following three categories.

I've never heard of this name or term.	I've heard of this name or term but don't know what it is.	I know this name or term.

Finally, define or identify each name or term you do not know well.

_____

_____

_____

_____

_____

_____

_____

The Federal Judiciary

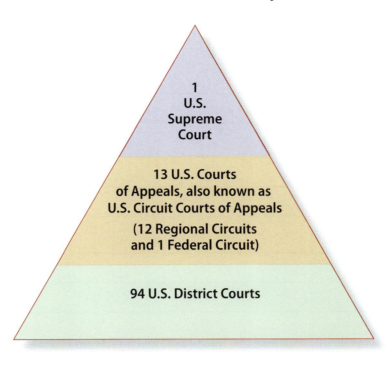

U.S. District Courts	▪ These are federal courts that try cases involving federal crimes, violations of federal law, or cases between parties from different states. ▪ U.S. District Courts are trial courts that hear witnesses, weigh evidence, and find facts. They can have juries.
U.S. Courts of Appeals	▪ These are appellate courts. ▪ They rule on appeals from decisions of the U.S. District Courts. They never have juries. ▪ These courts are organized into 12 geographic regions known as "Circuits." ▪ The U.S. Court of Appeals for the Federal Circuit reviews decisions concerning patents, claims against the U.S. government and other specialized matters.
U.S. Supreme Court	▪ The Supreme Court is the highest court in the land. ▪ It reviews decisions from the U.S. Courts of Appeal and can also review state supreme court decisions involving federal law. ▪ The Supreme Court also acts as a trial court in resolving disputes between different states of the United States, or in cases involving foreign ambassadors and other diplomats. ▪ The Supreme Court and other federal courts also have the power of judicial review: they can declare laws to be unconstitutional.

Chapter 7 | The Federal Courts: Our Judicial Branch

Name _____

Define each of the following:

Trial court _____
_____
_____

Jurisdiction _____
_____
_____

Chief Justice _____
_____
_____

Appeal _____
_____
_____

Writ of certiorari _____
_____
_____

Appellate court _____
_____
_____

Majority opinion _____
_____
_____

Dissenting opinion _____
_____
_____

Judicial review _____
_____
_____

Name _____

Describe the role of each of these courts in the federal system:

U.S. Supreme Court

_____
_____
_____
_____
_____
_____

U.S. Court of Appeals

_____
_____
_____
_____
_____
_____

U.S. District Court

_____
_____
_____
_____
_____
_____

Chapter 7 | The Federal Courts: Our Judicial Branch

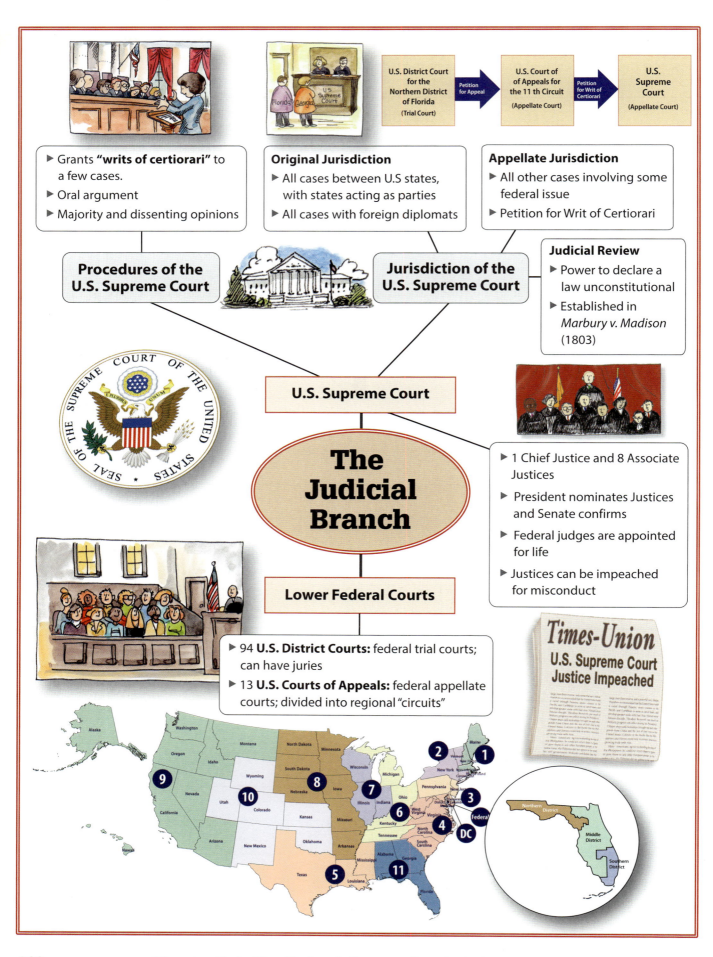

Review Cards: The Federal Courts

The Judicial Branch: The U.S. Supreme Court

- The **judicial branch** of our federal government is in charge of resolving disputes by interpreting and applying the law.
- The Constitution created our country's first national court, the **U.S. Supreme Court**.
- The Constitution also gave Congress the power to create "inferior" (lower) federal courts.
- The number of **Justices** on the Supreme Court has increased over time. There are now 8 **Associate Justices** and 1 **Chief Justice**. The Chief Justice presides over the Court and acts as its spokesperson. The Chief Justice also swears the President into office and presides over any Presidential impeachment trial.
- Supreme Court Justices are nominated by the President and confirmed by a majority vote in the Senate. This is an example of our system of **checks and balances**.
- All federal judges are appointed for life, so long as they maintain "**good behavior**" (do not commit "high crimes" or other misconduct, for which Congress can impeach them) or until they resign. This system of appointment for life helps federal judges to act independently of popular and political pressures. It helps to protect the independence of the judiciary and the separation of powers.
- Supreme Court Justices can be impeached by Congress, although no Supreme Court Justice has ever been removed from office.

Jurisdiction

- There are many different types of courts in the United States. The territory and type of cases over which a court exercises its authority is called its **jurisdiction**. The word *jurisdiction* comes from: "to say the law."
- Federal courts have **limited jurisdiction**. They can only decide (1) cases involving federal law; (2) cases involving the United States, individual states or foreign powers as parties; or (3) cases involving citizens from different states.
- The U.S. Supreme Court has **original jurisdiction** in all cases involving foreign representatives (ambassadors, consuls, and other diplomats) or states (such as Florida) as parties. In these cases, the Supreme Court is the original, or first, court that the parties turn to. In these cases, it acts as a **trial court**. The Supreme Court considers the evidence in these cases and reaches its decision.
- In all other cases, the Supreme Court exercises **appellate jurisdiction**. In these cases, it acts as an **appellate court**. It reviews appeals from the decisions of lower courts, rather than trying the case itself.

The "Lower" Federal Courts

- The Constitution gave Congress the power to create "inferior"—or lower—federal courts. The **Judiciary Act of 1789** created the first lower federal courts.
- Today, there are 94 U.S. District Courts and 13 U.S. Courts of Appeals.

Chapter 7 | The Federal Courts: Our Judicial Branch

U.S. District Courts

- Each state has at least one U.S. District Court. Florida has three. These are the only federal **trial courts**. This means they can have juries. These courts resolve disputes over federal law. They can also resolve disputes based on state law when these disputes are between citizens from different states.

U.S. Courts of Appeals

- The **U.S. Courts of Appeals** are appellate courts: they review cases on appeal, but do not try them.
- Each U.S. Court of Appeals (also known as "Circuit Courts") covers the U.S. District Courts in its "Circuit." For example, the U.S. Court of Appeals for the 11th Circuit covers the U.S. District Courts for Florida, Alabama and Georgia. The Court of Appeals for the 11th Circuit reviews appeals from all the U.S. District Courts in those three states.

How a Case Proceeds through Federal Court

- First, the parties file the case in U.S. District Court. The District Court is a trial court.
- The losing party can appeal the decision to the U.S. Court of Appeals for that Circuit.
- The appellate court may agree with the lower court or it could reverse the lower court and send the case back with instructions for a retrial.
- The party losing the appeal can petition for a writ of certiorari from the U.S. Supreme Court.

Review by the Supreme Court

- Each year, the U.S. Supreme Court receives thousands of requests for review—called petitions for a **writ of certiorari**. Only about a hundred of these are usually granted.
- In a typical case, the Supreme Court Justices read briefs from both sides of the case. Then they hear **oral arguments** by the attorneys from both sides, where the Justices ask questions. The Justices then discuss the case among themselves and reach their decision. One Justice writes a **majority opinion**, which is published. Justices who disagree with the majority opinion may write their own separate, **dissenting opinions**, which are also published.

Judicial Review

- In the case *Marbury v. Madison* in 1803, Chief Justice John Marshall established the power of **judicial review**. This is the power of the U.S. Supreme Court and other federal courts to declare that a law or executive order is unconstitutional.
- Federal courts can only declare laws unconstitutional if they are brought before them in actual court cases.

What Do You Know?

SS.7.C.3.11

1. Sam Morgan is convicted of committing mail fraud by the U.S. District Court for the Southern District of Florida. Sam believes the judge was unfairly biased against him. To which court should he send his appeal?
   A. U.S. Supreme Court
   B. Florida Circuit Court
   C. U.S. Court of Appeals
   D. Florida Supreme Court

SS.7.C.3.11

2. Article III of the Constitution established the U.S. Supreme Court. Why does this article refer to this court as "supreme"?
   A. It hears more cases than any other court.
   B. It has authority over all other courts in the United States.
   C. Its officers are appointed by the President of the United States.
   D. It has authority over both the executive and legislative branches.

SS.7.C.3.8

3. Why are federal judges appointed for life?
   A. to ensure the system of checks and balances
   B. to strengthen their jurisdiction over state courts
   C. to limit the power of the legislative and executive branches
   D. to maintain the independence of the judiciary and the separation of powers

SS.7.C.3.11

4. An oil barge belonging to the State of Alabama has a massive oil leak in the Gulf of Mexico. The leaked oil damages the beautiful beaches of Destin, Panama City, and Ft. Walton. The oil also endangers the shrimp and crab industry of Florida. The State of Florida sues the State of Alabama. Which court has jurisdiction over the case?
   A. U.S. Supreme Court
   B. Florida Supreme Court
   C. U.S. Court of Appeals for the 11th Circuit
   D. U.S. District Court for the Northern District of Florida

SS.7.C.3.11

5. How does an appellate court differ from a trial court?
   A. An appellate court usually has a jury.
   B. An appellate court decides issues of fact.
   C. An appellate court examines more witnesses.
   D. An appellate court reviews another court's decision.

Chapter 7 | The Federal Courts: Our Judicial Branch

SS.7.C.3.3

6. The Rio Grande forms the international border between Texas and Mexico. Over the years, the Rio Grande has changed its course several times. This has led to a number of disputes between Texas, New Mexico, and Mexico. The Country Club dispute between Texas and New Mexico was decided by the U.S. Supreme Court in 1927.

   Why did the Supreme Court act as a trial court in this case?
   A. The case involved federal law.
   B. The case was between several states as parties.
   C. The case was between citizens of different states.
   D. The case involved foreign ambassadors and other diplomats.

SS.7.C.3.11

7. Which are the only federal courts to have juries?
   A. U.S. District Courts
   B. U.S. Supreme Court
   C. U.S. Courts of Appeals
   D. U.S. District Courts of Appeals

SS.7.C.3.8

8. What kind of order does the U.S. Supreme Court issue to indicate that it will review a case?
   A. writ of certiorari
   B. majority opinion
   C. summary judgment
   D. writ of *habeas corpus*

SS.7.C.3.3

9. The headline on the left appeared in a newspaper.

   Which statement would most likely follow this headline?
   A. "Justice discovered to be ruling on cases solely to win votes."
   B. "Justice found to be opposing the President's views on the case."
   C. "Justice accused of accepting secret payments from a party in the case."
   D. "Justice committed treason by ruling in favor of a foreign diplomat against the United States."

SS.7.C.3.11

10. The diagram below provides details about the U.S. court system.

    Which court completes the diagram?
    A. Circuit Court
    B. Supreme Court
    C. Municipal Court
    D. Court of Veterans Appeals

Chapter 7 | The Federal Courts: Our Judicial Branch

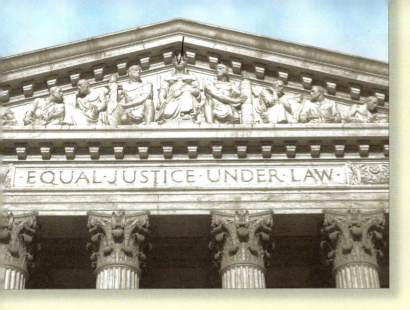

CHAPTER 8

The Rule of Law

SS.7.C.1.9   Define the rule of law and recognize its influence on the development of the American legal, political, and governmental systems.

SS.7.C.2.6   Simulate the trial process and the role of juries in the administration of justice.

SS.7.C.3.8   Analyze the structure, functions, and processes of the legislative, executive, and judicial branches. (See also Chapters 4–7.)

SS.7.C.3.10   Identify sources and types (civil, criminal, constitutional, military) of law.

SS.7.C.3.11   Diagram the levels, functions, and powers of courts at the state and federal levels. (See also Chapter 7.)

Names and Terms You Should Know

Law	Precedent	Trial
Rule of law	Case law	Jury
Accountability	Civil law	Summary judgment
Consistent Application	Criminal law	Appeal
Due process	Constitutional law	Arrest
Transparency	Military law	Florida County Court
Law code	Juvenile law	Florida Circuit Court
Statute	Court	Florida District Court of Appeal
Statutory law	Judge	Florida Supreme Court
Common law	Court order	

Chapter 8 | The Rule of Law

Florida "Keys" to Learning

1. A law is a rule that is enforced by the government and includes some penalty (*punishment*) for breaking it. Laws help a community to organize and protect itself, to settle disputes, and to punish crimes.

2. In many nations, the ruler's will (*desire*) is law. In contrast, Americans live under the rule of law. This means we live under a system of written laws that make it clear how people should behave with one another. Our government leaders are subject to the same laws. No one is above the law.

3. The rule of law requires: accountability to the law; fair and impartial procedures; decisions based on the law; the consistent application of the law to all parties; enforcement of the law; and the transparency, or openness, of institutions and processes (such as public trials).

4. Laws have evolved over time. Codes of written laws, from ancient times to the present, have played an important role in the development of the law. There are many sources of American law. Laws passed by a legislature are known as statutes. Medieval England established the common law—laws based on customs and the earlier decisions of judges in similar cases. Case law is law based on past court decisions. The Constitution is also a source of law.

5. There are many types of laws. These include criminal laws to punish those who commit crimes, and civil laws to resolve disputes between parties over accidents, property damage and other issues. There are also constitutional, military, and juvenile laws.

6. Laws are enforced in courts by the decision of a judge or a judge and jury. A jury is a panel of impartial citizens (*peers or equals*).

7. A civil case concerns a dispute or injury between two parties. It begins when one party files a "complaint" against the other. During pretrial discovery, both sides must produce evidence. Lawyers investigate and take depositions by interviewing witnesses. A lawyer can file a motion for summary judgment to dismiss the case if overwhelming evidence favors one side. If a trial occurs, a jury is then chosen. During the trial, each side makes its case. Lawyers present evidence from witnesses, documents and photographs, and they examine and cross-examine witnesses. Lawyers then make closing statements. The judge gives jury instructions. The jury's role is to decide the facts based on the evidence. Their decision is the verdict.

8. If one side is not satisfied with the verdict, it can appeal to an appellate court. The appellate court reviews the case for errors in law and decides whether to have a retrial.

9. A criminal case begins with the investigation of a crime. When a suspect is found, there is a hearing to decide if there is "probable cause" to arrest the suspect. If probable cause exists, the suspect is arraigned and can plead guilty or not guilty. Then bail is set: if paid, the person is freed until trial. If not, the person stays in jail. After a period of plea-bargaining, the case goes to trial. In a criminal case, the "burden of proof" is on the prosecution. The defendant is presumed not guilty unless the evidence shows otherwise beyond a reasonable doubt. If found guilty by the jury, the judge imposes a sentence. The defendant can appeal both the verdict and the sentence.

10. Florida has four levels of courts. Florida county courts hear civil cases for under $15,000 and cases of lesser crimes (misdemeanors). Florida circuit courts hear civil cases for more than $15,000 and more serious crimes (felonies). They also review appeals from the county courts. Florida District Courts of Appeal review cases from the circuit courts. Lastly, the Florida Supreme Court acts as the highest court in the state. It hears appeals from the lower state courts, including all death penalty cases, and can also issue some advisory opinions.

In the last chapter, you learned about the organization of the judicial branch of our federal government. In this chapter, you will look more closely at how laws are applied to specific situations by both state and federal courts.

Welcome to Law School!

You may only be in the middle grades, but in this chapter you are about to enter law school. You have probably already seen imaginary trials on television. What courts do is to interpret and apply the law. Therefore, you cannot truly understand what courts do—what happens in either a trial or an appellate court—until you first understand what a law is.

So, what exactly is a law?

A **law** is a type of rule, such as having to stop at a stop sign. Unlike other rules, a law is enforced by the government. There is almost always some penalty (*punishment*) for breaking a law. If a driver doesn't stop at a stop sign, the driver may get a traffic ticket and have to pay a fine.

Laws help a community to organize and protect itself. They allow community leaders to take those steps needed to achieve cooperation for the common good. They also help the community to settle disputes without violence. Laws protect the safety of individuals and their property. Laws against crimes serve special purposes. They help the victims of a crime overcome their grief by punishing the criminal. They discourage potential criminals from committing future crimes. And finally, the experience of punishment can lead some individuals to reform and give up their criminal behavior.

Interpreting the Law

Although the wording of a law may seem clear at first, difficulties often arise in applying it to specific situations. Take, for example, the case of a town that decides to put up a sign in a local park. The sign says "No Vehicles Permitted in the Park." This seems clear enough. The town doesn't want cars, trucks, motorcycles or buses driving through the park.

But Ms. Smith wants to take her toddler in a stroller into the park. Is her stroller a "vehicle"? Would this action violate the rule? And her husband, Mr. Smith, is in a wheelchair. Is his wheelchair a "vehicle"? Can Mr. Smith take his wheelchair into the park?

Several school children are playing in the same park. They were looking forward to a visit by the local ice-cream truck. Is an ice-cream truck a "vehicle"? Is it permitted to enter the park?

Jack and Jill ride their bicycles to school. Can they take a shortcut through the park? Is a bicycle a "vehicle," as intended by the sign?

These are examples of the kinds of problems that can arise in interpreting the language of a particular law. It is the job of courts to interpret laws and to apply them to specific situations.

Chapter 8 | The Rule of Law

As one of the most famous U.S. Supreme Court Justices once explained:

> "It is emphatically (clearly; without a doubt) the province and duty of the judicial department to say what the law is. Those who apply the rule to particular cases must of necessity [explain] and interpret that rule."
>
> —Chief Justice John Marshall, *Marbury v. Madison* (1803)

The Rule of Law and Due Process

What is so special about having laws? As you can see, laws make it clear how we should conduct ourselves. Because of laws, we know how we should behave and how others can be expected to behave.

Laws are generally written and available in public so that everyone can know about them. We expect our laws to be fair and reasonable in general. Even if we disagree with a specific law, we are still willing to obey it.

In many societies throughout history, the ruler's will has been law. Whatever the ruler desires at any moment suddenly becomes the law. In this kind of society, citizens cannot easily make future plans. From moment to moment, they do not know what they are permitted or not permitted to do. At any time, they may face harsh penalties. In this kind of society, everyone except the ruler is at risk.

Laws are therefore especially important in placing curbs on government. In a democratic society, the government itself is subject to the law. We say that we live under **the rule of law**. This means that we are ruled by laws rather than by our rulers' whims. Our laws protect us from arbitrary (*dictatorial; unfair*) and oppressive acts by government. Government leaders can only do what the law permits them to do. The police, for example, must follow the law when questioning or arresting suspects. Judges must also follow the law when deciding whether to fine or imprison someone. Finally, our government leaders are themselves subject to the rule of law, just like everyone else.

The rule of law actually consists of six principles:

Accountability to the law

Each of us is "accountable" to the law. We must answer to it. Our conduct is subject to written laws that

> No one is above the law. The **rule of law** is based on these six principles:
> - Accountability to the law
> - Fair procedures
> - Decisions based on law
> - Consistent application of the law
> - Enforcement of the law
> - Transparency (openness) of institutions

everyone knows and that everyone is subject to. We are legally responsible for our actions. No one is permitted to break the law without consequence. People who break the law must pay a penalty of some kind—either they pay a fine or go to prison. This even applies to our public officials.

Fair procedures

Procedures are the steps the government takes to carry out its decisions. The procedures used to decide whether an accused person has violated the law, or to settle a dispute between people or groups, should be fair and impartial.

These fair procedures are sometimes known as our **"due process" rights**. We are "due" a fair process if we risk losing our freedom or our property in a court or government proceeding. These "due process" rights include the right to a public trial or proceeding before our freedom or property can be taken away. A person accused of a crime has the right to see any evidence the police have collected and to question any witnesses. An accused person also has the right to the help of an attorney. If the police question a suspect, that suspect must be told of his or her right to remain silent and to consult with an attorney before answering any questions the police may have. These "due process" rights make the law more fair and impartial for all of us.

Decisions based on the law

When a court reaches a decision, such as to punish someone accused of a crime, this decision must be based on the law.

Consistent application of the law

The law should be applied to everyone in the same manner, no matter how poor or rich they are or where they come from. Everyone should be treated the same under the law.

For this reason, the Supreme Court has held that even those who cannot afford to pay for a lawyer are entitled to the help of one if they are accused of a serious crime. If an accused person cannot afford a lawyer, then the court must provide one for free.

To make sure the law is applied consistently, our court decisions are recorded. Judges consider what was done in the past and try to apply the law to new cases in a similar way.

Enforcement of the law

Our government enforces the laws we decide to have. That means it must carry them out. Our government officials, including the police, have a responsibility to enforce the law to protect citizens from violence and crime.

Transparency (*openness*) of institutions

Proceedings and most government decisions are made openly and in public, not in secret. This is known as **transparency**. It means everyone can see what is going on. Something is transparent if we can see through it. All our laws are public and all our court proceedings, such as trials, are public and transparent. This way, everyone can see that the law is applied fairly and consistently, and that government decisions are based on the law.

Where Do Laws Come From? How Laws Developed in Western Society

From the very earliest times, people have had laws. One of the earliest known written law codes was issued more than 3,700 years ago by Hammurabi, the ruler of Babylonia. With this written law code, people in ancient Babylon knew the laws to which they were accountable:

> These excerpts from famous law codes are offered as examples. This one was written many thousands of years ago. You may find it difficult to read. **You will not have to know any specific law codes for the EOC test.**

THE CODE OF HAMMURABI

22. IF ANY ONE IS COMMITTING A ROBBERY AND IS CAUGHT, THEN HE SHALL BE PUT TO DEATH . . . .

196. IF A MAN DESTROYS THE EYE OF ANOTHER MAN, THEY SHALL DESTROY HIS EYE. IF ONE MAN BREAKS ANOTHER'S BONE, THEY SHALL BREAK HIS BONE. IF ONE MAN DESTROYS THE EYE OF A FREEMAN OR BREAKS THE BONE OF A FREEMAN, HE SHALL PAY ONE MINA OF SILVER.

IF HE DESTROYS THE EYE OF A MAN'S SLAVE OR BREAKS THE BONE OF A MAN'S SLAVE, HE SHALL PAY ONE-HALF HIS PRICE . . . .

265. IF A HERDSMAN OR SHEPHERD, TO WHOSE CARE CATTLE OR SHEEP HAVE BEEN ENTRUSTED, BE GUILTY OF FRAUD . . . THEN HE SHALL BE CONVICTED AND PAY THE OWNER TEN TIMES THE LOSS . . . .

Word Helper

a code = a set of rules or laws
to commit = to do something
to destroy = here, to injure or damage
a freeman = a person who is not a slave
a mina of silver = an amount of money at that time; a coin
a herdsman = someone watching cattle
a shepherd = someone watching sheep
entrusted = to be trusted with something
fraud = cheating, lying or deceiving

Chapter 8 | The Rule of Law

The Active Citizen

Ancient law codes can be hard to read and understand. See if you can answer any of these questions.

▶ Were the penalties (*punishments*) for crimes in ancient Babylonia harsher than today? How would you explain the differences?

▶ Which of the laws above were to deter (*discourage*) crime, and which ones were to compensate (*reimburse; repay*) a victim for losses? Explain your answer.

▶ How were the penalties for hurting another person different, depending on his or her social status?

▶ Why were the penalties for fraud (*cheating; deceit*) in caring for animals so strict?

▶ What was the significance of written law codes like the Code of Hammurabi to the development of the rule of law?

Ancient Roman Law

In ancient Rome, the representatives of the common people insisted that their laws be written and displayed in a public place, so that the people would know what they could and could not do. These laws were written on **Twelve Tables** and placed on the main public square of Rome, known as the Forum, in 450–449 B.C.

The Roman Forum was a public square where the government made announcements.

Samples of Roman Laws from the Twelve Tables

Enrichment

Just like Hammurabi's Code, these ancient Roman laws may be difficult to understand. The rules here were used by Romans more than 2,000 years ago to resolve disputes and punish wrongdoers. You do not need to know about Roman law for the EOC test.

Table VII

Law II.

If you cause any unlawful damage . . . accidentally and unintentionally, you must make good the loss, either by offering what has caused it, or by payment.

Law XIII.

If anyone knowingly and intentionally kills a freeman, he shall be guilty of a capital crime. If he kills him by accident, without malice or intention, let him substitute a ram to be sacrificed publicly to seek forgiveness . . .

Word Helper
- **intentionally** = purposefully; deliberately
- **ram** = male sheep
- **capital crime** = crime punishable by death
- **malice** = ill will; bad feeling
- **reparation** = compensation; repayment

Table IX

Law III.

When a judge appointed to hear a case accepts money, or other gifts, for the purpose of influencing his decision, he shall suffer the penalty of death.

Table XII

Law III.

If a slave, with the knowledge of his master, commits a theft or causes damage to anyone, his master shall be given up to the other party by way of reparation for the theft, injury, or damage committed by the slave.

Enrichment

The Active Citizen

- Why was it advantageous for Roman commoners (*plebeians*) to have these laws publicly displayed?
- Select two of these laws and explain them in a letter to a relative in a different part of the ancient world.
- What common principles can you find in these laws?

The Romans expanded their territories to create a far-flung empire that dominated the ancient world. With so many peoples and traditions under their rule, the Romans needed a well-organized set of laws that everyone could easily follow. Romans introduced many important legal concepts, such as the enforcement of **contracts**—solemn agreements made by private parties that can be publicly enforced in courts of law. In a contract, one party often promises to pay another party to do something. The Romans also improved procedures for investigating and prosecuting crimes and for resolving commercial disputes.

Between 529 and 534 A.D., the **Emperor Justinian** took all the known laws of the Roman Empire and brought them together into a single law code—the **Code of Justinian**. This made them easier to refer to.

Law in the Middle Ages

During the Middle Ages in Europe (from 500 A.D. to about 1400 A.D.), laws came from many different sources. Some laws dated back to Roman times; others came from popular tradition.

A third group of laws came from the king. You already know, for example, that King John I of England signed *Magna Carta* in 1215. This royal charter gave certain rights to every freeborn Englishman. One of these rights was the right to a trial by jury.

Later in English history, laws were mainly passed by Parliament and approved by the king. Laws passed by Parliament or any other legislature such as Congress are known as **statutes**, or **statutory law**.

In the Middle Ages, England also established the **common law**. King John's father, Henry II, sent royal judges around the English countryside for part of each year in order to hear and decide cases. Henry told his judges to consider both local customs and past judgments in deciding cases. Later, these judges returned to London, where they discussed their cases and recorded their most important decisions.

> You should know the differences between statutory and common law for the EOC test.

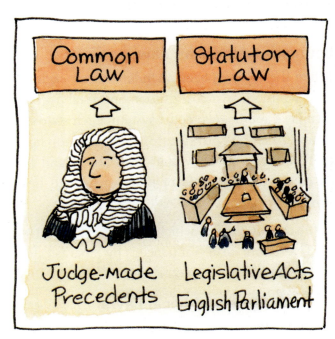

Two Sources of Law

Chapter 8 | The Rule of Law

173

Henry's goal was to create a system of laws "common" to the entire kingdom. The common law thus took into account not only laws passed by the king and Parliament, but also customs and decisions reached by earlier judges on the same issue.

People believed it was more just and fair when the law was applied consistently: all those in similar situations should receive the same treatment from the courts. The common law thus looked to **precedents**—previous decisions by courts, which served as models to guide later ones dealing with similar situations.

The common law came to be seen as a powerful force independent of the king's own authority. Chief Justice Sir Edward Coke (1552–1634) called the law "the perfection of reason." Coke considered the common law to be the "most general and ancient law of the realm."

The Active Citizen

- What is meant by the "common law"?
- How does statutory law differ from the common law?

> For the EOC test, you should be sure to know the different types of law—civil, criminal, constitutional, military and juvenile—as well as the different sources of law—statutory law, common law, case law, and constitutional law.

Sources and Types of American Law

Americans inherited all of these traditions—Judeo-Christian teachings, Roman law, English common law, and statutory law issued by the king and Parliament. In addition, colonial legislatures enacted many of their own laws.

Sources of American Law

When the colonies became independent, each new state wrote its own constitution and established its own laws and its own court system. Each state continued to rely on both **statutory** and **common law**—that is, laws passed by state legislatures and laws based on the decisions of judges who had heard similar cases in the past.

In the case of Florida, which became a state in 1845, its laws were also influenced by Spanish legal traditions.

Federal, State and Local Laws

As you learned in the last chapter, federal courts can only decide some kinds of cases, such as those con-

Sources of Law

Statutory Law	Statutory laws are all the laws passed by legislatures, also known as **statutes**.
Common Law	The common law is based on customs, traditions, and prior court decisions (*precedents*) on similar cases. Judges often have to fill gaps in the law in making their decisions. The common law is the sum of all these interpretations of laws.
Case Law	Case law is actually part of the common law. It is law based on prior court decisions (precedents).
Constitutional Law	These are laws based on the U.S. Constitution, including the Bill of Rights, and the state constitutions.

Chapter 8 | The Rule of Law

cerning federal law. State courts, in contrast, are more general. They can hear almost any type of case. Most legal matters today are, in fact, handled by state courts applying state law:

- If you are accused of committing a crime in Florida, you will be tried in a Florida state court for having broken a Florida law.

- If you have a contract dispute with a local business, you will seek to resolve your dispute in a Florida state court based on Florida law.

- If you suffered a personal injury in Florida because of someone else's carelessness, you seek compensation in a Florida state court.

As you know, our federal government also creates its own laws. Whenever Congress passes a bill and the President signs it, it becomes a new federal law. Local governments also pass their own laws. We are thus surrounded by a web of laws. American citizens are subject to **federal**, **state**, and **local laws**.

Local, State, and Federal Laws

Local Laws	These laws are passed by local governments and only concern the local community. An example might be the speed limit on a local street. Local laws are often known as "ordinances."
State Laws	These laws are passed by state governments. They affect the citizens, residents and visitors in a single state. An example of a state law might be the speed limit on state highways or the requirements for graduating from a public high school in that state.
Federal Laws	These laws are passed by Congress, based on the powers granted to Congress by the U.S. Constitution. Federal laws concern the entire nation. An example of a federal law might be a law limiting air pollution from trucks used in interstate trade.

Types of American Law

Besides different sources of law, we also have several types of laws today:

Civil Law—Civil law concerns everyday relations between citizens. Citizens can sue one another for personal injures or for violations of contract in order to obtain compensation for their losses. Civil law also covers family matters, such as divorce, or the inheritance of property when someone dies.

Criminal Law—Criminal law concerns the prosecution and punishment of individuals for crimes. The state has an interest in the enforcement of justice to protect society from criminal behavior. If a person commits a crime, the state puts the person on trial and punishes the person, if convicted, with a fine or imprisonment. Criminal laws thus punish those who have committed crimes and help to deter future crimes.

Constitutional Law—Constitutional law consists of the Constitution itself, including the Bill of Rights, and those federal laws that protect our rights under the Constitution. Laws based on state constitutions are also a form of constitutional law.

Military Law—Military law consists of the special laws and procedures that apply to the armed services. All members of the armed forces are subject to these special laws, found in the *Uniform Code of Military Justice*. These laws help to maintain discipline and security among our troops. For example, soldiers are tried by a special military tribunal, known as a **court-martial**, rather than by a jury. The rules of evidence, standards of proof, and punishments differ from those followed by civilian (*non-military*) courts.

Juvenile Law. Juvenile law consists of the special laws and procedures that apply to minors—those under the age of 18. Because of their younger age, minors are often not subject to the same penalties as adults. They are tried by judges in special juvenile courts.

The different types of laws can sometimes overlap. Suppose that Sandy steals Sarah's car. Sandy is arrested and prosecuted by the State of Florida for theft. This is a violation of the criminal laws of the State of Florida. But Sarah has also lost the use of

Chapter 8 | The Rule of Law

her car for several days when it was stolen. Sandy may have also damaged Sarah's car. Sarah can therefore sue Sandy in state court in a civil suit, seeking money in compensation for her losses (known as monetary "damages"). All of these violations are matters of state law.

Examples Illustrating the Sources and Types of Laws

		Sources of Laws	
Types of Laws	**Common law/Case law**	**Statutory law**	**Constitutional law**
Civil	A past decision by a state court about the conditions in which a driver is responsible for causing accidental injuries to another.	A law passed by Congress on how banks and other lenders must explain their finance charges to consumers.	A provision in the U.S. Bill of Rights stating that a person is entitled to just compensation when the government takes his or her property.
Criminal	A past decision by a state court about when to excuse someone for acting in self-defense.	A law passed by the Florida Legislature about the punishment for robbing a store.	A provision in the U.S. Bill of Rights stating that a person accused of a crime is entitled to the assistance of an attorney.
Military	A past decision by a court martial about when a soldier may lawfully disobey an unreasonable order.	A law passed by Congress about the rights of soldiers on the battlefield.	A provision in the U.S. Constitution stating the President is the Commander in Chief.
Juvenile	A decision by the U.S. Supreme Court about the protections that minors (juveniles) should receive in juvenile courts.	A law passed by the Florida Legislature setting the maximum time that a minor can be kept in a juvenile detention center.	A section of the Florida Constitution stating when a child accused of breaking the law may be charged as a juvenile committing an act of delinquency.
Constitutional	A decision by the U.S. Supreme Court stating that the police must inform suspects of their right to speak to an attorney.	A law passed by Congress to enforce voting rights under the Fifteenth Amendment.	Each of the amendments in the U.S. Bill of Rights.

The Active Citizen

How well can you identify the different sources and types of laws? Check all those that apply to each of the following excerpts from actual laws. Then explain why you made those selections.

Florida Statutes, § 812.014   Theft

(1) A person commits theft if he or she knowingly obtains or uses, or endeavors to obtain or to use, the property of another with intent to, either temporarily or permanently:

(a) Deprive the other person of a right to the property or a benefit from the property.

(b) Appropriate the property to his or her own use or to the use of any person not entitled to the use of the property. . . .

(2)(e) Except as provided in paragraph (d), if the property stolen is valued at $100 or more, but less than $300, the offender commits petit theft of the first degree, punishable as a misdemeanor of the first degree, as provided in §775.082 or §775.083.

Source: ☐ Common law/Case law   ☐ Statutory law   ☐ Constitutional law
Type: ☐ Criminal law   ☐ Civil law   ☐ Military law   ☐ Juvenile law
Level: ☐ Federal law   ☐ State law

Explain your selections. _____

10 U.S. Code, § 838. Article 38. Duties of Trial Counsel and Defense Counsel

(a) The trial counsel of a general or special court-martial shall prosecute in the name of the United States, and shall, under the direction of the court, prepare the record of the proceedings.

(b) (1) The accused has the right to be represented in his defense before a general or special court-martial or at an investigation under section 832 of this title (article 32) as provided in this subsection.

(2) The accused may be represented by civilian counsel if provided by him.

(3) The accused may be represented—(A) by military counsel detailed under section 827 . . . or (B) by military counsel of his own selection if that counsel is reasonably available.

Source: ☐ Common law/Case law   ☐ Statutory law   ☐ Constitutional law
Type: ☐ Criminal law   ☐ Civil law   ☐ Military law   ☐ Juvenile law
Level: ☐ Federal law   ☐ State law

Explain your selections. _____

Florida Statutes, § 768.81 Comparative fault. (c) "Negligence action" means, without limitation, a civil action for damages based upon a theory of negligence, strict liability, products liability, professional malpractice whether couched in terms of contract or tort, or breach of warranty and like theories. The substance of an action, not conclusory terms used by a party, determines whether an action is a negligence action. . . .

(2) Effect of Contributory Fault.—In a negligence action, contributory fault chargeable to the claimant diminishes proportionately the amount awarded as economic and noneconomic damages for an injury attributable to the claimant's contributory fault, but does not bar recovery.

Source: ☐ Common law/Case law   ☐ Statutory law   ☐ Constitutional law
Type: ☐ Criminal law   ☐ Civil law   ☐ Military law   ☐ Juvenile law
Level: ☐ Federal law   ☐ State law

Explain your selections. _____

How Our Laws Are Interpreted and Applied: the Job of Courts

Just as there are different sources of law, there are different places where these laws are applied:

- State laws are generally applied by state courts.
- Federal laws are generally applied by federal courts.
- Military laws are applied by military tribunals (courts-martial).

So, what happens when a case is tried in court?

You've seen plenty of courtroom dramas on television, but have you ever stopped to think about what a court really is? A **court** is a public place where disputes are resolved according to law. Every court has both a courtroom and a judge. In many cases, the judge alone makes the decision. In other cases, a jury decides the case. A **jury** is a panel of impartial, neutral citizens, chosen at random from the locality where the trial takes place. In cases submitted to a jury, the judge oversees the trial and instructs the jury to make sure the trial is reasonable and fair.

A court has special powers. It can issue **court orders**, which must be obeyed. These orders have the force of law. For example, court can compel parties to produce documents and can compel witnesses to appear. It can order individuals to behave in the courtroom and can even fine or imprison those who disobey for "contempt of court." When a verdict is reached, the court issues a judgment that must be enforced.

The Organization of Florida's State Courts

The organization of the judicial branch in most states is similar in many ways to that of the federal government. Florida's state courts were reorganized in 1972. The number of types of state courts was then reduced from ten to four:

> "The judicial power shall be vested in a supreme court, district courts of appeal, circuit courts and county courts. No other courts may be established by the state, any political subdivision or any municipality"
>
> —Florida State Constitution, Article V, Section 1 (as amended)

Florida's State Court System

- The **county courts** are at the bottom level of Florida's court system. The county courts handle lesser crimes (known as "misdemeanors"), small claims and civil cases involving less than $15,000. A misdemeanor is any crime punishable by no more than one year in prison.

- At the next level, Florida is divided among 20 **circuit courts**. These courts handle more serious crimes (known as "felonies"), civil cases for more than $15,000, and family law matters. A felony is any crime punishable by more than one year in prison. These courts also review appeals from the county courts. Florida's circuit courts thus serve as both trial and appellate courts.

- Just above Florida's circuit courts are the state's five **District Courts of Appeal**. These are appellate courts. They review appeals from cases decided by the circuit courts. They do not try cases.

- Lastly, at the very top of Florida's court system is the **Florida Supreme Court**. It is the highest authority on Florida law: its decisions are binding on all other Florida courts (and on federal courts applying Florida laws). The Florida Supreme Court consists of seven Justices. The Justices are initially appointed by the Governor, based on the recommendations of a separate judicial qualifications commission. Justices can then remain in office after being elected for six-year terms. Each appellate district has at least one Justice.

The Florida Supreme Court reviews cases from the District Courts of Appeal. In a few special situations, the Florida Supreme Court can also review a case directly from one of the state's circuit courts. Like the U.S. Supreme Court, it does not need to accept for review all the cases that are appealed to it. However, it must review all death penalty cases.

The Florida Supreme Court is generally an appellate court but has original jurisdiction in a limited number of cases. Like the U.S. Supreme Court, it has the power of judicial review. Unlike the U.S. Supreme Court, the Florida Supreme Court can issue **advisory opinions** to the Governor or Attorney General. These are the opinions of the court on whether a law or proposed law is constitutional.

The Chief Justice of the Florida Supreme Court is chosen by a majority of the Florida Supreme Court Justices and oversees Florida's entire state court system.

As you can see, Florida state courts differ from the federal system in several important respects:

▶ The federal court system has three levels of courts, while Florida has four levels of courts.

▶ The Florida Supreme Court can give advisory opinions when asked by the Governor; the U.S. Supreme Court can never give advisory opinions.

▶ U.S. Supreme Court Justices and all federal judges are appointed for life; Florida judges may initially be appointed but then must be elected to retain their office.

▶ The Chief Justice of the U.S. Supreme Court is nominated by the President of the United States; the Chief Justice of the Florida Supreme Court is chosen by the Justices themselves.

▶ In the federal system, "circuit courts" (U.S. Courts of Appeals) are above "district courts" (U.S. District Courts); in Florida, the opposite is true: "district courts" (Florida District Courts of Appeal) are above "circuit courts" (Florida Circuit Courts).

▶ Florida's trial courts are **courts of general jurisdiction**: they can try all kinds of cases. Even at the bottom level of the federal court system, the U.S. District Courts are more limited: they can only try cases on issues of federal law or between parties from different states.

The Active Citizen

Complete the diagram below.

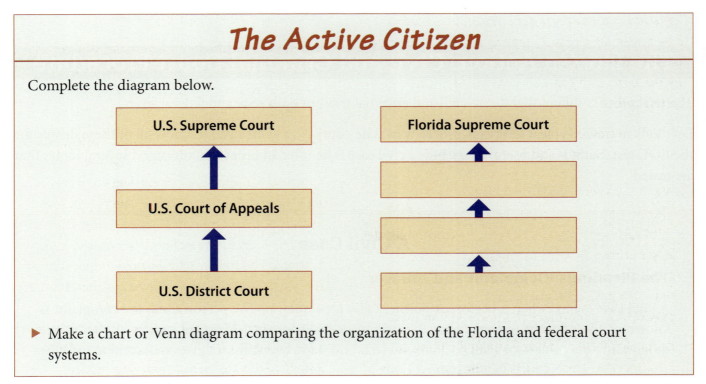

▶ Make a chart or Venn diagram comparing the organization of the Florida and federal court systems.

Chapter 8 | The Rule of Law

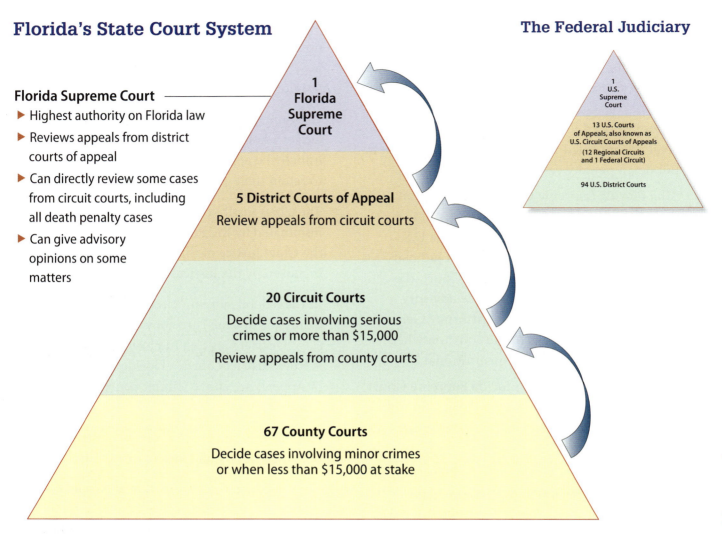

The Law in Action: Civil and Criminal Court Procedure

The **trial process** differs slightly for civil and criminal trials in both state and federal court.

Let's look at how a typical **civil case** proceeds in state court. You won't need to know all of these details for the EOC test, but it is still useful to see how a civil case is handled in order to understand several topics that are tested.

A Civil Case

The Pleadings: Complaint and Answer

A civil case begins when a person or business files a **complaint**. The person filing the complaint is known as the **plaintiff** (*complainer*). The person or business sued in a civil case is known as the **defendant**. The complaint gives background facts and states the plaintiff's grievances and request for

Chapter 8 | The Rule of Law

relief. The defendant must file an **answer** with the court admitting or denying the claims made in the complaint.

Pretrial Discovery

Next comes a period of pretrial "**discovery**." Each side must turn over all relevant documents to the other side. Each side also has a chance to demand written responses to questions they ask.

Meanwhile, the attorneys conduct their own investigations. For example, they may look at police and hospital reports. They also interview witnesses.

Each party can also take **depositions**. This is a formal interview of a witness with a court reporter and all attorneys present. The court reporter types up the deposition. Evidence from depositions can be used later at the trial.

Pretrial Motions

> Be sure to know what a summary judgment is for the EOC test.

A "motion" is a document requesting the court to do something. Before the trial, either party can file a "**motion for summary judgment**" if the evidence in its favor is so overwhelming that the other side cannot reasonably win. The motion for summary judgment could be on particular points, or on the whole case. The trial judge will grant the motion only if the evidence is so strong that any other outcome at trial would be unreasonable. Once a motion for summary judgment is granted, a trial on that point—or sometimes, on the whole case—becomes unnecessary. The court decides the issue without a trial because the evidence is so overwhelming.

The trial court will also encourage the parties to "settle" the case (*come to an agreement*) without the expense of a trial. Usually, the parties must have a settlement conference.

> Be sure to know the role of the jury in the trial process for the EOC test.

Jury Selection

Before the trial can begin, the court must select a **jury**. A number of local citizens eligible for jury duty are chosen by the court at random. The citizens on this list must come to the courthouse. The lawyers then have an opportunity to strike off any jurors whom they think might be **biased** (*favor one side over the other*).

Continued ▶

Chapter 8 | The Rule of Law

The Trial

At the trial, each side presents its case. First, each lawyer will make an **opening statement**. The opening statement explains what the lawyer thinks the evidence will show.

Then the attorneys present their witnesses. Each side asks questions to its own witnesses (known as examination). It also asks questions to the opposing witnesses (known as **cross-examination**).

The attorneys also introduce documents and photographs, which must be identified by witnesses to show they are authentic. The lawyers may bring in qualified **expert witnesses**, such as doctors or professors, who give their opinions on what the evidence shows.

All of these proceedings must follow strict rules of evidence. A witness can say what he has personally seen, for example, but cannot tell the jury what he thinks his neighbor might have been thinking.

At the end of the trial, the attorneys present their **closing statements**.

Jury Instructions and the Role of the Jury

After the lawyers have finished, the trial judge instructs the jury on what they must decide. This advice is known as **jury instructions**.

> Here is more important information about the role of the jury.

The main role of the jury is to act as a "**fact-finder**." They must decide if the claims made in the complaint are true, whether they were a violation of the law, if the plaintiff is entitled to any compensation, and if so, how much money should be awarded.

Jury Deliberations and Verdict

The jury next goes into the jury room, where they discuss the case privately among themselves. Eventually, they reach a **verdict** (*decision or judgment in a court case*).

> Be sure to know the difference between a trial court and appellate court for the EOC test.

Appeal

In any lawsuit, the losing party can **appeal** the judgment to an **appellate court**. As you know from the last chapter, an appellate court reviews the decisions of trial courts. The appellate court does not retry the case on the basis of the facts. It does not take away the important job of the jury as "fact-finder." The only job of an appellate court is to **review how the law was applied to the facts of the case.** If the trial court made an error in its conduct of the trial or in its application of the law, the appellate court can send the case back with instructions for a retrial, or it can even reverse the decision.

How can a trial court make a mistake in its application of the law? It might, for example, have allowed the jury to hear evidence at the trial that should not have been admitted. This evidence might have unfairly prejudiced the jury. Or, the trial judge might have interpreted the law incorrectly in the court's instructions to the jurors.

Chapter 8 | The Rule of Law

The Active Citizen

▶ Have your class simulate a civil trial. One student should act as the judge, two students should act as attorneys, one student should act as the plaintiff, one student should act as the defendant, one student should act as the court bailiff, six students should act as jurors, and several other students should act as witnesses. Use the imaginary complaint below as the basis for your class's mock trial.

▶ Be sure to include all of the steps listed above for the trial: opening statements, submission of documents, examination and cross-examination of witnesses, closing statements, jury instructions from the judge, jury deliberations, and a final verdict.

▶ Make a chart or Venn diagram comparing the processes in a trial and appellate court.

▶ Interview a friend, relative or neighbor who has been involved in a civil case.

The Beginning of a Lawsuit in Civil Law

```
Smith and Smith
Attorneys at Law

         NINTH CIRCUIT COURT FOR THE STATE OF FLORIDA

Leo Montague            ) Case No.: 303
                        )
           Plaintiff,   ) Complaint for Personal Injury
                        )
vs.                     )
                        )
Mary Capulet,           )
                        )
           Defendant    )
                        )

NOW COMES LEO MONTAGUE, hereinafter Plaintiff, by and through his attorneys,
John Smith and Joan Smith, and complaining of MARY CAPULET, hereinafter
called Defendant, respectfully states as follows:
                              I
1. Plaintiff Leo Montague is an individual, and resident at 212 Sunshine
Drive, Sarasota, Florida
2. Defendant Mary Capulet is an individual, and resident, who may be served
at 3200 Orange Drive, Apartment 5B, Orlando, Florida.
                              II
1. That on April 8, 2018, at approximately 3:15 p.m., Defendant was driving
southbound on Bullfrog Creek Road.
2. Plaintiff was a pedestrian who stepped into Bullfrog Creek Road at
approximately 3:15 p.m. in order to cross to the other side of the road.
3. Defendant was talking on her cell phone prior to the accident.
4. Defendant continued driving and hit Plaintiff with her car.
5. Plaintiff could see that, immediately prior to the accident, Defendant was
talking on her cell phone.

                    Complaint for Personal Injury - 1
```

```
                              III
6. The Defendant breached the duty of care owed to Plaintiff by failing to
use reasonable care while driving her automobile, by talking on a cell phone
while driving and by failing to pay attention to the road.
6. Immediately after the accident, Plaintiff was rushed to General Hospital.
7. As a result of Defendant's negligence, Plaintiff suffered personal
injuries in the form of whiplash, cuts, scratches and bruises, and damage to
his left leg.
8. Plaintiff was examined by Dr. William Jersey of General Hospital, who
concluded that Defendant's left leg was badly damaged in the accident.
5. Despite physical therapy, Plaintiff has been unable to run again because
of injuries sustained in his left leg, and will, in reasonable probability,
incur a loss of earning capacity in future.
6. Defendant also experienced physical pain and suffering and mental anguish
because of Defendant's negligence.
By reason of the foregoing, Plaintiff has been damaged by an amount of one
million dollars ($1,000,000).
WHEREFORE, Plaintiff prays a Judgment be entered against Defendant for
recovery of damages as set forth above.

                         Dated this 21 of July, 2018
                         John Smith
                         John and Joan Smith
                         Attorneys for Plaintiff

                    Complaint for Personal Injury - 2
```

Chapter 8 | The Rule of Law

A Criminal Case

Criminal cases follow somewhat different procedures from civil ones. In a criminal case, the state itself is a party to the proceeding. It acts in the interest of protecting society. In serious offenses, the defendant risks the loss of liberty through imprisonment.

Again, you won't need to know all of the following details for the EOC in Civics. However, knowing something about how a criminal case is handled will be useful, especially for understanding the Bill of Rights. Many of the rights in the Bill of Rights protect those accused of committing a crime.

Criminal Investigation

When a crime is first reported to the police, the police conduct an investigation. They may obtain a **search warrant** from a judge to search places they have good reason to believe may provide important evidence. They will interview witnesses and possible suspects.

The Arrest

As a result of their investigation, the police may arrest a suspect if they have "**probable cause**" to believe this person committed the crime. The police cannot obtain a confession without first informing the suspect of his or her rights. Among these are the right to remain silent and the right to have an attorney present during questioning.

An informal hearing is held to decide whether there is "**probable cause**" to keep the suspect in custody. A person being charged with murder must be indicted by a **grand jury**—a group of 15 to 21 citizens.

Arraignment

If there are sufficient grounds to hold the suspect, the suspect is **arraigned**, or charged, in open court. The suspect is asked to plead "guilty" or "not guilty" to the charges. Then the court sets **bail**. This is an amount to be paid by the defendant to ensure that he or she will appear at trial. If bail is paid, the defendant is released until trial. If no bail is set or paid, the defendant must remain in jail until trial.

Plea-Bargaining

The defendant may enter into negotiations with the district attorney before trial. This process is known as **plea-bargaining**. The defendant may admit to a lesser crime if the charges against the defendant are dropped. If no plea bargain is made, the case goes to trial.

The Trial

In Florida, if a defendant could go to prison for six months or more, the defendant has the right to a **jury trial**. In criminal cases, the state (or the "People") is always against the defendant.

As in civil cases, both sides—the state and the defendant—have the right to strike off (*eliminate*) potential jurors during jury selection.

Once the case goes to trial, an attorney from the district attorney's office—the **prosecutor**—presents the state's case against the accused. Very special rules control the admission of evidence in a criminal trial. The district attorney's office is required to hand over to the defendant all the relevant evidence that the police have gathered. The police cannot use any evidence at trial that has been tampered with or obtained by them unlawfully.

The defendant has the right to face and question all witnesses. If the defendant cannot afford an attorney and has been accused of a serious crime, the court is required to appoint an attorney for the defendant, known as the "public defender."

In a criminal case, the "**burden of proof**" is on the prosecution. It is presumed that the defendant is innocent until proven guilty. If it cannot be shown beyond a reasonable doubt that the accused committed the crime, then the jury should find the defendant not guilty.

After the evidence is presented and the attorneys make their closing statements, the judge will give instructions to the jury. The jury then deliberates in private to reach a **verdict**. The jury could decide to **convict** the defendant on all charges, it could find the defendant guilty of lesser crimes, or it could decide that the defendant is not guilty at all.

Sentencing

If the jury finds the defendant guilty, then the judge decides what the punishment should be. This process is known as **sentencing**. No cruel or unusual punishments are permitted. The amount of punishment should be in proportion to the severity of the crime. In sentencing, a judge must take into account many factors, including the severity of the crime, whether the defendant has previously been convicted of a crime, and whether the defendant shows any **remorse** (*sorrow for having committed the crime*).

Appeal

As with civil cases, the defendant has the right to appeal the verdict or sentence to an appellate court.

Mary Smith was walking home when she saw a wallet on the street. She picked it up and continued on her way. In fact, Hector Garcia had slipped on the wet pavement and was lying on the ground around the corner. He saw Mary leave with his wallet and called the police with his cellphone to say it was stolen. Officer Sheila Swift read the message from the local police department and saw and arrested Mary. Mary said she was going to call the owner of the wallet once she reached home. Mary had a prior conviction for theft so the local district attorney decided to charge her.

Your class should simulate her questioning, arrest, arraignment and trial. Your teacher should select students to act as Mary, Mr. Garcia, Officer Swift, the judge, attorneys, witnesses and jurors.

The Active Citizen

▶ Create two separate flow charts showing civil and criminal procedures. The first chart should show the main steps of a civil case from pretrial to final judgment: occurrence of an injury or dispute, the filing of a complaint, an answer from the defendant, pretrial discovery, motions for summary judgment, settlement conference, the trial (opening statements, examination and cross-examination of witnesses, closing statements), jury instructions, jury deliberation, verdict, and appeal. The second chart should show the main steps of a criminal case: the occurrence of a crime, a criminal investigation, an arrest, arraignment, plea-bargaining, the trial, jury deliberations, the verdict, sentencing, and appeal. Describe each step on your flow charts.

▶ In your opinion, is the use of different procedures for civil and criminal cases justified? Explain your answer.

▶ Imagine you have been unfairly accused of a crime. Write a letter to a friend describing your ordeal.

Complete the chart below by describing the six principles of the rule of law.

The Rule of Law

Principle	Description
Accountability to the law 	
Fair and impartial procedures 	
Decisions based on the law 	
Consistent application of the law to all parties 	
Enforcement of the law 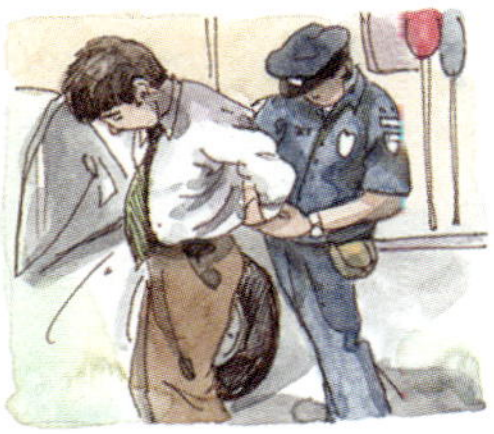	
Transparency of Institutions 	

Chapter 8 | The Rule of Law

Name _____

Complete the chart by describing the different sources and types of law:

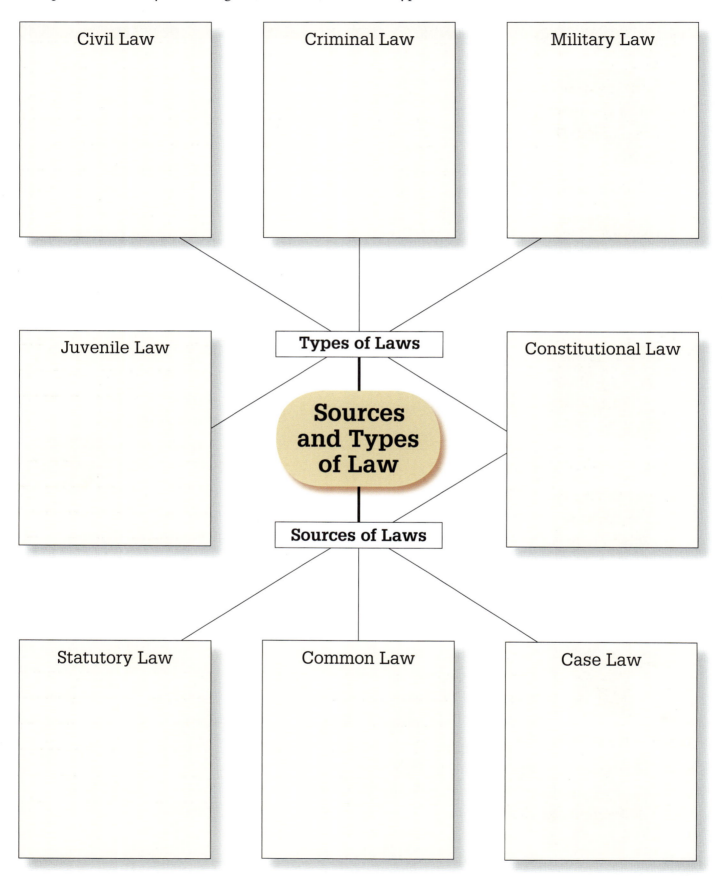

Name _____

Make a question relating to each of the following clusters of terms and phrases:

| Accountability to the law |
| Fair procedures |
| Decisions based on the law |
| Consistent application |
| Enforcement of the law |
| Transparency |

| "Due process" rights |
| Right to a hearing |
| Right to legal counsel |
| Right to see the evidence |
| Right to face accusers |
| Right to a decision based on the law |

| Historic law codes |
| Code of Hammurabi |
| Twelve Tables |
| Code of Justinian |

| Statutory law |
| Common law |
| Case law |
| Constitutional law |

Chapter 8 | The Rule of Law

Name _____

Make a question relating to each of the following clusters of terms and phrases:

| Civil law |
| Criminal law |
| Constitutional law |
| Military law |
| Juvenile law |

_____
_____
_____
_____
_____
_____
_____

| Florida Supreme Court |
| Florida District Courts of Appeal |
| Florida circuit courts |
| Florida county courts |

_____
_____
_____
_____
_____
_____

| Civil case |
| Trial court |
| Summary judgment |
| Jury |
| Judge |
| Appeal |

_____
_____
_____
_____
_____
_____
_____

Now exchange your questions with a partner in your class. Each of you should answer the other's questions.

Name _____

Define each of the following:

Rule of law _____
_____
_____

"Due Process" rights _____
_____
_____

Statutory law _____
_____
_____

Common law _____
_____
_____

Civil law _____
_____
_____

Florida Supreme Court _____
_____
_____

Florida District Courts of Appeal _____
_____
_____

Florida Circuit Courts _____
_____
_____

Jury _____
_____
_____

Chapter 8 | The Rule of Law

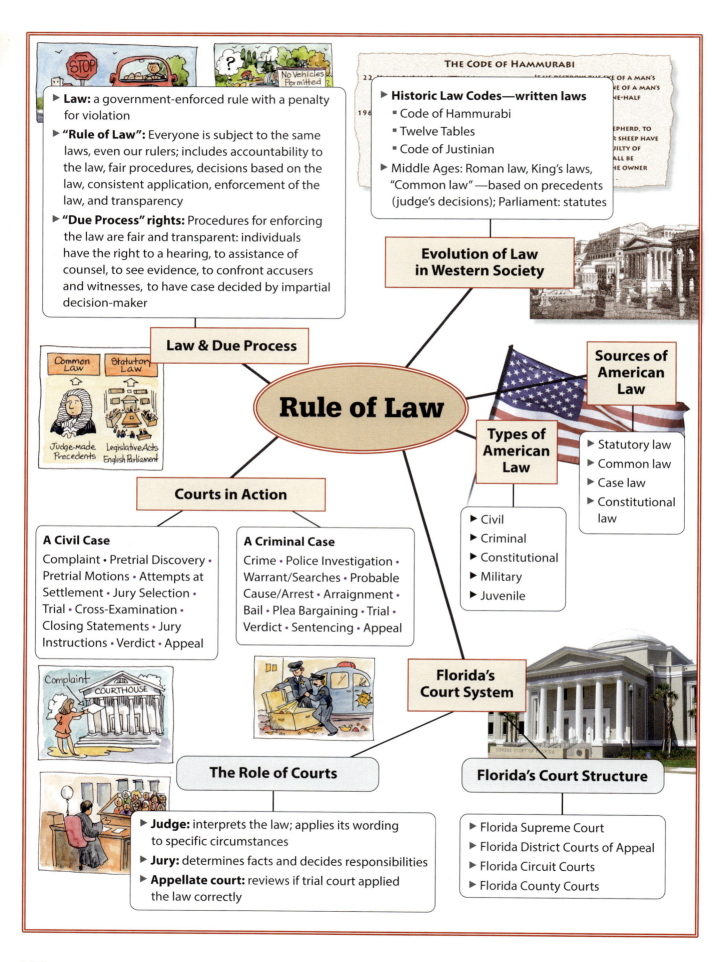

Review Cards: The Rule of Law

What is Law?

- A **law** is a rule that is enforced by government and that has a penalty for breaking it.
- Laws help the members of a community organize and protect themselves, settle disputes and punish those who commit crimes.
- Laws may seem clear but often need to be interpreted to see how they apply to specific situations.

The Rule of Law

- In some societies, the ruler's will is law. Ordinary subjects have little control over their lives. They are always subject to their ruler's desires.
- Americans live under the **rule of law**. This means we live under a system of written laws. These laws make it clear how we should behave and how we can expect others to behave.
- It also means that our government leaders cannot just do anything they please. They are subject to the rule of law like everyone else. No one is above the law.

Six Principles of the Rule of Law

- **Accountability to the law:** Our conduct is subject to written laws that everyone knows and that everyone is subject to.
- **Fair procedures:** The procedures used to decide whether an accused person has violated the law, or to settle a dispute between two or more parties, must be fair and impartial. For example, an accused person has the right to see the evidence, hear witnesses and receive the help of an attorney. Fair procedures are known as our **"due process" rights**.
- **Decisions based on the law:** When a court reaches a decision, such as to punish someone accused of a crime, the decision must be based on the law.
- **Consistent application of the law:** The law should be applied to everyone in the same way. If two people commit the same crime, they should receive the same punishment.
- **Enforcement of the law:** Our government must enforce those laws we decide on. That means it carries them out. Enforcement of the law protects ordinary citizens from violence and crime.
- **Transparency (*openness*) of institutions:** Proceedings should be open and in public. This is known as transparency because it means everyone can see what is going on. It is important that our procedures, such as trials, are public and transparent so that we can see that decisions are based on a fair and consistent application of the law.

How Laws are Consistently Applied in the United States: the Work of Courts

- Laws are enforced in **courts**. Decisions of courts are recorded and serve as **precedents** for later cases.
- Sometimes court decisions are made by judges, and sometimes by a **jury**, a panel of impartial local citizens who decide on the facts of the case.

Chapter 8 | The Rule of Law

Examples of Historical Law Codes: How Laws Developed in Western Society

- **Hammurabi** of Babylonia established one of the earliest known written law codes, more than 3,700 years ago. One of its basic principles was that punishments should equal crimes—"an eye for an eye." Having written laws that all could see was an important step in developing the rule of law. It meant that people knew what the laws permitted them to do and what they prohibited.
- Early Roman laws were displayed publicly on **Twelve Tables**, so everyone could see them. Because the Roman Empire grew so vast with so many different peoples, it was important to have a set of standardized, public laws. Roman law established rules that still influence modern law, such as the enforcement of **contracts**, investigation and prosecution procedures, rules for resolving commercial disputes, and the requirement of evidence in court cases.
- The Middle Ages had many sources of law. Laws came from old Roman codes, popular traditions, and kings. Laws passed by a legislature like Parliament were called **statutes.** Medieval England established the **common law**: laws based on customs and **precedents** (*earlier decisions made in courts*) found throughout the kingdom.

Sources of American Law

Americans today have several sources for their laws:
- **Constitutional law:** These are laws found directly in the U.S. Constitution or state constitutions. They are the highest form of law.
- **Statutory law:** These are laws, known as **statutes**, passed by legislatures, such as by Congress or the Florida Legislature.
- **Common law:** These are laws based on customs and judicial precedents (the decisions of courts looking at similar cases).
- **Case law:** These are laws based on court decisions in prior cases.

Types of Laws

There are several different types of American laws:
- **Civil law:** concerns disputes between private parties. For example, two passengers may claim they were injured by another driver's carelessness, or one business may sue another for breaking a contract.
- **Criminal law:** concerns crimes. The government charges the accused of committing a crime.
- **Constitutional law:** concerns the U.S. Constitution (including the Bill of Rights) or a state constitution.
- **Military law:** concerns the armed forces. Stricter rules apply in military courts. "Martial law" is enforced by a "court martial."
- **Juvenile law:** concerns minors (those under 18 years of age). Juvenile courts take into account the younger age of minors accused of committing crimes.

How a Case Proceeds in Criminal Court

- Police respond to a crime report with an investigation, sometimes with a **search warrant**.
- If a suspect is detained, an informal hearing decides if there was **probable cause** of a crime.
- If there is probable cause, the suspect is **arraigned** (*charges are read*).
- **Bail** is set: if paid, the person is released until trial. If not, he or she stays in jail awaiting trial.
- After a period of **plea bargaining**, when charges may be reduced for a plea of guilty, the case goes to trial. If a potential prison sentence is six months or more, a jury is assigned.
- During the trial, the police present their evidence. Lawyers for each side question witnesses. The "**burden of proof**" that the crime was committed is on the district attorney.
- The jury deliberates and reaches a verdict on the defendant's guilt.
- If guilty, the judge imposes a **sentence**. A defendant can choose to appeal.

How a Case Proceeds in Civil Court

Pretrial:
- In a civil case, a **complaint** is first filed by one side against another.
- In the **discovery** period, both sides must produce evidence.
- A lawyer can file a **motion for summary judgment** if there is overwhelming evidence for one side. This may end the trial or take care of some of the disputed issues.
- The court will also encourage both sides to "**settle**" outside of court.

The Trial:
- If a trial occurs, a **jury** is then chosen.
- During the trial, each side makes its case. Lawyers present evidence from witnesses, documents and photographs. Witnesses are questioned by both lawyers (**examined** and **cross-examined**). After all the evidence is presented, lawyers make closing statements.
- The judge then gives the jury their **jury instructions** on what they must decide. The judge tells the jury what law to apply to the case. The role of the jury is to decide on facts based on the evidence.

Appeals:
- If one side is not satisfied with the decision, it can **appeal** to an **appellate court**.
- The appellate court reviews the decision and decides if the trial court applied the law correctly or if there should be a retrial.

The Organization of Florida's Courts

- **Florida county courts:** Hear civil cases for less than $15,000, or lesser crimes (misdemeanors). A **misdemeanor** is any crime that is punishable by no more than one year in prison.
- **Florida circuit courts:** Hear civil cases when more than $15,000 is at stake, and more serious crimes (felonies). A **felony** is any crime that is punishable by more than one year in prison. These courts also review cases from the county courts.
- **Florida District Courts of Appeal:** Appellate courts that review cases from the circuit courts.
- **Florida Supreme Court:** The highest court in the state; hears appeals from the lower state courts, including all death penalty cases; can also issue some advisory opinions (advising the Governor or Attorney General if certain laws are constitutional).

What Do You Know?

SS.7.C.3.10

1. Connie Hargrave's tree fell in the last storm and damaged the car of her neighbor, Andy Collin. Connie did not have insurance that covered this type of accident and has not paid Andy for the damage. Andy decides to sue Connie in court. Which type of lawsuit will this be?

   A. civil
   B. military
   C. criminal
   D. constitutional

SS.7.C.1.9

2. Which actions reflect a fundamental principle of the rule of law?

   A. Decisions by the government are based on the law.
   B. Government leaders can change the law without notice.
   C. People accused of crimes against the state are tried in secret.
   D. Different social classes enjoy different legal rights and privileges.

SS.7.C.3.10

3. Why were historical law codes like Hammurabi's Code, the Twelve Tables and the Code of Justinian significant?

   A. They established official religions.
   B. They established new economic systems.
   C. They established democratic governments.
   D. They established written laws for the entire community.

SS.7.C.3.8

4. Jack sues Jill in Florida Circuit Court for a personal injury. Jack claims Jill hit him while she was driving carelessly and texting on her cell phone. Jill denies his claim. On what grounds could the judge grant Jack's request for summary judgment on this claim?

   A. The judge doesn't think that Jill's witnesses are very believable.
   B. The jury has indicated that it prefers Jack's version of the accident.
   C. Many experts believe that texting while driving is likely to cause accidents.
   D. The evidence in Jack's favor is so overwhelming that it would be unreasonable to think otherwise.

SS.7.C.3.11

5. Which statement correctly compares judges at the state and federal levels?
   A. Florida judges must retire after ten years on the bench because of strict term limits.
   B. Individuals must first serve as state judges before they can be appointed as federal judges.
   C. Florida judges are often more politically active since they are elected, while federal judges are appointed for life.
   D. Neither federal nor Florida judges can lawfully serve in any other political office once they leave service in the judicial branch.

SS.7.C.3.10

6. The diagram below shows details about the law.

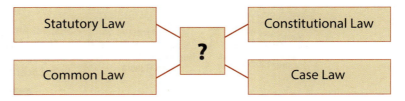

Which phrase completes the diagram?
A. Historical Law Codes
B. Sources of American Law
C. The Separation of Powers
D. The Enforcement of Contractual Agreements

SS.7.C.3.11

7. Jack lives in Miami. He has a contract dispute with a hotel owner in Tampa for less than $15,000. In which court should Jack seek help?
   A. U.S. District Court
   B. Florida Circuit Court
   C. Florida County Court
   D. Florida District Court of Appeal

SS.7.C.3.11

8. The diagram below shows steps in a civil case in Florida.

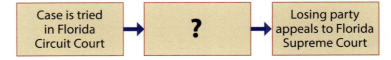

Which statement completes the diagram?
A. Losing party appeals to U.S. District Court
B. Losing party appeals to Florida County Court
C. Losing party appeals to U.S. Circuit Court of Appeals
D. Losing party appeals to Florida District Court of Appeals

Chapter 8 | The Rule of Law

SS.7.C.1.9

9. The drawing on the left shows Abraham Lincoln as a young lawyer, presenting his client's case to a judge.

   Which conclusion can best be drawn from this drawing?
   A. Americans live under the rule of law.
   B. Judges make better fact-finders than do jurors.
   C. More court cases involve state law than federal law.
   D. Civil cases are more difficult to defend than criminal ones.

SS.7.C.3.10

10. The four headlines below deal with incidents involving laws.

1.   2.   3.   4.

Which correctly identifies the type of law involved in each headline?

A. 1. civil law   2. state law   3. military law   4. federal law
B. 1. civil law   2. federal law   3. state law   4. military law
C. 1. state law   2. civil law   3. criminal law   4. federal law
D. 1. federal law   2. state law   3. military law   4. civil law

SS.7.C.1.9

11. Which characteristic does the U.S. Constitution have in common with historic law codes like the Twelve Tables of ancient Rome?
    A. It establishes harsh punishments for crimes.
    B. It protects ordinary citizens with the rule of law.
    C. It describes detailed procedures for court proceedings.
    D. It is more concerned with property rights than with individual freedom.

SS.7.C.1.9

12. Which consequence is an important benefit of the rule of law?
    A. Bureaucratic government procedures are reduced.
    B. Government decisions are based on the will of the majority.
    C. Government officials can act on their own instincts in emergencies.
    D. Citizens are protected from arbitrary and oppressive uses of government power.

CHAPTER 9

The Bill of Rights and Later Amendments

SS.7.C.2.4 Evaluate rights contained in the Bill of Rights and other amendments to the Constitution.

SS.7.C.2.5 Distinguish how the Constitution safeguards and limits individual rights. (See also Chapters 8 and 12).

SS.7.C.3.5 Explain the constitutional amendment process.

SS.7.C.3.6 Evaluate constitutional rights and their impact on individuals and society. (See also Chapter 12.)

SS.7.C.3.7 Analyze the impact of the 13th, 14th, 15th, 19th, 24th, and 26th amendments on participation of minority groups in the American political process.

Names and Terms You Should Know

Amendment	Double jeopardy	14th Amendment
Ratification	"Pleading the Fifth"	Equal protection under the law
States' rights	Due process of law	
Bill of Rights	Eminent domain	15th, 19th, 24th and 26th Amendments
Freedom of religion	Property rights	Political process
Free speech	Trial by jury	Poll taxes
Freedom of the press	Right to legal counsel	Suffrage
Freedom of assembly	Cruel and unusual punishments	Civil disobedience
Freedom to petition	Forced internment	Equal Rights Amendment
Right to bear arms	Unenumerated rights	Civil Rights Act of 1964
To quarter soldiers	Reserved powers	Voting Rights Act of 1965
Search and seizure	13th Amendment	Civil Rights Act of 1968
Privacy		

Florida "Keys" to Learning

1. Amending the Constitution is more difficult than passing an ordinary law. It is a two-step process. First, an amendment must be proposed. This has always been done by a vote of two-thirds of each house of Congress. Then the proposed amendment has to be ratified by three-fourths of the state legislatures. (An amendment can also be approved by special state ratifying conventions, but this has also never been done.)

2. The first ten amendments to the Constitution are known as the "Bill of Rights." They were passed to meet the demands of Anti-Federalists during the debate over ratification of the Constitution.

3. The First Amendment establishes five freedoms: freedom of religion, speech, the press, assembly and to petition. Congress cannot establish a state religion, cannot prohibit (*forbid*) the free exercise of religion, cannot limit freedom of speech, cannot limit freedom of press, cannot stop people from holding assemblies, and cannot prevent people from petitioning the government.

4. The Second Amendment establishes the right to bear arms (*guns and other weapons*).

5. The Third Amendment prohibits the sending of soldiers to live in homes without the consent (*agreement*) of the owners in peacetime. This practice is known as quartering.

6. The Fourth Amendment protects us from unreasonable searches and seizures. A search occurs when police enter a house or look through something like a purse or car. A seizure occurs when the police seize our belongings or arrest us. In general, a warrant must be issued by a judge in advance, based on "probable cause" (reasonable grounds for suspicion).

7. The Fifth Amendment states that a serious criminal case may not go to trial unless a grand jury has determined there is sufficient evidence; no person can be tried twice for the same crime ("double jeopardy"); no person can be deprived of life, liberty, or property without "due process" (a process that is fair, just and reasonable); and government can take private property for public purposes ("eminent domain") but must provide fair compensation.

8. The Sixth Amendment gives those accused of a crime the right to a speedy and public trial by an impartial jury as well as the right to be informed of the charges, to face accusers and witnesses, to compel witnesses to appear in court to testify, and to the help of an attorney.

9. The Seventh Amendment provides the right to a jury trial in many civil cases.

10. The Eighth Amendment forbids excessive bail, excessive fines, and cruel and unusual punishments.

11. The Ninth Amendment states that the enumeration of specific rights in the Constitution does not mean that there are not also other rights. These are known as unenumerated rights.

12. The Tenth Amendment provides that any rights not granted (*given*) to the federal government are reserved for the states or the people.

13. The balance between protecting individual rights and giving government enough power to govern effectively is found in the separation of powers and the system of checks and balances. Our rights are also limited by the rights of others.

14. Several amendments to the Constitution have extended the rights of minorities and women, giving them the ability to participate fully in the political process.

15. The Thirteenth Amendment abolished slavery.

16. The Fourteenth Amendment defined U.S. citizenship. It also required that states provide "due process of law" and the "equal protection of the laws" to all citizens.

17. The Fifteenth Amendment prohibited federal and state governments from denying the right to vote on the basis of race. The Nineteenth Amendment gave women the right to vote. The Twenty-fourth Amendment prohibited any requirement to pay poll taxes to vote in federal elections. The Twenty-sixth Amendment lowered the voting age to 18 years of age.

18. Civil rights acts passed by Congress guarantee minorities equality under the law and the right to participate in the political process.

In this chapter, you will learn how the U.S. Constitution can be changed through the process of amendment, and how amendments have increased the protection of our individual rights and expanded our democracy.

Amending the Constitution

The authors of the Constitution knew that they could not anticipate all future circumstances. Times and society change. If the Constitution were to succeed, it would have to be able to adapt to new realities and circumstances.

The authors therefore provided procedures for the Constitution to be **amended** (*added to or changed*). However, this was made more difficult than passing an ordinary law. Article V established a two-step process for amendments. The first step was to introduce an amendment proposal. The second step was to **ratify** (*approve*) it.

Step 1. Proposing the Amendment

This can be accomplished in either of two ways:

1. **By a two-thirds vote of both houses of Congress.** All amendments of the Constitution so far have used this method.

or

2. There is a second way of introducing a proposal. On the request of two-thirds of the state legislatures, Congress can call for a national convention to amend the Constitution.

Step 2. Ratifying the Amendment

There are also two ways to ratify a proposed amendment:

1. **Ratification by three-fourths of the state legislatures.**

or

2. Ratification by special ratification conventions in three-fourths of the states.

For each proposed amendment, Congress will select one of these methods for ratification—so far, only the first has been used. The amendment process has been used successfully just 27 times since 1791.

Ways of Amending the Constitution

Proposes the Amendment

2/3 of each House of Congress proposes the amendment

or

2/3 of State Legislatures request a National Convention, which proposes amendments

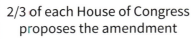

Ratifies (*approves*) the Amendment

3/4 of the State Legislatures

or

3/4 of special State Conventions ratify the amendment

The Active Citizen

Did the authors of the U.S. Constitution make it too hard to amend? Hold the following debate in your classroom: "Resolved: That the process of amending the Constitution should be the same as the process for passing an ordinary law."

Chapter 9 | The Bill of Rights and Later Amendments

The Bill of Rights: Our First Ten Amendments

In the debate over ratification of the Constitution, Anti-Federalists loudly raised the criticism that the Constitution needed a bill of rights to protect the American people from a central government that might abuse its power. On June 8, 1789, James Madison, one of the leading Federalists, introduced 22 amendments in Congress. After some deletions and with many changes, these became the first ten amendments to the Constitution, known as the **Bill of Rights**.

The First Amendment

Congress shall make no law respecting an establishment of religion, or prohibiting the free exercise thereof; or abridging the freedom of speech, or of the press; or the right of the people peaceably to assemble, and to petition the government for a redress of grievances.

The First Amendment set the tone for the Bill of Rights. It told the Congress what it could **not** do. This amendment placed a limit on the new federal government's exercise of power. The amendment actually establishes *five freedoms*:

1. **Freedom of Religion:** Congress cannot establish an official religion. At a time when England and other countries in Europe had established churches, this was interpreted to mean that there could be no law creating a national religion. Congress also cannot prohibit (*forbid*) the free exercise of religion by individual citizens. Americans are free to worship any faith or religion, or to have no religion at all.

2. **Freedom of Speech:** Congress cannot **abridge** (*cut short or limit*) freedom of speech. People can express themselves in any way they choose: by speaking, making signs, or taking actions. Even "symbolic speech" actions are protected, such as wearing armbands or burning the American flag to protest American foreign policy. However, there are limits to free speech where public safety and the rights of others are involved. For example, one cannot "falsely shout fire in a crowded theatre." Speech is limited where it poses a clear and present danger.

3. **Freedom of the Press:** We have freedom of expression in print as well as in our spoken words. Congress cannot limit our freedom to write and publish our opinions or observations.

4. **Freedom of Assembly:** Congress also cannot prevent people from exercising their right to **assemble** peaceably. Without this right, the

value of free speech is greatly weakened. It is especially with an audience that political speech has the greatest impact.

5. **Freedom to Petition:** A petition is a written request, usually signed by many people. Government cannot deny people the right to **petition** the government. If the government is to serve the people, people must be able to communicate their concerns to their government officials and leaders.

The Second Amendment

Word Helper
bear arms = carry guns
infringed = limited; weakened

A well regulated militia, being necessary to the security of a free State, the right of the people to keep and bear arms, shall not be infringed.

The Second Amendment gives individuals the right to own and carry firearms (*guns*). In the case of the *District of Columbia v. Heller* (2008), the U.S. Supreme Court ruled that the Second Amendment guaranteed the right to use arms for "traditional purposes," such as the defense of one's home.

The Third Amendment

No soldier shall, in time of peace be quartered in any house without the consent of the owner, nor in time of war, but in a manner to be prescribed by law.

prescribed = laid down; stated

The Third Amendment was prompted by bitter memories of the British government's practice of quartering troops in the homes of American colonists without their consent before and during the Revolutionary War. This grievance was one of those listed in the Declaration of Independence. This amendment prohibits the quartering of soldiers in peacetime without the owner's permission.

The Fourth Amendment

The right of the people to be secure in their persons, houses, papers, and effects, against unreasonable searches and seizures, shall not be violated, and no warrants shall issue, but upon probable cause, supported by oath or affirmation, and particularly describing the place to be searched, and the persons or things to be seized.

This amendment protects our homes, the places where we work, our possessions, and our persons from unreasonable searches and seizures. A "**search**" occurs when police enter a place to look for evidence. A "**seizure**" occurs when police either seize (*take*) something or arrest a person. If police officers want to make a search or seizure, they must first apply, under oath, to obtain a warrant. This is a document, signed by a judge, that permits police officers to conduct a search. In making their request for a warrant, the police must show "probable cause"—reasonable grounds for having suspicions and making the request.

In some cases, searches and seizures are permitted without a warrant. For example, if a police officer is in "hot pursuit," chasing a suspect who is fleeing the scene of a robbery in a car, it would be unreasonable to expect the officer to find a judge and obtain a

Chapter 9 | The Bill of Rights and Later Amendments

warrant before continuing the chase. Searches without warrants are permitted in these cases.

Any evidence that the police gather in a criminal case in violation of this amendment cannot be used in a court of law. The Fourth Amendment also protects our right to **privacy**—our ability to conduct our private lives without the interference of government.

The Fifth Amendment

No person shall be held to answer for a capital, or otherwise infamous crime, unless on an ... indictment of a Grand Jury ... nor shall any person be subject for the same offen[s]e to be twice put in jeopardy of life or limb; nor shall be compelled in any criminal case to be a witness against himself, nor be deprived of life, liberty, or property, without due process of law; nor shall private property be taken for public use, without just compensation.

indictment = formal accusation
jeopardy = danger
compelled = forced
compensation = payment

Like the First Amendment, the Fifth Amendment provides five separate rights. Four of these concern the rights of the accused:

1. A person cannot be charged for murder without an indictment by a grand jury. You already know that a jury is made up of a group of impartial local citizens. A grand jury is usually made up of 16 to 23 jurors (in Florida, 15 to 21). It provides a screening process to determine if there is enough evidence to make criminal charges and send a case to trial. The grand jury can call witnesses, examine evidence, and make an investigation to assist in its determination.

2. No person can be tried twice for the same crime. This is known as "**double jeopardy**" because the accused's liberty and life would be placed in danger twice.

3. No one accused of a crime can be forced to testify against himself or herself (self-incrimination). This is to prevent authorities from using pressure to frighten suspects into making false confessions or false testimony. Refusing to answer questions because the answers may be self-incriminating is sometimes called "**pleading the Fifth**."

4. No one can have life, liberty, or property taken away by government without "**due process of law**." Due process means fairness. It means that one cannot lose life, liberty or property unless the procedures applied to the case are fair.

5. The last part of the Fifth Amendment focuses on **property rights** (*the right to be secure in the ownership of property*). It states that government can take private property for a valid public use (such as building a major highway), but the property owner must receive "just compensation." This means that the property owner must be paid what the property is truly worth. The right of government to take over private property for public purposes is called **eminent domain**.

The Sixth Amendment

In all criminal prosecutions, the accused shall enjoy the right to a speedy and public trial, by an impartial jury of the State and district wherein the crime shall have been committed ... and to be informed of the nature and cause of the accusation; to be confronted with the witnesses against him; to have compulsory process for obtaining witnesses in

confront = face
compulsory = involving compulsion; ability to compel

204 Chapter 9 | The Bill of Rights and Later Amendments

counsel = a lawyer

his favor, and to have the Assistance of Counsel for his defen[s]e.

The Sixth Amendment also provides a person accused of a crime with several rights. In this amendment, these rights are focused on the trial itself:

1. The right to a **speedy** and **public trial**.

   The key words here are, "speedy and public." If one is accused of a crime and placed in jail, unless the case proceeds quickly to trial, the accused may have to wait in jail a long time before guilt or innocence is determined.

   The accused must not be tried in an isolated, secret court, but in a place where the public can see that the accused is fairly treated. Too often in dictatorships, innocent people are locked up while their cases are delayed for years without trial. Even if there is a trial, it is held in a hidden or secret place where no one can witness the unfair procedures that may result in sentencing the accused to long years of imprisonment or even death.

2. The right to trial by an **impartial jury**.

   The accused is entitled to a trial by a group of **"peers"** or equals, known as **jurors**. They should be impartial and not be biased.

3. The right **"to be informed of the nature and cause of the accusations."**

   People have a right to hear the charges against them so that they can defend themselves. Charges must be stated at the time of any arrest or before any **forced internment** (*captivity or imprisonment*).

4. The right to "confront" witnesses.

   We have the right to face and question our accusers, in order to prove our innocence.

5. The right to require witnesses to appear in court for the accused.

6. The right to have the assistance of **counsel** (*an attorney*) for the **defendant** (*the person accused of committing the crime*).

In Chapter 10, you will learn how the U.S. Supreme Court interpreted this amendment in two cases: *Gideon v. Wainwright* and *Miranda v. Arizona*.

The Seventh Amendment

In suits at common law, where the value in controversy shall exceed twenty dollars, the right of trial by jury shall be preserved …

This amendment guarantees the right to a jury trial in many civil (*non-criminal*) cases.

The Eighth Amendment

Excessive bail shall not be required, nor excessive fines imposed, nor cruel and unusual punishments inflicted.

There are three parts to this amendment:

1. The first part deals with the right of an individual accused of crime while awaiting trial. A defendant can usually remain outside of prison before trial by giving **bail** (*something of value, usually money, that the defendant gives the court to guarantee that he or she will come to the trial*). The Eighth Amendment requires that the bail not be "excessive" (*too high in proportion to the charges against the defendant*).

2. The amendment further provides that any fines on the defendant should also not be excessive.

3. Finally, the amendment guarantees that we should not have to suffer any **"cruel and unusual punishments."**

Chapter 9 | The Bill of Rights and Later Amendments

The Active Citizen

Enrichment

Do you think that capital punishment (*execution*) should be prohibited as a "cruel and unusual punishment" in today's society? Write a persuasive essay with four paragraphs giving your point of view. In the first paragraph, write your introduction. In the second and third paragraphs, give your arguments with evidence to back them up. In the fourth paragraph, write your conclusion. Then exchange your persuasive essay with a partner from your class. After you read each other's papers, see if you influenced your partner's point of view. Which arguments did you both feel were most persuasive? Which arguments needed more support?

The Ninth Amendment

enumeration = listing
construed = interpreted
retained = kept

The enumeration in the Constitution, of certain rights, shall not be construed to deny or disparage others retained by the people.

When someone makes a list, others may think that whatever is not on the list is deliberately left off or excluded. The Ninth Amendment makes it clear that this is not the case for the individual rights listed in the Constitution and Bill of Rights. Other rights *not* listed in the Constitution may still exist and remain with the people. These are known as **unenumerated rights**.

The Tenth Amendment

The powers not delegated to the United States by the Constitution, nor prohibited by it to the States, are reserved to the States respectively, or to the people.

This amendment makes it clear that all rights and powers not granted to the federal government by the Constitution are "reserved" to the states and to the American people. This amendment supports **states' rights**—the rights and powers of states in our federal system. You will learn more about this amendment in Chapter 11 on **federalism**—the division of power between the federal government and the states.

The Active Citizen

▶ Select your favorite amendment and draw your own political cartoon illustrating that amendment.
▶ Make a poster showing the rights of an accused person provided by the Bill of Rights.
▶ You may be surprised by how many of the rights in the Bill of Rights concern individuals accused of crimes. How are these rights about criminal procedure actually important safeguards of our political freedoms and our democratic system of government?

The Impact of Constitutional Rights on American Society

The individual rights guaranteed by the Constitution and Bill of Rights have helped to shape our nation's political, economic and social systems.

Political System: Our Constitution established a representative form of government. Ordinary citizens were given the final say in selecting their government

Summary: Individual Rights in the Bill of Rights

First Amendment Rights: The "Five Freedoms"

- **Freedom of religion:** People have the right to belong to any religion and to worship as they please; Congress cannot establish an official religion.

- **Freedom of speech:** People are free to say what they wish, including criticizing the government (but we cannot endanger the safety of others or violate their rights).

- **Freedom of the press:** People can write and publish what they wish, including criticism of the government (without violating the rights of others).

- **Freedom of assembly:** People have the right to meet publicly in groups.

- **Freedom to petition:** People have the right to write to their government officials to ask for change.

Rights of the Accused

- **No unreasonable search and seizure:** Police must have reasonable grounds for searching a place, taking goods, or arresting a person.

- **The right to due process:** The government must follow fair, public and transparent procedures before taking away someone's life, liberty or property.

- **The right to "plead the Fifth":** We cannot be forced to testify against ourselves.

- **The right to a trial by jury:** If accused of a crime, we have the right to be tried publicly by a group of impartial citizens.

- **The right to the assistance of legal counsel:** A person accused of a crime has the right to the help of a lawyer.

- **No cruel and unusual punishment:** A person cannot be tortured or suffer a cruel and unusual punishment.

- **No double jeopardy:** A person cannot be tried twice for the same crime.

Other Rights in the Bill of Rights

- **The right to bear arms:** A person has the right to have a gun for self-defense.

- **The right to privacy:** We have a right to conduct our private lives without government interference.

- **The right to just compensation for property taken by eminent domain:** If the government takes our property for public use, it must pay us what it is worth.

> You won't have to know the numbers of amendments for the EOC test, but you should know these key groups of rights.

leaders through periodic elections. The Bill of Rights further guaranteed freedom of speech and of the press. This gave ordinary citizens the power to criticize government leaders without fear. The free press kept citizens informed about the actions of their leaders. People have the right to assemble and to organize protests against government policies. They can even engage in peaceful **civil disobedience**—refusing to

Name _____

Our individual rights are precious. We cannot protect our rights, however, if we cannot recognize when those rights are violated. Complete the chart below by identifying which rights in the Bill of Rights have been violated in each scenario.

Events	Which rights have been violated and how
Sarah robs a bank. The police arrest her and interrogate her. No lawyer is present and the police do not tell her about her rights. Sarah confesses to the crime.	
Jasmine writes an article in the newspaper about corruption in her local government. The mayor orders the police to arrest her for publishing her article. Jasmine is arrested and sent to jail without a trial.	
Edgar wants the United States to withdraw its troops from a Middle Eastern country. He writes to his member of Congress. He also meets with other people to demonstrate in the street against the government's actions. The police arrest Edgar for participating in a demonstration against government policy.	
Jim lives in a state that decides to tax its citizens to provide funding for religious schools. All different types of religious schools can request funding from this new tax, so state officials feel the tax is fair. Jim, however, refuses to pay the tax.	
Sandra is accused of shoplifting. She is placed on trial and the jury finds her "not guilty." Shortly after the trial, the store finds a videotape showing Sandra committing the crime. The District Attorney decides to charge her again for shoplifting. Sandra is put on trial a second time for the same crime.	
Leroy is arrested for causing a public nuisance when he repeatedly refuses to stop playing loud music after 10:00 pm at night. The judge refuses to set any bail before his trial. After Leroy is found guilty, the judge sentences him to three years in prison.	

© FTE ■ Unlawful to photocopy without permission

obey laws that they think are wrong, in order to persuade others to change those laws.

The Bill of Rights also gave rights to those accused of crimes. Government leaders could not forcibly detain (*imprison*) critics without cause. We can only be imprisoned if, after a fair and public trial, we have been convicted of a serious crime by an impartial jury. In dictatorships, citizens do not enjoy many of these rights. Dictators often outlaw opposition parties, prohibit free speech, and send critics into **forced internment** (*imprisonment*).

Economic System: Americans also enjoy **property rights**—the right to own private property. The Bill of Rights stated that the government could not take away a person's private property unless it was needed for a public purpose and the owner was fairly paid for its value. The Thirteenth Amendment later abolished slavery and involuntary servitude. We cannot be forced to work for someone else against our will. These individual rights form the basis of our **economic freedom**—our freedom to buy and own private property, to make agreements with others, to choose what we want to do for a living, and to choose where and how we want to live. We are free to buy or not to buy any goods and services we can afford. The American system of free enterprise—one in which people can run their own private businesses—depends on both our property rights and on our system of economic freedom.

Social System: The Bill of Rights, later amendments and civil rights acts have led to a society in which all Americans enjoy equal rights and opportunities under the law. With free speech and freedom of the press, Americans are also able to communicate information freely, bringing about a more informed society. The individual rights guaranteed by the Constitution and Bill of Rights thus play an essential role in protecting our democratic form of government and way of life.

How the Constitution Both Safeguards and Limits Our Individual Rights

The Constitution tries to strike a balance that gives our government leaders enough power to govern effectively and yet protects our individual rights and liberties. This balance is found in our constitutional structure, which includes the separation of powers, the system of checks and balances, the division of power between the federal government and the state governments, and the guarantees of individual rights found in the Constitution and the Bill of Rights. The Constitution, Bill of Rights, and several later amendments guarantee individual rights that our government must respect. The result is a government that acts to safeguard (*protect*) our individual rights.

At the same time, the creation of a stronger federal government limited individual rights in some ways. To protect our rights, we have certain responsibilities. We must obey the law, pay taxes, defend the nation, and fulfill our other obligations as citizens (see Chapter 12).

Furthermore, our individual rights are not unlimited. We cannot enjoy our own rights without respecting the rights of others. Courts have placed certain common-sense restrictions on the exercise of our individual freedoms. Courts have held, for example, that:

- Free speech does not permit us to create an immediate danger to others or to publish harmful lies about others.
- The right to bear arms does not mean we can carry dangerous guns in all public places.
- Protection against unreasonable searches and seizures does not mean the police need to get a court warrant if they are chasing a suspect they just saw commit a robbery.

Chapter 9 | The Bill of Rights and Later Amendments

Name _____

Complete the Internet chat below by filling in the text messages on some of the limits placed on the rights guaranteed by the Bill of Rights.

What the amendment says

Limits on the right

The First Amendment guarantees free speech.

Yes, but _____
_____
_____
_____

The First Amendment also guarantees a free press.

Yes, but _____
_____
_____
_____

The Second Amendment says that we have the right to bear arms.

Yes, but _____
_____
_____
_____

The Fourth Amendment says that the police need to obtain a warrant before searching a place or seizing a suspect.

Yes, but _____
_____
_____
_____

210   Chapter 9 | The Bill of Rights and Later Amendments

- The freedom of religion does not allow us to interfere with others' rights.

You will learn more about some of these interpretations of the Bill of Rights by the judicial branch in the next chapter. The limits that we place on ourselves and the powers that we grant our government to safeguard our rights are, in fact, closely related. We cannot have one without the other.

The Impact of Later Amendments on American Democracy

One key to the success of American democracy has been the involvement of citizens in the **political process**. At first, however, many groups were excluded from American political life: African Americans, women, those who could not pay poll taxes, and those under 21 years of age could not vote. In order to participate fully in American life, these groups needed to gain the rights and responsibilities of citizenship, including the right to vote.

The ability of our Constitution to change through the power of amendment opened the door to the granting of equal political rights to all these groups. The amendments described below made it possible for these groups to enter into the political process.

The 13th, 14th, and 15th Amendments

These three amendments were passed during and just after the Civil War, the great conflict between North and South that ended the practice of slavery.

The Thirteenth Amendment

servitude = state of being a servant or slave

Neither slavery nor involuntary servitude, except as a punishment for crime whereof the party shall have been duly convicted, shall exist within the United States, or any place subject to their jurisdiction.

Impact: The Thirteenth Amendment abolished slavery and involuntary servitude. **Involuntary servitude** is any form of forced labor.

Despite the abolition of slavery, some minorities were still treated as second class citizens. In Florida, many African Americans were forced to labor in camps under harsh conditions where they made turpentine, a major commercial product of the state. This form of involuntary servitude survived in Florida until the 1940s, despite the Thirteenth Amendment.

The Fourteenth Amendment

Section 1. All persons born or naturalized in the United States, and subject to the jurisdiction thereof, are citizens of the United States and of the State wherein they reside. No State shall make or enforce any law which shall abridge the privileges or immunities of citizens of the United States; nor shall any State deprive any person of life, liberty, or property, without due process of law; nor deny to any person within its jurisdiction the equal protection of the laws.

Impact: The Fourteenth Amendment guaranteed equality to African-American freedmen (*freed slaves*). It was ratified in 1868, just after the end of the Civil War. It further guaranteed all U.S. citizens certain rights against the actions of state governments.

Citizenship. The first section of this amendment stated that all persons born or naturalized in the United States were citizens of the United States and of the state in which they lived. Its purpose was to make it clear that the freed slaves were U.S. citizens with all the rights of citizenship.

Privileges and Immunities. The amendment also stated that no state could pass laws that limited the benefits of citizenship. These benefits are referred to as the "privileges and immunities" of citizenship.

"Due Process" Rights. The amendment further guaranteed citizens their "due process" rights in actions by state governments. The Fourteenth Amendment forbids any state government from taking "life, liberty, or property without due process of law." Both the procedures used and the laws applied must be fair, reasonable, and just. Based on the Fourteenth Amendment, the Bill of Rights applies to the states as well as to the federal government.

Equal Protection Clause. Lastly, the Fourteenth Amendment stated that all citizens are entitled to the "equal protection of the laws." This means that states must treat all people equally. It reflected the concerns of Congress over the treatment of African-American freedmen in Southern states. The Equal Protection Clause said that states could not legally discriminate against any citizen. It became a pillar in the struggle for civil rights in America.

The Fifteenth Amendment

The right of citizens of the United States to vote shall not be denied or abridged by the United States or by any State on account of race, color, or previous condition of servitude.

abridged = limited

Impact: Despite the Fourteenth Amendment, many African Americans were still denied the right to vote. The Fifteenth Amendment addressed this problem directly. The Amendment forbade the federal and state governments from denying any citizen the right to vote on the basis of race, color, or having once been a slave.

The First Vote

The Expansion of Democracy: the 19th, 24th, and 26th Amendments

The Nineteenth Amendment

The right of citizens of the United States to vote shall not be denied or abridged by the United States or by any State on account of sex.

Impact: Throughout the nineteenth century, American women were denied the right to vote, known as **suffrage**, in most states. Women reformers sought an amendment that would give women the right to vote across America. They used many tactics on behalf of women's suffrage, including, in some cases, **civil disobedience** (*refusing to obey laws considered unjust*). After many campaigns and struggles, women finally secured the right to vote in all states with the ratification of the Nineteenth Amendment in 1920.

While women secured suffrage with the Nineteenth Amendment, women reformers in the 1960s and 1970s wanted greater equality of opportunity. They failed, however, to achieve adoption of the **Equal Rights Amendment**. This amendment was proposed by Congress in 1972, but was never ratified by enough states. It stated that "Equality of rights should not be denied . . . on account of sex." Women themselves became divided over whether to support the amendment, and many claimed it was unnecessary.

The Twenty-fourth Amendment

The right of citizens of the United States to vote in any primary or other election for President or Vice President, for electors for President or Vice President, or for Senator or Representative in Congress, shall not be denied or abridged by the United States or any State by reason of failure to pay any poll tax or other tax.

Impact: Tactics such as **poll taxes** (*a special tax paid in order to vote*) were once used, even as late as the 1960s, by Southern states to discourage African-American voters. The Twenty-fourth Amendment prohibited any state from requiring the payment of a poll tax for citizens to vote in federal elections.

The Twenty-fourth Amendment was ratified at the height of the Civil Rights Movement of the 1960s. African-American leaders like Dr. Martin Luther King, Jr., held rallies and demonstrations, conducted boycotts, went on marches, and committed acts of **civil disobedience**. Their actions led to several laws that helped end racial discrimination and promoted greater social justice. These included:

The Civil Rights Act of 1964. Many restaurants and hotels in the South would not serve African Americans. This law prohibited such discrimination in restaurants, hotels and many forms of employment on the basis of race, sex (*gender*), religion or ethnic origin.

The Voting Rights Act of 1965. This law echoed the Fifteenth and Twenty-fourth Amendments. It prohibited poll taxes and racial discrimination in voting, and permitted special federal officials to register voters.

The Civil Rights Act of 1968. This law prohibited racial discrimination in the sale or rental of housing.

Twenty-sixth Amendment

The right of citizens of the United States, who are eighteen years of age or older, to vote shall not be denied or abridged by the United States or by any State on account of age.

Impact: During the War in Vietnam, young men were being **drafted** (*conscripted for compulsory military service*) at the age of 18 years, but they were not permitted to vote until they reached 21 years of age. Critics argued that if an 18-year-old man was old enough to be required to fight and die for his country, then surely he was old enough to vote. The amendment process again made it possible to expand voting rights by lowering the minimum voting age from 21 years to 18 in the Twenty-sixth Amendment.

◆ ◆ ◆

The general impact of these amendments has been to make women, young adults and minorities equal partners with other voters in the American system of democracy. We now see representatives of every race, ethnic background, gender and age at every level of our government. This was not always the case. There was a bitter struggle to provide the rights of citizenship to all, thus permitting Americans to live up to their original creed, that all people are created equal. The ability of Americans to amend the Constitution has helped to make this transformation possible.

| Enrichment | # The Active Citizen |

▶ Choose one of the amendments in this section and conduct research using your school library and the Internet. Learn about the historical circumstances that led to the amendment and the changes that it brought about, especially in the expansion of American democracy. Then give an oral presentation, PowerPoint or Prezi presentation, or make and show a video, to your class.

▶ Pretend to be a freedman, a woman at the turn of the century, a poor voter in the South in 1960, or an 18-year-old about to be drafted to serve in Vietnam in 1970. Then give a speech to your class in favor of the appropriate constitutional amendment.

Name _____

Complete the chart below by describing each right and evaluating how it influences people's actions.

First Amendment: "Five Freedoms"	Description/Influence
Freedom of religion 	
Freedom of speech 	
Freedom of the press 	
Freedom of assembly 	
Freedom to petition 	

Name _____

Complete the chart below by describing each right and evaluating how it influences people's actions.

Rights of the Accused	Description/Influence
No unreasonable search and seizure 	
Right to "due process" 	
Right to "Plead the Fifth" 	
Right to a trial by jury 	
Right to the assistance of legal counsel 	

Chapter 9 | The Bill of Rights and Later Amendments

Name _____

Complete the chart below by describing each right and evaluating how it influences people's actions.

Rights of the Accused	Description/Influence
No "double jeopardy" 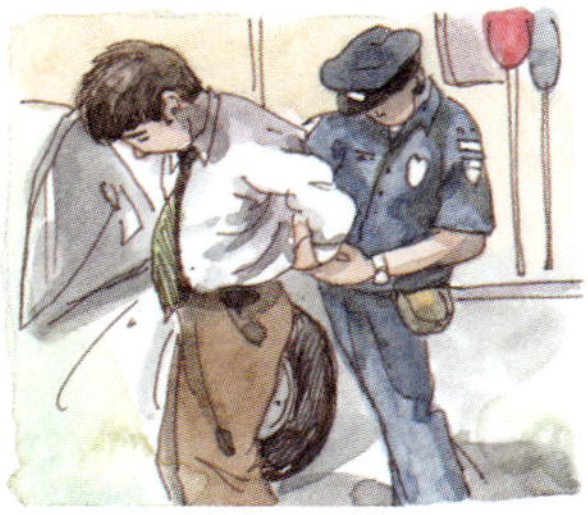	
No "cruel and unusual" punishment 	

Other Rights in the Bill of Rights	Description/Influence
Right to bear arms 	
Right to privacy 	
Right to just compensation for property taken by eminent domain 	

Name _____

Complete the chart below on the later amendments and laws expanding American democracy.

Amendment	What it says	Impact on role of minorities and women in the political process
Thirteenth Amendment		
Fourteenth Amendment		
Fifteenth Amendment		
Nineteenth Amendment		
Twenty-fourth Amendment		
Twenty-sixth Amendment		
Civil Rights Act of 1964		
Voting Rights Act of 1965		
Civil Rights Act of 1968		

Chapter 9 | The Bill of Rights and Later Amendments

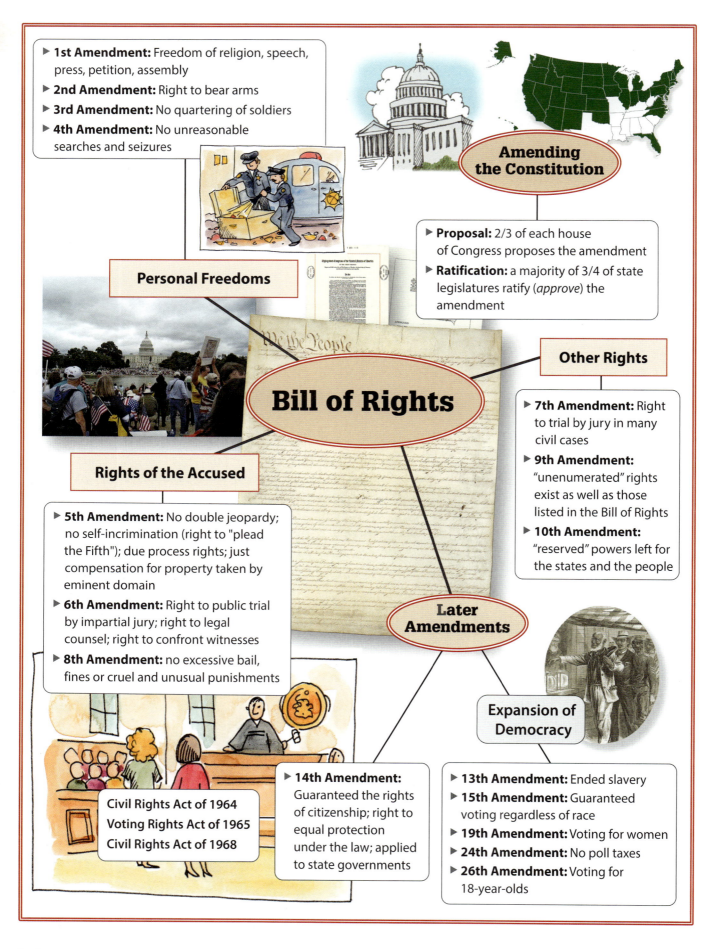

Review Cards: The Bill of Rights and Later Amendments

Amending the Constitution

The Constitution allows for changing times through the amendment process. However, to amend the Constitution is more difficult than passing an ordinary law.

Article V of the Constitution established a two-step process for amendments:

Step 1. Proposing the Amendment

First, it must be **proposed**. An amendment can be proposed in either of two ways:

1. By a two-thirds vote of both Houses of Congress. All amendments of the Constitution so far have used this method.

   or

2. On the request of two-thirds of the state legislatures, Congress can call for a national convention to amend the Constitution.

Step 2. Ratifying the Amendment

Then it must be ratified. There are two ways to **ratify** (*approve*) an amendment. Congress selects which one to apply:

1. Ratification by three-fourths of the state legislatures. So far, only this method has been used.

   or

2. Ratification by special ratification conventions in three-fourths of the states.

The Bill of Rights: The First Ten Amendments

The **Bill of Rights** consists of the first ten amendments to the Constitution. They were proposed by the first Congress to meet the demands of the Anti-Federalists, who had demanded a bill of rights during the debate over ratification of the Constitution. The Bill of Rights originally just protected individuals from actions by the federal government. Only later did the Fourteenth Amendment apply these rights to actions by state governments.

First Amendment

Establishes five freedoms. Congress *cannot*:
1. limit freedom of religion or establish a state religion
2. limit freedom of speech
3. limit freedom of the press
4. prevent people from holding assemblies
5. prevent people from petitioning the government.

Second Amendment

Protects citizens' **right to bear arms**.

Third Amendment

Prohibits (*forbids*) government from **quartering** (*sheltering*) soldiers in citizens' homes in peacetime without the owners' consent.

Chapter 9 | The Bill of Rights and Later Amendments

Fourth Amendment

Protects citizens from unreasonable **searches** and **seizures** of their persons, houses, papers and other belongings.

Fifth Amendment

Provides several rights, most of which protect those accused of a crime:

1. **"Double Jeopardy"**: No person can be tried twice for the same crime.
2. Freedom from **Self-Incrimination**: No person can be compelled to testify against himself or herself (**"Pleading the Fifth"**—refusing to answer questions where the answers might be self-incriminating).
3. **"Due Process" rights**: No person can be deprived of life, liberty, or property without **due process**— a process that is fair and that respects the person's rights.
4. **Eminent Domain**: Private property may be taken over by government for public use, but the owner must be fairly compensated (*paid*).

Sixth Amendment

Guarantees rights of the accused in criminal proceedings. These rights are:

1. The right to a **speedy** and **public trial**
2. The right to be tried by an **impartial jury**
3. The accused must be informed of the charges
4. The **right to face witnesses** against the accused
5. The right to require witnesses to come to the court, who can testify in the accused's favor
6. The right to the assistance of **legal counsel** (*an attorney*)

Seventh Amendment

Provides the right to a jury trial in many civil cases.

Eighth Amendment

1. Prohibits excessive **bail** (*money given by the accused to guarantee appearance at trial*).
2. Prohibits excessive fines.
3. Prohibits **cruel and unusual punishments**.

Ninth Amendment

The **enumeration** (*listing*) of some rights in the Constitution does not mean that other rights may not also exist. These other rights are known as **unenumerated rights**.

Tenth Amendment

Any rights not given to the federal government or prohibited to the states are reserved for the states or for the people. These powers are known as the **"reserved"** powers.

Later Amendments Contributed to the Expansion of Democracy

Later amendments have played an important role in the expansion of democracy by bringing previously excluded groups into the American political process. The **impact** of these amendments has been to expand American democracy.

- The **13th Amendment** abolished slavery and involuntary servitude in the United States.
- The **14th Amendment** protected the rights of freedmen and other citizens:
  1. It made all persons born or naturalized in the United States into citizens of the United States.
  2. No state can limit the benefits of citizenship (**"privileges and immunities"**).
  3. **Due Process Clause** prohibits any state from taking "life, liberty, or property without due process of law." Courts have interpreted this to mean the Bill of Rights applies to the state governments.
  4. **"Equal protection of the laws"** requires states to treat people equally under the law. The Equal Protection Clause became an important weapon in the struggle for civil rights in America.
- The **15th Amendment** prohibited the federal and state governments from denying the right to vote to any citizen on the basis of race, color, or having been a slave.
- The **19th Amendment** gave women the right to vote (known as *suffrage*).
- The **24th Amendment** abolished **poll taxes** as a requirement to vote in federal elections. Poll taxes had been used to deny African-American citizens their right to vote.

The 24th Amendment was passed at the time of the Civil Rights Movement when African-American leaders were using **civil disobedience**, demonstrations, and other efforts to end racial segregation and achieve equality. This amendment was accompanied by the **Civil Rights Act of 1964** (banning discrimination in restaurants, hotels, and most employment), **Voting Rights Act of 1965** (enforcing the 15th and 24th Amendments), and **Civil Rights Act of 1968** (banning discrimination in housing). An **Equal Rights Amendment**, guaranteeing equality to women, was never ratified.

- The **26th Amendment** lowered the voting age to 18 years old.

How the Constitution Safeguards and Limits Individual Rights

- The Constitution seeks to find a balance between limiting government power to protect individual rights and allowing government sufficient power to govern effectively.
- The balance is found in a constitutional structure that has a separation of powers, checks and balances, the division of power between the federal government and the state governments, and the guarantees of individual rights found in the Constitution, Bill of Rights and state constitutions.
- Courts have upheld individual rights but have also placed certain common-sense restrictions on our exercise of them to protect the rights of our fellow citizens: for example, free speech does not permit us to create an immediate danger to others or to tell lies about others; freedom of religion does not allow us to interfere with others' rights; the right to bear arms does not mean we can carry any kind of gun into every public place; protection against unreasonable searches does not mean the police have to get a court warrant if they are engaged in a chase.
- Our constitutional rights are accompanied by responsibilities, such as to obey the law.
- Our constitutional rights give us our **economic freedom** and have shaped our political, economic and social systems. Our democracy survives, for example, because we cannot be imprisoned just for disagreeing with government policies.

Chapter 9 | The Bill of Rights and Later Amendments

What Do You Know?

SS.7.C.2.4

1. What is one of the five freedoms protected by the First Amendment?
   A. Freedom of speech
   B. Freedom from self-incrimination
   C. Freedom from unreasonable search and seizure
   D. Freedom from cruel and unusual punishments

SS.7.C.3.5

2. What is usually the first step in amending the U.S. Constitution?
   A. Three-fourths of the state legislatures propose the amendment.
   B. Two-thirds of each house of Congress propose the amendment.
   C. Conventions in three-fourths of the states propose the amendment.
   D. The President, after consulting with the U.S. Supreme Court, proposes the amendment.

SS.7.C.2.4

3. Juanita owns unused property in her town. Her city council decides to use part of her property to build a new bus terminal. The council votes to give Juanita $20,000 for this part of her property. She claims her land is worth much more. The city clerk sends her a check for $20,000, and the city starts building the terminal. Which two rights of Juanita have been violated?
   A. to assistance of counsel and to a trial by jury
   B. to privacy and to protection from unreasonable seizure
   C. to due process and to just compensation in case of eminent domain
   D. to equal protection of the law and to a prohibition of double jeopardy

SS.7.C.3.5

4. The diagram below shows the most common method of amending the U.S. Constitution.

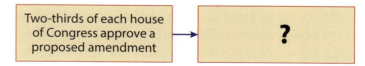

   Which completes the diagram?
   A. Two-thirds of the states hold a constitutional convention
   B. Three-fourths of the state legislatures ratify the amendment
   C. The President of the United States approves the amendment
   D. Three-fourths of both houses of Congress ratify the amendment

SS.7.C.2.4

5. Which of these rights from the Bill of Rights helps people accused of crimes?
   A. the right to bear arms for self-defense
   B. the right to have the assistance of counsel
   C. the right not to have troops quartered in one's home
   D. the right to petition government for a redress of grievances

SS.7.C.2.4

6. While Alex was at school, police officers broke into his home and took his computer. They did not have a warrant and there was no reason to believe that Alex had broken any laws. Alex was not avoiding the police or planning to move away from his home. Which right did the police officers violate?
   A. the right to due process of law in the Fourteenth Amendment
   B. the right to assistance of legal counsel in the Sixth Amendment
   C. the right to the equal protection of the laws in the Fourteenth Amendment
   D. the right against unreasonable searches and seizures in the Fourth Amendment

SS.7.C.2.4

7. The statement below was made by Benjamin Franklin in the *Pennsylvania Gazette* in 1737.

   > *Freedom of speech is the pillar of a free government. When this support is taken away, the constitution of a free society is dissolved and tyranny is erected.*

   What makes this freedom so essential to a successful democracy?
   A. It helps the government to enforce the law.
   B. It provides new ideas to government leaders.
   C. It promotes patriotic activities in times of war.
   D. It permits citizens to criticize government actions.

SS.7.C.3.6

8. Which statement best defines "due process" of law?
   A. Decisions affecting individuals are made by a jury of peers.
   B. Procedures used to enforce the law are fair, reasonable and just.
   C. People have guaranteed rights that can only be taken away in emergencies.
   D. Government decisions affecting individuals are made in secret to avoid publicity.

Chapter 9 | The Bill of Rights and Later Amendments

SS.7.C.2.4

9. What was the main purpose for the Bill of Rights?
   A. to establish a republican government in America
   B. to guarantee individual freedoms against abuses of power
   C. to announce the reasons for separating from Great Britain
   D. to establish a stronger central government in the United States

SS.7.C.3.6

10. Why is freedom of the press so important to democratic government?
    A. It keeps talented and creative writers employed.
    B. It helps government officials keep track of public opinion.
    C. It keeps citizens informed about the acts of their government leaders.
    D. It provides a place where candidates can advertise in election campaigns.

SS.7.C.3.6

11. Which statement describes an impact of the Due Process and Equal Protection Clauses of the Fourteenth Amendment?
    A. Women were guaranteed the right to vote in all states.
    B. African-American freedmen were guaranteed the right to vote.
    C. Americans were protected against abuses by state governments.
    D. Opponents of the government no longer feared forced internment.

SS.7.C.3.7

12. The newspaper headline on the left announces an amendment to the U.S. Constitution.

    What was the impact of the passage of this amendment to the U.S. Constitution on the American political process?
    A. Women were allowed to vote in elections in all states.
    B. Citizens from 18 to 20 years of age were allowed to vote in elections.
    C. Those who could not afford to pay poll taxes could still vote in federal elections.
    D. Restaurants and hotels could not practice discrimination against Vietnam veterans.

SS.7.C.2.5

13. The statement below about free speech is from the Supreme Court decision of *Schenck v. United States* (1919).

    The most stringent protection of free speech would not protect a man in falsely shouting fire in a theater and causing a panic.

    Which conclusion can be drawn from this reasoning?
    A. Our constitutional rights are limited by the rights of others.
    B. Not all Supreme Court decisions uphold the U.S. Constitution.
    C. Since 1917, Americans no longer enjoy the freedom of speech.
    D. The U.S. Supreme Court generally favors the powers of the federal government over the rights of individuals.

CHAPTER 10

"May It Please the Court": The Supreme Court in Action

SS.7.C.2.4 Evaluate rights contained in the Bill of Rights and other amendments to the Constitution. (See also Chapter 9.)

SS.7.C.3.12 Analyze the significance and outcomes of landmark Supreme Court cases including, but not limited to, *Marbury v. Madison*, *Plessy v. Ferguson*, *Brown v. Board of Education*, *Gideon v. Wainwright*, *Miranda v. Arizona*, *In re Gault*, *Tinker v. Des Moines*, *Hazelwood v. Kuhlmeier*, *United States v. Nixon*, and *Bush v. Gore*.

Names and Terms You Should Know

Marbury v. Madison	*Gideon v. Wainwright*	Segregation
Judicial review	Right to legal counsel	*Plessy v. Ferguson*
Tinker v. Des Moines	*Miranda v. Arizona*	Equal protection under the law
Hazelwood v. Kuhlmeier	*In re Gault*	*Brown v. Board of Education*
District of Columbia v. Heller	Juvenile rights	*United States v. Nixon*
Rights of the accused	Due process	*Bush v. Gore*

© FTE ▪ Unlawful to photocopy without permission

Florida "Keys" to Learning

1. The U.S. Supreme Court interprets and enforces rights promised by the Constitution. Its power of judicial review often helps it to protect those rights.

2. In *Marbury v. Madison* (1803), the Court firmly established the power of judicial review: the principle that the Supreme Court has the power to rule that laws passed by Congress are unconstitutional and that it can invalidate (*cancel; overturn*) them.

3. In *Tinker v. Des Moines Independent School District* (1969), a group of students in Des Moines, Iowa, wore black armbands to protest the Vietnam War. School authorities suspended these students. The students sued the school for violating (*denying; failing to respect*) their free speech rights. The Court established that students were citizens entitled to the freedom of speech guaranteed by the First Amendment, and that wearing armbands as a protest was a form of speech.

4. In *Hazelwood School District v. Kuhlmeier* (1988), the Court placed limits on students' free-speech rights. It stated that school officials could censor (*examine and edit*) school-sponsored student publications so long as such restrictions served a proper educational purpose.

5. In *District of Columbia v. Heller* (2008), a police officer applied to have a handgun at home but was denied a permit due to a prohibition of private handguns in Washington, D.C. The Court ruled that a prohibition of handgun ownership for self-defense in the home violated the Second Amendment's right to bear arms.

6. Several of the rights in the Bill of Rights protect the rights of the accused (those accused of a crime). In *Gideon v. Wainwright* (1963), the Court ruled that the Sixth Amendment guarantees the right to a legal counsel (*a lawyer*) to a defendant charged with a felony (*a serious crime*) who is too poor to afford one.

7. In *Miranda v. Arizona* (1966), the Court ruled that suspects must be informed of their Fifth and Sixth Amendment rights before being questioned. Suspects have the right to remain silent and to have a lawyer. Police now must read suspects their "Miranda" rights.

8. In *In re Gault* (1967), a juvenile (*minor*) was imprisoned after an unfair process under juvenile law. He was denied "due process" rights and was given an unjustly harsh penalty for supposedly making an obscene phone call he said he did not make. The Court ruled that "due process" rights apply to minors as well as to adults.

9. In *Plessy v. Ferguson* (1896), the U.S. Supreme Court affirmed the constitutionality of state segregation laws, so long as the facilities offered to each race were of "equal standards." This became known as the "separate-but-equal" doctrine.

10. In *Brown v. Board of Education* (1954), the Court ruled that racial segregation in public schools violated the Equal Protection Clause of the Fourteenth Amendment. The *Brown* decision was the first step toward ending racial segregation in the South.

11. In *United States v. Nixon* (1974), President Nixon's claim of "executive privilege" was overruled by the U.S. Supreme Court, which ordered the President to hand over tapes of White House conversations to investigators. The Supreme Court's decision proved that even the President of the United States is not above the "rule of law."

12. In *Bush v. Gore* (2000), the U.S. Supreme Court halted the recount of manual votes in Florida. As a result, George W. Bush won Florida's electoral votes and became the next President, even though his opponent, Al Gore, had received a larger share of the nation's popular vote.

Imagine a close relative promised you a special present: a favorite book or computer game, a trip to an amusement park, or tickets to a baseball game or musical. Such a promise would surely be wonderful, but if you never actually received the present, you would soon become disappointed.

The Bill of Rights was a splendid promise made to the American people. But without a means of enforcement, the Bill of Rights would have become an empty promise and nothing more. What made the Bill of Rights and later constitutional rights so effective was the fact that these promises were combined with the active protection of the federal courts, and especially by the U.S. Supreme Court.

In Chapter 7, you learned how the U.S. Supreme Court manages its workload. In this chapter, you will witness the Supreme Court in action. You will see how the Court has interpreted and enforced rights promised by the Constitution, especially those rights found in the Bill of Rights and the Fourteenth Amendment.

The Power of Judicial Review

Marbury v. Madison (1803)

This decision, perhaps the single most important one in the history of the Supreme Court, took place against a background of political rivalry. *Marbury v. Madison* was not about individual rights, but about the powers of the Court itself. It laid the foundation for many later decisions by the Court.

The Political Background

John Adams was the second President of the United States. Adams was defeated by Thomas Jefferson in the Presidential election of 1800. In December 1800, Adams' party in Congress passed laws creating new judicial posts. Their aim was to fill the judiciary with sympathetic judges before Jefferson took power.

President Adams nominated new judges from his own political party to fill all of these posts. The Senate only completed confirmation of his new appointments on March 3, 1801—Adams' last day in office. The new appointments were quickly signed by Adams and sealed by his Secretary of State, **John Marshall**. Most of the new commissions (*official signed documents of the appointment*) were delivered (*handed over*), but in the last-minute rush, a few were not.

Meanwhile, the Chief Justice of the Supreme Court had resigned in January. Adams appointed John Marshall to take his place. In February 1801, Marshall assumed office as Chief Justice of the Supreme Court. Marshall also remained as Secretary of State during Adams' final month in office.

On March 4, 1801, Thomas Jefferson took the oath of office as the third President of the United States. He appointed James Madison as his Secretary of State. Jefferson and Madison refused to deliver any remaining last-minute commissions made by Adams. One of these undelivered commissions was to William Marbury.

Marbury's Lawsuit

After writing to Madison, Marbury applied to the Supreme Court for the delivery of his commission.

The **Judiciary Act of 1789** had given the U.S. Supreme Court the power to issue a court order to a government official to perform his duties (*writ of mandamus*). Marbury filed his suit in the Supreme Court, seeking such an order to Madison, requiring him to deliver the commission.

The lawsuit placed Chief Justice Marshall in a delicate situation. As former Secretary of State, Marshall had set the seal of the United States on the very commission he was now asked to enforce. Could his decision be impartial in these circumstances?

Chapter 10 | "May It Please the Court": The Supreme Court in Action

The Legal Issues

The case brought two issues before the Court:

1. Should the Supreme Court issue a court order to Madison, as Secretary of State, requiring him to deliver the commission to William Marbury?
2. Can the Supreme Court rule on the constitutionality of a law passed by Congress?

The Decision/Outcome

Marshall found an ingenious solution to his situation in this case.

First, Marshall made it clear that Marbury was fully entitled to his appointment, which had already been signed and sealed.

Then Marshall turned to the question of enforcement. Did the Supreme Court actually have the power to order the Secretary of State to deliver Marbury's commission?

Marshall explained that the Constitution had given the U.S. Supreme Court "original jurisdiction" in only a small number of cases. Congress did not have the right, under the Constitution, to enlarge this original jurisdiction. Only a constitutional amendment could do this. Therefore, the section of the Judiciary Act of 1789 that gave the Supreme Court the power to issue court orders to officials to perform their duties was an "unconstitutional" expansion of the Court's original jurisdiction.

Since this section of the Judiciary Act was unconstitutional, Marshall concluded that it could not be enforced. Therefore, the Supreme Court lacked the power to order Madison to deliver Marbury's commission.

This raised a second issue, which was actually far more important than the first: **Which branch of government had authority to determine the constitutionality of laws?** Marshall explained that it was the U.S. Supreme Court that held the final power in determining whether or not a law, or parts of it, were constitutional.

Here was his argument:

1. The Constitution was the fundamental (*basic*) law of the United States.
2. When the Constitution and an ordinary law were in conflict, the Constitution had to be upheld.
3. It was the job of the U.S. Supreme Court to interpret and apply the law.
4. It was therefore the job of the Supreme Court to interpret both the Constitution and individual laws passed by Congress.
5. The Supreme Court could declare laws unconstitutional if it found them to be in conflict with the Constitution.
6. Finally, unconstitutional laws were invalid (*not valid; not lawful*) and could not be enforced.

Ironically, Marshall had limited the Supreme Court's authority by denying it the power to issue certain types of court orders (*writ of mandamus*). At the same time, Marshall had greatly expanded the Court's authority by establishing the principle of judicial review.

Justice John Marshall

Significance

The decision in *Marbury v. Madison* firmly established the principle of judicial review: the principle that the Supreme Court has the power to rule that laws passed by Congress are unconstitutional and to invalidate (*cancel; overturn*) them.

With this decision, the Supreme Court took on the role of "guardian" of our Constitution. The Court uses its power of judicial review to protect our individual rights. But remember: the U.S. Supreme Court only determines the constitutionality of a law if it comes before the Court in a real case.

Case Summary

Summarize this case and the Court's decision in your own words.

What constitutional principle did this case establish? What impact has this case had on American society and government?

The Active Citizen

"It is emphatically the province and duty of the Judicial Department to say what the law is. Those who apply the rule to particular cases must, of necessity, expound and interpret that rule. If two laws conflict with each other, the Courts must decide on the operation of each. So, if a law be in opposition to the Constitution: if both the law and the Constitution apply to a particular case, so that the Court must either decide that case conformably to the law, disregarding the Constitution; or conformably to the Constitution, disregarding the law: the Court must determine which of these conflicting rules governs the case. This is of the very essence of judicial duty . . ."

—*Marbury v. Madison*, 1803

Word Helper
- **emphatically** = unmistakably; without a doubt
- **province** = area of responsibility
- **expound** = explain
- **in opposition to** = in disagreement with
- **conformably** = in agreement with
- **disregarding** = ignoring; paying no attention to
- **essence** = the very core; the most basic part

▶ Do you agree with John Marshall that the Supreme Court is the branch of government best suited to determine the constitutionality of laws? Write an editorial for a newspaper in 1803, in which you either support or attack his reasoning in *Marbury v. Madison*. An **editorial** is a type of newspaper article presenting an opinion on an issue.

▶ How did Marshall's reasoning in *Marbury v. Madison* make it difficult for his opponents in Congress to attack his decision?

▶ Why was this decision so important for later ones?

Main Events behind *Marbury v. Madison*

1787: Article III of the Constitution defines the "original jurisdiction" of the U.S. Supreme Court. These are situations in which the Court has immediate authority to take action.

1789: The first Congress passes the Judiciary Act of 1789, creating lower federal courts. The same act expands the "original jurisdiction" of the U.S. Supreme Court. It gives the Court the power to issue orders to federal officials.

1796: John Adams is elected second President of the United States.

June 6, 1800: John Marshall takes office as President Adams' Secretary of State.

October-December 1800: John Adams loses the Presidential election to Thomas Jefferson. Adams and Jefferson lead opposing political parties.

February 4, 1801: John Marshall becomes Chief Justice of the Supreme Court, while also remaining Secretary of State in the final month of Adams' Presidency.

March 2, 1801: Two days before he leaves office, President John Adams nominates William Marbury as a judge.

March 3, 1801: On Adams' last day in office, the Senate confirms Marbury's appointment. President Adams signs and Secretary of State John Marshall puts the seal of the United States on Marbury's commission (*a signed official document with the appointment*) along with 41 others. Marshall's brother James Marshall is unable to take all of the commissions for delivery. He fails to deliver the commission to Marbury and two other appointees.

March 4, 1801: Thomas Jefferson becomes President. He finds Marbury's undelivered commission on the table in the office of the Department of State.

March 5, 1801: Jefferson appoints James Madison as his Secretary of State. Jefferson and Madison refuse to deliver Marbury's commission.

December 16, 1801: Marbury writes to Madison that he will seek an order from the U.S. Supreme Court forcing Madison to deliver Marbury's commission.

December 17, 1801: Marbury applies to the Supreme Court for an order requiring Madison to deliver his commission. His application is based on the Court's power to issue such orders under the Judiciary Act of 1789.

February 24, 1803: Fourteen months later, Chief Justice Marshall issues his decision. Marshall rules that part of the Judiciary Act of 1789 is **unconstitutional**. Congress cannot expand the "original jurisdiction" of the Court, which is stated in the Constitution. This can only be changed by a constitutional amendment. Therefore, the Supreme Court has no power to issue orders to federal officials to perform their duties. This means the Court cannot order Madison to deliver the commission. In this decision, Marshall further explains that the Supreme Court must have the power to overturn any laws that it believes are in conflict with the Constitution. This is the power of **judicial review**.

▶ Based on his earlier involvement in Marbury's appointment, should Chief Justice Marshall have excused himself from ruling on the case?

▶ How did Marshall's decision expand the power of the Supreme Court?

A List of Landmark Supreme Court Cases

Judicial Review

▶ *Marbury v. Madison* (1803): In this case, the U.S. Supreme Court established its power of judicial review—the right to overturn laws it finds unconstitutional.

First Amendment – Free Speech

▶ *Tinker v. Des Moines Independent School District* (1969): Students in public schools have freedom of speech, and wearing an armband as a protest is a form of speech.

▶ *Hazelwood School District v. Kuhlmeier* (1988): School authorities can edit/censor school-supported student newspapers, consistent with their educational mission.

Second Amendment – Right to Bear Arms

▶ *District of Columbia v. Heller* (2008): The Second Amendment guarantees citizens the right to have guns for lawful purposes such as self-defense. Local governments can impose reasonable restrictions but they cannot totally ban handguns.

Rights of the Accused

▶ *Gideon v. Wainwright* (1963): Poor defendants charged with committing serious crimes have a right to be provided with free legal counsel.

▶ *Miranda v. Arizona* (1966): Police must inform suspects of their rights before questioning them. These rights include the right to remain silent and the right to have the assistance of an attorney.

▶ *In re Gault* (1967): Juveniles (those under 18) in juvenile law proceedings are entitled, just like adults, to reasonable "due process" rights when facing possible detention (*imprisonment*).

Racial Segregation

▶ *Plessy v. Ferguson* (1896): State segregation laws do not violate the Equal Protection Clause of the Fourteenth Amendment if the state offers "separate but equal" facilities to members of each race.

▶ *Brown v. Board of Education* (1954): Since separate schools are by their very nature unequal, segregation has "no place" in public education. This decision ended racially segregated schools.

The Presidency

▶ *United States v. Nixon* (1974): The Supreme Court denied President Nixon's claim of "executive privilege" and ordered Nixon to hand over White House tapes to investigators. The decision showed that the President of the United States is not above the rule of law. It led to President Nixon's resignation rather than face impeachment.

▶ *Bush v. Gore* (2000): The Supreme Court stopped a manual recount of votes in Florida in the 2000 Presidential election because there were no clear standards for the recount; the decision gave the votes to George W. Bush, making him the next President.

First Amendment Rights

As you learned in the last chapter, the First Amendment guarantees American citizens the right to free speech: "Congress shall make no law . . . abridging (limiting) the freedom of speech." But does this right extend to students?

Tinker v. Des Moines Independent School District (1969)

The Facts

In the 1960s, the United States was involved in an unpopular war in Vietnam. Americans were sharply divided. A group of junior high and high school students in Des Moines, Iowa, decided to show their opposition to the war by wearing black armbands to school. Their parents supported their protest. School officials feared a disruption and banned the wearing of armbands two days before the students had planned their demonstration. When the students still wore the armbands, school authorities suspended them from school until they returned without the armbands. Even though their protest was a silent, symbolic act rather than spoken words, the students claimed that the school authorities had violated their "free speech" rights under the First Amendment.

The Legal Issues

1. Do students have the right to free speech guaranteed in the First Amendment?
2. Was the wearing of armbands to school an exercise of "free speech"?

The Decision/Outcome

The Supreme Court ruled that the actions of school officials had indeed violated the students' First Amendment rights. First, the students were individuals entitled to the protections of the First Amendment. Students and teachers did not "shed their constitutional rights to freedom of speech or expression at the schoolhouse gate." The wearing of armbands was seen as an expression of the student's views on a public issue and therefore a form of "pure speech" entitled to the protections of the First Amendment. School officials had not shown that the wearing of armbands by the students had threatened such a disruption that the prohibition was necessary:

> "Clearly, the prohibition of (forbidding) expression of one particular opinion, at least without evidence that it is necessary to avoid material and substantial interference with schoolwork or discipline, is not constitutionally permissible. . . .
>
> In our system, state-operated schools may not be enclaves (areas) of totalitarianism (dictatorship). School officials do not possess absolute authority over their students. Students in school as well as out of school are 'persons' under our Constitution. They are possessed of fundamental (basic) rights. . . . In the absence of a specific showing of constitutionally valid reasons to regulate their speech, students are entitled to freedom of expression of their views."
>
> —*Tinker v. Des Moines*, 1969

Significance

The decision established that students were citizens entitled to the freedom of speech guaranteed by the First Amendment. Students do not lose their free speech rights just because they are in school.

Case Summary

Summarize the case by completing the paragraph frame below.

The Facts:
In the late 1960s, Americans were divided over the war in _____.
Mary Beth Tinker wore an armband to her public school to protest the war. School officials feared unrest and suspended her from school. Tinker sued the school for violating her right to free speech.

The Decision/Outcome:
The Supreme Court ruled that wearing an armband in protest was an exercise of the right to _____. It also ruled that even in public schools, students have _____.

Impact on Society:
The case was important because it established that _____
_____.

In *Tinker*, the Supreme Court held that "Students don't shed (*lose*) their constitutional rights at the schoolhouse gate." What do you think the Court meant by this comment? _____
_____.

Hazelwood School District v. Kuhlmeier (1988)

In the aftermath of *Tinker*, there was a flourishing (*thriving*) of student expression. Several lower courts ruled against censorship of school-sponsored student publications. **Censorship** refers to the revising of a publication (such as a magazine or book) by authorities before it is made public, or even a refusal to permit its publication at all. In *Kuhlmeier*, the U.S. Supreme Court defined some of the limits on students' free-speech rights.

The Facts

Students in a journalism class in Hazelwood East High School in Missouri published their own student newspaper. The school district paid for the printing as well as their academic adviser's salary. In 1983, the academic adviser showed the next issue to the school principal for approval. The principal objected to a story on teenage pregnancy in which student reporters had interviewed three pregnant students. The principal also objected to a story about divorce. The paper was printed without the two stories.

Cathy Kuhlmeier, the student editor of the newspaper, and the two student reporters sued the school district for violating their free speech rights. Their claims were upheld by the U.S. Court of Appeals for the Eighth Circuit.

The Legal Issue

Does the First Amendment protect school-sponsored publications from censorship by school authorities?

The Decision/Outcome

The Supreme Court reversed the ruling of the U.S. Court of Appeals.

According to the Supreme Court, the right to publish in a school-sponsored newspaper was not the same as the right to wear armbands in *Tinker*. In the case of school-sponsored activities, school officials have the right to exercise control "so long as their actions are reasonably related to legitimate pedagogical (*educational*) concerns." The situation was seen as different from *Tinker* because in this case the school was actually promoting the publication through its sponsorship: "A school need not tolerate student speech that is inconsistent with its basic educational mission, even though the government could not censor similar speech outside the school."

> **Word Helper**
> **legitimate pedagogical concerns** = valid educational concerns; concerns about teaching
> **tolerate** = permit; put up with
> **mission** = purpose; goal
> **inconsistent with** = in conflict with; in disagreement with
> **censor** = when officials examine and edit a writing, taking out any unacceptable parts, before it is published
> **contempt** = dislike; hatred

The Supreme Court concluded that school-sponsored student publications were *not* protected by the First Amendment. The school principal's refusal to publish the three articles thus did not violate the student's rights. Three of the Justices dissented from the majority opinion, arguing that it showed an "unthinking contempt for individual rights."

Significance

Kuhlmeier qualified some of the free speech rights given to students by *Tinker*. It stated that school officials could censor school-sponsored student publications so long as such restrictions served a valid educational purpose. In decisions since *Kuhlmeier*, the Supreme Court has further explained that "the constitutional rights of students in public school are not [the same as] the rights of adults in other settings." While students do not lose their rights when they enter school, "the nature of those rights is what is appropriate (*proper*) for children in school."

Case Summary

Summarize the facts of this case and the Court's decision in your own words.

_____
_____
_____
_____

The Active Citizen

▶ Imagine you are presenting oral argument before the U.S. Supreme Court for either of the parties in *Hazelwood v. Kuhlmeier*. What points would you emphasize?
▶ Complete the Venn diagram below.

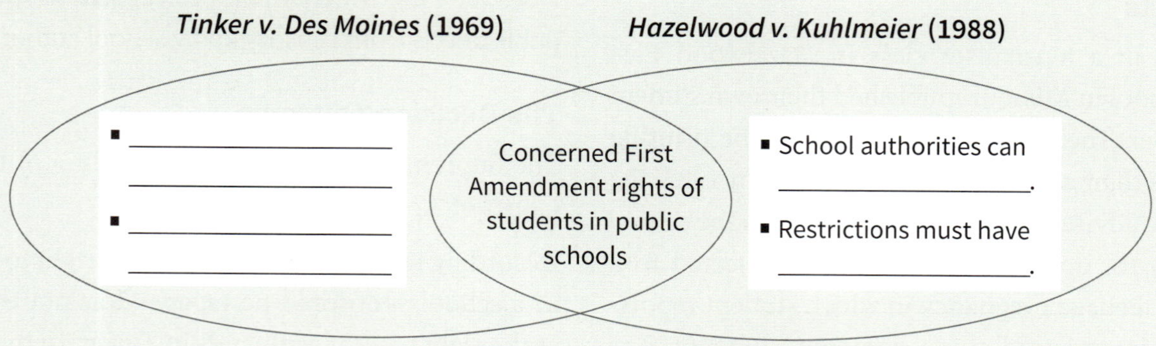

Tinker v. Des Moines (1969) — **Hazelwood v. Kuhlmeier (1988)**

- _____
- _____

Concerned First Amendment rights of students in public schools

- School authorities can _____.
- Restrictions must have _____.

234 | Chapter 10 | "May It Please the Court": The Supreme Court in Action

Second Amendment Rights

We occasionally learn of tragic assaults (*attacks*) against students by intruders with handguns and other dangerous weapons. Such events are often followed by demands for stricter gun control.

At the same time, the Second Amendment guarantees our right to "bear arms." How far should the right to buy and bear arms go? Does this constitutional right prevent local governments from banning certain types of guns?

District of Columbia v. Heller (2008)

In 1975, Washington, D.C., passed its Firearms Control Regulations Act. This law prohibited residents from registering or carrying handguns. In addition, all lawfully owned firearms had to be kept unloaded and disassembled (*taken apart*) or bound by a special trigger lock when in the owner's home. Richard Heller, a police officer, applied for a handgun permit for his home and was denied. He challenged the law in court.

The Legal Issue

Do local laws prohibiting handgun ownership violate Second Amendment rights to keep handguns and other firearms for private use in one's home?

The Decision/Outcome

The Second Amendment protects an individual's right to bear arms and to use those arms for lawful purposes, such as self-defense. The Supreme Court criticized Washington, D.C.'s total ban on handgun ownership in the home because it prohibited guns in the very place where they were most needed for the lawful defense of self, family, and property. Such a prohibition was therefore not permitted under the Second Amendment.

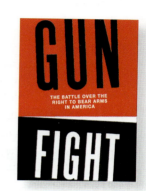

The Court also ruled against the city's requirement that all lawful firearms at home be disassembled or bound by a trigger lock. This requirement made it impossible for citizens to use arms quickly for the lawful purpose of defending themselves. The Court therefore held that this requirement was also unconstitutional.

Significance

The right to bear arms under the Second Amendment is an individual right closely tied to the right of self-defense. Based on the decision in *Heller*, local governments cannot totally ban handguns, although they can control licensing procedures and impose other reasonable requirements.

Case Summary

Summarize the facts of this case and the Court's decision in your own words. _____

_____

_____

What has been the impact of this decision on society? _____

_____

_____

Rights of the Accused

Several of the rights in the Bill of Rights protect those who have been accused of a crime. These safeguards serve two purposes:

1. They protect innocent persons who may be wrongfully accused; and
2. They protect us all from arbitrary (*dictatorial; unfair*) actions by the government.

Although the rights of the accused were established by the Bill of Rights, several Court decisions were needed to determine how these rights applied to specific situations.

Gideon v. Wainwright (1963)

The Facts

Clarence Gideon was arrested in Florida. He was accused of robbing the jukebox in a pool hall. A witness had seen Gideon walking from it with a bottle of wine and change in his pockets. Gideon faced a prison sentence but was too poor to afford a lawyer. He requested a lawyer but was told that, under the laws of Florida, the court would only pay for a lawyer if he faced the death penalty. Gideon defended himself and was sentenced to five-years imprisonment. From prison, Gideon appealed his case in a hand-written letter to the U.S. Supreme Court.

The Legal Issue

Does the Sixth Amendment require a court to provide legal counsel (*a lawyer*) to an indigent (*poor*) defendant accused of a felony (*a crime punishable with imprisonment of more than one year*)?

The Decision/Outcome

The U.S. Supreme Court heard Gideon's case. It then held that the government must provide a lawyer to anyone accused of a felony who is too poor to afford one. The right to a lawyer was a fundamental right, essential to a fair trial. The Sixth Amendment guaranteed this right, while the Fourteenth Amendment placed this requirement on state as well as federal courts. When he was tried again with the help of a lawyer, Gideon was acquitted (*found to be innocent*) and released.

Significance

Based on the decision in *Gideon*, states must now provide free lawyers to defendants charged with felonies who cannot pay for their own attorney. Public defenders, special court-appointed lawyers who are paid by the government, generally fill this role.

Case Summary

Summarize the facts of this case and the Court's decision in your own words. _____

_____

_____

What is your opinion? Should the rest of society have to pay for a lawyer to defend a poor person who may have actually committed a crime? _____

_____

_____

Miranda v. Arizona (1966)

The Fifth Amendment protects us from self-incrimination (*making a statement that incriminates ourselves*), and the Sixth Amendment guarantees a person accused of a serious crime the right to an attorney.

The Facts

In 1963, Ernesto Miranda was arrested in Arizona for kidnapping and rape. After two hours of police questioning, Miranda signed a confession (*a statement admitting he had committed the crime*).

However, Miranda was never told that he had the right to remain silent or to have a lawyer present during the questioning. Miranda was convicted and sentenced to 20 to 30 years imprisonment. Miranda appealed on the grounds that he had not been informed of his rights to remain silent or to see an attorney before he gave his confession.

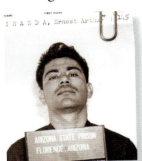

The Legal Issue

Can the police **interrogate** (*question*) a suspect without informing him of his rights to remain silent and to have a lawyer present?

The Decision/Outcome

The U.S. Supreme Court overturned Miranda's conviction on the grounds that Miranda had not been properly informed of his rights:

> *"The person in custody must, prior to interrogation, be clearly informed that he has the right to remain silent, and that anything he says will be used against him in court; he must be clearly informed that he has the right to consult with a lawyer and to have the lawyer with him during interrogation, and that, if he is indigent, a lawyer will be appointed to represent him...."*
>
> —*Miranda v. Arizona*, 1966

> **Word Helper**
>
> **custody** = under police control
> **interrogation** = questioning
> **to be informed** = to be told
> **to consult** = to discuss with; to get advice from
> **indigent** = poor

Significance

The rights established by the Supreme Court in this case are now referred to as "Miranda" rights. Police must state these rights before questioning a suspect; otherwise, any self-incriminating statements or confession cannot be used in court. These requirements reduce the risk that police treat suspects unfairly.

Miranda himself was retried and convicted a second time without the use of his confession. Miranda was released in 1972, but he was killed in a fight four years later.

> "You have the right to remain silent. Anything you say can and may be used against you in a court of law. You have the right to talk to a lawyer before we ask you questions. You also have the right to have a lawyer present during questioning. If you cannot afford a lawyer, you have the right to have one appointed at public expense."
>
> —Miranda rights

Case Summary

Summarize the facts of this case and the Court's decision in your own words.

Chapter 10 | "May It Please the Court": The Supreme Court in Action

In *Miranda*, the Court ruled that before the police question someone, the person must "be clearly informed that he has the right to remain silent, and that anything he says will be used against him in court." Explain, in your own words, what the Court meant. _____

_____

_____

Did the Court in *Miranda* make it too difficult for police to convict criminals? _____

_____

_____

In re Gault (1967)

States have different procedures and penalties for criminal offenses committed by minors (those under 18 years old) and by adults. *In re*, "in the matter of," is used in juvenile proceedings to indicate that there are no opposing parties as there are in adult criminal cases. **Juvenile** means having to do with minors.

In the 1960s, juvenile courts had no attorneys or juries. Decisions were made by juvenile court judges. The reasons for these differences were generally to protect children, to keep them from being branded as criminals, and to discourage them from becoming criminals. The existence of a separate juvenile justice system permitted some states, however, to act without fully respecting the rights of minors.

The Facts

Gerald Gault was 15 years old when he was accused of making an obscene telephone call to a neighbor. Gault was arrested and taken to a children's detention home. Gault's parents were away at work when he was arrested, and no notice was left for them.

A hearing was scheduled for the next day without notice and without sufficient time to prepare. The hearing was informal: Gault was questioned by a judge from the superior court acting as a juvenile judge. Gault denied making the obscene remarks. No witnesses were present at the hearing.

A second hearing was held the following week. The neighbor again did not appear for the hearing, and no transcript was made of either hearing. Gault never had the benefit of an attorney. Gault was convicted of making the obscene call and sentenced to a juvenile detention home until he was 21 years old—a period of six years. The maximum penalty for an adult making an obscene phone call at that time was only $50 and two months' imprisonment. Moreover, under Arizona law, a juvenile court order could not be appealed.

To release their son, the parents petitioned for a *writ of habeas corpus* (a special court procedure for the release of someone unjustly imprisoned). Their petition was denied by the Arizona Supreme Court on the grounds that the procedures applied to Gault's case had met "due process" requirements.

Legal Issue

What "due process" rights are owed to a **juvenile** (*a minor*) facing a possible loss of liberty?

The Decision/Outcome

The U.S. Supreme Court overturned the decision by an 8 to 1 vote. While there are good reasons for treating juveniles and adults differently, the Court held that juveniles were still entitled to all reasonable "due process" rights when facing possible detention (*imprisonment*).

These "due process" rights include: (1) timely notice of criminal charges; (2) the right to face and question witnesses; (3) the right against self-incrimination; (4) the right to counsel (*an attorney*); (5) the right to a transcript (*typed record*) of the proceedings; and (6) the right to appellate review. Gerald Galt had been denied all of these rights.

> "Due process of law is the primary and indispensable foundation of individual freedom. It is the basic and essential term in the social compact which defines the rights of the individual...."

Word Helper

due process of law = the right to a fair, public and just procedure
primary = main; most important
indispensable = something we cannot do without
social compact = social contract; agreement to form a community

The Supreme Court considered how Gault would have been treated if he had been tried as an adult instead of as a juvenile. It began with the fact that his maximum punishment would have been far less:

> The essential difference between Gerald's case and a normal criminal case is that safeguards available to adults were discarded in Gerald's case. The summary procedure as well as the long commitment was possible because Gerald was 15 years of age instead of over 18. If Gerald had been over 18, he would not have been subject to Juvenile Court proceedings. For the particular offense immediately involved, the maximum punishment would have been a fine of $5 to $50, or imprisonment in jail for not more than two months. Instead, he was committed to custody for a maximum of six years.

discarded = thrown out
summary procedure = shortened procedure
long commitment = long imprisonment
maximum = the greatest amount
committed to custody = imprisoned; put under the control of authorities

The Court continued by listing the many "due process" rights that Gault would have enjoyed as an adult:

> If he had been over 18 and had committed an offense to which such a sentence might apply, he would have been entitled to [important] rights under the Constitution of the United States as well as under Arizona's laws and constitution. The United States Constitution would guarantee him rights and protections with respect to arrest, search and seizure, and pretrial [questioning]. It would [give him] specific notice of the charges and adequate time to ... prepare his defense. He would be entitled to clear advice that he could be represented by counsel, and, at least if a felony were involved, the State would be required to provide counsel if his parents were unable to afford it.... If the case went to trial, confrontation and opportunity for cross-examination would be guaranteed.

offense = crime
sentence = punishment given by a court
specific notice of the charges = provide specific information about what one is accused of
adequate time = enough time
be entitled to = have a right to
felony = a crime punishable by imprisonment for more than one year
confrontation = facing accusers
cross-examination = questioning of opposing witnesses

All of these "due process" rights had been denied to Gault. Instead, special procedures that were supposed to protect juveniles from the harshness of adult courts had in fact been abused.

Although Arizona claimed its juvenile law system was designed to protect minors accused of a crime, the U.S. Supreme Court found the very opposite to be true:

> So wide a gulf between the State's treatment of the adult and of the child requires a bridge sturdier than mere verbiage, and reasons more persuasive than cliché can provide."
>
> —*In re Gault*, 1967

gulf = divide; space between
sturdier = stronger; more sturdy
mere verbiage = words and nothing else
cliché = an overused phrase or saying

Chapter 10 | "May It Please the Court": The Supreme Court in Action

Significance

As a result of Gault's case, state juvenile justice systems must now provide minors with the "due process" rights guaranteed by the Constitution and listed in the Court's decision. These rights are known as juvenile rights.

Case Summary

Summarize the facts of this case and the Court's decision in your own words. _____

_____

_____

What was the impact of this decision on American society? _____

_____

_____

Racial Segregation and "Equal Protection"

One of the most important issues ever to face American courts has been that of racial segregation—the separation of people by race. Following the Civil War and period of Reconstruction, Southern states passed "Jim Crow" laws imposing racial segregation on public places, such as trains, buses, parks and schools. These laws required African Americans to use different facilities than whites did.

Yet the Fourteenth Amendment had promised all American citizens the "equal protection of the laws."

White Southerners argued that so long as the facilities offered to African Americans were "separate but equal," the requirements of the Fourteenth Amendment were satisfied.

In the following two cases, you will see how the Supreme Court's views on the meaning of "equal protection" under the Fourteenth Amendment have shifted over time. These two court cases were among the most influential in all of American history.

Plessy v. Ferguson (1896)

The Facts

In 1890, Louisiana passed a "Jim Crow" law requiring railroad companies to "provide equal but separate" passenger cars to members of different races. Opponents of segregation persuaded Homer Plessy, who was one-eighth African American and appeared to be white, to challenge this law. Plessy sat in a railroad passenger car reserved for whites. He told the conductor of his mixed ancestry and was arrested. He fought this case all the way up to the U.S. Supreme Court.

The Legal Issue

Can a state impose racial segregation by offering "separate-but-equal" facilities, without violating the Equal Protection Clause of the Fourteenth Amendment?

The Decision/Outcome

The U.S. Supreme Court saw nothing in the Louisiana law itself that stated that some races were inferior (*below; not as good as*) to others. Therefore, the separation of races it required did not violate the Equal Protection

240 Chapter 10 | "May It Please the Court": The Supreme Court in Action

Clause of the Fourteenth Amendment. If African Americans or others chose to see themselves as inferior, the Court said, this had nothing to do with the law itself. The law merely separated these races without indicating that either one of them was superior or inferior.

"We cannot say that a law which requires the separation of two races is unreasonable. We consider the [error] of [Plessy's] argument to consist in the assumption that the enforced separation of the two races stamps the colored race with a badge of inferiority. If this be so, it is not by reason of anything found in the act, but solely because the colored race chooses to put that construction upon it. . . .

When the government … has secured to each of its citizens equal rights before the law, and equal opportunities for improvement and progress, it has accomplished the end for which it was organized, and performed all of the functions respecting social advantages with which it is endowed …

If the civil and political rights of both races be equal, one cannot be inferior to the other civilly or politically. If one race be inferior to the other socially, the constitution of the United States cannot put them upon the same plane."

—*Plessy v. Ferguson*, 1896

> **Word Helper**
> *assumption* = belief
> *inferior* = of lesser quality
> *badge of inferiority* = sign or mark of lesser quality
> *construction* = interpretation
> *secured* = obtained
> *end* = purpose; goal
> *functions* = tasks; responsibilities
> *respecting* = having to do with
> *endowed* = given
> *same plane* = same level

Significance

In *Plessy v. Ferguson*, the U.S. Supreme Court upheld the constitutionality of state segregation laws, so long as the facilities offered to each race were of "equal standards." This became known as the "separate-but-equal" doctrine. In *Plessy*, the Court held that such segregation did not violate the Equal Protection Clause of the Fourteenth Amendment. As a result of this decision, states across the South strengthened their segregation laws.

Case Summary

Summarize the facts of this case and the Court's decision in your own words. _____

What was the impact of this decision on American society between 1896 and 1954? _____

Chapter 10 | "May It Please the Court": The Supreme Court in Action

Brown v. Board of Education (1954)

For the next 50 years after *Plessy v. Ferguson*, white and African-American children continued to attend separate public schools across the South.

Starting in the 1930s, African-American lawyers at the National Association for the Advancement of Colored People, or "NAACP," began challenging the "separate-but-equal" doctrine in public education. They launched an ambitious strategy by filing a series of lawsuits challenging state laws.

The Facts

Linda Brown was a schoolgirl in Topeka, Kansas. Her father sued the local school board because Linda was forced to attend an all-black school when an all-white school was closer to their home. Brown lost the case in state court. In 1953, the NAACP appealed Linda Brown's case along with a number of others to the U.S. Supreme Court.

The Legal Issue

Did racial segregation in public schools violate the Equal Protection Clause of the Fourteenth Amendment?

The NAACP's Legal Argument

Thurgood Marshall, the NAACP lawyer handling the case, did not argue that the facilities given to African-American children were inferior (although this was generally the case). Instead, he argued that the system of segregated education was, by its very nature, unequal because it sent a psychological message to African-American children that they were not "good enough" to be taught with whites.

Marshall supported his argument with the findings of an African-American psychologist, Dr. Kenneth Clark. Clark showed white and black dolls to young African-American children and found that these children preferred the white dolls to black ones. Clark concluded that the system of racial segregation had led to this painful sense of inferiority. It denied these children "equal protection."

The Decision/Outcome

Earl Warren, a former Governor, had only just been appointed as Chief Justice of the Supreme Court. Warren wanted to avoid a divided decision. With great effort, he obtained the support of all nine Justices. They were persuaded in part by Thurgood Marshall's reasoning. Warren wrote the Court's unanimous opinion, which declared racial segregation in public schools to be a violation of the Fourteenth Amendment:

> "Does segregation of children in public schools solely on the basis of race, even though the physical facilities and other 'tangible' factors may be equal, deprive the children of the minority group of equal educational opportunities? We believe that it does. . . . Segregation of white and colored children in public schools has a detrimental effect upon the colored children. The impact is greater when it has the sanction of the law, for the policy of separating the races is usually interpreted as denoting the inferiority of the [African-American] group. A sense of inferiority affects the motivation of a child to learn. . . .
>
> We conclude that, in the field of public education, the doctrine of 'separate but equal' has no place. Separate educational facilities are inherently unequal."
>
> —*Brown v. Board of Education*, 1954

Word Helper

solely = only
tangible = things you can touch; physical
deprive = deny; keep from having
detrimental = harmful
sanction = blessing; approval
denoting = meaning
affects = influences
motivation = desire; willingness
doctrine = principle; belief
inherently = see *The Active Citizen* at the top of the next page

The Active Citizen

▶ Look up the word "inherent" in the dictionary. Why did Chief Justice Earl Warren conclude that segregated schools were "inherently" unequal? Why did this mean that "in the field of public education, the doctrine of 'separate but equal' has no place"? How was this conclusion important to the Supreme Court's judgment?

Significance

The *Brown* decision had an enormous impact. It required the entire system of public education in the South to change. Southern Senators in Congress immediately signed a public protest against the *Brown* decision. Local officials across the South swore they would never enforce it. Violence in the South increased.

Southern resistance required the U.S. Supreme Court to make a separate ruling on how the *Brown* decision was to be carried out a year later. Enforcement of the *Brown* decision was handed over to the lower federal courts, which were to see that local school districts carried out the desegregation order "with all deliberate speed."

The *Brown* decision would take many years to carry out. As a result of the *Brown* decision, the first steps were taken towards ending racial segregation in the South and creating the more equal, multicultural society we enjoy today.

Case Summary

Summarize the facts of this case and the Court's decision in your own words.

_____

_____

_____

What was the impact of the *Brown* decision on American society? _____

_____

_____

The Active Citizen

▶ Complete the Venn diagram below comparing the two decisions, *Plessy* and *Brown*. How would you account for the differences in outcome?

Plessy v. Ferguson (1896)   **Brown v. Board of Education** (1954)

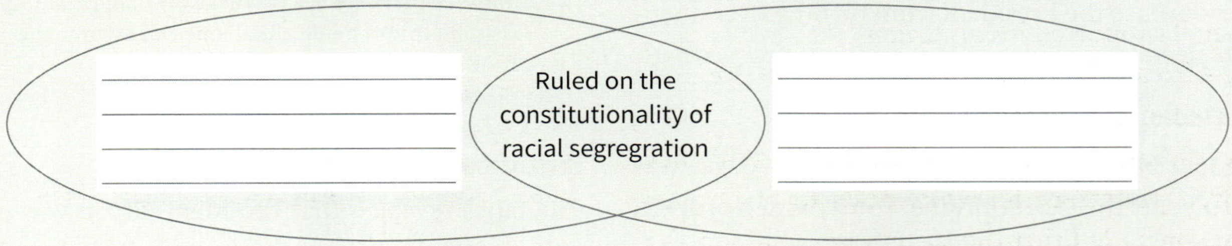

(Venn diagram: center overlap reads "Ruled on the constitutionality of racial segregation")

Continues ▶

Chapter 10 | "May It Please the Court": The Supreme Court in Action

- Imagine you are presenting oral argument to the Supreme Court in the case of *Brown v. Board of Education*. Which points would you emphasize?
- Prepare an oral presentation, PowerPoint or Prezi presentation, or video on the impact of either of these two decisions on American society.

The Presidency

The Supreme Court has only occasionally ruled on questions of Presidential power. In the next two cases, the Court ruled on whether "executive privilege" allowed a President to avoid handing over documents in a criminal investigation, and whether an inconsistent recount of votes could be permitted in the most closely contested Presidential election in U.S. history.

United States v. Nixon (1974)

The Facts

During the Presidential election campaign of 1972, a group of former government agents broke into Democratic Party headquarters in the Watergate Hotel and office complex in downtown Washington, D.C. President Nixon, a Republican, tried to protect these agents from investigation by claiming that they were acting for national security. At Congressional hearings, it was revealed that Nixon had taped all his conversations in the White House. Nixon refused to hand over the tapes to investigators, claiming that as President of the United States, he was entitled to "executive privilege."

"A President and those who assist him must be free to explore alternatives in the process of shaping policies and making decisions, and to do so in a way many would be unwilling to express except privately. These are the considerations justifying a presumptive privilege for Presidential communications. . . . But this presumptive privilege must be considered in light of our historic commitment to the rule of law . . . To ensure that justice is done, it is imperative to the function of courts that compulsory process be available for the production of evidence needed either by the prosecution or by the defense."

—*United States v. Nixon*, 1974

The Legal Issue

Does "executive privilege"—the need of the President of the United States for privacy and confidentiality in making high-level decisions of national importance—excuse the President from turning over documents needed as evidence in a criminal proceeding?

> **Word Helper**
> *alternatives* = options; other choices
> *compulsory process* = ability of the courts to give orders
> *production of evidence* = handing over of documents; appearance of witnesses
> *presumptive privilege* = a privilege one can presume exists; all things being equal, one can assume the President has this privilege

The Decision/Outcome

President Nixon's claim of "executive privilege" was overruled by the U.S. Supreme Court, which ordered the President to hand over the tapes.

Significance

The tapes revealed that President Nixon was indeed behind the Watergate "cover-up." President Nixon resigned rather than face impeachment. The decision proved that even the President of the United States is not above the "rule of law."

Case Summary

Summarize this case by completing the paragraph frame below.

In 1972, Richard Nixon faced re-election as President. A special unit in the White House was created to conduct secret investigations. Members of this unit broke into the headquarters of the _____ Party at the Watergate Hotel to spy on their campaign activities.

When they were caught and arrested by police, President Nixon tried to cover up their ties to the _____. White House officials told the FBI not to investigate the break-in. The White House secretly tried to pay the arrested men to lie about their connections.

A special independent prosecutor was appointed to investigate the break-in. Congress also conducted its own investigation. A former member of Nixon's staff told a Congressional committee that the President had _____.

President Nixon denied this.

The same staff member next revealed that Nixon had taped all his White House conversations. Congress and the special prosecutor demanded to listen to these tapes. Nixon refused to hand over the tapes, claiming "executive privilege." By this he meant the right of the President to _____ _____.

The demand for the tapes reached the U.S. Supreme Court. The Court weighed the President's need for freedom in making decisions of national importance with the needs of investigators for evidence in a criminal proceeding. In the end, the Court ordered President Nixon to hand over the tapes. These proved that he was lying all along. Nixon resigned the Presidency rather than face impeachment.

The great significance of the decision was that it showed that even the President is not above the _____. This is an essential part of our legal system, in which all citizens alike live under the rule of _____.

The Active Citizen

▶ In *United States v. Nixon*, did the U.S. Supreme Court strike the right balance between the needs of the executive and judicial branches? Or did their decision upset the traditional separation of powers? Write a short essay of two to three paragraphs giving your views on whether the Supreme Court was right in ordering President Nixon to turn over his tapes.

Bush v. Gore (2000)

The Facts

In 2000, Americans experienced the closest Presidential contest in their history. When Americans went to bed that election night, it was still unclear who their next President would be. In the end, the election hinged on which candidate—Vice President Al Gore or Texas Governor George W. Bush—had won Florida's electoral votes.

The award of Florida's votes was delayed because of errors that had been made in the voting and counting of votes, especially on many paper ballots. A recount was started in some districts because of disputed votes. George W. Bush filed to stop the recount. The Florida Supreme Court ruled against Bush, and ordered a count by hand of all the ballots in the state. However, there were no uniform standards for determining when a ballot would be counted and when it should be rejected. Moreover, such a count could not have been completed before Florida was required to report its vote to the Electoral College. Bush filed a petition with the U.S. Supreme Court to halt the recount.

The Legal Issue

Did the lack of standards for a manual recount (*recount by hand*) of the vote violate the Equal Protection Clause of the Fourteenth Amendment?

The Decision/Outcome

The Supreme Court was sharply divided. By a 5 to 4 vote, it halted the recount because of the absence of uniform standards and the fact that legally questionable votes might have been included in the recount.

The Court was sensitive to the fact that it was sharply divided and also interfering with the people's selection of their next President. The majority opinion pointed out that seven of the Justices agreed that a manual recount in Florida would have been full of problems:

> "Seven Justices of the Court agree that there are constitutional problems with the recount ordered by the Florida Supreme Court that demand a remedy.... The only disagreement is as to the remedy.... None are more conscious of the vital limits on judicial authority than are the members of this Court, and none stand more in admiration of the Constitution's design to leave the selection of the President to the people, through their legislatures, and to the political sphere. When contending parties invoke the process of the courts, however, it becomes our unsought responsibility to resolve the federal and constitutional issues the judicial system has been forced to confront."
>
> —*Bush v. Gore*, 2000

Word Helper

recount = counting the votes again
remedy = solution to a problem; cure; fix
conscious = aware
political sphere = area left to politics
contending parties = opposing parties
invoke = call on; appeal to
unsought responsibility = a responsibility the Court did not seek or want

The dissenting Justices felt that the recount could have been properly handled by the Florida courts, and that denying this fact was an attack on the judiciary itself:

> "Although we may never know with complete certainty the identity of the winner of this year's Presidential election, the identity of the loser is perfectly clear. It is the Nation's confidence in the judge as an impartial guardian of the rule of law."
>
> —*Justice J.P. Stevens, Dissenting Opinion, Bush v. Gore*, 2000

Significance

In *Bush v. Gore* (2000), the U.S. Supreme Court halted the recount of manual votes in Florida. As a result, George W. Bush won Florida's electoral votes and became the next President, even though his opponent, Al Gore, had received a larger share of the nation's popular vote.

Case Summary

Summarize the facts of this case and the Court's decision in your own words.

_____
_____
_____
_____

Why did the dissenting Justices argue that the real "loser" in the majority opinion was the "nation's confidence in the judge as an impartial guardian of the rule of law"?

_____
_____
_____
_____

The Active Citizen

In the 2000 Presidential election, it was clear that if the manual recount of votes in Florida were stopped, candidate George W. Bush would become the next President. If the manual count continued, it was less clear who the winner might be. If the U.S. Supreme Court Justices had voted in the election, could they consider themselves as impartial, disinterested parties? What about the Justices of the Florida Supreme Court? Were these courts therefore wrong to intervene in the electoral process? Did they have a choice once both candidates sought court action to resolve the dispute? Hold a class discussion on whether the Florida state court system and the U.S. Supreme Court should have become involved in this dispute.

Enrichment | ## Other Supreme Court Cases

In addition to the issues above, the U.S. Supreme Court has ruled on many other matters. These include:

- ▶ The Rights of Students
- ▶ Political Campaign Contributions
- ▶ Privacy Rights
- ▶ Individual Rights in Wartime
- ▶ The Powers of the Federal Government
- ▶ Freedom of Speech
- ▶ Legislative Representation
- ▶ Freedom of Religion

Chapter 10 | "May It Please the Court": The Supreme Court in Action

The Active Citizen

Enrichment

▶ Your teacher should divide your class into groups. Each group should select one of these topics and research two cases in that area. For each case, they should investigate the background facts, the legal issues, the reasoning of the Supreme Court, the Court's decision, and the significance of the case. Then each group should make an oral presentation, a PowerPoint or Prezi presentation, or a video to share what they have learned with the rest of the class.

▶ Turn your classroom into the U.S. Supreme Court! Select one of the cases discussed in this chapter. Your teacher should appoint nine students to act as the Justices of the U.S. Supreme Court, and should appoint a group of students to represent the team of attorneys on each side of the case. Attorneys from each team should take turns in representing their case before the Justices, while the Justices should ask penetrating questions during oral argument. Then the Justices should confer among themselves to see if they reach the same decision that the Supreme Court did in the actual case, and briefly present their "majority opinion" to the class. Finally, the rest of the class should complete a questionnaire evaluating how well each of the participants performed his or her part.

How well can you recognize these excerpts from several of the most famous decisions of the U.S. Supreme Court?

> "First Amendment rights, applied in light of the special characteristics of the school environment, are available to teachers and students. It can hardly be argued that either students or teachers shed their constitutional rights to freedom of speech or expression at the schoolhouse gate."

▶ From which decision is this excerpt taken? _____

▶ Which clues helped you to identify this case? _____

_____

_____

> "So wide a gulf between the State's treatment of the adult and of the child requires a bridge sturdier than mere verbiage, and reasons more persuasive than cliché can provide."

▶ From which decision is this excerpt taken? _____

▶ Which clues helped you to identify this case? _____

_____

_____

> "The person in custody must, prior to interrogation, be clearly informed that he has the right to remain silent, and that anything he says will be used against him in court; he must be clearly informed that he has the right to consult with a lawyer and to have the lawyer with him during interrogation, and that, if he is indigent, a lawyer will be appointed to represent him."

▶ From which decision is this excerpt taken? _____

▶ Which clues helped you to identify this case? _____

_____

_____

> "We cannot say that a law which requires the separation of two races is unreasonable. . . . If the civil and political rights of both races be equal, one cannot be inferior to the other civilly or politically."

▶ From which decision is this excerpt taken? _____

▶ Which clues helped you to identify this case? _____

_____

_____

> "We conclude that, in the field of public education, the doctrine of 'separate but equal' has no place. Separate educational facilities are inherently unequal."

▶ From which decision is this excerpt taken? _____

▶ Which clues helped you to identify this case? _____

_____

_____

> "These are the considerations justifying a presumptive privilege for Presidential communications . . . But this presumptive privilege must be considered in light of our historic commitment to the rule of law . . . To ensure that justice is done, it is imperative to the function of courts that compulsory process be available for the production of evidence."

▶ From which decision is this excerpt taken? _____

▶ Which clues helped you to identify this case? _____

_____

_____

Chapter 10 | "May It Please the Court": The Supreme Court in Action

Name _____

Complete the chart below and on the following pages.

Case	Background Facts	Legal Issue(s)	Decision/Outcome	Significance
Marbury v. Madison (1803)				
Tinker v. Des Moines (1969)				
Hazelwood v. Kuhlmeier (1988)				

Chapter 10 | "May It Please the Court": The Supreme Court in Action

Name _____

Case	Background Facts	Legal Issue(s)	Decision/Outcome	Significance
District of Columbia v. Heller (2008)				
Gideon v. Wainwright (1963)				
Miranda v. Arizona (1966)				
In re Gault (1967)				

Name _____

Case	Background Facts	Legal Issue(s)	Decision/Outcome	Significance
Plessy v. Ferguson (1896)				
Brown v. Board of Education (1954)				
United States v. Nixon (1974)				
Bush v. Gore (2000)				

Name _____

Imagine you are making an argument before the U.S. Supreme Court for one of the cases that you read about in this chapter.

Name of case: _____

Mr. Chief Justice and may it please the Court.

I come today representing _____.

We believe that _____

_____

_____

_____

_____

_____

_____

_____

In conclusion, we firmly believe that the Court should rule that _____

_____

_____

_____

because _____

_____

_____

_____

Thank you for this opportunity to appear before the Court.

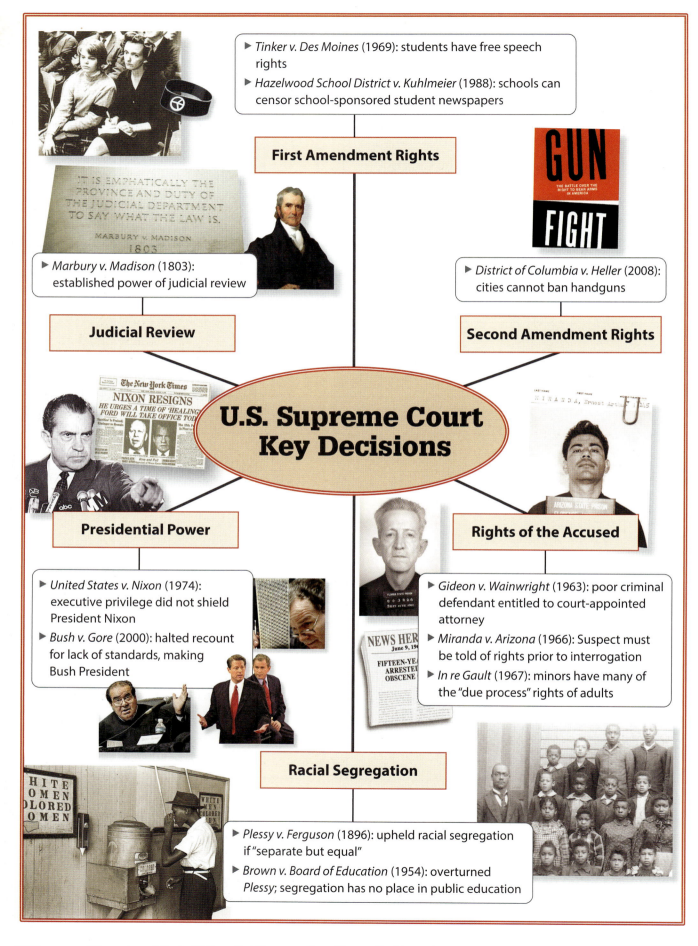

Review Cards: The Supreme Court in Action

Judicial Review

The Supreme Court is the final authority in interpreting the Constitution. It interprets and protects constitutional rights, especially those in the Bill of Rights and the Fourteenth Amendment.

Marbury v. Madison (1803)
- **Facts:** William Marbury sued the Secretary of State, James Madison, for failing to deliver his commission.
- Marbury filed his suit directly with the Supreme Court so that it would order Madison to send the commission. In the Judiciary Act of 1789, Congress had given the Supreme Court the power to issue such orders (*writs of mandamus*).
- **Issues:** (1) Should the Supreme Court issue a court order to Madison, as Secretary of State, requiring him to deliver the commission to William Marbury? (2) Can the Supreme Court rule on the constitutionality of a law passed by Congress?
- **Decision/Outcome:** Chief Justice John Marshall believed that Marbury was entitled to his commission. However, the Supreme Court did not have the power to order its delivery. The Constitution had defined the "original jurisdiction" of the Supreme Court, and Congress had no power to enlarge it. The section of the Judiciary Act giving the Court the power to issue *writs of mandamus* thus conflicted with the Constitution.
- The Court had the duty of interpreting the law, and where it saw that a law was in conflict with the Constitution, the law was invalid. The Court's power to overturn laws it views as unconstitutional is known as **judicial review**.
- **Significance:** The case established the Court's power of judicial review.

First Amendment Rights (Free Speech)

Are students entitled to the same "free speech" rights as adults?

Tinker v. Des Moines Independent School District (1969)
- **Facts:** Students were sent home and suspended from school for wearing black armbands, which they were wearing as a protest against the Vietnam War. Students claimed the school violated their First Amendment right to free speech.
- **Issues:** (1) Do students have the right to "free speech" guaranteed in the First Amendment? (2) Was the wearing of armbands to school an exercise of "free speech"?
- **Decision/Outcome:** The Supreme Court ruled that First Amendment rights applied to students, and that the wearing of armbands was a form of symbolic speech that the First Amendment protected.
- **Significance:** The case made it clear that students had free speech rights.

Hazelwood School District v. Kuhlmeier (1988)
- **Facts:** Two articles in a school-sponsored student newspaper were censored by the school principal. The students claimed this violated their First Amendment rights.
- **Issue:** Does the First Amendment protect school-sponsored publications from censorship by school authorities?
- **Decision/Outcome:** The Supreme Court ruled that schools have the right to censor speech in activities they sponsor (*pay for*), if the restrictions are for valid educational purposes.
- **Significance:** *Kuhlmeier* restricted the *Tinker* ruling by allowing censorship in this case. It gave school officials the right to limit student speech in some circumstances.

Chapter 10 | "May It Please the Court": The Supreme Court in Action

Second Amendment Rights (The Right to Bear Arms)

District of Columbia v. Heller (2008)
- **Facts:** Policeman Richard Heller claimed that a local law prohibiting residents from owning handguns violated his Second Amendment rights.
- **Issue:** Do local laws prohibiting handgun ownership violate the Second Amendment?
- **Decision/Outcome:** The Supreme Court ruled that the Second Amendment applied to guns kept at home for family protection. The amendment guarantees the right to have firearms for self-defense. Local governments therefore had no power to ban handguns, although they could set limitations.
- **Significance:** States cannot prohibit handgun ownership, although they can set reasonable restrictions.

Fifth and Sixth Amendment Rights (Rights of the Accused)

Several rights in the Bill of Rights protect the accused. This is to protect innocent people who have been wrongfully accused of a crime, and to guard against government abuse.

Gideon v. Wainwright (1963)
- **Facts:** Clarence Gideon, a poor defendant, was accused of robbery. He asked the court to provide him with a free lawyer, but was refused. At the time, Florida only provided a free lawyer in capital (*death penalty*) cases.
- **Issue:** Does the **Sixth Amendment** require a court to provide **counsel** (*a lawyer*) to a poor defendant accused of a **felony** (*a crime punishable with imprisonment of one year or more*)?
- **Decision/Outcome:** The Supreme Court ruled that the Sixth Amendment guarantees the right to a lawyer. Governments are therefore required to provide one to defendants too poor to afford one if they are charged with a felony.
- **Significance:** States now offer poor defendants the services of a public defender.

Miranda v. Arizona (1966)
- **Facts:** Ernesto Miranda was convicted for kidnapping and rape after he confessed during police interrogation. He appealed the case because he had not been informed of his Fifth and Sixth Amendment rights to remain silent and to have a lawyer present before his confession.
- **Issue:** Can the police **interrogate** (*question*) a suspect without informing him of his rights to remain silent or to have a lawyer present?
- **Decision/Outcome:** The Supreme Court ruled that suspects must always be informed of their Fifth and Sixth Amendment rights before interrogation; otherwise their confession cannot be used in court.
- **Significance:** Police now must read suspects their "Miranda" rights.

In re Gault (1967)
- **Facts:** Gerald Gault's parents appealed a case where a juvenile court had denied Gault's "due process" rights and given him an unjustly harsh penalty. He was accused of making a single obscene call to a neighbor, which he denied. He was sent away to a juvenile home with no right of appeal. Gault was given no advance notice of his hearing, faced no witnesses, had no lawyer, had no transcript of the hearing, and had no right of appeal. The maximum penalty for an adult was 2 months, yet he was sent away for 6 years.
- **Issue:** What "due process" rights are owed to a **juvenile** (*a minor*) facing a possible loss of liberty?
- **Decision/Outcome:** The Supreme Court ruled that although juvenile courts should have different procedures than adult courts, normal "due process" rights still applied to minors.
- **Significance:** Because of *In re Gault*, states reformed their juvenile justice procedures.

Fourteenth Amendment Rights (Racial Segregation and "Equal Protection")

These two cases, for and against segregation, are among the most influential in U.S. history.

Plessy v. Ferguson (1896)

- **Facts:** An African-American man, Homer Plessy, appealed his arrest for ignoring Louisiana's "Jim Crow" **segregation** laws by sitting in the "whites only" passenger car of a train. Plessy himself was seven-eighths white.
- **Issue:** Can a state impose racial segregation by offering "separate-but-equal" facilities, without violating the Equal Protection Clause of the Fourteenth Amendment?
- **Decision/Outcome:** The Supreme Court ruled against Plessy: it held that racial segregation did *not* violate the **Fourteenth Amendment's** right to "equal protection," so long as the facilities provided to each race were "**separate but equal**." The Louisiana law itself, said the Court, did not say that one race was either superior or inferior to the other.
- **Significance:** As a result, segregation laws were further strengthened across the South.

Brown v. Board of Education (1954)

- **Facts:** The **NAACP** (National Association for the Advancement of Colored People) appealed a case in which an African-American girl, Linda Brown, was forced to attend a segregated, African-American public school when a white school was closer to her home.
- **Issue:** Does racial segregation in public schools violate the Equal Protection Clause of the Fourteenth Amendment?
- **NAACP's Legal Argument: Thurgood Marshall**, the NAACP lawyer, argued that segregated education sent young African-American children the message that they were inferior to whites. Psychologist Dr. Clark supported this claim with a study in which African-American children preferred white dolls. Therefore racial segregation in public schools was "inherently unequal."
- **Decision/Outcome:** Chief Justice Earl Warren wrote the unanimous Court decision: racially segregated public schools violated the Fourteenth Amendment because they made African-American children feel inferior, not equal.
- **Significance:** The Supreme Court ruled that the lower federal courts should enforce the decision "with all deliberate speed." Though it took many years, the *Brown* decision was the first step toward ending racial segregation in the South. It led to a transformation of American society.

Before *Brown v. Board of Education*

After *Brown v. Board of Education*

Presidential Power

Despite the separation of powers, the Supreme Court has occasionally ruled on issues concerning Presidential power.

United States v. Nixon (1974)

▸ **Facts:** In 1973, a group was caught breaking into Democratic headquarters in the Watergate Hotel and office complex. Journalists and Congressional hearings gradually learned that the White House might be involved. They also discovered that President Nixon had taped all his White House conversations. Nixon claimed he had "executive privilege" and refused to hand over tapes of White House conversations to investigators.

▸ **Issue:** Does "executive privilege"—the need of the President of the United States for privacy and confidentiality in making high-level, national decisions—excuse the President from turning over documents needed as evidence in a criminal proceeding?

▸ **Decision/Outcome:** The Supreme Court ruled that "executive privilege" did not justify withholding the tapes in these circumstances. The President was ordered to hand over the tapes.

▸ **Significance:** The tapes were handed over and President Nixon was implicated in the Watergate scandal. Nixon resigned rather than be impeached. The decision emphasized that even the President is not above the rule of law.

Bush v. Gore (2000)

▸ **Facts:** In November 2000, the Presidential election between candidates George W. Bush and Al Gore was extremely close. The outcome depended on which candidate won Florida's electoral votes. Florida election officials were ready to certify Bush as the winner, but there had been significant irregularities in voting practices and the counting of ballots. The Florida Supreme Court ordered a manual recount. Bush filed a petition with the U.S. Supreme Court to halt the recount because of a lack of uniform standards.

▸ **Issue:** Did the lack of standards for a manual recount of voters' ballots violate the Equal Protection Clause of the Fourteenth Amendment?

▸ **Decision/Outcome:** A sharply divided U.S. Supreme Court ruled (5 to 4) that the lack of standards and possibility of illegal votes violated the Equal Protection Clause. It halted the recount.

▸ **Significance:** As a result of this decision, George W. Bush won the Presidential election.

What Do You Know?

SS.7.C.3.12

1. What was the significance of the U.S. Supreme Court decision in *Marbury v. Madison* (1803)?
    A. It gave the Court the power to mediate disputes between different states.
    B. It gave the Court original jurisdiction in disputes involving foreign governments.
    C. It established the power of the Court to declare an act of Congress unconstitutional.
    D. It established the right of the Court to advise Congress in advance on the validity of proposed laws.

SS.7.C.3.12

2. The passage below is from the 1969 U.S. Supreme Court decision in *Tinker v. Des Moines.*

    > *Clearly, the prohibition of expression of one particular opinion, at least without evidence that it is necessary to avoid material and substantial interference with schoolwork or discipline, is not constitutionally permissible.*

    What did the Court conclude on the basis of this reasoning?
    A. School authorities could censor school-sponsored publications.
    B. Students were entitled to free speech rights even in a school setting.
    C. Students could not publish statements that criticized government policies.
    D. Students could not publish statements that identified other students by name.

SS.7.C.3.12

3. Which statement describes the significance of the U.S. Supreme Court's decision in *Miranda v. Arizona* (1966)?
    A. Southern states could no longer maintain racially segregated public schools.
    B. States could no longer have racial quotas as part of their affirmative action programs.
    C. Individuals accused of serious crimes unable to pay for an attorney were entitled to a state-sponsored one.
    D. Suspects had to be told of their right to have an attorney present or to remain silent during police interrogations.

SS.7.C.3.12

4. Which statement identifies the significance of the U.S. Supreme Court decision in *Brown v. Board of Education* (1954)?
    A. It overturned racial segregation in public schools.
    B. It overturned the earlier decision of *Gideon v. Wainwright.*
    C. It upheld state laws requiring the payment of poll taxes to vote.
    D. It upheld state laws requiring racial segregation on railroad cars.

Chapter 10 | "May It Please the Court": The Supreme Court in Action

SS.7.C.3.12

5. The passage below is from the U.S. Supreme Court decision *In re Gault* (1967).

   > *From the inception of the juvenile court system, wide differences have been tolerated . . . between the procedural rights accorded to adults and those of juveniles. In practically all jurisdictions, there are rights granted to adults, which are withheld from juveniles. . . .*
   >
   > *[H]istory has again demonstrated that unbridled discretion, however benevolently motivated, is frequently a poor substitute for principle and procedure. . . .*

   Which conclusion did the Court draw from this reasoning?

   A. Evidence cannot be presented in a court of law if obtained by police in an unlawful search.
   B. States must provide minors accused of crimes with most of the same "due process" rights given to adults.
   C. Suspects must be informed of their Fifth and Sixth Amendment rights prior to police interrogation.
   D. A person accused of a felony who is unable to afford an attorney is entitled to have one provided by the court.

SS.7.C.3.12

6. In which U.S. Supreme Court decision did Chief Justice John Marshall establish the power of the Court to invalidate a "law repugnant to [*in conflict with*] the Constitution"?

   A. *Bush v. Gore*
   B. *Miranda v. Arizona*
   C. *Marbury v. Madison*
   D. *Brown v. Board of Education*

SS.7.C.3.12

7. What lesson did state courts learn from the 1963 U.S. Supreme Court case *Gideon v. Wainwright*?

   A. Minors are entitled to many of the same "due process" rights as adults.
   B. Evidence cannot be presented in a court trial if obtained by police in an unlawful search.
   C. Suspects must be informed of their 5th and 6th Amendment rights prior to police interrogation.
   D. A person accused of a felony who cannot afford an attorney is entitled to have one appointed by the court.

SS.7.C.3.12

8. The passage below is from the U.S. Supreme Court decision in *Plessy v. Ferguson* (1896).

> *We consider the underlying fallacy of the plaintiff's argument to consist in the assumption that the enforced separation of the two races stamps the colored race with a badge of inferiority. If this be so, it is not by reason of anything found in the act, but solely because the colored race chooses to put that construction upon it. . . .*
>
> *If the civil and political rights of both races be equal, one cannot be inferior to the other civilly or politically. If one race be inferior to the other socially, the constitution of the United States cannot put them upon the same plane.*

What was the impact of the reasoning above?

A. Racial segregation remained in place in the South for another half century.
B. Southern state governments were forced to end their practice of racial segregation.
C. State governments had to ensure the economic and social equality of their residents.
D. State governments no longer had to provide equal facilities to members of different races.

SS.7.C.3.12

9. The passage below is from the U.S. Supreme Court case *Tinker v. Des Moines* (1969).

> *In our system, state-operated schools may not be enclaves of totalitarianism. School officials do not possess absolute authority over their students. Students in school as well as out of school are "persons" under our Constitution. They are possessed of fundamental rights .... In the absence of a specific showing of constitutionally valid reasons to regulate their speech, students are entitled to freedom of expression of their views.*

Based on this reasoning, what did the U.S. Supreme Court conclude?

A. Students have the right to wear armbands in school to express their political beliefs.
B. Students can express their political views in student newspapers but not in classrooms.
C. Students will cause too much disruption if they wear armbands to school.
D. Students have the right to express their political opinions at home but not in school.

Chapter 10 | "May It Please the Court": The Supreme Court in Action

SS.7.C.3.12

10. How did the Supreme Court's decision in *Bush v. Gore* (2000) differ from its decision in *Brown v. Board of Education* (1954)?
    A. The *Brown* decision was unanimous, while the Justices divided along suspected party lines in *Bush v. Gore*.
    B. *Bush v. Gore* affected the entire nation, while *Brown* only had an impact on a handful of people.
    C. *Brown* was decided at a time of economic prosperity, while *Bush v. Gore* was decided during an economic depression.
    D. *Bush v. Gore* prohibited racial segregation in schools, while *Brown* affected state voting procedures.

SS.7.C.3.12

11. The passage below is from the U.S. Supreme Court decision in *Brown v. Board of Education* (1954).

    > Segregation of white and colored children in public schools has a detrimental effect upon the colored children. The impact is greater when it has the sanction of the law, for the policy of separating the races is usually interpreted as denoting the inferiority of the [African-American] group .... We conclude that, in the field of public education, the doctrine of 'separate but equal' has no place.

    What was the impact of this reasoning by the U.S. Supreme Court?
    A. Racial segregation was discontinued in public elementary schools but continued in higher grades.
    B. Southern states were forced to end all racial segregation in public schools.
    C. Southern states were required to ensure the economic and social equality of all races.
    D. Southern states could maintain separate schools for African-American and white children if they were of equal quality.

SS.7.C.3.12

12. What was the outcome of the U.S. Supreme Court's decision in *Bush v. Gore* (2000)?
    A. A recount of votes in Florida was stopped and George W. Bush became the next President.
    B. The U.S. Supreme Court confirmed the ruling of the Supreme Court of Florida to conduct a recount.
    C. The U.S. Supreme Court used the results of the popular vote in place of the Electoral College.
    D. The U.S. Supreme Court ordered a new election to be held in Florida.

CHAPTER 11

Federalism:
Federal, State and Local Governments Acting Together

Florida Governor Ron DeSantis

SS.7.C.2.3 Experience the responsibilities of citizens at the local, state, or federal levels. (See also Chapter 12.)

SS.7.C.3.4 Identify the relationship and division of powers between the federal government and state governments. (See also Chapter 4.)

SS.7.C.3.9 Illustrate the lawmaking process at the local, state, and federal levels. (See also Chapter 5.)

SS.7.C.3.13 Compare the constitutions of the United States and Florida.

SS.7.C.3.14 Differentiate between local, state, and federal governments' obligations and services.

Names and Terms You Should Know

- Federalism
- Enumerated (Expressed or Delegated) powers
- Concurrent powers
- Reserved powers
- Tenth Amendment
- Supremacy Clause
- Supreme law of the land
- Level of government
- Constitution
- Florida Constitution
- Preamble
- Articles
- Amendments
- Florida Declaration of Rights
- State legislators
- Statute
- Governor
- County
- Municipality
- Ordinance
- City/County Commissioners
- Council members
- School board
- Government obligations
- Government services

© FTE • Unlawful to photocopy without permission

Florida "Keys" to Learning

1. The Constitution spelled out with precision which powers were granted to the new central government and which were left to the states. Those powers granted to the federal government are known as the "enumerated" powers. These powers are also sometimes called the "expressed" or "delegated" powers. The powers left for the states are known as the "reserved" powers. Examples of reserved powers are the control of elections and public education within a state. Powers given to both the federal government and the states, such as the power to tax, are known as "concurrent" powers.

2. This division of power is known as federalism.

3. The Supremacy Clause—Article VI of the Constitution—declares the supremacy of federal law over state law. Federal law is the "supreme law of the land"—our highest law.

4. There are many important similarities between the U.S. Constitution and the later Florida Constitution. Both have a preamble, articles and amendments. Both view the people as the ultimate source of all governmental power. The Florida Constitution includes the Florida Declaration of Rights, which echoes the U.S. Bill of Rights. Both documents create governments with similar structures. The U.S. Constitution created a national legislature, Congress, with a Senate and House of Representatives. Florida has its own state legislature, with the Florida Senate and Florida House of Representatives. Both constitutions created executive branches led by a chief executive (the President at the federal level and the Governor of Florida at the state level), and court systems with trial courts, appellate courts, and a supreme court.

5. There are also important differences between the two constitutions. The U.S. Constitution addresses the concerns of the nation, such as defense and foreign affairs. The Florida Constitution focuses on matters specific to Florida, such as elections and voting, state finances, taxation, local government, and public education.

6. The Florida Constitution also has several unique provisions, such as its taxpayer's bill of rights. The Florida Constitution establishes English as the official language and prohibits state income taxes on individuals. The Florida Cabinet has several elected officials, such as the state attorney general.

7. The Florida Constitution is also easier to amend than the U.S. Constitution. An amendment can be proposed in five different ways and requires only 60% of the voters to ratify it. In contrast, the U.S. Constitution needs approval in three-fourths (75%) of the states.

8. There are two main forms of local government in Florida: counties and municipalities. They address local needs.

9. County governments are operated by elected commissioners and make laws for the whole county, known as ordinances. Counties provide health services, maintain county courts and jails, supervise local elections, and maintain county records. They may also handle waste disposal, maintain local roads, and have police and fire departments. They collect property tax and sales tax to pay for county services. Each county is also a public school district, which has its own elected school board to oversee the management of the district's schools.

10. A municipality is a city, town or village with its own separate government. A municipality often has an elected mayor. The elected members of the city council or city commission make local laws, also known as ordinances. Some municipalities appoint a city manager to serve as their executive. Municipal governments serve many of the same functions as county governments. They often maintain police and fire departments, manage public parks and recreation areas, operate waste disposal, issue building permits, and collect local taxes.

The authors of the U.S. Constitution not only separated government powers among three branches but also created a system for the new federal government and state governments to share power. This division of power is known as **federalism**. In this chapter, you will study federalism and the role of state and local governments in our federal system.

The Division of Power in the Federal System

The Enumerated and Reserved Powers

From the beginning, our federal government has only had limited powers. These are the "**enumerated**" powers listed in the Constitution. These listed powers are also known as the "**delegated**" or "**expressed**" powers. (You can look back at Chapter 5 to see examples of these powers.)

All other powers are "reserved" (*saved for*) the states. **The Tenth Amendment**, the last amendment in the Bill of Rights, makes this clear:

> "*The powers not delegated to the United States by the Constitution, nor prohibited by it to the States, are reserved to the States…or to the people.*"
> —Tenth Amendment (1791)

Because of the words used in the Tenth Amendment, the powers left to state governments are frequently called the "**reserved powers**."

The Supremacy of Federal Law

In all areas where the federal government lawfully exercises power, federal law is **supreme**. It is treated as superior to state law.

This principle was established by the **Supremacy Clause** of the Constitution:

> "*This Constitution, and the Laws of the United States … and all treaties made… under the authority of the United States, shall be the supreme law of the land; and the judges in every state shall be bound thereby…*"
> —U.S. Constitution, Article VI, Clause 2

If a state law and federal law are seen to be in conflict, judges are required by the Supremacy Clause to rule in favor of the federal law. Federal law is considered to be the "**supreme law of the land**." For example, some states had once allowed poll taxes (*special taxes paid in order to vote*). The Twenty-fourth Amendment to the U.S. Constitution outlawed poll taxes in 1964. Because of the supremacy of federal law, this amendment made all state poll taxes invalid.

The Concurrent Powers

Under our federal system, many of the enumerated powers (like the power to declare war) are exclusive: they are held **only** by the federal government. Other government powers are reserved **just** for the states. There is a third group of powers that are actually **shared** by state governments and the federal government. These shared powers are known as the "**concurrent powers**." Several of the enumerated powers, like the power to tax, are also concurrent powers. Both the federal government and the state governments have the power to tax their citizens.

Several examples of enumerated, concurrent and reserved powers are shown on the chart below:

Exclusive Enumerated Powers	Concurrent Powers	Reserved Powers
Coin and print money	Tax	Regulate elections
Regulate interstate commerce	Borrow money	Regulate a state's internal commerce
Declare war	Provide for the general welfare	Establish local governments

Continues on next page ▶

Chapter 11 | Federalism: Governments Acting Together

Exclusive Enumerated Powers	Concurrent Powers	Reserved Powers
Manage relations with foreign nations	Legislate and enforce laws	Establish and maintain state militia
Punish counterfeiters of U.S. securities and money	Create and maintain court systems	Provide for the health, safety, and education of state residents
Raise, maintain, and command the military forces of the United States		Ratify amendments to the Constitution
Establish systems of patents and copyrights		Regulate the practice of law and medicine
Establish standard weights and measures		Keep all powers not granted to the federal government (10th Amendment)
Make naturalization rules for immigrants to become U.S. citizens		
Establish post offices		

The Active Citizen

▶ Classify the power to conduct each of the following government activities by type:

	Exclusively Federal	Concurrent	Reserved
Set the requirements for the practice of medicine in Florida	☐	☐	☐

Explain your choice: _____

| Set the speed limits on a state highway | ☐ | ☐ | ☐ |

Explain your choice: _____

| Set requirements for the safety of meat products sold in several states | ☐ | ☐ | ☐ |

Explain your choice: _____

| Collect taxes to pay for government services | ☐ | ☐ | ☐ |

Explain your choice: _____

| Sell bonds to finance government programs | ☐ | ☐ | ☐ |

Explain your choice: _____

266   Chapter 11 | Federalism: Governments Acting Together

	Exclusively Federal	Concurrent	Reserved
Sign a nuclear arms treaty with Russia	☐	☐	☐

Explain your choice: _____

Set standards for high school graduation	☐	☐	☐

Explain your choice: _____

Negotiate a treaty of commerce with Singapore	☐	☐	☐

Explain your choice: _____

Require all U.S. citizens to have health insurance	☐	☐	☐

Explain your choice: _____

Require bicycle riders to wear helmets	☐	☐	☐

Explain your choice: _____

▶ "You've Got the Power!" Complete the table below by defining the various types of government powers in our federal system. Then provide one example of each.

Type of Power	Definition	Example
Enumerated Powers (also known as Expressed or Delegated Powers)		
Implied Powers (see Chapter 5)		
Concurrent Powers		
Reserved Powers		

Chapter 11 | Federalism: Governments Acting Together

Levels of Government

In the rest of this chapter, you will learn how these different levels of government—federal and state—work together. You will also learn about a third level of government: local government. Finally, you will see that citizens have two responsibilities in common at each of these levels of government: to obey the law and pay taxes.

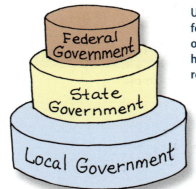

Under our system of federalism, each "layer" of our government has has its own powers and responsibilities.

A Comparison of the Florida Constitution and the U.S. Constitution

A written constitution actually serves several purposes at the same time: (1) it provides a framework or blueprint for government; (2) it limits the authority and power of government; and (3) it protects individual rights.

Like our federal government, state and local governments in Florida are based on a written constitution: the **Constitution of the State of Florida**. This document is the source of authority for Florida's state government.

The current state constitution was adopted in 1968. This constitution is similar to the U.S. Constitution in many ways. Both documents begin with a **preamble** followed by a series of **articles**. Finally, both include **amendments**. The U.S. Constitution ends with a series of amendments. In the Florida Constitution, amendments lead to changes in the text of the Constitution rather than to a separate list of amendments at the end.

The Florida Constitution begins with this Preamble:

We, the People of the State of Florida, being grateful to Almighty God for our constitutional liberty, in order to secure its benefits, perfect our government, insure domestic tranquility, maintain public order, and guarantee equal civil and political rights to all, do ordain and establish this constitution.

This is, in fact, very similar to the Preamble to the U.S. Constitution, which you have studied in Chapter 4. Both Constitutions begin with "*We the People*"—a recognition that the powers of government in a democratic society are based on the consent of the people. It is the people who, in the spirit of John Locke's social contract, form the government.

The Florida Constitution further provides these basic definitions:

"Section 1. **Political power**—All political power is inherent in the people."

"Section 2. **Basic rights**—All natural persons, female and male alike, are equal before the law and have inalienable rights, among which are the right to enjoy and defend life and liberty, to pursue happiness, to be rewarded for industry, and to acquire, possess and protect property . . ."

Much of this language is borrowed directly from the U.S. Declaration of Independence.

Both constitutions follow this opening statement with a list of their purposes. The Florida Constitution borrows many of its purposes directly from the U.S. Constitution. To these, it adds the goals of maintaining public order and guaranteeing equal civil and political rights to all.

A Comparison of the U.S. Constitution and Florida Constitution

U.S. Constitution	Florida Constitution
Preamble Begins: "We the People" Describes purposes of government	**Preamble** Begins: "We, the people of the State of Florida..." Describes purposes of government
Articles (7 Articles) (**Bill of Rights**: see Amendments I-X below) **Article I Legislature** ◆ Congress ▪ Senate ▪ House of Representatives **Article II Executive** ◆ President and Vice President **Article III Judiciary** ◆ U.S. Supreme Court Article IV States **** **Article V Amending Process** ◆ Proposing the amendment: 2/3 vote of both houses of Congress ◆ Ratifying the amendment: ¾ of state legislatures (or special state conventions) **** **Article VI Supremacy Clause** ◆ Federal law is "supreme law of the land" **Article VII Ratification of Constitution**	**Articles (12 Articles)** **Article I Declaration of Rights** **Article II General Provisions** ◆ Section 1 State boundaries ◆ Section 9 English is official language **Article III Legislature** ◆ Florida State Legislature: ▪ Senate ▪ House of Representatives **Article IV Executive** ◆ Governor, Lieutenant Governor and Cabinet **Article V Judiciary** ◆ State courts, judges, attorneys and public defenders **Article VI Suffrage and Elections** ◆ Regulations; term limits for state offices; campaign spending **Article VII Finance and Taxation** ◆ Taxes, bonds ◆ Section 5: no personal income tax **Article VIII Local Government** ◆ Counties, municipalities **Article IX Education** **Article X Miscellaneous** **** **Article XI Amending Process** ◆ Proposing amendments (five methods): ▪ 3/5 of each house of legislature proposes ▪ Constitutional convention ▪ Voter initiative ▪ Constitution Revision Commission ▪ Taxation and Budget Reform Commission ◆ Approving amendments: 60% of voters must approve most amendments in referendum **** **Article XII Schedule** (transition from older constitution to new one of 1968)
Amendments ◆ Only 27 Amendments ▪ **Bill of Rights** (1791): First Ten Amendments ▪ 13th Amendment ended slavery ▪ 14th Amendment defined the rights of U.S. citizens ▪ 15th, 19th, 24th and 26th Amendments—expanded the right to vote	**Amendments** ◆ The Florida Constitution has been amended more than 100 times since 1968. ◆ Once approved, amendments are placed as changes in the text of the Florida Constitution itself.

Chapter 11 | Federalism: Governments Acting Together

Florida Declaration of Rights

The first article of the Florida Constitution is the Florida "Declaration of Rights." This Declaration is very similar to the U.S. Bill of Rights. It guarantees the following rights and freedoms to the citizens of Florida:

- Freedom of religion
- Freedom of speech and the press
- Freedom of assembly
- The right to bear arms
- The right to due process
- The right to be secure against unreasonable searches and seizures
- No *ex post facto* laws*
- No laws reducing contract obligations
- A guarantee of the right to a writ of *habeas corpus*, except in times of invasion or rebellion*
- Protection against double jeopardy
- One cannot be forced to testify against oneself (no self-incrimination)
- No cruel or unusual punishment
- The right to bail
- The right to an attorney if accused of a crime
- The right to a speedy and public trial by an impartial jury

*For the meaning of these rights, see Chapter 12.

Ties between the Florida and U.S. Constitutions are so close that in several places the Florida Constitution adopts standards from the U.S. Constitution by reference. For example, it provides that Florida's rules against unreasonable searches and seizures should "be construed (*interpreted*) in conformity with the 4th Amendment to the United States Constitution, as interpreted by the United States Supreme Court" (Florida Constitution, Article I, Section 12).

How Florida's State Government Is Organized

In Articles II–IV, the Florida Constitution establishes the organization of its state government. There are many similarities between Florida's state government and the federal government. Like the federal government, Florida's government has three branches: legislative, executive, and judicial. Also like the federal government, the three branches of Florida's state government serve to check one another to prevent abuses of government power.

The Legislative Branch: The Florida State Legislature

Composition. *The legislative power of the state shall be vested in a legislature of the State of Florida, consisting of a senate composed of one senator elected from each senatorial district and a house of representatives composed of one member elected from each representative district.*

—Florida Constitution, Article I, Section 1

The Florida State Legislature, like Congress, has two houses. It consists of:

1. the **Florida House of Representatives**, with up to 120 members; and
2. the **Florida Senate**, with up to 40 members.

These **state legislators** are known as State Representatives and State Senators. A Florida State Representative is elected for a term of two years and a

	Federal Government	Florida State Government
Legislative Branch	Congress: U.S. Senate U.S. House of Representatives	Florida State Legislature: Florida Senate Florida House of Representatives
Executive Branch	President Vice President Appointed Cabinet Members	Governor Lieutenant Governor Elected Cabinet Members (Attorney General, etc.)
Judicial Branch	U.S. Supreme Court U.S. Circuit Court of Appeals U.S. District Court	Florida Supreme Court Florida District Courts of Appeal Florida Circuit Courts Florida County Courts

Florida State Senator is elected for a term of four years. To be a legislator in either house, a candidate must:

- be 21 years old;
- be a resident of Florida for at least two years; and
- be a resident of the district he or she will represent.

Florida's legislative branch has the power to make laws, just as Congress does at the federal level. Laws made by Congress or the state legislature are known as **acts** or **statutes**.

Like Congress, the Florida Legislature also has investigative powers. It can order the appearance of witnesses and documents to assist state legislators in deciding which state laws to pass.

And like Congress, the Florida Legislature can override a veto by the executive with a two-thirds majority vote in each house. It also has the power to impeach officials in the other two branches of government for wrongdoing, corruption, or crime.

The Executive Branch: The Governor, Lieutenant Governor and Cabinet

Both Florida and the federal government have one individual in charge of the executive branch. Instead of a President, Florida has a **Governor**; and instead of a Vice President, Florida has a **Lieutenant Governor**.

"The supreme executive power shall be vested in a governor, who shall be commander-in-chief of all military forces of the state not in active service of the United States. The governor shall take care that the laws be faithfully executed, commission all officers of the state and counties, and transact all necessary business with the officers of government. The governor may require information in writing from all executive or administrative state, county or municipal officers upon any subject relating to the duties of their respective offices. The governor shall be the chief administrative officer of the state responsible for the planning and budgeting for the state."

—Florida Constitution, Article IV, Section 1

The Governor of Florida has many powers and responsibilities similar to those of the President of the United States. The Governor serves as chief executive of the state government, can veto proposed legislation, commands the state militia, and can pardon those convicted of state crimes. The Governor oversees a large number of departments and administrative agencies, including the Florida Citrus Commission, the Florida Department of Health, the Florida Department of Elder Affairs, the

Florida State Board of Education, and the Florida Fish and Wildlife Conservation Commission.

Just as the President represents the United States, the Governor represents the State of Florida.

One additional power that the Governor has, which the President lacks, is the power to request advisory opinions from the Florida Supreme Court.

To serve as Governor or Lieutenant Governor, an individual must:

- be at least 30 years old
- have lived in Florida for the past 7 years before the election.

While the Cabinet is not even mentioned in the U.S. Constitution, it is described in the Florida Constitution, where its three members are listed:

> "There shall be a cabinet composed of an attorney general, a chief financial officer, and a commissioner of agriculture."
>
> —Florida Constitution, Article IV, Section 4

Unlike the federal government, these three members of the Cabinet in Florida are elected officials. Each must meet the same minimum qualifications for office as the Governor, except that the Attorney General needs only to have lived in Florida for the five years before the election. The Governor, Lieutenant Governor and Cabinet members are all elected to 4-year terms in office.

The Judicial Branch

Florida's court system likewise has several similiarities to the federal one, although Florida has four—not three—levels of courts.

> "**Courts.** The judicial power shall be vested in a supreme court, district courts of appeal, circuit courts and county courts. No other courts may be established by the state, any political subdivision or any municipality."
>
> —Florida Constitution, Article IV, Section 4

At the very top of Florida's court system sits the Florida Supreme Court; just below that are Florida's five District Courts of Appeal; below these are two levels of trial courts—20 circuit courts for more important cases and 67 county courts for less important ones. You can review Florida's court structure in Chapter 8.

Other Differences between the U.S. and Florida Constitutions

There are many other differences between the Florida Constitution and the U.S. Constitution. The most important is that the U.S. Constitution addresses the concerns of our nation as a whole, while the Florida Constitution addresses matters specific to the State of Florida. Some of these more specific concerns are found in the Florida Constitution's provisions for:

- elections and voting (Article VI)
- state finances and taxation (Article VII)
- local government (Article VIII)
- public education (Article IX)

In general, the Florida Constitution is more detailed than the U.S. Constitution. The U.S. Constitution lays out broad principles and concepts. The Florida Constitution includes broad principles but frequently enters into specific details. This is typical of most state constitutions.

Enrichment

Many of the similarities between the Florida Constitution and the U.S. Constitution can be traced to the history of the state constitution. In 1838, Florida was still a territory. To become a state, Florida had to submit a written constitution to Congress for approval. Using the constitutions of several Southern states as models, Floridians developed a constitution that included many concepts already found in the U.S. Constitution.

There have actually been six Florida constitutions. The first was the one drafted in 1838 and approved by Congress when Florida became a state in 1845. It was repealed in 1861 when Florida became one of the first states to secede from the Union just before the Civil War.

After the Civil War, Florida sought to rejoin the Union. In 1868, Congress required a new constitution from Florida. The new state constitution had to conform to the U.S. Constitution, especially the 13th and 14th Amendments, which ended slavery. John Pope, commander of the Union occupation force in Florida, ordered the election of delegates to attend a state constitutional convention. This assembly drafted the Florida Constitution of 1868. Reconstruction (the period just after the Civil War) ended shortly afterwards and Florida was readmitted to the Union.

The state constitution was revised again in 1885. Florida's present-day constitution was adopted in 1968. While later constitutions introduced several changes, most of the basic principles of the current constitution can be traced back to the Constitution of 1838.

Florida's first Constitution (1838).

The Florida Constitution thus has many provisions without any equivalent in the U.S. Constitution:

- It specifically names English as the "official language of the State of Florida" (Article II, Section 9).

- It prohibits the collection of any state personal income taxes or inheritance taxes (Article VII, Section 5). Florida is one of only a handful of states that do not collect personal income taxes. However, Florida does collect corporate income tax.

- It requires the state legislature to draft and adopt a Taxpayer's Bill of Rights.

- It gives the state legislature the power to create the Department of Veterans Affairs and the Department of Elder Affairs.

- It permits the Governor to reduce expenditures whenever there is less state revenue (*income*) than expected.

- It creates a trust fund to conserve and protect the Florida Everglades.

- It provides for the licensing of professionals, such as attorneys and doctors.

- It places limits on marine net fishing in Florida waters.

- It provides for education about tobacco and the prevention of smoking.

- It places restrictions on smoking in indoor workplaces.

Chapter 11 | Federalism: Governments Acting Together

The Active Citizen

▶ Complete the Venn diagram below comparing the organization of the federal government and the state government of Florida.

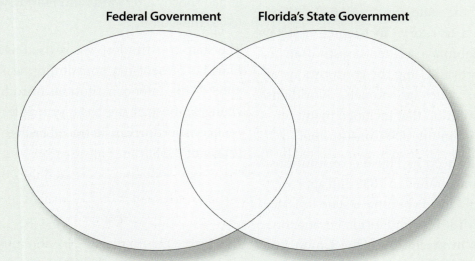

▶ Why do you think the Florida Constitution and the constitutions of most states are more specific than the U.S. Constitution?

The Amendment Process: Florida vs. United States

One area in which the U.S. Constitution and the Florida Constitution are especially different is the amending process. You will recall that "**to amend**" is to revise, add to, or change. Both the U.S. Constitution and the Florida Constitution permit amendments so that these constitutions can change along with society's changing needs. However, amending each constitution was deliberately made more difficult than passing an ordinary law.

As you learned in Chapter 9, the U.S. Constitution can be amended through a two-step process. First, proposals for amendments are made either by a vote of two-thirds of each house of Congress, or by a national convention that can be called for by two-thirds of the state legislatures. Then the proposed amendment must be ratified by three-fourths of the state legislatures or by special conventions in three-fourths of the states.

The Florida Constitution can also be amended through a two-step process. In the first step, an amendment is proposed; in the second step, the proposed amendment is approved by voters and adopted.

In Florida, however, there are more ways for proposing amendments than in the federal system. In Florida, final adoption of an amendment is also not as difficult as at the federal level. As a result, there have been many more amendments to the Florida Constitution than to the U.S. Constitution.

Thousands of amendments to the U.S. Constitution have been suggested. However, only 17 amendments have actually been added to the U.S. Constitution since the ratification of the Bill of Rights in 1791.

In contrast, there have already been more than 100 amendments to the Florida Constitution since 1968. With five methods for proposing amendments and the requirement that only 60% of the voters need to approve most amendments, the Florida Constitution is just much easier to amend.

Chapter 11 | Federalism: Governments Acting Together

For example, Florida voters amended the Florida Constitution in 2000 to require high-speed rail throughout the state. Then in 2004, another amendment successfully repealed that provision. Even an amendment to care more humanely for pigs has become part of Florida's State Constitution (Article X, Section 21). There is no equivalent in the U.S. Constitution and none is likely.

Amending the Florida Constitution

Step 1. Proposal

There are five ways in which a constitutional amendment may be proposed:

1. By a three-fifths (3/5) vote of both houses of the Florida legislature.
2. By a Constitutional Revision Commission, which meets every 20 years. Its members are the Florida Attorney General and 36 members selected by the Speaker of the Florida House of Representatives, the President of the Florida Senate, the Chief Justice of the Florida Supreme Court, and the Governor.
3. By the Taxation and Budget Reform Commission, which also meets every 20 years. It has members appointed by the Governor, the Speaker of the House, and the President of the Senate.
4. By voters directly proposing an amendment. (At least 8% of voters in the last election must sign petitions proposing the amendment.)
5. By a majority of voters calling for a constitutional convention to revise the constitution.

Step 2. Adoption

1. To adopt a proposed amendment, sixty percent (60%) of the voters must approve the amendment in a referendum, held in the next general election after it is proposed.
2. If the proposed amendment concerns taxes, then the approval of two-thirds (66.7%) of the voters is required for the amendment to be adopted.

The Active Citizen

Make a chart or Venn diagram comparing how an amendment is proposed and adopted at the federal level and in Florida.

The Lawmaking Process at the State Level

The Florida Legislature meets for regular session, starting in March, for 60 days each year. The Governor can also summon special sessions.

The lawmaking process in Florida is quite similar to the process at the federal level (see Chapter 5). A bill can be introduced in either house when the legislature is in session. As in Congress, committees are a part of the legislative process. After a bill is introduced, it is referred to a committee, where the bill is discussed and may be changed. The committee can report the bill favorably, amend the bill, or report the bill unfavorably. If the bill is killed in committee, it is dead for the rest of the legislative session.

Chapter 11 | Federalism: Governments Acting Together

If the bill is reported favorably by the committee, it is then placed on the calendar for a discussion on the floor of the house. This is followed by a vote. Passage of the bill requires a simple majority vote in support of the bill.

Once a bill has passed in one house, it is sent to the other house. If it passes in the other house without amendment, the bill can be immediately sent to the Governor. However, if the bill is amended in the second house, it is then sent to a conference committee, just as bills are in Congress. The members of the conference committee iron out the differences in the two versions of the bill and the new bill is sent to both houses. They must approve or reject the revised bill in its entirety.

Once the bill has passed in both the Florida Senate and the Florida House of Representatives, it is submitted to the Governor for approval. The Governor can sign the bill, making it into a law. The Governor can also veto the bill. If the Governor vetoes the bill, the legislature can override the veto by a two-thirds vote in each house. The Governor must sign or veto the bill within 7 days if the legislature is in session. If the legislature has adjourned, the Governor must sign or veto the bill within 15 days. Otherwise, it immediately becomes law.

How a Bill in the State Legislature becomes a Law

A bill is introduced in the Florida Senate or House of Representatives.	The bill goes to a committee; if approved, it goes back to the house.	Bill is debated and voted on by the house.	Bill goes to the other house and passes through the same stages.	If approved in different form, bill goes to conference committee and back to each house to be passed in same form.	If the bill is approved by a majority in both houses, it is sent to the Governor, who signs or vetoes it.

The Active Citizen

- Imagine that you are a Florida State Senator. Write to a friend or colleague describing a bill you have sponsored and its progress in becoming a law.
- You can check on current bills being considered by the Florida Legislature by going to flsenate.gov or myfloridahouse.gov.

> Be sure to know what ordinances, city and county commissioners, and school boards are for the EOC test. You do **not** need to know the differences between county and municipal governments.

Local Government in Florida

Local government is the level of government that is closest to us. It affects our daily lives. There are two main types of local governments in Florida: counties and municipalities. These local governments handle such matters as local roads and bridges, public schools, public parks, libraries, garbage collection and recycling, building permits, and providing police and fire protection.

County Governments

The largest unit of local government in Florida is the county. Florida is divided into 67 counties. The citizens of each county elect a sheriff, tax collector, county clerk, property appraiser, and other county officials. They also elect five to seven **commissioners**. These form a **board of commissioners**, which makes laws for the county. The commissioners deal

Florida's Ten Largest Municipalities

Municipality	Type of Government
Jacksonville	Mayor-council
Miami	Mayor-commission
Tampa	Mayor-council
St. Petersburg	Mayor-council
Orlando	Mayor-commission
Hialeah	Mayor-council
Tallahassee	Commission-manager
Fort Lauderdale	Commission-manager
Port St. Lucie	Council-manager
Pembroke Pines	Commission-manager

with matters affecting residents of the county. Laws passed by county commissioners are known as **ordinances**. The county also collects property tax and sales tax to pay for county services.

County governments provide health care, offer assistance to the homeless, maintain county courts and jails, supervise elections, and keep records for the county, including births, deaths, marriages and divorces. They also provide garbage collection, recycling and utilities in some areas.

School Boards

Each county in Florida also forms its own public school district. Voters in the county elect five or more members to a **school board** for the district. The school board operates and supervises all public schools in the district. The school board also sets the rates of local school district taxes to support its schools.

Municipal Governments

A **municipality** is any city, town or village that establishes its own government. Municipalities are formed within counties, but they are considered to be separate. There are hundreds of incorporated municipalities in Florida. The government of a municipality is known as a **municipal government**.

There are several different forms of municipal government. The most common has a **mayor** and a **city council** or **commission**. The mayor is elected by all of the voters of the town or city. He or she acts as the chief executive—appointing other city officials, preparing a budget, enforcing city laws, and proposing new laws. The city council or commission acts as a legislature. Its members are also elected. The city council or commission passes local laws. Like county laws, these are also known as **ordinances**.

Jacksonville, for example, has an elected mayor. The city has 19 elected members on its city council. Miami has an elected mayor and five elected commissioners. Tampa has an elected mayor and a city council with seven council members.

Some cities in Florida have a special city manager. In these cities, voters elect commissioners. The commissioners in turn appoint the city manager and other officials to run the administration of the city. Both Tallahassee and Fort Lauderdale have city managers. In these cities, the elected commissioners set policies but the city manager heads the city administration. Both cities also have an elected mayor, who sits on the commission. The mayor represents voters from throughout the city, but does not act as a chief executive.

The Active Citizen

What form of local government do you live under? Research your local government on the Internet and write a brief description for a friend in another part of Florida.

Chapter 11 | Federalism: Governments Acting Together

Government Obligations and Services

Our three levels of government—local, state and federal—work together to provide services to their citizens. Each level of government has an **obligation** (*requirement*) to provide particular services. Local governments provide services to local residents, while state governments meet statewide needs. The federal government promotes the general welfare of the nation as a whole. Sometimes the services offered by these different levels of government overlap.

Federal Government. Our federal government provides services at the national level. These include maintaining the armed forces, controlling immigration into the United States, conducting relations with foreign countries, and regulating trade between the states. The federal government checks the quality of food and drugs sold in the United States to protect consumer safety. It also regulates banks and the stock market. The federal government operates U.S. Post Offices, prints money, issues passports, and operates U.S. embassies in other countries. It collects taxes and pays social security benefits, Medicare and Medicaid. In cases of natural disaster such as hurricanes, the federal government provides emergency relief. Its courts enforce federal laws and protect the constitutional rights of U.S. citizens. Its prisons hold criminals who have broken federal laws.

State Government. The state government of Florida protects the lives and property of Florida citizens. It provides necessary statewide services, works to improve the state's economy, and promotes the general welfare of the people of Florida.

Florida's state government regulates business, industry, and insurance in the state. It establishes licensing requirements for professions (doctors, lawyers and teachers). It maintains state highways and enforces statewide rules for safe driving. The state government issues driving licenses, marriage licenses, hunting licenses and fishing licenses. It regulates utilities in the state such as electricity and natural gas; establishes statewide building codes; sets statewide education requirements; and supervises public education across the state. The state government establishes standards for hospitals and public health; looks after the special needs of veterans, disabled workers, and the elderly in Florida; operates state parks; and performs other vital services that affect all Floridians.

Local Government. Florida's county and municipal governments provide services to their residents. They run the public schools. They provide police and fire protection. They provide garbage collection and recycling. They make local zoning decisions (how property can be used in an area),

enforce state building codes, and issue building permits to allow new construction. Local governments build and maintain local roads and bridges. In some places, local governments provide forms of public transportation, such as buses or trolleys. They provide health care; issue business licenses; license and inspect local restaurants; operate local parks and beaches; and record births, marriages, divorces and deaths. What all these services have in common is that they concern citizens in a smaller area than services provided by the state or federal government.

Overlapping Services. When the powers of the federal government and state governments are concurrent, their services can sometimes overlap.

- Federal, state and local governments each offer their own court systems for the administration of justice.

- Federal, state and local governments provide their own forms of law enforcement. The federal government has the FBI, Florida has its own Department of Law Enforcement, and many counties and municipalities have their own police departments.

▶ Federal, state and local governments maintain their own parks and recreation areas. The federal government has the National Park Service, Florida has its own state parks, and many counties and municipalities have their own local parks and recreation areas.

The Active Citizen

Which level of government would be primarily responsible for providing this service?

	Local	State	Federal
Defending American ships attacked overseas in neutral waters	☐	☐	☐
Providing summer school programs for middle school students in your town	☐	☐	☐
Negotiating changes to trade agreements with Mexico	☐	☐	☐
Setting health and safety standards for amusement parks throughout Florida	☐	☐	☐
Building a new town hall	☐	☐	☐
Repairing a state highway that crosses several counties	☐	☐	☐
Providing disability payments to injured workers	☐	☐	☐
Building a new firehouse for a major city	☐	☐	☐
Introducing a new recycling program to accompany garbage collection	☐	☐	☐
Establishing new civics requirements for all Florida middle school students	☐	☐	☐
Introducing a zoning ordinance that creates a new shopping district in your town	☐	☐	☐
Making rules for banks with branches in several states	☐	☐	☐
Setting rules for visitors to Everglades National Park	☐	☐	☐
Issuing driving licenses to residents of Florida	☐	☐	☐

Services Typically Provided by Local Governments

- Building and maintaining local roads and bridges
- Law enforcement
- Fire protection
- Regulating local business and industry/ issuing business licenses
- Zoning and building permits
- Regulating utilities (electricity, gas, water)
- Garbage collection/sanitation
- Collecting property and sales taxes
- Supervising elections
- Operating public schools
- Maintaining public libraries
- Managing local parks and recreation areas
- Keeping public records: births, marriages, divorces, deaths

Chapter 11 | Federalism: Governments Acting Together

Name _____

Which term or phrase does not fit with the others found in the same box? In the space to the right of each box, write the term or phrase that does not belong. Then use the same term or phrase in a sentence.

Preamble
Congress
Florida Constitution
Florida Declaration of Rights
Organization of Florida's state government

Federalism
County
Reserved Powers
Tenth Amendment
Concurrent Powers

Mayor
City Manager
State legislators
Council members
City Commissioners

President
Florida Senate
Lieutenant Governor
Florida Supreme Court
Florida House of Representatives

Law
Statute
Ordinance
Appointment

280   Chapter 11 | Federalism: Governments Acting Together

Name _____

Which term or phrase does not fit with the others found in the same box? In the space to the right of each box, write the term or phrase that does not belong. Then use the same term or phrase in a sentence.

| Supremacy Clause |
| No personal income tax |
| Elected Cabinet members |
| English is the official language |

| School Board |
| Ordinance |
| Governor |
| County Government |
| Municipal Government |

| Issues driving licenses |
| Regulates voting in elections |
| Takes charge of national defense |
| Establishes statewide building codes |
| Sets statewide education requirements |

| State Board of Education |
| Fish and Wildlife Conservation Commission |
| Department of Elder Affairs |
| U.S. Department of Defense |
| Citrus Commission |

Chapter 11 | Federalism: Governments Acting Together

Name _____

Complete the chart below comparing the organization of our federal and state governments.

	Federal government	Government of the State of Florida
Legislative Branch		
Executive Branch		
Judicial Branch		
Other Features		

Describe the powers, organization and responsibilities of local governments in Florida.

Local Governments in Florida

Type	Description
County Government	
Municipal Government	

Name _____

In this chapter you learned about the system of federalism: how our local, state and federal governments have both different and overlapping powers and responsibilities. Complete the chart below by showing the obligations of each level of government and some of the services it provides.

Obligations and services of the federal government

_____
_____
_____
_____
_____
_____
_____
_____

Obligations and services of Florida's state government

_____
_____
_____
_____
_____
_____
_____
_____

Obligations and services of your local government

_____
_____
_____
_____
_____
_____
_____
_____

Chapter 11 | Federalism: Governments Acting Together

Federalism and State and Local Governments

Federalism
- Division of power between federal and state governments
- "Enumerated" (delegated or expressed) powers held by federal government
- "Reserved" powers (left to the states) - 10th Amendment
- "Concurrent" powers (shared by federal and state)
- Supremacy Clause

Obligations and Services of Governments
- Federal government meets national needs, such as defense & foreign policy
- State governments meet statewide needs, such as educational requirements
- Local governments meet local concerns, such as running a school district

The U.S. Constitution vs. Florida Constitution

U.S. Constitution
- Preamble: "We the People"; purposes
- Government of 3 branches:
  - Congress
  - President and Vice President
    Appointed Cabinet (not in Constitution)
  - Federal Courts: 3 levels

Florida Constitution

- Preamble: "We the People of Florida"; purposes
- Florida Declaration of Rights (like Bill of Rights)
- State Government of 3 branches:
  - Governor and Lt. Governor
  - Elected Cabinet
  - Florida State Legislature
    Florida House of Representatives: up to 120 members
    Florida Senate: up to 40 members
  - Florida Courts: 4 levels

Local Governments in Florida
- **County Governments**
  Largest unit of local government; cover the entire state
- **Municipal Governments**
  Governed by mayor and a council or commission; sometimes has city manager

Differences between Florida and U.S. Constitutions
- Elected Cabinet in Florida
- No state income tax in Florida
- English is the official language in Florida
- Florida Constitution is easier to amend
  - 5 ways to propose amendment
  - 60% of voters must approve for adoption
- Florida Constitution is more detailed

Chapter 11 | Federalism: Governments Acting Together

Review Cards: Federalism—Federal, State and Local Governments Acting Together

Division of Power between the Federal and State Governments

Federalism = Division of power between the federal government and the state governments.

"Enumerated" powers = The powers granted to the federal government and listed in Article I, Section 8 of the Constitution. Also known as the **"delegated" powers** or **"expressed" powers**.

Examples: power to declare war; power to regulate interstate commerce; power to coin money

"Reserved" powers = The powers held back from the federal government and reserved for the state governments. The **Tenth Amendment** specifically states that these powers are **"reserved"** for the states and the people.

Examples: power to establish local government; power to provide public education

"Concurrent" powers = The powers shared by the federal and state governments. Both can exercise these powers.

Examples: power to tax; power to borrow money

Supremacy Clause (Article VI of the Constitution) = states that whenever there is a conflict between federal and state law, the federal law is supreme.

A Comparison of the Florida Constitution and the U.S. Constitution

Similarities

1. Both Constitutions acknowledge the people as the source of all government power. This is acknowledged in their Preambles and in Article I of the Florida Constitution: "All political power is inherent in the people." Both Preambles also identify the purposes of the government they establish.
2. Both Constitutions state that all people are equal before the law and have inalienable rights.
3. The Florida **Declaration of Rights,** found in the first article of the Florida Constitution, echoes the U.S. Bill of Rights.
4. Ties between the two Constitutions are so close that the Florida Constitution adopts several standards from the U.S. Constitution by reference.
5. Both Constitutions establish similar government structures with three branches.
6. Both the Florida Legislature and the U.S. Congress have two houses: the Senate and House of Representatives.
7. Both the U.S. President and the Florida Governor are chief executives, who serve as Commanders in Chief of their armed forces, are assisted by a Cabinet, hold veto power, and have the right to pardon. Each executive oversees a great number of departments.
8. Both the federal and state judicial branches have several levels. Both have a supreme court, appellate courts, and trial courts.

A Comparison of the Florida Constitution and the U.S. Constitution

Differences

1. The U.S. Constitution and the federal government it created address national concerns, such as foreign affairs, while the Florida Constitution and state government focus on matters specific to Florida, such as elections and voting, state finances and taxation, local government and public education.
2. Like most state constitutions, the Florida Constitution is more detailed than the U.S. Constitution.
3. The Florida Constitution has some provisions without any equivalent in the U.S. Constitution, such as identifying English as the official language, prohibiting state income taxes, having elected Cabinet officials, and providing a taxpayer's bill of rights.
4. Amending the Florida Constitution is easier than amending the U.S. Constitution. There are five ways to introduce an amendment to the Florida Constitution and only a 60% majority of voters is needed for ratification. At the federal level, three-fourths of the states must approve for ratification.

Local Governments in Florida

Local governments make decisions that affect all Floridians, such as operating schools, parks, libraries, and fire and police departments. There are two main kinds of local governments in Florida:

1. **County Governments**

   Florida has 67 counties. Citizens in each county elect a sheriff, tax collector, and other officials. They also elect **commissioners** to serve as members of the county **board of commissioners,** which make laws—known as **ordinances**—for the county. They also pass zoning ordinances, which govern land use. County governments provide health services, maintain county courts, supervise local elections, and maintain records of birth, death, marriages and divorces.

   Each county also forms its own **school district**. Voters elect members to a **school board,** which oversees the management of all public schools in the district.

2. **Municipal Governments**

   They are formed for cities, towns and villages that wish to set up their own local government. Voters in a town or city may elect a chief executive, known as the **mayor**, who is assisted by a **city council** or **city commission**, whose members are also elected. In some municipalities, the city council or city commission appoints a **city manager** to head the city administration. The city council or commission passes local laws, known as **ordinances**. There may still be a mayor, who serves on the city council or commission but is elected by all the voters in the municipality.

   Municipal governments are usually responsible for fire and crime prevention, maintaining local roads, zoning and granting building permits, collecting garbage and recycling, supervising local elections, managing local parks and recreation areas, and providing other local services.

Government Obligations and Services

Federal Government
The federal government handles national issues, such as national defense, foreign policy, and the American economy. Federal courts protect the rights of citizens guaranteed by the Constitution and the Bill of Rights, and interpret federal law.

State Government
Florida's state government regulates state businesses and insurance, licenses professionals (such as teachers, lawyers and doctors), builds and maintains state highways, issues and enforces rules for traffic safety, licenses drivers, regulates state utilities, and creates building construction codes. It also operates the state's public education system and regulates conservation, pollution, and public health throughout the state.

Local Government
Florida's local governments address the daily local needs of their people, such as operating their public school districts, managing local police and fire departments, and overseeing local sewage and garbage disposal.

What Do You Know?

SS.7.C.3.4

1. Which is an example of a reserved power?
   A. the power to collect taxes
   B. the power to establish post offices
   C. the power to educate young citizens
   D. the power to declare war on foreign enemies

SS.7.C.3.4

2. Which is an example of a concurrent power?
   A. the power to borrow money
   B. the power to regulate interstate commerce
   C. the power to set admission requirements for state universities
   D. the power to make naturalization rules for immigrants

SS.7.C.3.13

3. How does the process for amending the Constitution of Florida compare to that of amending the U.S. Constitution?
   A. It is more difficult to amend the Florida Constitution than to amend the U.S. Constitution.
   B. It is more difficult to amend the U.S. Constitution than to amend the Florida Constitution.
   C. The Florida Constitution and the U.S. Constitution follow the exact same procedures for amendment.
   D. The U.S. Constitution requires two steps for amendment, while the Florida Constitution can be amended in just a single step.

Chapter 11 | Federalism: Governments Acting Together

SS.7.C.3.14

4. Which obligation is owed by state governments to their citizens?
   A. making local zoning ordinances
   B. defending the nation against foreign attack
   C. negotiating trade agreements with foreign nations
   D. regulating the activities of professionals such as doctors and lawyers

SS.7.C.3.14

5. Which is an obligation owed by local governments to their citizens?
   A. the operation of public school districts
   B. the establishment of statewide curricular requirements
   C. the provision of professional certification requirements for teachers
   D. the setting of national economic policies to promote full employment

SS.7.C.3.14

6. The table below identifies services provided by different levels of government.

Level of Government	Federal	State	Local
Service Provided	Provides for the national defense	?	Operates public school districts

   Which completes the diagram?
   A. Enforces local building codes
   B. Operates police and fire departments
   C. Conducts diplomacy with foreign leaders
   D. Establishes high school graduation requirements

SS.7.C.3.14

Use the chart below to answer Questions 7 and 8.

Levels of Government		
I	II	III
U.S Government	Government of the State of Florida	County and Municipal Governments

7. Which governments provide garbage collection services to homes and businesses?
   A. I only
   B. I and II
   C. III only
   D. I, II, and III

288   Chapter 11 | Federalism: Governments Acting Together

SS.7.C.3.14

8. Which levels of government establish and implement educational requirements for minors?
   A. I only
   B. I and II
   C. II and III
   D. I, II, and III

SS.7.C.3.13

9. Which statement identifies a basic similarity between the U.S. and Florida Constitutions?
   A. Both have a preamble, articles and amendments.
   B. Both prohibit the collection of personal income taxes.
   C. Both provide details on the qualifications for voting in elections.
   D. Both have detailed provisions on public education and local government.

SS.7.C.3.13

10. Which document does the Florida Declaration of Rights most closely resemble?
    A. *Magna Carta*
    B. The Bill of Rights
    C. The U.S. Constitution
    D. The Declaration of Independence

SS.7.C.3.13

11. What is one way that the government of the State of Florida differs from the federal government?
    A. Florida judges hold their positions with lifetime appointments.
    B. Members of the Cabinet in Florida also sit in the state legislature.
    C. Several Cabinet members in Florida are elected rather than appointed.
    D. Unlike the Vice President of the United States, the Lieutenant Governor of Florida is appointed.

SS.7.C.3.9

12. What is a law passed by a Florida county or municipality called?
    A. an act
    B. a statute
    C. a precedent
    D. an ordinance

SS.7.C.3.4

13. What is guaranteed by the "Supremacy Clause" of the U.S. Constitution?
    A. the supremacy of federal over state law
    B. the supremacy of individual rights over government power
    C. the supremacy of Congress over the President
    D. the supremacy of the people over their government

Chapter 11 | Federalism: Governments Acting Together

SS.7.C.3.9

14. The diagram below shows several steps in how a bill becomes a law in Florida.

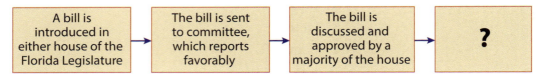

What is the next step in this process?

A. The bill is sent to a conference committee.
B. The bill is sent to the Governor for approval.
C. Two thirds of both houses need to support the bill.
D. The bill is sent to the other house of the legislature.

SS.7.C.3.4

15. Which statement identifies a similarity between state and federal governments?

A. Both levels of government can borrow money for paying expenses.
B. Both levels of government can establish post offices for sending mail.
C. Both levels of government can determine rules for the naturalization of citizens.
D. Both levels of government can establish systems for granting patents to inventors.

SS.7.C.3.4

16. Based on the Tenth Amendment to the U.S. Constitution, which powers belong to either state governments or individual citizens?

A. all powers needed to conduct U.S. foreign policy
B. all powers needed by Congress to carry out its enumerated powers
C. all powers not delegated to the federal government by the Constitution
D. all powers needed to prevent corruption and abuse by the federal government

SS.7.C.3.13

17. Which goal identifies one of the main purposes of a constitution?

A. to limit government authority
B. to raise money for government officials
C. to make it more difficult to pass new laws
D. to prevent citizens from interfering with the government

Chapter 11 | Federalism: Governments Acting Together

CHAPTER 12

The Obligations, Responsibilities, and Rights of Citizens

SS.7.C.2.1 Define the term "citizen," and identify legal means of becoming a U.S. citizen.

SS.7.C.2.2 Evaluate the obligations citizens have to obey laws, pay taxes, defend the nation, and serve on juries.

SS.7.C.2.3 Experience the responsibilities of citizens at the local, state, or federal levels. (See also Chapter 11.)

SS.7.C.2.4 Evaluate rights contained in the Bill of Rights and other amendments to the Constitution. (See also Chapters 9 and 10.)

SS.7.C.2.5 Distinguish how the Constitution safeguards and limits individual rights. (See also Chapter 9.)

SS.7.C.2.14 Conduct a service project to further the public good.

Names and Terms You Should Know

Citizen	Resident	Civic meetings
Fourteenth Amendment	Obligation of citizenship	Common good
Naturalized citizen	Taxes	Voting
Naturalization process	Jury service	Running for office
Alien	Summons	Petitioning government
Immigrant	Selective service	*Ex post facto* law
Law of Blood	Responsibility of citizenship	*Habeas corpus*
Law of Soil	Civic participation	

Florida "Keys" to Learning

1. An American citizen is a legally recognized member of the United States. U.S. citizenship is obtained by birth or by becoming a citizen through the naturalization process.

2. Citizenship is obtained at birth either by the "Law of Soil" or the "Law of Blood." The "Law of Soil" is that any child born on American soil automatically becomes an American citizen. The "Law of Blood" is that if a child is born in another country and both his or her parents are American citizens, the child is also an American citizen.

3. Naturalization is the process by which someone who does not have U.S. citizenship at birth can become a U.S. citizen. To become a naturalized citizen, a person must be lawfully admitted to the United States, reside in the United States for five years, take a citizenship test, be of good character, and swear an oath of allegiance to the United States.

4. A person does not need to become a citizen to live and work lawfully in the United States. Many people from other countries living in the United States—known as "aliens"—are lawful permanent residents. Their permanent residence permit is sometimes known as a "green card."

A naturalization ceremony

5. American citizens have obligations and responsibilities as well as rights. The obligations of American citizens are the things they *must* do. These obligations are to obey the law, pay taxes, serve on a jury if summoned, and register with the Selective Service (if male and aged 18–25) in order to defend the nation if called on.

6. American citizens also have responsibilities. These are things they *should* do to make our democratic system effective. They promote the common or public good. Citizens should be informed about local, state and national public affairs, and vote in elections. They can also join a political party, run for political office, serve on local committees, attend public meetings, petition government by writing to government officials, and volunteer for local public service projects.

7. Americans have individual rights guaranteed in the Constitution. These include the right to request a writ of *habeas corpus*. The Constitution also provides that no citizen will ever be subject to an *ex post facto* law (*a law punishing acts that occurred before the law was passed*).

8. As you learned in Chapter 9, Americans also have individual rights guaranteed by the Bill of Rights. These include freedom of speech and the press, freedom of religion, the right to bear arms, the prohibition against unreasonable searches and seizures, the ban on "double jeopardy" (*being tried twice for the same crime*), and the right to a public trial by an impartial jury.

9. The most important rights held exclusively by U.S. citizens are the right to vote and the right to run for political office. Other benefits of U.S. citizenship include the right to carry a U.S. passport, the ability to serve on a jury, a preference in bringing relatives into the United States, and the ability to hold many government jobs.

In the introduction to this book, you learned what a "citizen" is: a legally recognized member of a nation like the United States. Such citizenship brings with it obligations, responsibilities and rights.

After the Civil War, leaders in Congress wanted to make it clear that all Americans—including the freed slaves—were U.S. citizens with the same rights as other citizens. This principle was established by the Fourteenth Amendment:

"All persons born or naturalized in the United States, and subject to the jurisdiction thereof, are citizens of the United States and of the State wherein they reside."

This Amendment made it clear that there were actually two paths to U.S. citizenship: (1) by birth; or (2) by becoming a citizen through the naturalization process.

American Citizenship

Citizenship at Birth

In fact, there are even two ways to become an American citizen at birth, based on where you are born and who your parents are.

▶ The "Law of Soil": Any person born on American soil is automatically an American citizen.

▶ The "Law of Blood": A baby born in another country is still an American citizen at birth if both parents are American citizens, or if one parent is an American citizen who has lived at least one year continuously in the United States. If the father but not the mother is an American citizen and the parents are **not** married, special rules will apply. For the child to qualify for U.S. citizenship, the father has to provide convincing evidence of fatherhood.

Enrichment

The Active Citizen

Here is a part of the current law, passed by Congress, on citizenship at birth:

"The following shall be nationals and citizens of the United States at birth:

(a) a person born in the United States, and subject to the jurisdiction thereof;

(b) a person born in the United States to a member of an Indian, Eskimo, Aleutian, or other aboriginal tribe . . .

Continues ▶

Chapter 12 | The Obligations, Responsibilities and Rights of Citizenship

(c) a person born outside of the United States ... of parents both of whom are citizens of the United States and one of whom has had a residence in the United States ..., prior to the birth of such person;

(d) a person born outside of the United States ... of parents, one of whom is a citizen of the United States who has been physically present in the United States ... for a continuous period of one year prior to the birth of such person, and the other of whom is a national, but not a citizen of the United States ...."

—8 U.S. Code §1401

- Sandra's father works for a large company with offices all around the world. Sandra was born while her parents were living in Costa Rica for more than a year. Her father is a U.S. citizen, but her mother is from Costa Rica and is not a U.S. citizen. Her father grew up overseas and has never actually lived one year continuously in the United States. However, her American grandmother came to Costa Rica when Sandra was born. Sandra's parents are married. Based on these facts and the law above, was Sandra a U.S. citizen at birth? Explain your answer.

- James was born overseas while his parents were visiting his father's parents in Morocco. Both of James' parents were born overseas, but became naturalized American citizens before James was born. Was James an American citizen at birth? Explain your answer.

- Maria lives in Mexico. Both her parents are Mexican. Maria is a Mexican citizen. She was born in an American hospital while her parents were on a short vacation in San Diego, California. Was Maria an American citizen at birth? Explain your answer.

Naturalization

The **Fourteenth Amendment** provides a second pathway to citizenship: **naturalization**. This is the process by which an **immigrant** (a person who comes to the United States with an intent to stay) becomes a U.S. citizen. Those who acquire citizenship through this process are known as "**naturalized citizens**."

The Constitution gives Congress the power to regulate the naturalization process. To apply for naturalization, a resident alien (a foreign-born person) must be at least 18 years old, be a lawful permanent resident, have lived in the United States for five years, be of "good character," and know basic English. The candidate must complete an N-400 application form and submit the form with accompanying documents (such as a "green card" and two photographs). If the application is approved, the candidate is interviewed by the U.S. Citizenship and Immigration Services. At the interview, the candidate is given a brief oral test on American history and government. If the applicant knows enough English and passes the test, he or she can attend a naturalization ceremony to swear an oath of allegiance to the United States and become a U.S. citizen.

A person does not need to become a citizen to lawfully live and work in the United States. Many foreign nationals—known as "**aliens**"—are **lawful permanent residents**. This means they have been legally admitted into the United States and have permission to stay and work here. Their lawful permanent residence card is sometimes known as a "green card" because of its green color.

Lawful permanent residents—also known as "legal aliens"—have many rights. They have the right to live in the United States. They have the right to work. They have the right to become certified in professions like teaching and law. They generally have the right to leave and re-enter the United States. They also enjoy the guarantees of individual rights found in the Bill of Rights. However, there are some rights only citizens possess, such as the right to vote.

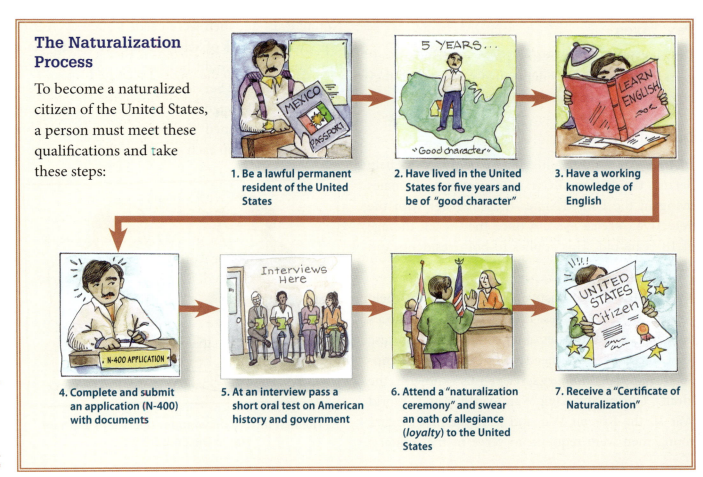

The Naturalization Process

To become a naturalized citizen of the United States, a person must meet these qualifications and take these steps:

1. Be a lawful permanent resident of the United States
2. Have lived in the United States for five years and be of "good character"
3. Have a working knowledge of English
4. Complete and submit an application (N-400) with documents
5. At an interview pass a short oral test on American history and government
6. Attend a "naturalization ceremony" and swear an oath of allegiance (*loyalty*) to the United States
7. Receive a "Certificate of Naturalization"

The naturalization process has had many positive effects on American government and society. It has meant that people arriving in the United States have the possibility of becoming citizens—full and equal partners in American society. It has meant that immigrants have a chance to contribute their talents and skills to government service and to American society as a whole. The fact that immigrants can become fully integrated into American society makes the United States very attractive to newcomers, who bring knowledge and skills. Finally, the arrival of so many people from foreign lands—with their own foods, languages, customs, and ideas—has greatly enriched American culture.

The Obligations of Citizenship

American citizens have **obligations** (or **duties**) as well as rights. These obligations are things that all citizens *must* do. Citizens can be fined or even imprisoned if they fail to meet the obligations of citizenship.

Obey the Law

Not only citizens but visitors to the United States and permanent residents must all obey the law.

The Obligations of Citizenship: the "Musts" of Citizenship

▶ Obey the law.
▶ Pay taxes.
▶ Register with the Selective Service and defend the nation if called upon.
▶ Serve on juries if summoned.

Pay Taxes

Citizens must pay taxes to support government services. Visitors and residents also pay taxes if they buy goods or earn income here.

Defend the Nation

In times of war, all citizens are required to help defend the nation. Even in peacetime, all males living in the United States must register with the Selective Service System once they reach the age of 18 years old. This applies to both residents and citizens.

The purpose of the Selective Service System is to help defend the United States. The Selective Service keeps the names and addresses of registrants on file in case the United States ever needs to re-establish conscription (*compulsory military service*)—also known as the "draft." During the Civil War, World War I, World War II, the Korean War and the War in Vietnam, young men were required to serve in the military.

If you are a man age 18 through 25 and living in the U.S., then you must register with Selective Service. It's the law. According to law, a man must register with Selective Service within 30 days of his 18th birthday. Selective Service will accept late registrations but not after a man has reached age 26. You may be denied benefits or a job if you have not registered. You can register at any U.S. Post Office and do not need a social security number.

Not all draft-age men were needed in every year of every war. The task of Selective Service was to select those men who would be required to serve. Typically, the Selective Service drew the days of the year at random and assigned each day a number. Those numbers determined the order in which eligible men were called up each year for military service.

The first lottery drawing for the War in Vietnam was in December 1969.

The last "draft" ended in January 1973. Since that time, the United States has had an all-volunteer military force. Citizens volunteer to serve in the armed forces out of patriotism (*love of country*) and to obtain the many benefits of military service—good pay, physical and vocational training, work experience, funding for future education, health benefits, and opportunities for travel. Of course, there is also hard work associated with a tour of military duty and the risk of injury or even loss of life in combat.

Although the draft has ended, all draft-age males living in America must still register with the Selective Service System in case the United States ever needs to draft its young men to help defend the nation again.

Serve on Juries

Only citizens are asked to serve on juries. For jury service, a court will usually choose names by lot (*at random*) from a list of licensed drivers and those with Florida identification cards who live in the

area. Courts have the power to summon individuals to appear before them. Potential jurors are sent a jury summons. A "summons" is an order to appear in court. The summons tells the potential juror where and when (both day and time) to appear. The citizen receiving the summons can ask for a postponement or to be excused from jury duty, but must provide a valid reason to the court.

When potential jurors arrive at the courthouse, they become part of a juror pool. Only some of them will ever serve on a jury. The actual jurors for each case are chosen at random from members of the juror pool. Lawyers have the right to question these citizens before they are placed on a specific jury. The lawyers may "strike" (*eliminate*) a number of potential jurors without giving any reason. They can also eliminate jurors on the grounds of possible juror prejudice.

If selected to serve on a jury, citizens attend a trial. They hear and see witnesses and evidence. Then they discuss the evidence with other jurors to reach a verdict. Good citizens pay attention at trial and try to reach fair conclusions without bias or prejudice.

By serving on juries, citizens help protect our constitutional right to be tried by our peers (*equals*). In this case, it is easy to see how our rights and obligations are closely related. The Sixth Amendment guarantees us the benefit of a trial by jury, but our help is needed to serve as jurors for others if this right is to be effective.

The Responsibilities of Citizenship

In addition to the legal obligations (or duties) of citizenship, citizens have responsibilities that are not enforced by penalties. These are things citizens *should* do. All of these are forms of "civic participation" (*participating in government*). They are ways of being an active citizen.

If ordinary citizens do not devote some of their time to public affairs, democracy simply cannot work. Passive citizenship cannot ensure the success of our democratic system of government. Our system depends on the willingness of its citizens to perform their responsibilities as well as their legal obligations.

Be Informed. To influence public policy and to make wise decisions when voting, citizens need to be informed. They should read or listen to reliable sources of information—such as books, newspapers and news magazines, radio, television, and the Internet.

Chapter 12 | The Obligations, Responsibilities, and Rights of Citizens 297

Vote. Democracy depends on citizens carefully choosing their own representatives. Good citizens therefore exercise their right to vote both by being informed and by voting in every election. When they cannot be at home on the day of an election, they send in an **absentee ballot** in advance. These are special ballots, usually sent by a voter by mail, when he or she cannot go in person to the **polling place** (*the place where voting takes place*) to vote on "**Election Day**" (*the day of the election*). You will learn more about elections in the next chapter.

Express Views. Good citizens actively communicate their views to others. They write letters, speak with friends, and voice their opinions at civic meetings. In fact, one of the easiest ways to participate in our democracy is by expressing your views in a letter to the newspaper, to a special interest group, or to one of your government representatives.

Join a Political Party/Run for Office. Good citizens join political parties and may even run for public office themselves. You will learn more about elections and political parties in the next chapter.

The Active Citizen

Enrichment

Select one local issue or one thing you would like to change in your community. Then write a letter expressing your views. Send your letter to a local newspaper, to your representatives in the Florida State Legislature, or to your member of Congress:

▶ First, think about the issue you would like to address. You might want to conduct some research to get details about the problem or situation you would like to change.

▶ Then think about the changes you would like to introduce. What evidence do you have that these changes would work? Can you explain why your ideas might help to solve the problem? Has your approach been used successfully elsewhere? Do you have the names of any experts who support your ideas? In writing your letter, be sure to introduce who you are, to describe the problem, to explain your solution, to provide evidence to support your ideas, and to conclude by showing how your solution will solve the problem. Then thank your reader.

▶ Next see what local newspapers might be interested in printing your letter. Search the Internet to find the names of local newspapers, or ask your school librarian.

▶ Then search the Internet to find the name of your representatives in the Florida House of Representatives and the Florida Senate. Also find the name of your member of Congress.

Attend Civic Meetings. Good citizens attend **civic meetings**—both to remain informed and to provide their views to government leaders who must make decisions. A civic meeting is a group of citizens meeting for a public purpose. These could be public meetings of the local school board, deciding which

programs to fund; or public meetings of the town planning commission, deciding where to build a new road; or "town hall meetings" called by your member of the state legislature or Congress, who is trying to sound out local opinion on future legislation.

Petition the government. Citizens have the right to petition their government. A **petition** is a formal written request to government officials to make some change. Usually a petition addresses a single issue. Most petitions are addressed to legislators--such as the members of the Congress. Petitions often include the signatures of other citizens who agree with the request. It takes time and effort to write a petition and obtain signatures. Good citizens are willing to make this effort to let their representatives know how they would like their government to act on important issues.

Volunteer. Finally, good citizens will **volunteer** from time to time on local projects for the good of the community—such as cleaning up local roads on a special "pick-up litter" day, working in a local school library, reading to elderly citizens at a local community center, or serving on a student or parent committee that is making recommendations to the local school board.

The aim of all of these forms of **civic participation** is to promote the "**common good**" or "**public good**"—simply, what is good for the community as a whole.

The Active Citizen

How important would you rate each of these obligations and responsibilities of citizenship?

	Not important	Important	Very important
Obeying the law	☐	☐	☐
Justify your evaluation _____			
Paying taxes	☐	☐	☐
Justify your evaluation _____			
Defending the nation	☐	☐	☐
Justify your evaluation _____			
Serving on a jury	☐	☐	☐
Justify your evaluation _____			
Voting in elections	☐	☐	☐
Justify your evaluation _____			

Continues ▶

Attending civic meetings	☐	☐	☐
Justify your evaluation _____			
Petitioning the government	☐	☐	☐
Justify your evaluation _____			
Running for office	☐	☐	☐
Justify your evaluation _____			

▶ Conduct a community service project with your classmates to promote the public good. Your teacher may divide your class into groups. Each group can search the Internet to find a good local community service project to undertake. Some possible ideas are to:
- organize an after-school event for local elementary school children;
- act as tour guides showing fourth and fifth graders your middle school;
- help the environment by picking up litter at a park, or by volunteering in a local recycling program;
- volunteer to read or talk to elderly patients at a local nursing home;
- volunteer at the local office of a nonprofit organization, such as Habitat for Humanity, the American Red Cross, or the American Cancer Society;
- volunteer at a local food bank or soup kitchen for the homeless;
- volunteer at a local museum or community center.

▶ What would be the consequences for American society if citizens **refused** to perform their citizenship responsibilities? Would society fall apart? Would the military or a dictator take over? Or would things continue nearly the same as they are today? Prepare an oral presentation, a skit, a PowerPoint presentation, or a video showing what would happen in the United States under these circumstances.

The Rights of Citizenship

Citizenship brings rights as well as obligations and responsibilities. Some of these rights are shared with visitors and lawful permanent residents. Other rights, such as voting, belong exclusively (*only*) to citizens of the United States.

Individual Rights Guaranteed in the Constitution

Some rights are guaranteed to all individuals by the text of the original Constitution:

"The Privilege of the Writ of Habeas Corpus shall not be suspended, unless when in Cases of Rebellion or Invasion the public Safety may require it. No Bill of Attainder or ex post facto Law shall be passed."

—U.S. Constitution, Article I, Section 9

Writ of *Habeas Corpus*

Article I, Section 9 prevents Congress from taking certain actions against citizens. These include sus-

pending the right to a writ of habeas corpus. "Habeas corpus" means to "have the body." A "writ of habeas corpus" is a type of court order. It is a court order to an official to bring an imprisoned person before the court. The court will then decide whether there is enough evidence to justify the imprisonment.

A lawyer or relative can request a "writ of habeas corpus" to free someone who has been wrongfully imprisoned.

Federal courts can use the "writ of habeas corpus" to order the appearance of someone imprisoned by a state court, even if that person has been imprisoned on the basis of state law. This provides a pathway for citizens to use the federal courts to challenge the imprisonment of individuals they believe are unjustly imprisoned by state courts. Thousands of petitions are filed in federal courts each year for a writ of habeas corpus to free prisoners in state prisons. The Constitution states that the right to petition for a writ of habeas corpus cannot be suspended unless the nation is threatened by rebellion or invasion.

No *Ex Post Facto* Laws

Ex post facto is a Latin phrase meaning "after the fact." An **ex post facto** law is a law condemning an action that is passed *after* the action was taken. For example, suppose Congress passed a new federal law on June 30th, placing a penalty on all those who failed to wear helmets while riding on motorcycles on interstate highways. If the law placed the penalty on all those who had not worn a helmet since last January 1st, even though the law itself was only passed on June 30th, this would be an *ex post facto* law. How could a motorcyclist on an interstate highway have known, on January 1st, the requirements that Congress would introduce six months later? *Ex post facto* laws are obviously unfair. For this very reason, the Constitution forbids *ex post facto* laws.

These two constitutional protections extend not just to U.S. citizens but to all individuals in the United States—visitors, lawful permanent residents, and citizens.

The Active Citizen

Which of these illustrates a writ of *habeas corpus* and which is an *ex post facto* law?

A. "This U.S. District Court orders the state prison to bring prisoner Daniel Jones before it."

B. "All those who entered this building last month after 5:00 p.m. shall pay a $200 fine."

Individual Rights Guaranteed by the Bill of Rights

Other individual rights were added to the Constitution by the Bill of Rights in 1791. You have already studied these rights in Chapter 9, and reviewed Supreme Court cases interpreting some of these rights in Chapter 10. A summary of those important citizenship rights appears on the next page.

Chapter 12 | The Obligations, Responsibilities, and Rights of Citizens

THE BILL OF RIGHTS

First Amendment	The right to freedom of speech, freedom of the press, freedom of religion, freedom of assembly, and freedom to petition the government.
Second Amendment	The right to bear arms.
Third Amendment	The right not to have troops quartered without permission in one's home in peacetime.
Fourth Amendment	No search or seizure (*arrest*) without a warrant or a reasonable exception.
Fifth Amendment	No "double jeopardy" (*being tried twice for the same crime*); no "self-incrimination" (*being forced to testify against ourself*); no taking away of "life, liberty or property" without "due process of law"; and no taking of property by eminent domain (*for "public use"*) without just compensation.
Sixth Amendment	The right to a speedy and public trial by an impartial jury for a criminal offense; the right to be informed of all criminal charges; the right to face and question witnesses; and the right to have legal counsel (*a lawyer*).
Seventh Amendment	The right to a trial by jury in some civil matters.
Eighth Amendment	No excessive bail; no excessive fines; and no "cruel and unusual punishments."
Ninth Amendment	People may have other, "unenumerated rights," which are not mentioned in the Constitution or the Bill of Rights. Just because individuals are given several specific rights does not mean that they do not also have other unlisted rights.
Tenth Amendment	Rights not given to the federal government are "reserved" for the states and the people.

These rights belong not only to American citizens but to all individuals present in the United States—visitors, lawful permanent residents, and citizens.

There are other rights and privileges, however, enjoyed only by American citizens.

For Citizens Only: The Benefits of U.S. Citizenship

The most important rights held **exclusively** (*only*) by U.S. citizens are: (1) the right to vote; and (2) the right to hold political office.

As you know, the 15th, 19th, 24th and 26th Amendments guaranteed the right to vote to several different groups of U.S. citizens (see Chapter 9).

In addition to these rights, only U.S. citizens have the right to carry a U.S. passport, to reenter the United States after living abroad, and to serve on juries. Most federal jobs and several other occupations also require U.S. citizenship. Only U.S. citizens, for example, can work in the U.S. Post Office. Lawful permanent residents are permitted to enlist in the armed services, but some positions in the U.S. military are only open to U.S. citizens.

The Exclusive Benefits of U.S. Citizenship

- Only U.S. citizens can vote in U.S elections or serve on juries.
- Only U.S. citizens can carry a U.S. passport.
- A U.S. citizen can never lose his or her right to reside in the United States.
- U.S. citizens have a priority over permanent residents when applying to bring family members to the United States.
- Only U.S. citizens can run for elective office in the federal government and most state and local government offices.
- Many federal government jobs and some state government jobs require U.S. citizenship.
- Many college financial aid programs are limited to U.S. citizens.
- Other government benefits may be open only to U.S. citizens.

The Active Citizen

Rights

Freedom to express yourself.
Freedom to worship as you wish.
Right to a prompt, fair trial by jury.
Right to vote in elections for public officials.
Right to apply for federal employment requiring U.S. citizenship.
Right to run for elected office.
Freedom to pursue "life, liberty, and the pursuit of happiness."

Obligations and Responsibilities

Support and defend the Constitution.
Stay informed of the issues affecting your community.
Participate in the democratic process (including voting and running for office).
Respect and obey federal, state, and local laws.
Respect the rights, beliefs, and opinions of others.
Participate in your local community.
Pay income and other taxes honestly, and on time, to federal, state, and local authorities.
Serve on a jury when called upon.
Defend the country if the need should arise.

The chart above was taken from the website of the U.S. Citizenship and Immigration Service. It has been changed slightly. (See https://www.uscis.gov/citizenship/learners/citizenship-rights-and-responsibilities). It lists the rights, obligations and responsibilities of U.S. citizenship.

- Select one right and one obligation/responsibility that apply to both U.S. citizens and to lawful permanent residents. Explain each one.
- Select one right and one obligation/responsibility from the chart above that apply to U.S. citizens but *not* to lawful permanent residents. Explain each one.
- Imagine that you have a friend whose parents are lawful permanent residents. They have already lived in the United States for 12 years. Write a letter explaining the benefits of U.S. citizenship to them and outlining what they must do to become naturalized citizens.

Name _____

Look at each of the scenarios below. Then explain the obligations and responsibilities of a good citizen in each situation.

Scenario	What a Good Citizen Would Do
The United States is under attack. The President of the United States has asked Congress for a declaration of war. Congress has declared war and has authorized the Selective Service System to call up all men between the ages of 18 and 25 for military service.	
A resident of Alcoma in Polk County has received a jury summons from the County Circuit Court. However, this resident has an operation scheduled for eye surgery the same day that cannot be easily changed.	
Andrew and Rachel Jackson have received a notice from the Internal Revenue Service that they have made an error in last year's income taxes. The notice states that they owe an additional $3,345 to the federal government, as well as a $600 penalty.	
A young hospital worker has registered to vote but has not had time to study the issues closely. The Presidential election is this coming Tuesday.	
The town is holding a civic meeting to decide whether to allow property developers to build a new entertainment complex and residential development of single-family homes.	
The local middle school is looking for parent chaperones so that fifth graders can take their annual trip to watch state government in action in Tallahassee.	
Stan is on a jury that has already been deliberating for two days. He believes that the accused is innocent, but he is tired of the jury deliberations. If he changes his vote to convict the accused, he can leave for home in a few hours. Stan believes the accused will only have to serve six months in prison at most, if convicted.	
Nancy is driving home after a long day at work. She is at a red light that always seems to take a long time to change. She notices there is no traffic and there are no police cars or police officers in sight.	
There is a leaky fire hydrant in Mr. Smith's neighborhood. It seems to be wasting water, but nothing has been done to fix it for more than three weeks.	
Ms. Jamie disagrees strongly with recent cuts in school funding, which have caused her local high school to eliminate its art program. Ms. Jamie is a professional artist. She believes that students should have the opportunity to study art in high school. She argues that art is important, not only for art appreciation and the enjoyment of life, but also to develop vital skills in spatial reasoning needed for engineering, artificial intelligence, computer programming, physics, anatomy, medicine, graphic design, architecture, interior design, and fashion.	

Name _____

Identify the terms and phrases in the concept circles below and explain how they fit together.

Circle 1:
- Five years residence
- "Good character"
- History and Government Test
- Oath of allegiance

_____
_____
_____
_____
_____
_____
_____
_____
_____

Circle 2:
- Trial by jury
- Jury summons
- Jury
- Peers

_____
_____
_____
_____
_____
_____
_____
_____
_____

Name _____

Identify the terms and phrases in the concept circles below and explain how they fit together.

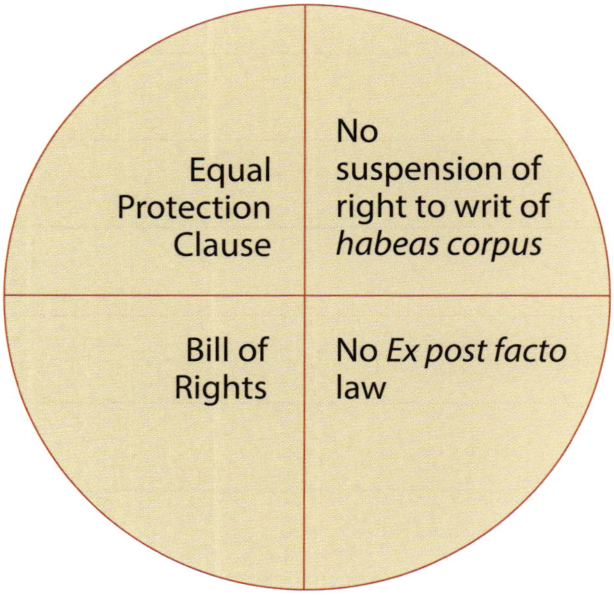

- Equal Protection Clause
- No suspension of right to writ of *habeas corpus*
- Bill of Rights
- No *Ex post facto* law

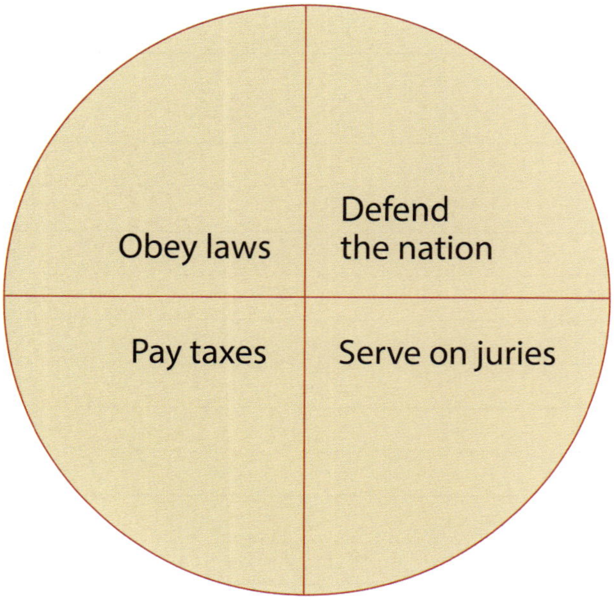

- Obey laws
- Defend the nation
- Pay taxes
- Serve on juries

306   Chapter 12 | The Obligations, Responsibilities, and Rights of Citizens

Name _____

Identify the terms and phrases in the concept circles below and explain how they fit together.

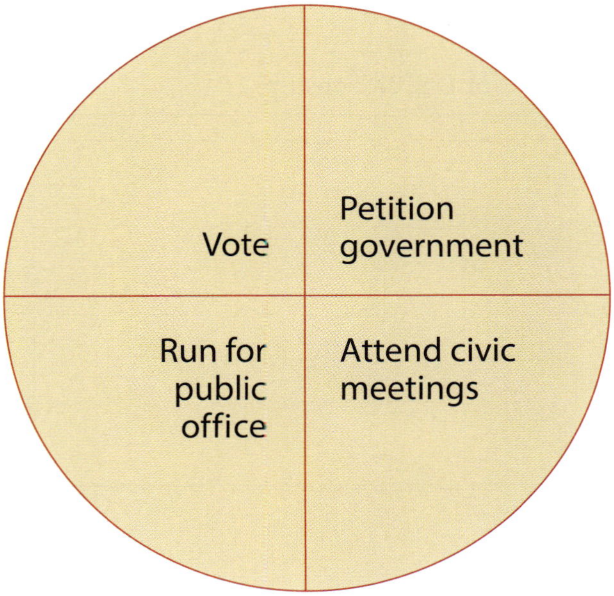

- Vote
- Petition government
- Run for public office
- Attend civic meetings

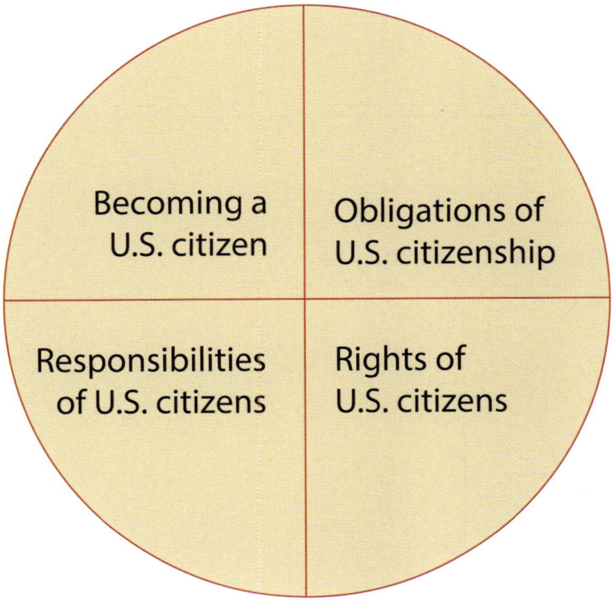

_____
_____
_____
_____
_____
_____
_____

- Becoming a U.S. citizen
- Obligations of U.S. citizenship
- Responsibilities of U.S. citizens
- Rights of U.S. citizens

_____
_____
_____
_____
_____
_____
_____

Chapter 12 | The Obligations, Responsibilities, and Rights of Citizens

Name _____

Imagine that you are making your own comic strip to explain the obligations, responsibilities and rights of U.S. citizenship to elementary school children. You can include captions, characters and speech bubbles in your comic strip.

In these panels, make your comic strip explaining the obligations of U.S. citizenship:

In these panels, make your comic strip explaining the responsibilities of U.S. citizenship:

In these panels, make your comic strip explaining the rights of U.S. citizenship:

Name _____

What are the basic steps for becoming a naturalized citizen of the United States? Complete the chart below. First list the qualifications you need to meet to be eligible for U.S. citizenship. Then identify the steps you would have to take to become a naturalized citizen.

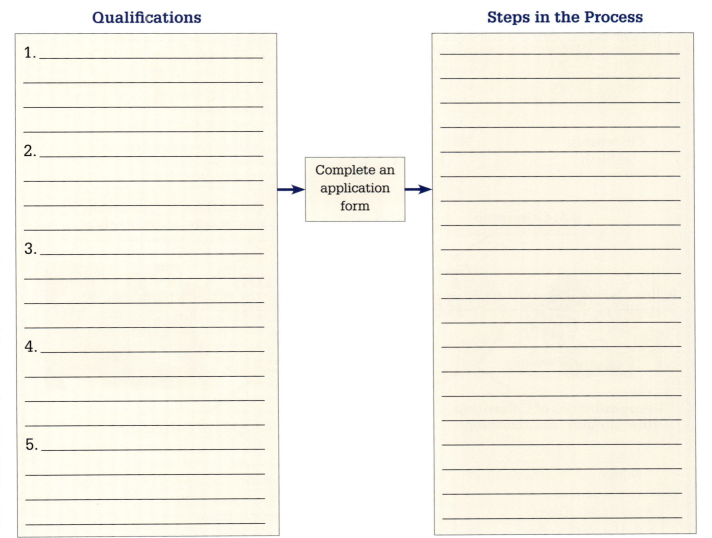

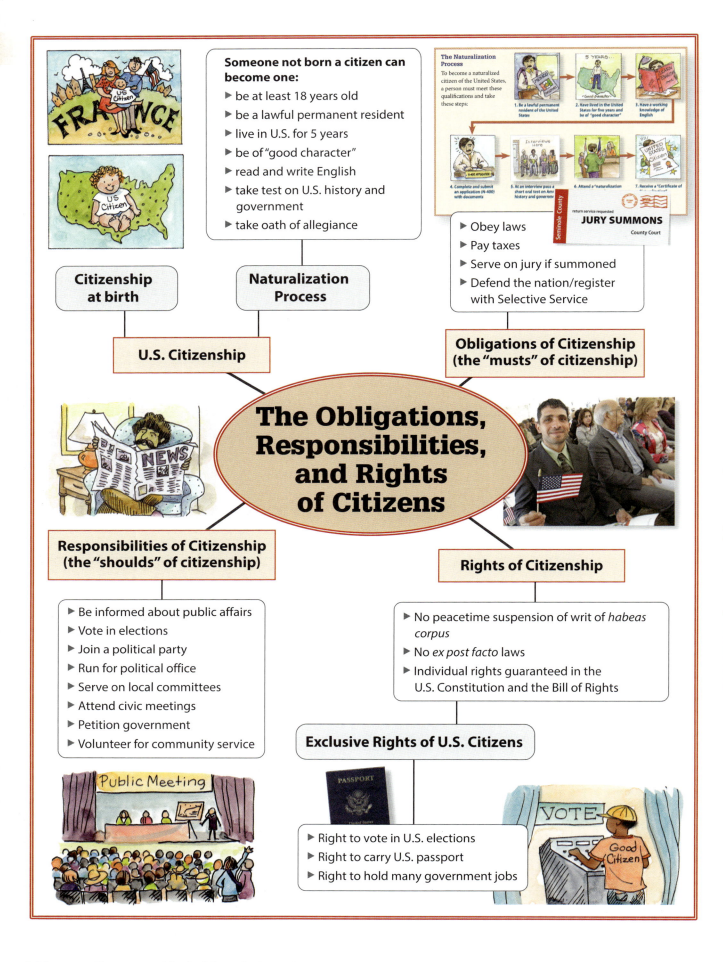

Review Cards: The Obligations, Responsibilities, and Rights of Citizens

Obtaining United States Citizenship

- A **citizen** is a legally recognized member of a nation.
- In the United States, the Fourteenth Amendment specifies two paths to citizenship: at birth and through naturalization.
- A person receives citizenship at birth by the "Law of Soil," if they are born in the United States, or by the "Law of Blood," if born outside but both parents are American citizens. If only one parent is an American citizen, the "Law of Blood" still applies if that parent has lived at least one year continuously in America.
- **Immigrants** to the United States (*those who come from other countries with an intent to live here*) can become citizens through **naturalization**. To become a "naturalized" U.S. citizen, a person must know English, be of good character, be at least 18 years old, and have been a lawful permanent resident for at least 5 years. Then he or she must complete an application, pass a test on American history and government, and swear an oath of allegiance.
- A person who is not a citizen but who lawfully lives and works in the United States is a "**lawful permanent resident**," or legal alien. Lawful permanent residents hold "green cards."
- Legal aliens have the right to live and work in the U.S., to receive professional certification, to leave and re-enter the United States, and to be protected under the Bill of Rights. They cannot vote.
- The naturalization process has made America more attractive to immigrants, who enrich America with their own talents, cultures and traditions.

The Obligations of Citizenship: What Citizens *Must* Do

- Citizens have an **obligation to obey the law, to pay taxes, to defend the nation,** and **to serve on juries**. Visitors must also obey the law and pay taxes, such as local sales taxes, or income taxes if they work. Citizens and visitors can be punished for failing to meet any of their obligations.
- Citizens have an obligation to help defend the nation. All draft-age males, whether citizens or residents, must register with the **Selective Service**. They also have an obligation to serve the military if **conscripted**; however, conscription has not happened since 1973.
- Citizens have an obligation to serve on juries when called. Citizens are called to jury duty with a **jury summons**.
- Trial by jury is a constitutional right. However, we can only preserve this right by meeting our obligation to serve as a juror when called.

The Responsibilities of Citizenship: What Citizens *Should* Do

- **Citizenship responsibilities** are not enforced by law, but they are encouraged. These include participation in and having knowledge of local, state, and national affairs and events.
- Responsible citizens who are **informed** and active in public policy ensure a working democracy.
- Citizens meet their **citizenship responsibilities** by **voting, running for office, attending civic meetings** and **petitioning the government**. They can also **volunteer** for local service projects to promote the **common** or **public good** (what is good for the community).

Chapter 12 | The Obligations, Responsibilities, and Rights of Citizens

The Rights of Citizenship

- U.S. citizens have rights as well as obligations and responsibilities.
- The U.S. Constitution guarantees certain rights to all people in America, both citizens and non-citizens. State constitutions, like the Florida State Constitution, also protect citizens' rights.
  - Everyone is guaranteed the right to apply for a **writ of *habeas corpus***, a court order to bring a prisoner before the court to determine if his or her imprisonment is lawful.
  - Everyone is protected against ***ex post facto*** **laws**. *Ex post facto* means "after the fact." An *ex post facto* law punishes people for doing something that only became illegal after they did it.
- The Bill of Rights applies to everyone in the United States—citizens and non-citizens alike.
- Some rights are only enjoyed by U.S. citizens. Only U.S. citizens can vote and hold political office in the United States.
- Other benefits of U.S. citizenship include the right to live permanently in the United States, the right to have a U.S. passport, the right to hold certain jobs and military offices that require citizenship, the right to have priority in applying to bring family members from other countries to the United States, and the right to enjoy certain other government and private benefits, such as some college scholarships.

What Do You Know?

SS.7.C.2.3

1. The list below identifies several activities.

   - Attending a school board meeting
   - Voting in a primary election
   - Sending a petition to local officials
   - Putting a candidate's sign in your yard
   - Registering voters at a community college

   What do these activities illustrate?

   A. ways that citizens can meet their citizenship obligations

   B. opportunities for citizens to participate in national elections

   C. opportunities for citizens to influence political action committees

   D. ways in which citizens can meet their citizenship responsibilities

SS.7.C.2.1

2. The diagram below shows the requirements for becoming a naturalized citizen.

Which statement completes the diagram?

A. Pay federal income tax
B. Have an annual income of $20,000 or more
C. Have resided in the United States for five years
D. Have a parent, spouse or child who is a U.S. citizen

SS.7.C.2.2

3. The document below was part of a summons to perform an important civic duty.

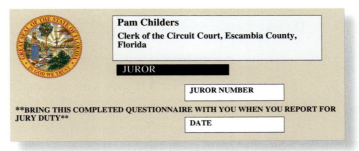

Why is it important for citizens to meet the obligation indicated in this document?

A. to guarantee our right to confront witnesses
B. to preserve constitutional limits on governmental power
C. to guarantee our right to be judged by a jury of our peers
D. to protect our right to petition for a writ of *habeas corpus*

SS.7.C.2.5

4. What protects a citizen from being punished for an act that only became a crime after the act was committed?

A. the right to petition for a writ of *habeas corpus*
B. the unenumerated rights of the Ninth Amendment
C. the Constitution's prohibition of *ex post facto* laws
D. the powers reserved to citizens by the Tenth Amendment

Chapter 12 | The Obligations, Responsibilities, and Rights of Citizens

SS.7.C.2.14

5. The notice below was posted by Florida Americorps.

May 8, 2014: Governor Announces a Disaster Fund for Floridians Affected by Flooding

The company, Florida Americorps, will coordinate the volunteers and donations in the disaster. They urge all Floridians to serve their local community. They raise funds to aid the Commission in accomplishing its goals of meeting human needs in Florida. They are guided by a voluntary Board of Directors.

What is an appropriate private community service project that responsible citizens might undertake in response to this notice?

A. organize a 10K bike race for breast cancer
B. establish a book club at the local high school
C. help repair a nursing home that has been flooded
D. take senior citizens to a Miami Heat basketball game

SS.7.C.2.1

Ester Tua Caballa becomes a citizen in the U.S. District Court in Pensacola, Florida in June 2014.

6. The photograph on the left shows an accomplishment of Ms. Ester Tua Caballa.

What are three of the requirements she had to fulfill for this accomplishment?

A. reside in the United States for five years; be of "good character"; pass a U.S. history test
B. be of "good character"; pass a test of general knowledge; have a high school diploma
C. be of "good character"; enter the United States lawfully; earn more than $20,000 annually
D. reside in the United States for five years; enter the United States lawfully; serve in the armed forces

SS.7.C.2.2

7. Which practice is part of the obligation of a U.S. citizen to help defend the nation?

A. serve on a jury
B. register for Selective Service
C. vote in all national elections
D. keep informed about national issues

314   Chapter 12 | The Obligations, Responsibilities, and Rights of Citizens

SS.7.C.2.14

8. The sign below was placed in public view by members of United Way.

> **GET CONNECTED!**
> **Powered by Orange County, Florida United Way Volunteers**
>
> **Commit to Help by:**
> ☑ Bagging & Distributing food
> ☑ Stocking shelves
> ☑ Tutoring a homeless child
> ☑ Mentoring, playing with children, ages 4–12, facing homelessness
> ☑ Helping sand and stain bunk beds inside the Thomas House Family Shelter

Which statement best describes the impact of such activities by private citizens?

A. They enable volunteers to earn more money.
B. They often lead to friction between volunteer groups.
C. They increase government involvement in people's lives.
D. They can make a positive difference in the lives of those they help.

SS.7.C.2.3

9. Which is considered a citizenship responsibility rather than an obligation?

A. paying taxes
B. obeying the law
C. attending civic meetings
D. registering for Selective Service

SS.7.C.2.3

10. The list below identifies several activities conducted by U.S. citizens.

> - Voting in elections
> - Attending civic meetings
> - Petitioning the government
> - Running for public office

Which is an important reason for citizens to engage in these activities?

A. to increase their wealth
B. to reduce their income tax
C. to promote the common good
D. to limit the powers of the government

SS.7.C.2.4

11. The Venn diagram below compares two means of becoming a U.S. citizen.

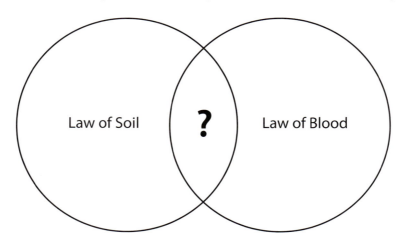

Which characteristic completes the Venn diagram?

A. Obtained at birth
B. Does not include voting rights
C. Obtained through naturalization
D. Requires residence in the United States

SS.7.C.2.3

12. What would be the most likely consequence to society if citizens began refusing to fulfill their citizenship responsibilities?

A. People would face the threat of losing their individual rights and freedoms.
B. People would have more free time because they would have fewer social obligations.
C. People would benefit from the direction of strong leaders who would guard their freedoms.
D. People would find that society was able to look after itself with the help of civic participation.

SS.7.C.2.5

13. Joe Smith was found not guilty of robbing a store. When Joe was tried in state court a second time for the same crime, he was found guilty and sent to state prison.

Joe's lawyer believes that Joe has been wrongly imprisoned. What can the lawyer do?

A. protest against an unfair *ex post facto* law
B. petition for a writ of *habeas corpus*
C. demand Joe's "due process" rights
D. petition for a writ of *certiorari*

SS.7.C.2.5

14. The diagram below shows some of the rights of U.S. citizens and of lawful permanent residents.

Rights of U.S. Citizens
- Right to vote
- Right to hold U.S. passport
- Priority in bringing relatives to the United States
- Right to work at jobs in the federal government

Rights of U.S. Citizens and Lawful Permanent Residents
- ?
- No ex post facto laws
- Rights in the Bill of Rights
- Right to work and reside in the United States

Which completes the diagram?

A. Right to refuse to pay taxes
B. Right to run for public office
C. Right to petition for *habeas corpus*
D. Right to work at the U.S. Post Office

SS.7.C.2.2

15. Which of these is a legal obligation of U.S. citizenship?

A. to reside in the United States
B. to save money for retirement
C. to vote in Presidential elections
D. to serve on a jury when summoned

SS.7.C.2.1

16. Which of these is one of the legal requirements for becoming a citizen?

A. registering to vote
B. paying income taxes
C. having relatives in the United States
D. living in the United States at least five years

SS.7.C.2.5

17. Which of these is an example of how the Constitution limits rights?

A. by prohibiting *ex post facto* laws
B. by giving citizens the right to vote
C. by giving government limited powers over us
D. by allowing people to apply for writs of *habeas corpus*

Chapter 12 | The Obligations, Responsibilities, and Rights of Citizens

SS.7.C.2.1

18. Which statement identifies a positive impact of the naturalization process on American society?

   A. It increases American power and influence overseas.
   B. It leads to greater divisiveness on domestic political issues.
   C. It attracts talented immigrants who contribute knowledge and skills.
   D. It costs taxpayers money to enforce immigration and naturalization laws.

Permanent residents about to become citizens of the United States at a naturalization ceremony. What new rights, obligations and responsibilities will they have as U.S. citizens?

CHAPTER 13

Political Parties and Elections

SS.7.C.2.8 Identify America's current political parties, and illustrate their ideas about government.

SS.7.C.2.9 Evaluate candidates for political office by analyzing their qualifications, experience, issue-based platforms, debates, and political ads.

SS.7.C.2.7 Conduct a mock election to demonstrate the voting process and its impact on a school, community, or local level.

Names and Terms You Should Know

Political party	Socialist Party	Experience
Platform	Communist Party	Debate
Democratic Party	Candidate	Political advertisement
Republican Party	Public office	
Libertarian Party	Campaign	

Florida "Keys" to Learning

1. A political party is a group of people who share political beliefs. They organize to promote their shared beliefs by electing some of their members to government.

2. Political parties have had an important impact on American society, government and the political system. They make citizens more aware of public issues, nominate candidates to public office, hold primary elections, finance political campaigns, write platforms expressing their political ideas and future plans, and help legislators to organize and pass their legislative programs.

3. Americans have a two-party system. Since 1860, the two main political parties have been the Democratic and Republican Parties.

4. The Democratic Party in general favors providing more government services in order to promote social justice and achieve full equality of opportunity. These additional government services often require higher taxes.

5. The Republican Party in general favors less government interference in people's lives, more private enterprise, lower taxes, a strong military, and an active foreign policy.

6. In addition to these two major political parties, there have been many smaller parties in American history. These include the Socialist Party, the Communist Party, and the Libertarian Party. These parties are often formed by citizens with strong feelings about particular issues.

7. The United States is a representative democracy. This means that citizens elect representatives to decide issues for them. Only U.S. citizens can vote and run for public office.

8. To prevent fraud (*cheating; deceit*) in elections, a citizen must be registered to vote in his or her county in order to participate in an election. To register to vote in Florida, a person must be a citizen, be at least 18 years of age, be mentally capable, not have been convicted of a felony, and provide a current and valid identification card, such as a driver license.

9. In the United States, political parties nominate candidates for election to public office. Often, individuals from the same party will compete in a primary election to obtain their party's nomination. The nominees from opposing parties then run against each other. During the election campaign, candidates use political advertisements and other tactics to gain support. On Election Day, registered voters go to their polling place to vote.

10. To run for a particular office, a candidate must meet the specific requirements for that office, such as age and residency. Voters should evaluate (*judge*) qualified candidates based on their experience, issue-based platforms, performance in debates and political advertisements:

- *Experience:* Have they held the same or similar offices and done a good job? Do they have other valuable experiences?
- *Issue-based Platforms:* What are their views on key issues? Do you agree with their positions?
- *Debates:* Which candidates seem to be more informed and better able to think "on their feet"?
- *Political "ads":* What information do they provide and what do they say about the candidate who approved them?

Political parties are groups of people who share political beliefs. Usually, their members hold similar ideas about the role of government in society. Political parties promote their beliefs and work to get some of their members elected into positions in government.

The Rise of Political Parties

Even in colonial times, political parties had existed in Great Britain. When the United States became independent, many American leaders, including George Washington, hoped that Americans would *not* form their own political parties. In fact, the Constitution makes no mention at all of political parties. Washington and others feared that rivalry between parties would threaten American unity.

Washington's wish was not realized. The first American political parties formed around Alexander Hamilton and Thomas Jefferson during Washington's own first term as President. Hamilton's followers, the Federalists, favored a powerful federal government that promoted American manufacturing and commerce. Jefferson's supporters, the Democratic-Republicans, favored a weaker federal government.

The names of American political parties have changed over time, but for most of American history, Americans have had a two-party system. This means that in every period, elected government officeholders have almost always come from just two political parties.

For the past 160 years, our two main political parties have been the Democrats and the Republicans. Andrew Jackson is generally considered as the founder of the modern Democratic Party in 1828. Abraham Lincoln helped to organize the Republican Party in 1854. The Republican Party was first formed to oppose the spread of slavery to Western territories.

In addition to these two major parties, there have been many smaller parties in American history. These are usually formed by citizens with strong feelings about particular issues—from the demand for women's suffrage to more recent concerns for the protection of the environment and outrage at high taxes.

Political parties play many important roles. They make citizens more aware of public issues. They nominate candidates to political office. They hold primary elections. They finance political campaigns. They write platforms (*formal policy statements*) expressing their political ideas and future plans. And they help legislators to organize and pass their legislative programs.

American Political Parties Today

In the United States today, there are two major political parties:

- The Democratic Party
- The Republican Party

There are also several smaller political parties, often called "third parties." These include:

Chapter 13 | Political Parties and Elections

In fact, almost any group of dedicated citizens can register to form a new political party.

The Democratic Party

The Democratic Party controlled Florida politics for almost a century—from 1877 until the Civil Rights Movement in 1967. In the 1930s and 1960s, Democratic leaders like Presidents Franklin D. Roosevelt and Lyndon B. Johnson introduced new ideas, making the Democratic Party the party of "big government." They favored using the power of government to solve social and economic problems and to improve peoples' lives.

The cartoonist Thomas Nast introduced the donkey as a symbol of the Democratic Party in 1870.

What do Democrats believe in?

Today, the Democratic Party especially represents the interests of workers, minority groups, women, children, and young people.

Democrats generally favor greater government intervention (*interference; involvement*) to promote social justice and equality of opportunity. They believe that government support is needed to help Americans who are less well off. Democrats are often more willing than members of other parties to increase taxes in order to support domestic programs and investment in the nation's infrastructure—such as schools, universities, roads, public works and research. They are also strong environmentalists. On foreign policy, Democrats are often divided between those who favor an active foreign policy and those who would prefer to see more resources spent on non-military purposes at home.

Under President Barack Obama, Democrats introduced health care and financial reforms, withdrew U.S. troops from foreign soil, and provided temporary federal support to American industries about to collapse.

According to their website, Florida Democrats believe in the following:

"Florida Democrats believe in effective and efficient government that prioritizes (moves up in importance) *quality education, affordable health care, and an economy in which anyone who works hard can succeed.*

Most importantly, we believe that we are stronger together. We believe the fundamental (basic; most important) *American promise—that you can go as far as your own hard work will take you—should shine brightest in Florida.*

That is why we champion the middle class and cherish the principle that all Floridians should have the opportunity to work hard and succeed. That is why we will never stop fighting for better public schools, because education is the surest path to a better life for millions.

From standing for affordable health care and better schools to fighting for civil rights and access to the ballot box, Florida Democrats are leading every day to move our state forward."

Democrats thus favor using the power of government to promote civil rights and to provide high quality public education, affordable health care, protection of the environment, and a growing economy. They are willing to have higher taxes to pay for these benefits. Democrats believe this approach best promotes the interests of hard-working, middle class Americans.

The Republican Party

The Republican Party first arrived in Florida in 1867, just after the Civil War. But after 1877, Florida became a part of the "Solid South"—for the next 90 years, all its elected officials were Democrats.

During the Civil Rights Movement, Florida's Republican Party gained new support. Today, Governor Ron DeSantis and a majority of both houses of Florida's state legislature are Republicans.

Cartoonist Thomas Nast also introduced the elephant to represent the Republican Party—known as the "GOP," or Grand Old Party.

What do Republicans stand for?

Since the 1950s, Republicans have been the party of less government interference, more private enterprise, lower taxes, less public debt, and a strong foreign policy. They believe private initiatives—from education to energy and the environment—can often do a better job than government programs. These ideas were famously expressed in 1981, when Republican President Ronald Reagan told the nation that "government is not the solution to our problem, government is the problem." Under a series of Republican Presidents, federal domestic programs were cut and power was returned to state governments. At the same time, most Republican Presidents have stood for a strong military and active foreign policy. Under President Donald Trump, Republicans have lowered federal taxes, renegotiated trade agreements with foreign countries, reduced government regulations, and imposed stricter immigration controls.

The Republican Party of Florida has adopted the following "Mission Statement":

"The Republican Party of Florida will promote the principles upon which our nation and our state were founded: freedom, liberty, personal responsibility, and accountability. We will advocate fiscally-sound, common-sense solutions that will promote job and economic growth, provide the best education to our children, and create a path to prosperity for Florida and America."

According to Florida Republicans:

"Our roots run deep, with a foundation built on the core principles of lower taxes, less government, and more freedom."

In summary, Republicans favor less government involvement in our lives, lower taxes, and greater personal freedom. They believe this approach best promotes economic growth and job creation.

Democrats and Republicans on the Role of Government

Democrats: Government intervention can overcome social inequalities, help the economy, and promote the common good.

- Federal government intervention is needed to help underprivileged groups and promote economic prosperity.
- Taxes may have to be increased to support domestic programs like public education and health care.
- Civil rights, women, young Americans, and environmental protection should be strongly supported.

Republicans: People are more successful with less government interference and greater freedom.

- There should be less government interference in people's lives and more personal freedom.
- Lower tax rates will stimulate the economy and promote individual initiative.
- Fewer regulations will stimulate the economy.
- Americans need a strong military establishment and an active foreign policy in defense of freedom.

Chapter 13 | Political Parties and Elections

The Active Citizen

- Write a letter to a friend comparing the views of Democrats and Republicans on the role of government in society.
- Interview a relative, friend or neighbor who supports one of the two major political parties. Ask this person why he or she prefers one major party to the other. Also ask how active he or she is in politics.

In addition to these two major parties, there are also several smaller "third parties" in the United States. These include the Socialist, Communist and Libertarian Parties.

The Socialist Party

Socialism developed in reaction to the Industrial Revolution. Industrial laborers worked in horrible conditions for long hours with low pay, while many business owners amassed vast fortunes. Socialists sought to correct these injustices by proposing public ownership of energy, resources, transportation, housing and other basic industries. They also favored providing free services in health and education.

After World War II, several countries in Western Europe adopted socialist systems. These proved less successful in promoting economic growth than systems with less government ownership. Several European countries began "privatizing" state-owned industries in the 1980s.

The Socialist Party of the United States of America favors more public services and a less active foreign policy. American Socialists were active in opposing American involvement in Iraq and Afghanistan. The Socialist Party also supported same-sex marriages and the free speech rights of minors. In Florida, the Socialist Party became inactive in 2011.

The Communist Party

Communism was a movement that was started in Europe in the 1840s by Karl Marx and Friedrich Engels. Communists believe that all history is the history of "class struggle." One social group, or "class," always exploits (*takes unfair advantage of*) another.

Communists claim that under the system of free enterprise (also known as capitalism), business owners exploit their workers for their own benefit. Industrial workers are paid barely enough to feed, clothe and shelter themselves. The extra value they add to the products they manufacture goes straight into the pockets of business owners. Communists believe that conditions for workers will eventually decline until angry workers finally rise up in revolt against their employers. After a violent revolution, the workers will abolish (*end*) private ownership of property and establish a communist society.

Communism was actually established in Russia after the Russian Revolution in 1917, but the experiment proved to be a terrible failure. Dictators seized control and persecuted political opponents. Communism was finally abandoned in Russia and Eastern Europe between 1989 and 1991. The failure of communism in Russia and Eastern Europe led to a loss of interest in communism in many parts of the world. However, communism still remains the official policy of some countries like China and

Cuba. There is also an active communist party in the United States.

The Communist Party USA believes in fighting racism, protecting the environment, and in organizing workers and others for social reform. The party opposes cuts to social services and education, and tax breaks to corporations, while it supports free health care for all. The slogan on their website is "People and Planet before Profits." They further explain that "We are a political party of the working class, for the working class, with no corporate sponsors or billionaire backers."

American communists believe that capitalism will eventually fail. But for the moment, they also believe in cooperating with other workers' groups and liberal Democrats. Such cooperation with other groups, they say, is needed until the oppressed classes are strong enough to overcome the forces of capitalism (free enterprise), such as large corporations. American communists today actually hope to see communism established by peaceful means:

> "During the current stage of struggle . . . , the strategy to win necessarily includes a section of . . . the Democratic Party. . . . [We] must be a party in which labor and the other core forces play the leading role, acting in alliance with all working people and progressive social movements."

Under communism, all private businesses will eventually be replaced by state ownership.

You will learn more about both socialist and communist forms of government in Chapter 16.

The Libertarian Party

The **Libertarian Party** is the third largest party in the United States today. It received more than four million votes in the 2016 Presidential election, about 3% of the total. The key word in libertarianism is "liberty." Libertarians favor less government interference in our lives and more personal freedom. They favor greater freedom of speech, freedom of religion, the free market economy, reduced taxation, reduced government spending, personal privacy, states' rights, and the right to carry guns.

The preamble (*introduction*) to the 2013 Platform of the Libertarian Party of Florida explains libertarianism as follows:

> "Libertarians seek a society based on personal liberty and responsibility—a society in which all individuals are sovereign (have final authority) over their own lives. . . . People have the right to engage in any activity that is peaceful and honest, and pursue happiness in whatever manner they choose so long as they do not forcibly or fraudulently interfere with the equal rights of others."

For example, Libertarians oppose having national education standards, which they see as unnecessary federal interference in education.

Because they oppose government interference in our lives, Libertarians oppose gun control laws. They are also against the government's "War on Drugs," which they see as government interference in people's personal choices and ineffective:

> "Libertarians believe that it is immoral for the government to dictate which substances a person is permitted to consume, whether it is alcohol, tobacco, herbal remedies, saturated fat, marijuana, etc. These decisions belong to individual people, not the government."

In summary, members of the Libertarian Party believe that we have our own lives, and that we should be free to pursue happiness in our own ways, with only very limited interference from the government.

Chapter 13 | Political Parties and Elections

The Libertarian Party of Florida promotes the following principles:

- "Recognizing absolute freedom of speech, religion, and association
- Demanding Constitutionally-limited government
- Ensuring minimal taxation and balanced budgets
- Defending property rights
- Asserting sovereignty of the State from unconstitutional federal interference
- Asserting sovereignty of the Republic from unconstitutional international interference
- Promoting a true free market economy
- Upholding the Second Amendment and the absolute right to self-defense
- Defending personal privacy and the Fourth Amendment
- Defending property rights
- Promoting strong national defense through a Constitutional foreign policy
- Ending government corruption
- Ensuring no individual, corporation or government is above the rule of law
- Ending prohibitions on all personal activities that do not infringe upon the rights of others."

Where the Political Parties Stand

Less government intervention / Lower taxes ←——————————→ More government intervention / Higher taxes

| Libertarian Party | Republican Party | Democratic Party | Socialist Party | Communist Party |

The Active Citizen

- Make a Venn diagram or chart comparing communism and Libertarianism.
- Do you support the views of the Libertarian Party? Why or why not?
- Write a letter to a friend explaining the views of either socialists, communists or Libertarians.

*You do **not** need to know about the Green Party for the EOC test.*

The Green Party   *Enrichment*

The Green Party is the fourth largest political party in the United States today. It received more than a million votes in the Presidential election of 2016. The party was originally formed to protect the environment. Green Party members oppose the competitiveness of modern society.

"Our first priority (goal) is to promote . . . a fundamental shift away from our current cultural system of exploitation (taking unfair advantage), excessive consumption and unregulated competition."

326 Chapter 13 | Political Parties and Elections

Enrichment

According to their platform, members of the Green Party support these ten "key values":

1. "Grassroots Democracy"
2. Social Justice and Equal Opportunity
3. Ecological Wisdom*
4. Non-Violence
5. Decentralization
6. Community-Based Economics and Economic Justice
7. Feminism and Gender Equity
8. Respect for Diversity
9. Personal and Global Responsibility
10. Future Focus and Sustainability**

Green Party

*"Ecological" refers to the relationship of living things to one another and the environment.

**Sustainability refers to the ability of a system to continue into the future.

The Active Citizen

▶ Which of the following political parties do you think you would most agree with—Democratic, Republican, Socialist, Communist, or Libertarian? Explain your answer.

▶ When you become old enough to register to vote, do you intend to join a political party? Explain your answer.

The Impact of Political Parties on Government and Society

Political parties have affected our government and society in both positive and negative ways.

Positive Effects of Political Parties	Negative Effects of Political Parties
Representation: Political parties represent the views of voters.	**Division:** Political parties divide Americans.
Participation: Political parties create opportunities for citizens to participate in government and politics.	**Bias:** Political parties present biased (*one-sided*) views of the issues.
Candidates: Political parties find and select candidates for elected public offices.	**Pressure:** Political parties pressure legislators and other elected officials to follow their party's program against their own beliefs.
Campaigns: Political parties manage and finance election campaigns.	**Distraction:** Legislators and other officials spend more time supporting their party, raising money and trying to get re-elected than they do on the work of government.
Voting: Political campaigns encourage people to vote in elections.	

Continues ▶

Chapter 13 | Political Parties and Elections

Positive Effects of Political Parties	Negative Effects of Political Parties
Education: Political parties educate voters by informing them about the issues. **Debate:** Political parties offer alternatives and encourage debate. **Legislation:** Political parties help members of local, state and federal lawmaking bodies organize themselves into groups on behalf of a legislative program. **Watchdogs:** Political parties serve as "watchdogs" by criticizing what opposing parties are doing. **Bridges:** Political parties serve as bridges uniting members of the executive and legislative branches of government. **Compromise:** Political parties sometimes encourage members to compromise their views.	**Self-Interest:** Political parties act to win votes, rather than doing what is really best. **Stalemate:** Divisions between competing political parties often prevent government from getting things done. **Monopolistic:** Political parties raise large sums of money for campaigns, making it hard for independent candidates to compete. 

The Active Citizen

▶ Which of these effects are the most important ones?
▶ Hold a classroom debate on the following: "Resolved: That political parties in the United States should be abolished."
▶ Make a chart illustrating the benefits and drawbacks of political parties.

*You do **not** need to know this section for the EOC test.*

Elections

Enrichment

The United States is a representative democracy. That means that rather than deciding issues directly, citizens elect representatives to decide these issues for them. In the United States, the Tuesday following the first Monday of November is known as "Election Day." Most important elections take place on that day.

You already know that one of the purposes of political parties is to organize citizens to win elections. But what exactly occurs in an election?

Voter Registration

Only citizens can vote. In order to vote in an election, a citizen must also be **registered**. To **register** is to enter information into an official record. Through this process, the government is able to prevent fraud (*cheating*) in elections. In Florida, voters register with their County Supervisor of Elections.

328   Chapter 13 | Political Parties and Elections

In all but six states, registration must take place before Election Day. The **National Voter Registration Act of 1993**, better known as the "Motor Voter" law, requires state governments to offer voter registration at the same time that someone applies for or renews his or her driver license. Most Americans now register to vote at this time. In addition, many states now allow voters to register online.

To register to vote in Florida, a person must:

- Be a citizen of the United States of America;
- Be a Florida resident;
- Be 18 years old (you may preregister if you are 16 years old);
- Not have been judged as mentally incapacitated (*incapable*) with respect to voting in Florida or any other state, without having had your voting rights restored;
- Not have been convicted of a felony in Florida, or any other state;
- Provide a current and valid Florida driver license number or Florida identification card number.

In Florida and most other states, voters can also declare a **party affiliation**. A person who declares a party affiliation is considered a "registered member" of that party and can vote in its primaries.

The Nomination Process

One important role played by political parties is finding good people to run for political office. During an election, each major party usually **nominates** (*names*) one candidate for each government office that is up for election. Smaller parties also offer candidates. An individual can even run for office as an independent candidate without the backing of any political party.

- **Primaries.** Often, individuals from the same party seeking the same political office will first compete in a **primary election** to obtain their party's nomination. A primary is a special election contested by members of the same party seeking their party's nomination. Usually it will be held several months before the general election.

  Florida has a **closed primary**. Only the registered candidates can vote in that party's primary election. All registered voters can participate, however, in non-partisan primary elections, such as for judicial offices or positions on local school boards.

- **Party Conventions.** Political parties hold state and national conventions. A convention is a large meeting. National conventions are usually held every four years to nominate candidates for President and Vice President. In August 2012, the Republican National Convention was held in Tampa, Florida.

  To win a party's nomination for President, a candidate needs the support of a majority of the delegates (*representatives*) at its national convention. Usually most of the delegates are already pledged to a candidate by the time the convention meets, based on the primaries.

  Party conventions also adopt a **party platform**—a detailed statement of the party's policies on key issues.

  A convention helps to ignite party enthusiasm behind a party's candidates for the campaign before the general election. It also provides opportunities to display party unity and strength, especially in the **media** (television, radio, newspapers and the Internet).

Chapter 13 | Political Parties and Elections

Political Campaigns

After a party chooses its nominees, its candidates campaign against the other parties for the final months before the general election. The methods that candidates use to win the nomination and to win the general election are basically the same:

- **Political Advertisements** Candidates purchase time on television and radio, or space in magazines and newspapers, in order to present their message to voters by advertising. Political advertising paid for by the candidate must include one of the following two statements:

    "Political advertisement paid for and approved by (name of candidate), (party affiliation) for (office sought)" or *"Paid by (name of candidate), (party affiliation), for (office sought)."*

    Political candidates sometimes attack opponents in their advertising. These efforts have been criticized as "negative campaign ads." Television advertising is also expensive, driving up the costs of election campaigns. At the same time, television advertising is one of the most effective means for building support.

- **Direct Mail and Telephone Campaigns** Candidates send out flyers or have volunteers call voters by telephone. Sometimes candidates will send recorded messages to large numbers of voters.

- **Canvassing Votes** Candidates and volunteers sometimes go house to house, knocking on doors in a targeted area to talk to voters. Supporters may arrange events at campaign headquarters, hotels or supporters' homes, where they discuss issues, or where candidates can meet directly with voters.

- **Reports in the Media** One of the best ways to advertise a candidate is by drawing the attention of the media to some newsworthy event.

- **Political Rallies and Demonstrations** Candidates hold political rallies in auditoriums, stadiums, or even in the street, where they give speeches to their supporters.

- **Volunteers** Unpaid volunteers play a special role in every campaign. They host meetings, contact voters, spread the messages of their candidates, make campaign contributions, and help raise additional funds.

- **Debates** In most elections, the candidates will hold public debates. A **debate** is a form of public speaking in which two sides face each other and take turns presenting their views. They also explain why they believe their opponent's views are mistaken. At these events, voters get to see the candidates face-to-face and judge for themselves how sincere the candidates are, what they know, and how quickly they think on their feet. Debates can have a significant impact on how viewers vote.

At the same time, surveys show that viewers often feel that the candidate they had already supported was the best one in the debate.

- **Online** Candidates today have their own websites to spread their campaign messages. They often post detailed policy statements on key issues on their websites.

Election Day

On "Election Day," registered voters go to their polling place to vote. A **poll** is the place where citizens vote. Polling places are usually a school, library or other public building located close to where the voter lives. No political campaigning is permitted in polling places.

When voters arrive, they proceed to a "check-in" table where poll workers check their names against an official list of registered voters in that area. In Florida, voters must show a current identification card with a picture and signature, such as a driver license, U.S. passport, or Florida identification card.

After checking in, the citizen is able to vote. The voter may be given a paper ballot and be taken to a booth where the ballot can be completed in private. Or the voter may be taken to a booth with a voting machine.

Campaign Finance

Political campaigns are paid for by private money, except for candidates for President of the United States, who may receive public money if they qualify. Presidential candidates accepting federal funds must limit their total spending in the election. Those who do not accept these funds have no limits on what they can spend from private financing. In the 2016 Presidential election, both Donald Trump and Hillary Clinton turned down public funds to avoid spending limits.

While there are limits on campaign contributions, individuals can form political committees. There are no limits to contributions made to some types of committees. Corporations and labor unions cannot make contributions to candidates, but they can make contributions to separate "political action committees," known as PACs. So long as a PAC acts independently of the candidate it supports, there is no legal limit to the amount it can spend on behalf of a candidate.

The Active Citizen

Enrichment

- Do you think there should be limits on campaign contributions?
- Why don't more citizens vote?

The table on the right shows that from 52% to 64% of all those eligible to vote in Presidential elections did so between 1948 and 2012. In 2016, only 56% of eligible voters actually voted. Why don't more eligible voters participate in Presidential elections? Conduct research on this question on the Internet and in your school library. Then give an oral presentation or PowerPoint presentation to your class. As part of your presentation, provide recommendations for increasing the number of people who come out and vote.

Source: United States Elections Project, George Mason University.

Year	Percent voting
1948	52
1952	62
1956	60
1960	64
1964	62
1968	61
1972	56
1976	55
1980	54
1984	55
1988	52
1992	58
1996	52
2000	54
2004	60
2008	62
2012	57

The EOC test requires you to know these factors for evaluating candidates.

Evaluating Candidates

In both primary and general elections, voters must make choices between candidates competing for the same position. What factors do voters consider in evaluating (*rating or judging*) candidates?

Constitutional Requirements

An initial consideration is whether the candidate meets all of the constitutional requirements for the office that he or she seeks. You learned about most of these requirements in earlier chapters.

Office	Requirements
United States (Federal)	
President	Be a "natural born citizen"; be at least 35 years of age; and have lived in the United States for 14 years.
U.S. Senator	Be at least 30 years of age; have been a U.S. citizen for nine years; and live in the state he or she will represent.
U.S. Representative	Be at least 25 years of age; have been a U.S. citizen for seven years; and live in the state from which he or she is chosen.
Florida (State)	
Governor, Lieutenant Governor and Cabinet Members	Be at least 30 years old and have been a resident of Florida for seven years.
Florida Senator	Be at least 21 years old; have been a resident of Florida for two years; and live in the district he or she will represent.
Florida Representative	Be at least 21 years old; have been a resident of Florida for two years; and live in the district he or she will represent.

Qualifications

Voters carefully consider each candidate's qualifications: where they grew up, where they were educated, what employment they had, and their past achievements. Are the qualifications of these candidates well suited to the political office they are seeking? Is there anything special about these candidates?

Experience

A closely related factor is experience. What work experience does each candidate have? What experience in public service does each have? Do any of the candidates have experience in the same or a similar office? Are any of the candidates already in office and seeking re-election? And how well did the candidates perform in their past positions? In general, voters consider how well the qualifications and experiences of the candidates have prepared them for the office they seek.

Issue-based Platforms

Where do each of the candidates stand on leading issues? Voters usually choose the candidate they most agree with on the leading issues of the campaign. Candidates usually release "issue-based platforms" of some kind—statements of where they stand on the major issues of the campaign. Candidates will repeat their positions on these issues at every available opportunity—in debates, village meetings, press conferences, political advertisements, rallies and demonstrations.

Voters must decide whether they agree with a candidate's positions. Even if they agree, voters must also consider whether the candidate will be able to meet these campaign promises if elected. A "campaign promise" is something a candidate promises to do while campaigning for election.

Performance in Debates

Candidates frequently debate one another when running for office. As you know, a debate is a form of public speaking in which candidates take turns presenting their views and challenging their opponents. Debates provide an opportunity to see candidates in action, close up. One can see how well informed they are, how quickly they can think, and how well they communicate ideas. Although the candidates have trained for the debate, what happens is always somewhat unpredictable. Voters get to see what candidates are really like as individuals, without the protection of the layers of advisers who often surround them. For this reason, voters may even be overly influenced by a candidate's performance in a debate. A candidate may make an error or appear nervous, when in fact that candidate would make an excellent leader.

Political Advertisements ("Ads")

Today, candidates present their views through television, radio, newspaper and Internet advertising. A good political advertisement presents a candidate's qualifications, experience, and views on the issues, while also showing why opponents are less qualified. They are therefore good sources of information.

Political advertisements not only serve to criticize opponents: they also reveal something about the sponsor of the ad. Does the advertisement distort or exaggerate the views and experiences of opponents? Does it make false claims about the candidate it supports? Can the ad be trusted or does it provide an example of "fake news"? Does it show that the candidate behind the ad is not completely honest or is too easily pressured by advisers? Political advertisements therefore provide additional information on whether a candidate should be supported.

	Candidate A	Candidate B
Qualifications		
Experience		
Issues		
Debate performance		
Political Advertisements		

Chapter 13 | Political Parties and Elections

Name _____

Evaluating Candidates

The following two candidates are running for the office of Senator in the Florida Senate, to represent District 34 (part of Broward County).

Kevin Smith is 32 years old and lives in Fort Lauderdale. He has lived his entire life in Florida. He grew up in Fort Lauderdale and attended public school there. Then he attended the University of South Florida in Tampa, where he studied computer systems technology and social science education. After college, Kevin returned to Fort Lauderdale and started a successful Internet company. One of his online products helps students to improve their study skills and grades. Kevin has never served in government before but welcomes the opportunity to introduce new ideas. He has released his own issue-based platform. He opposes any increase in sales taxes, property taxes, or corporate taxes. Kevin also wants to reduce air and water pollution. He promises that if elected, he will propose a reduction in licensing fees for the drivers of electric cars. Kevin has several political advertisements on television and on the Internet. In them, he is shown talking with seventh-grade students in civics classes about the future of Florida.

Maria Martinez is 45 years old. She also lives in Fort Lauderdale. Like Kevin, she has lived her entire life in Florida. Maria grew up in Miami. She attended public schools in Miami-Dade County and the University of Miami, where she studied business and accounting. Before moving to Fort Lauderdale, Maria served as an elected Miami-Dade County Commissioner for four years. She also worked full-time as an accountant for a small business. Before that, she was one of nine elected members of the Miami-Dade School Board. Maria has sponsored several political advertisements in the current campaign. They are on television and appear in newspapers and magazines. In them, she emphasizes her public service and experience. Maria has also released a seven-page issue-based platform, giving her views on public education, taxation, pollution, and tourism. In general, Maria believes that government should do more to help the underprivileged.

Last week Kevin and Maria engaged in a one-hour debate on television. Both candidates seemed relaxed and friendly. Observers generally agreed that Maria seemed to have more detailed knowledge about local government, while Kevin appeared to have more original ideas.

Compare the strengths and weaknesses of these two candidates. After evaluating the two candidates, decide which one you would vote for and explain why.

Qualifications:_____

Experience: _____

Issue-based platforms: _____

Performance in debate: _____

Political advertisements: _____

The candidate I would vote for would be _____ because _____
_____
_____.

The Active Citizen

▶ Evaluate and compare any two leading candidates in a recent election. Consider their qualifications, experience, views on issues, performance in debates, and the content of their political advertisements.

▶ Your class should conduct its own **mock election**. "Mock" means not real. A mock election is not a real election, but one organized for educational purposes.

1. Imagine your class is holding this election for the mayor of your town, or for a special administrator of your school. First, you must find suitable candidates. The class should be divided into two or three groups. Each group will form its own political party.

2. Each political party should hold a meeting, select a name, and draw up a party platform. If you choose to have a mock town election, your platform should identify problems in your town and propose solutions. If you choose to have a mock school election, your platform should identify problems facing your school and propose solutions.

3. Your political party should next select its nominees—either for town mayor or school administrator. First, your political party should elect a secretary. Then, all those who wish to run for office should identify themselves. Candidates should make short statements presenting their positions on the key issues.

4. The group should then hold a primary election to vote on which candidate should be the party's nominee. Voting can be done privately on slips of paper that are collected and counted by the party's secretary. The candidate with the most votes wins the party's nomination.

5. Now the candidates should campaign for the general election. Party members should design posters and write advertisements and letters on behalf of their candidates. Each party should hold one political rally at which their candidate speaks. The candidates should also hold at least one debate in front of the class. Other students should act as reporters, asking questions.

6. Your teacher should then hold the general election. Each party should make sure its members vote. Students should vote by writing their choice on a piece of paper, which they fold. The secretaries of the political parties should count the votes together. Then the teacher should announce the victor. The losing candidates should recognize the winner, while the winner should give a victory speech to the class thanking supporters and announcing new programs.

7. Finally, students should discuss how they felt about the mock election and what they learned from it about the election process. If this had been a real election, how important would the result have been to your town or school?

Chapter 13 | Political Parties and Elections

Name _____

Complete the exercise below.

ELECTION PROJECT

Evaluating Candidates for Public Office

INTRODUCTION:

In this project, you and your classmates will evaluate candidates running for office in the next election. Then you will create a candidate profile that appeals to young voters.

TASK:

1. Create a new notebook in OneNote for this project.

2. Select a public office, such as Governor of Florida or U.S. Senator, that is being decided in the next election.

3. Conduct Research:

   ▸ Identify the candidates from the two major parties (Democratic and Republican) who are running for that office.

   ▸ In your OneNote notebook, create two tabs (one for each candidate).

   ▸ Gather background information on each candidate and place findings in appropriate tabs.

   ▸ Evaluate how qualified each candidate is based on education, experience, and views on the issues.

   ▸ Some possible news sources: www.miamiherald.com/news/politics/ and www.cnn.com.

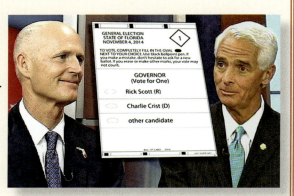

4. Now choose one candidate and form a part of that candidate's campaign team.

   ▸ Work in small groups. Your group should create a Facebook profile of your candidate that will appeal to young voters, ages 18–25. Your Facebook profile should include a photograph of the candidate and sections on the candidate's background and education, experience, views on key issues, and why that individual is the most qualified candidate for the office. Your Facebook profile should be aimed at young voters.

5. Finally, your group will make a presentation to the rest of the class on behalf of your candidate.

   ▸ Your group should base its presentation on its Facebook profile.

   ▸ Provide feedback to other groups in the form of written comments on how accurate you thought their presentation was, how polished and professional they appeared, and how compelling you think their case would have been to young voters.

(Adapted with permission from the Social Sciences Department of Miami-Dade County Public Schools.)

Name _____

1. What are the requirements for registering to vote in Florida?

2. Complete the chart below on the impact of political parties on government and society.

Positive Effects	Negative Effects

Chapter 13 | Political Parties and Elections

- **Democratic Party:** willing to have higher taxes to provide more government support for programs, such as health care and public education
- **Republican Party:** favors less government, lower taxes, less public debt, more freedom, and a strong foreign policy

- **Libertarian Party:** wishes to maximize human freedom and to reduce government and taxation
- **Socialist Party:** favors more public services, public ownership of utilities and some industries
- **Communist Party:** believes capitalists exploit workers; revolution may be needed to achieve change; Communist Party USA willing to cooperate with other progressive groups

Major Parties — **Other Parties**

Political Parties in Florida

Impact of Political Parties

Political Parties and Elections

Positive Effects
- Encourage citizens to participate in the political process
- Help government leaders to organize support
- Act as watchdogs over the opposing party

Negative Effects
- Divide Americans
- Place pressure on legislators

Voting — **Elections**

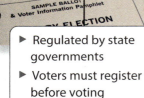

- Regulated by state governments
- Voters must register before voting

Factors in Evaluating Candidates

- Education
- Experience, especially in public office
- Their views on issues in issue-based platforms
- How capable they appear in debating
- How truthful and persuasive their political advertisements are

	Candidate A	Candidate B
Qualifications		
Experience		
Issues		
Debate performance		
Political Advertisements		

Review Cards: Political Parties and Elections

What are Political Parties?

Political parties are groups of people who share political beliefs and work to elect their candidates to public office.

Political Parties in the United States

- Americans have a **two-party** system.
- In the United States today, there are two major political parties: the **Democratic Party** and the **Republican Party**.
- There are also several smaller political parties (sometimes known as "third parties"), such as the **Socialist Party**, the **Communist Party**, the **Libertarian Party**.

The Democratic Party

- Democrats favor using the power of government to provide high quality public education, affordable health care, and a growing economy. They are also concerned about accountability of government, jobs, women and families, civil rights, immigration, and protecting land and water use.

The Republican Party

- Republicans stand for less government interference in our lives, more private enterprise, lower taxes, less public debt, a strong foreign policy, and greater personal freedom. They believe this approach will most promote economic growth and job creation, which will benefit all Americans.

Chapter 13 | Political Parties and Elections

The Socialist Party

- **Socialism** developed in reaction to the Industrial Revolution and the horrible social conditions it produced.
- Socialists sought to correct these injustices by having public ownership of energy, resources, transportation, housing and other basic industries, and by providing free services in health and education. In Europe, many countries adopted socialist beliefs. They offer free health care and free higher education to their citizens.
- In the United States, the Socialist Party opposed American involvement in Iraq and Afghanistan. The party became inactive in Florida in 2011.

The Communist Party

- **Communism** was a movement that was started in Europe in the 1840s by Karl Marx and Friedrich Engels. Communists believe that all history is the history of "class struggle" in which one social group, or "class," always exploits another. In the past, communists claimed a revolution would be necessary to free workers.
- The **Communist Party USA** opposes cuts to social services and education, and tax breaks to corporations, while it supports free health care and higher education. The party is willing to cooperate with other progressive groups to improve the conditions of American workers and oppressed groups.
- Communists believe that capitalism will eventually fail. Communists see themselves as representing the interests of workers. Under communism, private businesses will be replaced by state ownership.

The Libertarian Party

- The Libertarian Party is the largest "third" party in the United States today. The key word in **libertarianism** is "liberty." Florida Libertarians favor less government and more personal freedom. They favor freedom of speech, freedom of religion, the free market economy, reduced taxation, reduced government spending, personal privacy, states' rights, and the right to carry guns.

Constitutional Requirements for Major Public Offices

- **U.S. Representative**: Must be at least 25 years old, an American citizen for 7 years, and a current resident of that state.
- **U.S. Senator**: Must be at least 30 years old, an American citizen for 9 years, and a current resident of the state represented.
- **President of the United States**: Must be at least 35 years old, a "natural born" citizen, and have lived in the U.S. for at least 14 years.
- **Governor of Florida**: Must be at least 30 years old, and a resident of Florida for at least 7 years.
- **Florida Senator or Florida Representative**: Must be at least 21 years old, a resident of Florida for at least 2 years, and a current resident of the district represented.

Positive Effects of Political Parties

Representation: Political parties represent the views of voters.
Participation: Political parties offer opportunities for citizenship participation in government and politics.
Candidates: Political parties find and select candidates for elected offices.
Campaigns: Political parties manage and finance election campaigns.
Voting: Political campaigns encourage people to vote in elections.
Education: Political parties educate voters by informing them about the issues.
Debate: Political parties offer alternatives and encourage debate.
Legislation: Political parties help members of local, state and federal lawmaking bodies organize themselves into groups on behalf of a legislative program.
Watchdog: Political parties serve as "watchdogs" by criticizing what opposing parties are doing.
Bridge: Political parties serve as a bridge uniting members of the executive and legislative branches of government.
Compromise: Political parties encourage members to compromise their views.

Negative Effects of Political Parties

Division: Political parties divide Americans.
Bias: Political parties present biased views of the issues.
Pressure: Political parties pressure legislators and other elected officials to follow their party's program against their own beliefs.
Distraction: Legislators and other officials spend more time supporting their party, raising money and trying to get re-elected than they do on the work of government.
Self-Interest: Political parties act to win votes, rather than doing what is really best.
Stalemate: Divisions between competing political parties often prevent government from getting things done.
Monopolistic: Political parties raise large sums of money for campaigns, making it hard for independent candidates to compete.

The Nomination and Election Process

- Political parties must find suitable people to run for political office. Each party **nominates** (*names*) one candidate for each government office that is up for election.
- **Primaries**: When several individuals from the same party seek the same political office, they often compete in a **primary election** to obtain their party's nomination.
- **Party Conventions**: Political parties hold state and national **conventions**. National conventions are usually held every four years to nominate candidates for President and Vice President. Party conventions adopt a **party platform**—a detailed statement of the party's policies for the future.
- Party nominees then compete in a **general election campaign**. They hold rallies, make political advertisements, and have debates with other candidates.

Chapter 13 | Political Parties and Elections

Evaluating Candidates

Voters should **evaluate** (*judge*) candidates competing for the same political office based on these factors:
- **Qualifications**: The background, education, employment, and achievements of each candidate.
- **Experience**: Does the candidate have experience in this office or a similar one?
- **Issues**: Candidates usually release **issue-based platforms** filled with statements of where they stand on major issues and accompanying campaign promises. A **"campaign promise"** is something a candidate promises to do if he or she is elected.
- **Debates**: Candidates present their views face-to-face. Voters can judge a candidate in action, close up. They can consider how well informed, intelligent, and persuasive each candidate appears to be.
- **Political Ads**: A good political advertisement presents a candidate's qualifications, experience, and views on the issues, while also showing why opponents are less qualified. Political advertisements not only serve to criticize opponents, but also reveal something about the sponsor of the ad.

What Do You Know?

SS.7.C.2.8

1. Which issue represents a basic disagreement between socialists and communists?
   A. whether income taxes should be lowered
   B. whether conditions for workers should be improved
   C. whether all private businesses should be replaced by state ownership
   D. whether the government should provide public services like free education and health care

SS.7.C.2.8

2. Which statement reflects Republican views on the role of government?
   A. Republicans favor less government, lower taxes, and greater personal freedom.
   B. Republicans favor value-based governance, and oppose excessive consumption and unregulated competition.
   C. Republicans favor a national mass peoples' party, based on the working classes and opposition to monopoly capitalism.
   D. Republicans favor more affordable health care and increased public funding for education, even if it leads to higher taxes.

SS.7.C.2.8

3. Which issue represents a basic disagreement between Democrats and Republicans?
   A. whether monopoly capitalism should be replaced by state ownership
   B. whether Americans should unite behind the nation against global terrorism
   C. whether higher levels of taxation should be imposed to pay for more public services
   D. whether current uses of natural resources should be radically replaced by a greater focus on future sustainability

SS.7.C.2.8

4. The passage below is from a political party platform.

   > We believe we are stronger when we have an economy that works for everyone—an economy that grows incomes for working people, creates good-paying jobs, and puts a middle-class life within reach for more Americans. . . . [We] believe that in America, if you want a higher education, you should always be able to get one: money should never stand in the way. . . . [We] believe that health care is a right, not a privilege . . .

   Which major political party's views are represented in this platform?
   A. Democratic Party
   B. Constitution Party
   C. Libertarian Party
   D. Republican Party

SS.7.C.2.8

5. Which position would most likely be found in the Republican Party platform?
   A. support for the Affordable Care Act
   B. opposition to American intervention overseas in the War on Terror
   C. demand for increased taxation of corporations to support pre-school programs
   D. introduction of lower taxes for small businesses to encourage new job growth

SS.7.C.2.8

6. Which position would most likely be found in the Libertarian Party platform?
   A. support for the Affordable Care Act
   B. support for absolute freedom of speech and religion
   C. support for higher taxation to provide more government services
   D. support for increased regulation of business to curb the exploitation of natural resources

SS.7.C.2.8

7. Why does the Libertarian Party oppose having uniform national educational requirements?
   A. They feel such standards would probably be too difficult for most American students.
   B. They view such standards as unnecessary federal interference in education.
   C. They fear that national standards would cost taxpayers too much money to implement.
   D. They are afraid that national educational standards would not teach students enough about the environment.

Chapter 13 | Political Parties and Elections

SS.7.C.2.9

8. Azra is 29 years old. She was born in Istanbul, Turkey. Fifteen years ago, Azra moved to the United States with her family. She became a U.S. citizen eight years ago. Just last year, Azra moved to Florida. She has decided to run for public office. For which office is she qualified to run?

   A. Governor of Florida
   B. Florida State Senator
   C. U.S. Senator from Florida
   D. Member of U.S. House of Representatives

SS.7.C.2.9

9. George and Martha are both candidates for mayor in Jamestown's coming election. George is an engineer and Martha is a medical doctor. George has been on the Jamestown City Council for five years and Martha is the city's current mayor. Both George and Martha have acted as capable public servants in their roles. However, they strongly disagree on whether Jamestown should invest in building a new sports stadium, the main issue facing the city. What will probably be the most important factor for a voter in deciding which candidate to support in this election?

   A. which candidate has the most experience
   B. which candidate has better educational qualifications
   C. which candidate has spent more money in the election campaign
   D. which candidate shares the voter's views on building the stadium

SS.7.C.2.9

10. The fliers below were distributed by two candidates running for the Florida Senate.

    ELECT MARY LAMB AS STATE SENATOR!
    - State resident for 10 years
    - Graduate of the University of Central Florida in Orlando
    - 6 years on City Council
    - 2 years as State Representative

    ELECT TOM JONES AS STATE SENATOR!
    - State resident for 12 years
    - Graduate of the University of North Florida in Jacksonville
    - 1 year as volunteer worker for the Red Cross
    - 3 years as volunteer for the Florida Humane Society

    Based on the information on the fliers, why might Mary Lamb be considered more qualified than Tom Jones to be elected as State Senator?

    A. She has better views on the major issues.
    B. She has better educational qualifications.
    C. She has more experience in public office.
    D. She has spent more money in the election campaign.

CHAPTER 14

Interest Groups and the Media

SS.7.C.2.10 Examine the impact of media, individuals, and interest groups on monitoring and influencing government.

SS.7.C.2.11 Analyze media and political communications (bias, symbolism, propaganda).

Names and Terms You Should Know

Interest group	Special interest	Bias
Lobbying	Media	Symbolism
Lobbyist	Watchdog	Propaganda
Public interest group	Political Communications	Public opinion
Political Action Committee (PAC)		

Florida "Keys" to Learning

1. Individuals can influence government by speaking at meetings, sending letters, contributing to campaigns, petitioning government officials, and running for office.

2. An interest group is a group of individuals with common interests who seek to influence public policy. While political parties try to elect candidates and have positions on a wide number of issues, interest groups try to influence legislators and government officials directly, and only have positions on a narrow range of issues based on their specific interests.

3. A public interest group attempts to promote the common good—the interests of Americans as a whole rather than of any one specific group.

4. Interest groups often "monitor" (*keep track of*) developments in legislatures and government agencies, and report to their members or to the public.

5. Interest groups hire lobbyists, who speak to state legislators, members of Congress, or other government officials in order to influence new legislation or government regulations.

6. Interest groups also try to influence elections and election activities. Each interest group is allowed to form its own political action committee, or PAC, in order to help politicians get elected or re-elected.

7. Interest groups—particularly public interest groups and those supporting minority rights—sometimes promote their causes by filing lawsuits, also known as litigation.

8. Interest groups usually try to sway public opinion—the views of the general public—through advertising, press releases, publishing articles, and television and radio appearances. This is sometimes known as "grass roots" lobbying.

9. The media consist of newspapers, television, radio and the Internet. These are all ways of communicating with the public.

10. The media monitor and influence government. Newspapers and news agencies send reporters to follow government activities. People learn about their government from the media.

11. The media act as "watchdogs" over our government—questioning government leaders about their actions and exposing government wrongdoing.

12. Political communications appeal to both reason and emotion to persuade readers and viewers. They sometimes employ symbolism and bias. A symbol is something that represents something else, such as a flag, which represents a country. Being biased means being one-sided or prejudiced.

13. Political communications that are extremely biased and that appeal to fears and emotions in order to persuade public opinion are known as propaganda. Propaganda makes use of exaggerations, half-truths, name calling, glittering generalities, and over-simplification. The aim of propaganda and other forms of political communication is to influence public opinion.

Political parties are not the only groups not in the Constitution that influence government policies. Newspaper and television reporters and special interest groups are not mentioned there either. Yet they can have a tremendous impact on government decision-making. In fact, the press and other media are so influential they have even been called the "Fourth Branch" of government.

In this chapter, you will learn how individuals, interest groups, and the media monitor and influence government. You will also learn how they sometimes use bias, symbolism and propaganda to shape public opinion.

> To **monitor** the government means to closely observe what its different officials, agencies or branches are doing; for example, following a bill that is passing through Congress.
>
> To **influence** the government means to persuade members of the government to adopt policies or programs you prefer.

Individuals

In the United States, any individual can actually monitor and influence government policy. Often, individuals attempt to influence the government by running for elective office.

In fact, the U.S. Supreme Court has ruled that the First Amendment (free speech) protects an individual's right to spend unlimited amounts of his or her own money in an election campaign in which he or she is the candidate.

In recent years, Ross Perot and Ralph Nader both ran as independent candidates for the Presidency. Although there was little chance either would win the election, their campaigns brought greater attention to causes they believed in.

You don't have to run for President to influence government. You have already learned some of the ways that individuals can participate in civic life in Chapter 12. These are known as citizenship responsibilities. Here is a list of some of the ways that individuals can directly influence government decisions:

> **Some Ways Individuals Can Influence Government**
> ▶ Running for office
> ▶ Petitioning government officials
> ▶ Collecting signatures on issues
> ▶ Speaking at meetings
> ▶ Sending letters and e-mail messages
> ▶ Making campaign contributions
> ▶ Using social media

Interest Groups

We all have interests—some of us like sports while others enjoy music or being outdoors. An **interest group** is a group of individuals with common interests who seek to influence public policy. There are now thousands of such interest groups in the United States.

Many of these interest groups are based on common economic interests. For example, American manufacturers have formed an interest group known as the "National Association of Manufacturers." Other groups, such as the American Medical Association, the National Association of Home Builders, and the

Chapter 14 | Interest Groups and the Media

American Bankers Association, are focused on a single industry. The AFL-CIO (American Federation of Labor and Congress of Industrial Organizations) represents the interests of more than ten million workers. The National Education Association and the Service Employees International Union represent specific groups of workers.

Environmental interest groups, such as the Sierra Club, protect wildlife and attempt to reduce pollution. Other interest groups, like the NAACP (National Association for the Advancement of Colored People) and NOW (National Organization of Women) promote the interests of groups that were once disadvantaged in the past.

Some interest groups form over specific issues, such as the National Right to Life Committee and the American Israel Public Affairs Committee. The National Rifle Association is now largely concerned with protecting the right to own guns.

A public interest group attempts to promote the common good—the interests of Americans as a whole rather than of any specific group. A non-profit public interest group does not pay federal income tax.

An interest group differs from a political party. A political party focuses on electing its candidates to office. A political party usually has a platform addressing a large number of issues. An interest group attempts to influence public policies directly, rather than by electing its members as government officials. It generally focuses on a specific issue or area, rather than on all the problems facing our government leaders.

The Active Citizen

- Make a chart or Venn diagram comparing political parties and interest groups.
- Research one of the interest groups mentioned above. Give an oral presentation or PowerPoint presentation to your class describing how this group was formed, where it is located today, how many members it has, what its goals are, and what it has accomplished.

How Interest Groups Monitor and Influence Government

Interest groups have many ways to influence the government and further their goals.

Monitoring

To monitor something is to watch over it and check what is happening. Interest groups often "monitor" developments. This means they keep track of everything legislatures and government agencies are doing that might affect their area of focus. Interest-group officers or agents attend legislative sessions and committee hearings. They develop friendly relations with legislators and their staff to get copies of bills. Then the interest group sends newsletters to its members informing them of key developments. This keeps members informed and allows them to take steps to influence

348   Chapter 14 | Interest Groups and the Media

new laws or to react to new requirements. Some interest groups even rate legislators, based on how well they support the interest group's goals.

Lobbying

A lobby is a long hall or corridor. In the past, the hired representatives of interest groups often tried to corner legislators in the lobbies of their hotels or of legislative buildings to speak to them. Today, the paid agent of an interest group who speaks to state legislators, members of Congress, or government officials in order to influence new legislation or regulations is known as a **lobbyist**.

Lobbying is an activity protected by the right to free speech. Lobbyists must register with Congress, or with their state legislature. They also have to file reports showing how much each of their clients has paid for their lobbying services. All of this information is made available to the public.

At present, there are thousands of lobbyists working in Washington, D.C., and state capitals around the country. Some of these lobbyists are former legislators themselves. The main goal of these lobbyists is to influence members of Congress or state legislators. Very often lobbyists have special subject-area expertise and can provide very useful information to legislators. They may even help friendly legislators plan a strategy for passing or blocking proposed legislation.

individuals can contribute to candidates. However, the same law permits any interest group, including corporations and labor organizations, to form its own **political action committee**, or **PAC**. Each PAC must register with the Federal Election Commission. PACs can contribute larger sums of money to support candidates than individuals are permitted to do. PACs tend to favor **incumbents**—those already in office—since these candidates are more likely on average to win than their opponents. Some critics fear that PAC campaign contributions are corrupting the political system.

In addition to providing funds through PACs, interest groups provide endorsements to candidates and supply volunteers to work in election campaigns.

Litigation (lawsuits)

Litigation refers to filing and defending against lawsuits in court. One important way in which interest groups—particularly public interest groups and those supporting minority rights—promote their causes is by filing lawsuits. Civil Rights groups in the 1950s, such as the NAACP, used litigation to

Campaigning (helping candidates get elected)

Interest groups and their lobbyists also help politicians to get elected or re-elected. Campaign finance reform in 1974 limited the amount of money that

Chapter 14 | Interest Groups and the Media

overturn racial segregation in the South. Consumer groups and environmental groups also frequently use lawsuits. They may file a "class action" lawsuit, in which a large number of people are represented in one case. Even if an interest group has not filed its own lawsuit, it may file a friendly "brief" (a statement of written arguments) supporting one side or the other of an existing lawsuit filed by other parties. Even when they lose, lawsuits bring public attention to issues raised by interest groups.

Publicity

Interest groups also take other steps to win public support for their causes and to influence **public opinion** (*the views of the general public*). This is sometimes called "grass roots" lobbying. Interest groups may advertise in newspapers, magazines, radio or television. They may publish articles promoting their point of view. They may send out advertisements or persuasive literature by mail. They may even post videos on YouTube or phone members of the public directly in a telephone campaign. This puts pressure on lawmakers and other decision makers.

The Impact of Interest Groups

- There are many different types of interest groups, from those representing particular industries to public interest groups protecting the environment.
- Interest groups offer different points of view.
- Interest groups can be one-sided and biased.
- Interest groups encourage public participation in government.
- Interest groups help to provide specific details for proposed legislation.

- Interest groups bring subject-area expertise to legislators, government officials and the public.
- Interest groups help to monitor events in government for their members, for legislators and for the public.
- Interest groups can influence public opinion ("grass roots" lobbying).
- Interest groups can influence the legislative process.

The Active Citizen

- Imagine that you are a paid lobbyist. Write a newsletter to your clients (those who pay for your lobbying services).
- Are interest groups too powerful? Interview two adults (relatives, neighbors or friends) and ask them this question. Then share your results with your classmates.
- Identify the method—monitoring, lobbying, litigation, or publicity/"grass roots" lobbying—used by interest groups in each of the examples in the chart on the next page.

Scenario	Type of Interest Group Activity
The National Association of Armadillo Watchers, a public interest group, files a lawsuit to protect nine-banded armadillos in Florida from real estate developers.	
A hired representative of the Acme interest group contacts members of Congress, urging them to vote "yes" on a new bill.	
The staff of the Unicycle Association of America, an interest group, prepares its monthly newsletter telling its members about new legislation on unicycle lanes.	
The National Society of French Bakers of America starts a newspaper, radio and television campaign to increase public awareness of new government regulations on French breakfast pastries.	

The Media

> You do not need to know the history of the media for the EOC test, but you do need to know how the media influence government.

The term **"media"** refers to "mass media"—methods of communicating to large numbers of people. The media include newspapers, magazines, radio and television programs, Internet websites and "blogs," and "social media" like Facebook and Instagram.

Like political parties and interest groups, the media are not mentioned in the Constitution. And yet they have played just as important a role in American politics and government from the very beginnings of our nation.

At one time, most Americans learned about current events and politics from newspapers. In the early nineteenth century, newspapers were often filled with the debates of Congress and state legislatures. By the 1930s, Americans started learning about public events from the radio. President Franklin D. Roosevelt appealed directly to Americans in his weekly "Fireside Chats," broadcast over the radio. Most Americans listened by radio to President Roosevelt's speech on December 8, 1941, the day after the attack on Pearl Harbor, when he asked Congress for a declaration of war on Japan. Americans also saw occasional current events on newsreels when they went to the movies.

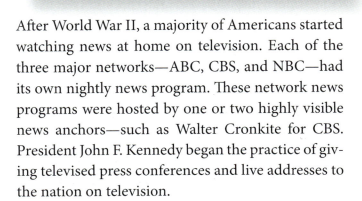

After World War II, a majority of Americans started watching news at home on television. Each of the three major networks—ABC, CBS, and NBC—had its own nightly news program. These network news programs were hosted by one or two highly visible news anchors—such as Walter Cronkite for CBS. President John F. Kennedy began the practice of giving televised press conferences and live addresses to the nation on television.

Chapter 14 | Interest Groups and the Media

Even as recently as 1981, when President Reagan addressed Congress for the very first time, almost two-thirds of the public watched his address that evening on one of the three major networks. Half of the public read about Reagan's speech the next day in the newspaper.

This situation has greatly changed in recent years with the rise of cable television and the Internet. There are now more television stations reporting the news than ever before. Many people also learn about current events from the Internet, which is being constantly updated, instead of watching news programs on television.

News Articles and Editorials

The media have two main kinds of articles or programs for their readers. Most articles are intended to inform readers. These informational articles tell readers the "who," "what", "when," "where," "how," and "why" of an event or news story. These articles attempt to give a balanced picture, often reporting more than one point of view.

Newspapers, magazines, the Internet and even television programs also sometimes present a second kind of article (or television segment): "opinion" pieces. These tell the opinions of the writer or producer. They are often in the form of "letters to the editor"—letters from outsiders who write to a newspaper or magazine to give their views. "Opinion" pieces might also be "editorials"—statements giving the viewpoint of the editors (*the people managing the newspaper or magazine*). The purpose of these "opinion" pieces is not to give balanced, informative reporting but to persuade readers to a particular point of view.

Investigative Journalism: The Media as "Watchdog"

Like interest groups, the media act as "**watchdogs**" of our government. They question government officials and research government activities to identify issues and to expose possible wrongdoing by government officials.

This has always been one of the roles of the media. The "muckrakers" of the Progressive Era (1890-1920), for example, exposed the abuses of rapid industrialization. Upton Sinclair reported that meat packers put dead rats and other impurities into their sausages in the chapters of a novel he first published in a newspaper in 1905. Outrage over his reports led Congress to pass the Meat Inspection Act in 1906.

Upton Sinclair

The role of the media as "watchdog" became especially significant when public mistrust of government grew during the Vietnam War in the 1960s and early 1970s. Investigative journalists played an important role in the Watergate scandal. Reporters from the *Washington Post* investigated and reported a break-in into Democratic Party national headquarters in the Watergate Hotel and office complex in 1972. Their newspaper articles led to Congressional hearings. These hearings eventually exposed the White House cover-up of the break-in. President Nixon resigned from office rather than face impeachment.

Journalists are considered "watchdogs" because they watch over public officials and report what they see to the public. Without their oversight, the public would have far less information about the workings of our government. Politicians and government leaders would then be able to act without the same accountability to the public.

The Impact of the Media

The media monitor and influence government in many ways:

- Newspapers, television stations and news agencies assign reporters to monitor the Presidency, Congress and key agencies as well as state and local governments. They follow their activities and report them to the American people. Other reporters investigate unfolding news stories.
- Reporters need information and interviews for their news stories. Legislators need to communicate their views and activities to the public. By giving an interview, a politician or legislator can often reach millions of voters. The media therefore make it easier for government leaders to communicate with the public.
- Government officials, legislators and politicians are less likely to be dishonest because they know that they are being constantly monitored by journalists. Politicians also try to act in a way that will be favorably shown in the media.
- Some critics fear that politicians have become more concerned with "photo opportunities" or tweets than with serious issues or making hard choices. The presence of the media forces politicians to be always thinking about re-election and short-term rather than long-term goals.
- The constant pressure of the media and the increased prying into private life discourages some talented individuals from entering politics or government service.

The Active Citizen

- Write one or two paragraphs describing what American politics would be like if there were no journalists, newspapers, radio, television, or the Internet.
- In the past, reporters focused on public issues but overlooked officials' private lives. This is no longer true. Should journalists be able to report on the private lives of public leaders? Write a short essay giving your views on this topic. First identify your point of view. Then give your reasons with supporting facts.

Evaluating the Impact of Bias, Symbolism and Propaganda on Public Opinion

Political communications are statements from political parties, interest groups and others. They provide information but are mainly designed to persuade readers and listeners. **Editorials** in newspapers and other media have the same purpose.

These types of communications use special persuasive techniques to influence public opinion. Three of the most important of these techniques are **bias**, **symbolism**, and **propaganda**.

- **Bias** is a prejudice in favor of or against something. People are **biased** when they favor one side over another without really looking at an issue or situation carefully. They may have a personal or economic interest in the issue.

Chapter 14 | Interest Groups and the Media

Political communications and media are biased when they give only one point of view on an issue or situation. They focus on information that favors their position while they ignore opposing information. They also show bias when they repeat popular prejudices and stereotypes (*general beliefs about different groups of people*).

▸ **Symbolism** is the use of symbols in speech or writing. A **symbol** is something that actually stands for or represents something else. For example, an eagle in a political cartoon could represent the United States, a donkey in a political poster could represent the Democratic Party, and an elephant could represent the Republican Party.

How many of the following symbols can you identify?

People trying to persuade others often associate themselves with a popular symbol. They try to link themselves to the positive feelings that the audience has about that symbol. For example, when American politicians appear on television, they often show the American flag in the background. They hope their viewers will associate them with the flag as a symbol of patriotism.

▸ **Propaganda** is a form of public communication that provides biased and one-sided information. The purpose of propaganda is to influence and persuade "public opinion"—the views of ordinary citizens.

Propaganda is always one-sided. It gives evidence in support of its point of view but not evidence for other points of view. Usually it is exaggerated and misleading.

Propaganda appeals to people's emotions rather than to their reason. It may, for example, encourage people's fears. Propaganda relies on emotionally charged "loaded language," rather than presenting logical reasoning and actual facts.

> You will not need to identify specific propaganda techniques on the EOC but you will need to recognize propaganda, symbolism and bias.

Some of the ways that propaganda attempts to influence public opinion are the following:

- **Opinions disguised as facts:** The propaganda presents opinions as though they were facts.

  "People on food stamps are clearly too lazy to work."

- **Endorsements:** The propaganda emphasizes the support of famous people, suggesting that this makes something reasonable or right.

  "Jennifer Lawrence, Lady Gaga and Taylor Swift support Amendment 10 as the best choice. Shouldn't you support it, too?"

Fact or Opinion?

A **fact** is a statement that can be verified by checking with other sources. It is either true or false. An **opinion** is an expression of belief. There are different kinds of opinions. Some opinions are mere expressions of taste: "I like the taste of a fresh, crisp apple." No one can dispute that the speaker likes apples. Other opinions are statements of belief about the future, or about factual matters where the facts remain unknown: "I think people will watch less television in the future" or "I believe Al Gore actually had more votes in Florida than George W. Bush in the 2000 election."

---

354 Chapter 14 | Interest Groups and the Media

- **"Bandwagon" technique:** The propaganda points out that a large number of people are doing something, so the listener or reader should do the same.

  "Most Floridians support Amendment 10. Shouldn't you support it, too?"

- **"Labeling" or "name calling":** The propaganda puts down opponents or ideas by calling them names and making fun of them. It uses "loaded language" (*terms with emotional meanings*).

  "Those against sending more U.S. troops to Syria are cowards afraid of their own shadows."

- **"Glittering generalities":** The propaganda makes vague, general statements that sound good but that are not specific enough to be checked.

  "This is the best product ever invented. Everyone loves using it."

- **Oversimplification:** The propaganda makes a complex situation or problem seem simpler than it really is. The propaganda may propose a simple solution to a group of complex problems.

  "Drug companies are responsible for our current health care crisis."

- **Half-Truths and Exaggerations:** The propaganda makes statements that give part of the truth but that are not really accurate. Exaggerations (saying something is more of something—stronger, larger, smarter—than it actually is) are a form of half-truth. Images in visual propaganda often contain exaggerated features, based on common biases and stereotypes.

  "Our candidate risked his life in the military in the last war." (This is a half-truth if the candidate was in the military but was never actually sent into combat.)

The Active Citizen

Examine the following two American posters from World War II. During this war (1941–1945), American soldiers fought against soldiers from Imperial Japan and Nazi Germany. Look for examples of bias, symbolism, and propaganda in these posters.

1. How does the first poster show bias? Consider the images and expressions of the two soldiers, and the use of loaded language like "Murdering Jap."
2. How does the second poster use symbolism? Consider the helmet and the statue the figure is holding.
3. Which common propaganda devices do these two posters use?
4. What impact do you think posters like these had on public opinion in wartime?

Chapter 14 | Interest Groups and the Media

Name _____

Identify whether each of the following statements illustrates bias, symbolism or propaganda. The same example could illustrate more than one of these. Then explain how this example would be likely to affect public opinion.

Statement	Bias, Symbolism or Propaganda?	Probable Impact on Public Opinion
"Our community has done more to help the homeless than any other community in recorded history."		
"As we approached the house, we could tell that there was something wrong inside even before we got there."		
"The American taxpayer has suffered for far too long. It is time for us to object to all these unnecessary taxes that just encourage government waste. Stand up for yourself by joining our new political party!"		
"As the smoke cleared on the battlefield, we could see the American flag still waving proudly."		
"We need to send more of our troops to this foreign country. We have never been defeated in war before and we don't want to start here. Sending a few thousand more troops should do the job."		
"People in other countries don't share the same concerns that we do. A quick glance at history is all that is needed to see that."		
"Most of our problems are caused by lazy people who come from other countries. If we could stop them from coming here, prosperity would return to our nation."		
"There is a reason why the tasty orange is our state fruit. Florida is clearly the best state. All the nicest and smartest people live here."		

Chapter 14 | Interest Groups and the Media

Name _____

Fill in the boxes in the concept ladder below by adding your own descriptions and explanations.

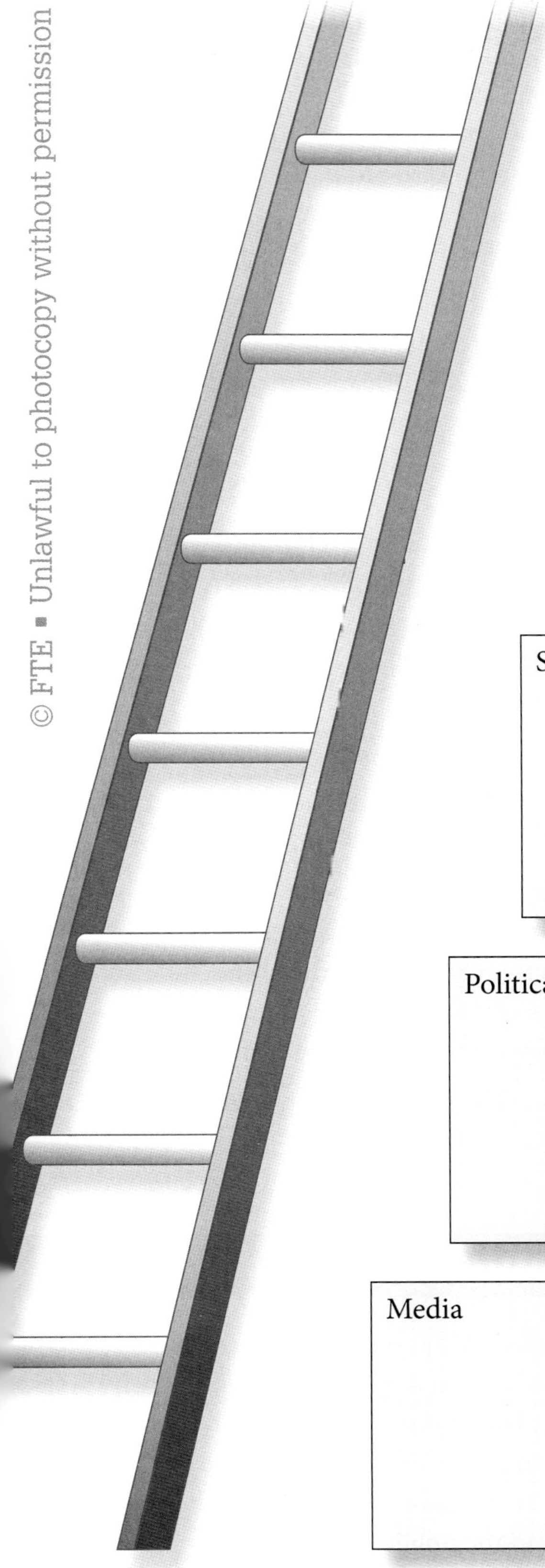

Propaganda

Bias

Symbolism

Political communications

Media

Chapter 14 | Interest Groups and the Media 357

Analyzing Media and Political Communications

As an active citizen, you may have to interpret communications from the media, interest groups, and political parties. Some of these communications may be speeches or written texts; others might be visual images, such as posters, signs or cartoons; still others could be moving images, such as political advertisements on television.

Remember that a political communication is not impartial. It is created by a specific political party or interest group, whose general aim is to persuade you to adopt their point of view. In particular, you should be able to identify any bias, symbolism or propaganda found in such communications.

1. The first step in analyzing any media or political communication is to see who created the message. Was it an individual, a reporter, a political party, or an interest group?

2. The second step is to determine the **purpose** of the article or communication. What were the authors of this communication trying to do? Remember that there are different types of communications, depending upon their purpose. Some articles, images or other communications are **informational**—their purpose is to give the reader impartial information. Other communications are **persuasive**—their purpose is to persuade the reader to adopt a particular point of view.

   How does this purpose influence what is said in the communication? In particular, does the communication show any bias? Does it make use of symbolism in order to persuade the reader? Is it actually a piece of propaganda—relying more on its appeal to emotions than on reasoning and facts?

3. Now read or listen to the text of the communication very carefully. What is the main idea it expresses? What arguments does the author use?

4. Next identify any facts or opinions in the communication. You should decide whether each of these facts is accurate. If the communication includes opinions, you should decide if those opinions are reasonable and justified by the evidence.

5. The final step is to **evaluate** (*determine the value of*) the reasoning in the communication. Is it logical? Or does it contain logical errors?

   ▶ Does it include any of the propaganda devices that you just read about? Is it one-sided? Does it contain "glittering generalities," half-truths, or exaggerations? Does it rely on endorsements or the bandwagon effect?

   ▶ How does it relate to other information you know about the topic?

The Impact on Public Opinion

The aim of propaganda and other forms of political communication is to influence public opinion. Yet no one can ever know for sure what the "public" is thinking. In fact, there really is no single public at all—only various groups of people within the public. To measure public opinion, experts take opinion polls. By selecting a sample that accurately represents a cross section of voters, an opinion poll can often predict voting results and measure popular attitudes. In this way, experts also try to determine how bias, symbolism, and propaganda have actually influenced the public.

Enrichment

The Active Citizen

Professor Joseph F. Truman includes several speeches in the appendix to his book, *Political Communication in American Campaigns*. Two of the speeches he includes are by President Ronald Reagan and Reverend Al Sharpton. The first excerpt below is from President Reagan's First Inaugural Address, given in January 1981. This was at a time when the country faced economic difficulties.

The second excerpt is from Reverend Sharpton's speech in favor of John Kerry at the Democratic National Convention in 2004. Kerry ran for President but lost to George W. Bush, who was seeking a second term. John Edwards was Kerry's running mate. He ran for the Vice Presidency.

In this activity, you are asked to compare the two speeches and the methods they use to persuade listeners. Both of these are examples of political communication.

President Reagan's First Inaugural Address

"The economic ills (problems) we suffer have come upon us over several decades. They will not go away in days, weeks, or months, but they will go away. They will go away because we as Americans have the capacity (ability) now, as we've had in the past, to do whatever needs to be done to preserve this last and greatest bastion (stronghold) of freedom.

In this present crisis, government is not the solution to our problem; government is the problem. From time to time we've been tempted to believe that society has become too complex to be managed by self-rule, that government by an elite group (top group of people) is superior to government for, by, and of the people. Well, if no one among us is capable (able) of governing himself, then who among us has the capacity to govern someone else? All of us together, in and out of government, must bear the burden. The solutions we seek must be equitable (fair), with no one group singled out to pay a higher price.

Summarize each paragraph in your own words:

_____
_____
_____
_____
_____
_____
_____
_____
_____
_____
_____
_____
_____
_____
_____
_____
_____
_____
_____
_____
_____
_____
_____
_____

Continues ▶

Summarize each paragraph in your own words:

We hear much of special interest groups. Well, our concern must be for a special interest group that has been too long neglected (ignored). It knows no sectional boundaries or ethnic and racial divisions, and it crosses political party lines. It is made up of men and women who raise our food, patrol our streets, man our mines and factories, teach our children, keep our homes, and heal us when we're sick—professionals, industrialists, shopkeepers, clerks, cabbies, and truck drivers. They are, in short, 'We the people,' this breed (type of people) called Americans.

Well, this [government's] objective will be a healthy, [strong], growing economy that provides equal opportunities for all Americans, with no barriers born of bigotry (bias; prejudice) or discrimination. Putting America back to work means putting all Americans back to work. With the idealism and fair play which are the core of our system and our strength, we can have a strong and prosperous America, at peace with itself and the world."

—President Ronald Reagan, First Inaugural Address (1981)

Reverend Al Sharpton's Speech to the Democratic National Convention

"I have come here tonight to say, that the only choice we have to preserve (keep) our freedoms at this point in history is to elect John Kerry the President of the United States.

(APPLAUSE)

Summarize each paragraph in your own words:

Summarize each paragraph in your own words:

I stood with both John Kerry and John Edwards on over 30 occasions during the primary season. I looked into their eyes. I am convinced that they are men who say what they mean and mean what they say.

(APPLAUSE)

I'm also convinced that at a time when a vicious (mean; cruel) spirit in . . . this country attempts to undermine America's freedoms—our civil rights, and civil liberties—we must leave this city and go forth and organize this nation for victory for our party and John Kerry and John Edwards in November.

(APPLAUSE)

And let me quickly say, this is not just about winning an election. It's about preserving (keeping) the principles on which this very nation was founded.

Look at the current view of our nation worldwide as a result of our unilateral (single-handed) foreign policy. We went from unprecedented (more than ever before) international support and solidarity (unity; agreement) on September 12, 2001, to hostility and hatred as we stand here tonight. We can't survive in the world by ourselves.

(APPLAUSE)

How did we squander (waste; fritter away) this opportunity to unite the world for democracy and to commit to a global fight against hunger and disease?"

—**Reverend Al Sharpton, Speech to the Democratic National Convention (2004)**

Continues ▶

▶ What was the purpose of each speech?

_____
_____
_____
_____

▶ What was the main message of each speech? What problem did each speaker address and how did he propose to solve it?

_____
_____
_____
_____

▶ Which of the following statements are opinions, and which are facts? Explain your answers.

President Ronald Reagan:

"*The economic ills* (illnesses; problems) *we suffer have come upon us over several decades.*"

Opinion ☐   Fact ☐

Explanation: _____
_____

"*In this present crisis, government is not the solution to our problem; government is the problem.*"

Opinion ☐   Fact ☐

Explanation: _____
_____

"*With the idealism and fair play which are the core of our system and our strength, we can have a strong and prosperous America, at peace with itself and the world.*"

Opinion ☐   Fact ☐

Explanation: _____
_____

Reverend Al Sharpton:

"I stood with both John Kerry and John Edwards on over 30 occasions during the primary season."

Opinion ☐   Fact ☐

Explanation: _____

_____

"We went from unprecedented (more than ever before) *international support and solidarity* (unity; agreement) *on September 12, 2001, to hostility and hatred as we stand here tonight.*

Opinion ☐   Fact ☐

Explanation: _____

_____

"We can't survive in the world by ourselves."

Opinion ☐   Fact ☐

Explanation: _____

_____

▶ What exaggerated statements, if any, were made in either speech?

_____
_____
_____
_____
_____

▶ How did these speeches appeal to listeners' emotions?

_____
_____
_____
_____
_____

Continues ▶

▶ Did either of these speeches show bias? Explain your answer.

▶ How did President Reagan use the phrase "We the People" and Reverend Sharpton use the expression "America's freedoms" as symbols? Explain your answer.

▶ Should either of these political communications be considered as an example of propaganda? Explain your answer.

Name _____

Complete the chart below by describing the different activities of interest groups and their impact in influencing government.

Activity	Description/Impact
Monitoring 	
Lobbying 	
Campaigning (helping candidates get elected) 	
Litigation (filing lawsuits) 	
Publicity (winning public opinion) 	

Chapter 14 | Interest Groups and the Media

Name _____

You are the chairperson of a nonprofit organization such as Habitat for Humanity, the American Red Cross, the American Cancer Society, the Make-A-Wish Foundation, the Girl Scouts of the USA, the Boy Scouts of America, or the American Society for the Prevention of Cruelty to Animals. Design a campaign to help you win support for your nonprofit organization—both in Congress and with the general public. Fill in the "action list" below.

Name of Nonprofit Organization: _____

Action List

1. Steps to take to lobby support in Congress:

_____
_____
_____
_____
_____

2. Steps to take to win support from the public:

_____
_____
_____
_____
_____

3. Ways to use the media in support of your cause:

_____
_____
_____
_____
_____

Can influence government through civic action:
- Run for office
- Petition government officials
- Speak at meetings
- Send letters
- Contribute to campaigns

- Organize to promote their common interests with legislators and public opinion
- Different types of interest groups: based on economic interests, unions, environmental protection, helping particular ethnic groups, etc.
- Activities of interest groups: monitoring, lobbying, litigation, campaigning, publicity
- Impact: Lobbyists often bring expert subject-matter knowledge to legislators; lobbyists can influence legislation; interest groups can sway public opinion

Individuals 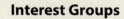 **Interest Groups**

The Impact of Individuals, Interest Groups, and the Media

The Media
- Television, newspapers, magazines, radio, the Internet
- News reporters monitor government activities
- People get their knowledge of public affairs from the media
- The media act as "watchdogs" exposing corruption, wrong-doing or error

Analyzing Political Communication/Advertising
- **Bias** = one-sided; not based on evidence
- **Symbolism** = represents something
- **Propaganda** = appeals to emotions: Look for bias, exaggeration, being one-sided, half-truths, glittering generalities

Fact or Opinion?
A **fact** is a statement that can be verified by checking with other sources. It is either true or false. An **opinion** is an expression of belief. There are different kinds of opinions. Some opinions are mere expressions of taste: "I like the taste of a fresh, crisp apple." No one can dispute that the speaker likes apples. Other opinions are statements of belief about the future, or about factual matters where the facts remain unknown: "I think people will watch less television in the future" or "I believe Al Gore actually had more votes in Florida than George W. Bush in the 2000 election."

Chapter 14 | Interest Groups and the Media

Review Cards: Interest Groups and the Media

How Individuals Can Affect Government

Individuals can influence government by:
- Running for office
- Petitioning government officials
- Collecting signatures on issues
- Speaking at meetings
- Sending letters
- Making campaign contributions

Interest Groups

- An **interest group** is a group of individuals with common interests who seek to influence public policy. Interest groups attempt to influence public policies directly, rather than by electing their members as government officials. Unlike a political party, an interest group tends to focus on a specific issue or area, rather than on all the problems facing government leaders.
- There are many different types of interest groups: environmental interest groups (which protect wildlife and reduce pollution), economic interest groups like the American Bankers Association and American Medical Association (which often focus on their single industry), civil rights interest groups, and interest groups that are formed over particular issues.
- A **public interest group** attempts to promote the **common good**—the interests of Americans as a whole rather than of any specific group.

How Interest Groups Monitor and Influence Government

- **Monitoring**: Interest groups often "**monitor**" developments. This means they keep track of everything legislatures and government agencies are doing that might affect their area of focus.
- **Lobbying**: Interest groups hire **lobbyists,** who speak to state legislators, members of Congress, and other government officials in order to influence new legislation or government regulations. **Lobbying** takes its name from the past when hired representatives of interest groups tried to speak to legislators in the lobbies of their hotels or of legislative buildings.
    Lobbyists usually specialize in a particular subject. They therefore bring subject-area expertise to legislators, government officials and the public. Interest groups often help to provide specific details for proposed legislation.
- **Campaigning**: Interest groups and their lobbyists also help politicians to get elected or re-elected.
    In 1974, a law was passed that allowed each interest group to form its own political action committee, or PAC. PACs can provide larger sums of money to political candidates than individuals are permitted to contribute.
- **Litigation** (lawsuits): Interest groups—particularly public interest groups and those supporting minority rights—sometimes promote their causes by filing lawsuits. Civil Rights groups in the 1950s, such as the NAACP, used litigation to help overturn racial segregation in the South. Consumer groups and environmental groups also frequently use lawsuits.
- **Publicity**: Interest groups usually try to influence **public opinion**—the views of the general public—through advertising, press releases, publishing articles, and television and radio appearances. This is sometimes known as "grass roots" lobbying.

The Media

The word "media" is the plural of "medium." A medium is something that transfers or carries something, including messages, from one place to another. Here, **"media"** refers to "mass media"—methods of communication to large numbers of people through television programs, newspapers, magazines, radio, Internet websites, Internet blogs, and social media.

- The media monitor and influence government. Media play an important role in our democratic system of government because they inform citizens what is happening in government. They also inform the public about current events more generally.
- The media act as a **watchdog** over our government, questioning government leaders about their actions and exposing government wrongdoing. "Investigative journalists" investigate issues or suspected wrongdoing through research and by interviewing witnesses and participants.

Political Communications: Bias, Symbolism and Propaganda

- Individuals, interest groups and political parties create political communications in order to persuade readers. Sometimes these communications show bias, make use of symbolism, or become a form of propaganda.
- Some communications show **bias**—they provide only a partial perspective and may be prejudiced for or against something. They may take advantage of popular beliefs and stereotypes.
- **Symbolism** refers to the use of symbols in a communication, like a donkey on a poster to represent the Democratic Party. The authors may try to associate themselves with popular symbols like the U.S. flag.
- Political communications that are very biased and that mainly appeal to fears and emotions are known as **propaganda**. Propaganda often relies on unsupported opinions, exaggerations, half-truths, name calling, stereotypes, oversimplifications, and "glittering generalities" (*claims that cannot be checked*).

Analyzing Media and Political Communications

To analyze a political communication, media message or political advertisement, take the following steps:

1. Determine who created the message.
2. Determine the purpose of the article or communication. Is it meant to be informational or persuasive? Does it show any obvious bias? Consider the use of any symbols in the article or communication.
3. Read or listen to the text carefully.
    - What is the main idea?
    - What arguments does the author use?
4. Identify facts and opinions in the communication.
    - Determine if its facts are accurate.
    - Decide if its opinions are reasonable, based on the evidence.
5. Evaluate the reasoning of the communication.

What Do You Know?

SS.7.C.2.10

1. What is an important difference between interest groups and political parties?
    A. Interest groups have more members than political parties.
    B. Interest groups have platforms addressing all issues of public concern.
    C. Interest groups are organized to elect their candidates to political office.
    D. Interest groups attempt to influence government directly on particular issues.

SS.7.C.2.10

2. Which of the following is NOT one of the ways in which the media influence government?
    A. by providing information to the public
    B. by contributing to election campaign funds
    C. by focusing public attention on particular issues
    D. by making public officials accountable for their actions

SS.7.C.2.10

3. The diagram below gives details about the American political system.

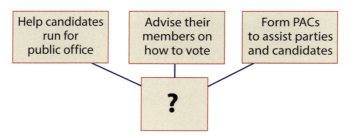

Which title completes the diagram?
    A. How interest groups monitor government activities
    B. How interest groups engage in campaigning
    C. How interest groups use publicity to win support
    D. How interest groups lobby state and federal legislators

SS.7.C.2.10

4. Sarah felt very strongly about an issue in the news. She wrote to her representative in Congress and expressed her feelings on the issue. Then she wrote a short editorial for the local newspaper and sent it off. Which statement describes Sarah's activities?
    A. She was acting as a lobbyist.
    B. She was forming her own political party.
    C. She was starting her own special interest group.
    D. She was influencing government as an individual.

SS.7.C.2.11

5. The graph below shows where Americans obtain their news.

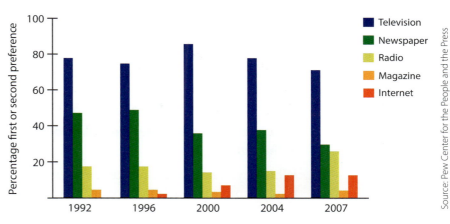

Based upon the information in the graph, where should a candidate spend the most campaign funds for advertising?

A. newspaper
B. television
C. Internet
D. radio

SS.7.C.2.10

6. "Italians make the best chefs in the world." What does this statement show?

A. a form of media
B. an example of bias
C. acting as a watchdog
D. an example of symbolism

SS.7.C.2.10

7. The table below describes four interest groups.

Interest Group 1	Supporters of the interests of workers
Interest Group 2	Activists who protect wildlife and struggle to reduce pollution
Interest Group 3	Defenders of the Second Amendment who protect the right to own guns
Interest Group 4	Advocates of greater equality for women through education and advocacy

Which group on the table would be mostly likely to support a ban on deepwater drilling in the Gulf of Mexico?

A. Interest Group 1
B. Interest Group 2
C. Interest Group 3
D. Interest Group 4

SS.7.C.2.10

8. Which best describes the main objective of a lobbyist?

A. to raise campaign funds for political parties
B. to influence public decision-making for the common good
C. to influence state legislators or members of Congress on issues
D. to advise political candidates on how to manage their election campaigns

Chapter 14 | Interest Groups and the Media

SS.7.C.2.10

9. What is one way that interest groups attempt to influence public policy?
   A. bribing legislators to support their proposals
   B. impeaching their opponents in the legislature
   C. sponsoring news programs on major television networks
   D. giving legislators the benefit of their subject-area expertise

SS.7.C.2.11

10. A U.S. government poster from World War I is shown at the right.

    Which evidence best supports the view that this poster is an example of wartime propaganda?
    A. its use of symbolism
    B. its mention of Liberty Bonds
    C. its use of bandwagon claims to influence the public
    D. its name-calling and the exaggerated characteristics of the soldier

SS.7.C.2.11

11. The sign shown at the right was posted all over the town of Mayberry.

    Which method does this political communication have in common with propaganda?

    > Vote for Joe Everyman for City Commissioner. He is the only candidate who truly cares about your future!

    A. using symbolism
    B. appealing to readers' fears
    C. name-calling of opponents
    D. presenting an opinion as a fact

SS.7.C.2.11

12. The statement below was made by President George W. Bush at the start of the 2004 Presidential election campaign against Democratic candidate Senator John Kerry.

    > It's a choice between keeping the tax relief that is moving the economy forward, or putting the burden of higher taxes back on the American people... It's a choice between an America that leads the world with strength and confidence, or an America that is uncertain in the face of danger.

    How was this political communication intended to win public support for President Bush?
    A. by using political symbolism
    B. by pointing to specific issues
    C. by labeling his opponent as uncertain
    D. by providing detailed evidence of his achievements

Chapter 14 | Interest Groups and the Media

CHAPTER 15

Public Policy

SS.7.C.2.12 Develop a plan to resolve a state or local problem by researching public policy alternatives, identifying appropriate government agencies to address the issue, and determining a course of action.

SS.7.C.2.13 Examine multiple perspectives on public and current issues.

SS.7.C.2.14 Conduct a service project to further the public good.

Names and Terms You Should Know

- Public policy
- Public policy alternatives
- Level of government
- Government agency
- Public policy solution
- Private community service solution
- Public good
- Issue
- Multiple perspectives
- Public perspective

Florida "Keys" to Learning

1. Actions taken by governments to solve problems and to achieve goals are known as public policy. In our system of democratic government, citizens can have a direct voice in public policy.

2. Public policy problems can often be addressed through the following steps: (1) identify a problem; (2) conduct research about the problem; (3) develop and evaluate various public policy alternatives; (4) identify the appropriate (*proper*) level of government and the right agency to address the problem; and (5) determine a course of action. Sometimes a private community service solution is the best alternative. These steps may vary depending on the problem faced.

3. Public issues are questions about which citizens may reasonably disagree. Knowing multiple perspectives on an issue helps us to take into account different interests and experiences, sometimes leading to a better solution.

4. Understanding multiple perspectives (*points of view*) can also help us develop compromises between different interests and concerns.

What is Public Policy?

Governments make laws, issue executive orders and regulations, and make other decisions that affect the public. Actions taken by governments to solve problems and achieve goals are known as **public policy**. This is because our government acts on behalf of the public. In this chapter, you will study public policy.

Public policy decisions can lead to new laws or actions by the government. Many of the examples in this book concern public policy decisions by our federal government. Congress may pass a new law. The President may issue an executive order affecting the national parks. The Environmental Protection Agency (EPA) may announce a new regulation changing air pollution standards.

State and local governments also make many public policy decisions. A state conservation commission may issue regulations banning (*prohibiting*) construction in an area in order to protect an endangered bird species. The Florida Department of Education may issue new academic requirements for student graduation from high school. A local town planning commission may approve a request to build a group of commercial buildings near the town center. A city council may raise local sales taxes to cover rising costs.

Citizens Influence Public Policy

In our system of democratic government, citizens can have a direct voice in public policy. Almost every important decision by government agencies allows some opportunity for public comment. Before a local committee or state or federal agency makes an order or regulation, it usually holds hearings. It may ask specific experts to testify and generally invites all interested citizens to submit oral or written comments.

In addition to these formal steps, citizens have the right to address their public officials and legislators by writing letters or sending **petitions** (*formal requests to government officials, signed by citizens who agree with the demand*). Citizens can also use political parties, interest groups and the media to draw attention to their concerns, to make new proposals, and to influence the public policy process.

Steps in the Public Policy Process: Developing a Plan to Resolve a State or Local Problem

The following steps are often used to address a public policy problem:

1. Identify a problem.
2. Conduct research about the problem. This research may focus on determining what has caused the problem.
3. Develop and evaluate various public policy alternatives (or "options"). Consider the pros and cons of each alternative.
4. Identify the appropriate (*proper*) level of government and the best agency to address the problem.
5. Determine your course of action. Consider private community service solutions along with public policy solutions. You may decide to present your policy alternative to the appropriate government agency or to take some other action.

> In answering questions about public policy on the EOC test, remember that you should first research the problem, then think of alternative solutions, and finally evaluate these alternatives before determining a course of action.

Chapter 15 | Public Policy

Now that you have learned the main steps for making a public policy decision, you are ready to develop a plan with your classmates to resolve a state or local problem.

Your teacher should divide your class into groups. Each group will identify a local or state problem and develop a solution to that problem. Then you will send your proposal (*suggested plan*) to the appropriate government agency.

1. Identify a Problem

First of all, your group should identify a local or state problem. Some examples of potential problems are listed below, but feel free to think of a different problem on your own. Be sure to select a problem that really concerns you.

The Environment
- How can local air, water and land pollution be reduced?
- How can local residents be encouraged to recycle waste?

Public Education
- How can students be better motivated?
- How can the local school district prevent bullying?
- How can class sizes be reduced?
- Should your school district offer after-school programs for children with working parents?

Safety and Crime
- How can local crime be reduced?
- How can homes and businesses be made safer?
- How can Florida prevent identify theft and Internet crime?

Bicycle Lanes, Roads, and Highways
- How can town roads be made safer for bicycle riders?
- How can traffic accidents in the community be reduced?
- How can local rush-hour traffic be reduced?

The Regulation of Retail Stores
- How can local shopping hours be made more convenient?
- How can the town attract more shoppers?

Parks and Recreation
- How can local parks be made more attractive?
- Which recreational facilities would local residents most enjoy?
- Should your town build a new sports center or outdoor stadium?

Insurance
- How can Florida reduce insurance rates for residents and businesses?

Taxation
- How can Florida improve its social services without raising sales taxes?

Real Estate Development and Construction
- How can your town or neighborhood promote development without damaging the environment?

Health and Food
- How can Florida let consumers know which foods are healthy choices?
- How can Florida help fight child obesity?
- How can Florida encourage children to be vaccinated?
- How can Florida help its residents obtain better health care?
- How can Florida help fight Alzheimer's disease?
- How can Florida reduce costs while maintaining quality health care?

Which local or state problem has your group identified?_____
_____
_____

2. Conduct Research

The next step is to conduct research about the problem. Be an aggressive researcher! Think of yourself as a reporter or a detective trying to solve a problem.

Your research might begin by defining the problem more precisely. Your group may wish to research the causes of the problem. Knowing what has caused a problem often helps in developing a solution to it. Then you should research different ideas for solving your problem. See whether any of these ideas have actually been tried.

There are many ways to find information about a problem and possible solutions. Members of your group may want to start by searching the Internet for information. You might also visit your school or local library for books, magazines and newspapers with information about the problem. Your school or local librarian should be able to help you locate good sources of information.

If your problem is a local one, you might look at local newspapers and community records at your local library or town hall. For example, there may have been a town meeting about the issue in the past. It could be helpful to see what solutions were discussed, what was tried, and what was rejected.

In addition to looking at the Internet and printed sources, you may want to interview experts or public officials about the problem your group has chosen. You might, for example, look at the website of a government agency that is related to the problem. Then you might look for "Contact Us" or "Staff" on that website. Once you click this link, you will often find the names and email addresses of one or more experts or government officials who have information about your problem. You can then email these experts. Be sure to introduce yourself and to ask specific, focused questions. Also be sure to send a thank you letter if one of these experts responds to your questions.

If your problem is a local one, you may also want to interview local community leaders in person or by telephone. You can ask them what they know about the problem and if there had been any efforts to solve the problem in the past. You can also ask these leaders for their ideas on what is causing the problem and what they think would be the best solution to the problem.

It may help for members of your group to put the information they find on index cards so that your group can bring all the results of its research together. Each index card should deal with a particular aspect of the problem—such as defining the problem, possible causes of the problem, previous attempts by officials to deal with the problem, and proposals to resolve the problem in the future. Be sure to record information about your sources on each card. Once your group has completed its

research, it can organize all the index cards from group members by topic—such as details about the problem, causes of the problem, and alternative solutions to the problem. Write three sources that your group has consulted (or plans to consult) below. These sources could be books, magazine articles, websites, or people that your group has interviewed.

_____
_____
_____

Complete one or two sample index cards from your own research:

Topic: _____
_____
_____
Source: _____
_____

Topic: _____
_____
_____
Source: _____
_____

3. **Develop and evaluate various public policy alternatives (or "options")**

Now comes the fun part! You should "brainstorm" with the other members of your group to think of possible solutions to your problem. When you brainstorm, you simply think of every idea you possibly can that might help to solve the problem. No reasonable idea is rejected. Sometimes hearing the ideas of classmates can even inspire you to think of new ideas.

- ☑ Think about what caused the problem. What solutions might eliminate the causes of the problem?
- ☑ Think about what has been proposed to solve the problem in the past, and why it wasn't tried or didn't work.
- ☑ Think about what has been proposed or tried successfully elsewhere, and how that might be adapted to your situation.
- ☑ Think about the resources you have and how they might be best used to solve the problem.

Try to be as creative as possible!

Because each proposal is an alternative solution to the problem, proposed solutions are sometimes called "**public policy alternatives**" or "**options**."

List two of the public policy alternatives that your group has developed in its brainstorming session on the top lines of the two cards on the next page.

Now you are ready to look at each public policy alternative more closely to evaluate it. You should consider the "pros" (*advantages*) and "cons" (*disadvantages*) of each alternative. "Pros" and "cons" may also be referred to as the "benefits" and "costs" of a proposed solution.

In thinking of pros and cons—or costs and benefits—begin by thinking how effective the proposed solution will be in solving the problem. Will it solve the problem completely? If not, will it help reduce the problem? Is the proposed solution something

378   Chapter 15 | Public Policy

that government agencies will be able to accomplish? Will the solution bring additional benefits besides solving the problem?

Then look at the disadvantages for each proposed policy alternative. What will each alternative cost? What resources would each require? What additional disadvantages might each bring?

Write down the pros and cons for two of the public policy alternatives you are evaluating:

Public Policy Alternative #1

Proposed Solution: _____
_____
_____
_____
_____

Pros: Cons:

_____   _____
_____   _____
_____   _____
_____   _____

Public Policy Alternative #2

Proposed Solution: _____
_____
_____
_____
_____

Pros: Cons:

_____   _____
_____   _____
_____   _____
_____   _____

Look again at all of the policy alternatives your group came up with during its brainstorming. Compare your evaluations with those of other members of your group and rank all the alternatives from best to worst.

▶ The *best alternative* is the one that brings the most benefits at the least cost.

▶ The *worst alternative* is the one that brings the least benefits for the most cost.

In the space below, write down your choice for the three best public policy alternatives from those proposed by your group. Put the one you consider the very best at the top of your list.

1. _____
_____

2. _____
_____

3. _____
_____

Explain why you feel the one at the top of your list is better than the other two.

_____
_____
_____
_____

Now give each of your top three alternatives a score:

Alternative 1	3 points
Alternative 2	2 points
Alternative 3	1 points

Compare your choices with those of your classmates. To calculate the score for each alternative, add together all the points it has received from all of the members of your group. The public policy alternative with the most points is the one your group has selected as the best course of action in response to the problem.

4. Identify the appropriate level of government and agency to address the problem

Now that your group has researched the problem and chosen its proposed solution, it is ready to identify which level of government and which particular government agency is best able to address the problem. In general, problems across the state are best handled by state agencies, while local problems are best handled by local agencies.

▶ Which level of government would best be able to deal with the problem your group has identified?

☐ State of Florida
☐ County Government
☐ Town, City or other Local Government

Once you determine the level of government for your problem, you should look on the Internet for the particular agency or department that would deal with this problem. Government agencies often deal with a specific subject matter. For example, a problem in a state forest area would be handled by the Florida Forest Service, while a problem with state educational requirements would be handled by the Florida Department of Education.

You can find a listing of major state agencies on the Internet by using the search term: "Florida state agencies."

You can usually find the names of local agencies by looking on your local government website.

▶ Which government agency would best be able to deal with this problem? Include contact information below.

Department, Agency or Office:
_____
_____

Email and/or Address:
_____
_____

Why is this the **appropriate** (*proper; suitable*) level of government and government agency? Explain your answer.
_____
_____
_____
_____

5. Determine a course of action

Now that you and the other members of your group have chosen the right agency, you can really go into action. This is when you implement your plan.

To "implement" means to put it into effect.

To implement a public policy solution, you usually have to win the support of the government agency in charge of that aspect of public policy.

There are many ways in which your group can directly influence such policy-makers. Members of your group can petition or write directly to the policy-makers in the government agency or department you have identified. You can offer to meet with these policy-makers to give them your opinions. You can even go to Tallahassee and visit the offices of your state legislators.

Your group can also try to build public support by writing letters to the editor of the local newspaper. You can create a campaign using social media like Facebook and Twitter, or create your own website or blog devoted to the problem. You can hold a public meeting or conference on the problem.

Not every problem requires a public policy solution. Some problems are better solved through the voluntary efforts of private individuals than they are by government. Many problems can be solved through **private community service solutions**—unpaid, voluntary efforts by private individuals.

For example, your community may have a food pantry or food bank. Food banks collect unsold food donated by grocery stores and restaurants. Food banks store and distribute this food to people in need. These food banks are private charities, usually run by unpaid volunteers. You can volunteer to work in your local food bank for community service after school. Other examples of community service are volunteering when there is an emergency such as a hurricane, or tutoring children in an after-school program.

Your group may decide to conduct its own private community service project to solve its problem, rather than to approach public policy decision-makers. For example, you might begin a voluntary recycling program, or create a registry of potential blood donors. For more information on conducting a community service project, see Chapter 12, page 300. All such public service projects aim to promote the "**common good**" (or "**public good**")—what is good for all the members of the community.

List three steps that you have taken with your group to implement (*put into effect*) your decision through a course of action.

1. _____
_____

2. _____
_____

3. _____
_____

Once you have implemented your plan, it is helpful to keep track of how well it works. This will help you become a better policy-maker in the future.

To evaluate the effectiveness of your plan, consider how well it works at solving the problem, what it costs (in time, money and other resources), and what additional advantages or disadvantages it brings.

How do you plan to keep track of the implementation of your plan?

_____
_____
_____

How well has it solved the problem?

_____
_____
_____

What have been its costs?

_____

_____

_____

What other advantages/disadvantages has it had?

_____

_____

_____

Addressing Public Issues

A **public issue** is a problem or decision facing the community about which citizens disagree on what should be done. There are at least two sides to every public issue. For example:

- Should Florida require special labels for genetically-engineered foods?
- Should Florida make talking on cell phones while driving a traffic violation?
- Should your town build a new sports complex?
- Should your town raise its local sales tax to provide more money for local public schools?
- Should your town create more bicycle lanes?
- Should your town require retail stores to stay open until 9:00 pm?
- Should your county introduce a new hotel tax to raise money for local services?

Multiple perspectives play an important role in how public issues are viewed, debated, and resolved. Each of us has different experiences. These experiences give each of us an ability to see things that others may not. Each of us looks at a problem from a unique **perspective**, or point of view. It is therefore important to consider the perspectives of others.

Groups often look at issues differently because of their different economic or cultural interests. To evaluate each group's perspective, always consider how the members of that group will be affected by any proposed solution to a problem or issue. Understanding multiple perspectives is especially useful for reaching compromises and resolving issues. A **public perspective** looks at an issue from the standpoint of the community as a whole.

Smithtown's Bicycle Lanes Controversy

For example, consider this issue: Should Smithtown introduce bicycle lanes?

For: A group representing local cyclists (bicycle riders) is strongly in favor of introducing bicycle lanes. They feel it is dangerous to ride their bicycles in Smithtown because they have to share lanes with cars, buses and trucks. It could be easy for any one of them to have an accident. If they do, the cost of Smithtown's insurance would probably go up. They also feel that Smithtown should have bicycle lanes to encourage more cycling. Riding a bicycle is healthy and does not burn fossil fuels or make pollution. Smithtown has two bicycle stores. Both stores have contributed large sums of money to the campaign to introduce bicycle lanes to Smithtown.

Against: The Smithtown Car and Truck Drivers Association ("SCTDA") is a private interest group. It strongly opposes introducing bicycle lanes to Smithtown. The association says that it would be very expensive to make bicycle lanes in Smithtown, while there are only a handful of bicycle riders living there. The money that would be spent in marking off roads for bicycle lanes could be better spent on the town's parks, police force or schools. Instead of helping Smithtown, the town would become a magnet for bicycle riders throughout the county. Every cyclist in nearby towns would come to Smithtown to use its new bicycle lanes. The roads would become crowded with cyclists and the chance of an accident involving a cyclist and a car would become greater, not less. In addition, there would be an increased chance of an accident between a cyclist and a pedestrian (*person on foot*). The association also argues that the creation of bicycle lanes would take space away from the shoulders of roads and narrow the driving space on existing automobile lanes. This would create a hazardous situation for automobile and truck drivers. Instead of making bicycle lanes in Smithtown, the SCTDA argues that bicycle owners from Smithtown go further inland for recreational cycling. Finally, they propose as an alternative that Smithtown dedicate a section of its public park to cycling. The SCTDA receives funds from several gasoline stations in Smithtown.

▶ How do the interests of the Smithtown cyclists and of the members of the Smithtown Car and Truck Drivers Association affect their perspectives on this issue?

_____
_____
_____

▶ How do the interests of the bicycle store owners and gasoline station owners affect their perspectives on this issue?

_____
_____
_____

▶ List two steps that either of these groups could take to win the support of the Smithtown City Council on this issue.

_____
_____
_____

Enrichment

The Active Citizen

You can discover some of the actual issues facing Florida today by looking at the websites of the Florida Senate (www.flsenate.gov) or the House of Representatives (www.myfloridahouse.gov). Click on "bills" on each website to find proposals currently before the state legislature. Many of these bills are attempts by legislators to resolve problems or to enact proposals on public issues.

1. Choose one of the bills on an issue that interests you.
2. Study both sides of the issue and write a letter to the editor of a local or regional newspaper giving your views.
3. Debate the issue in your class.
4. Contact your state legislator for his or her views on the bill.
5. Contact your local representatives of the two major political parties for their views on the bill.
6. Invite your legislator or a staff member to your class to explain his or her views on the issue and to answer questions.

Chapter 15 | Public Policy

Name _____

Complete the chart below by describing each of the steps for developing a plan to resolve a state or local problem.

Step	Description
Identify a problem 	
Conduct research 	
Develop and evaluate policy alternatives 	
Identify level of government and agency 	
Determine a course of action 	

384   Chapter 15 | Public Policy

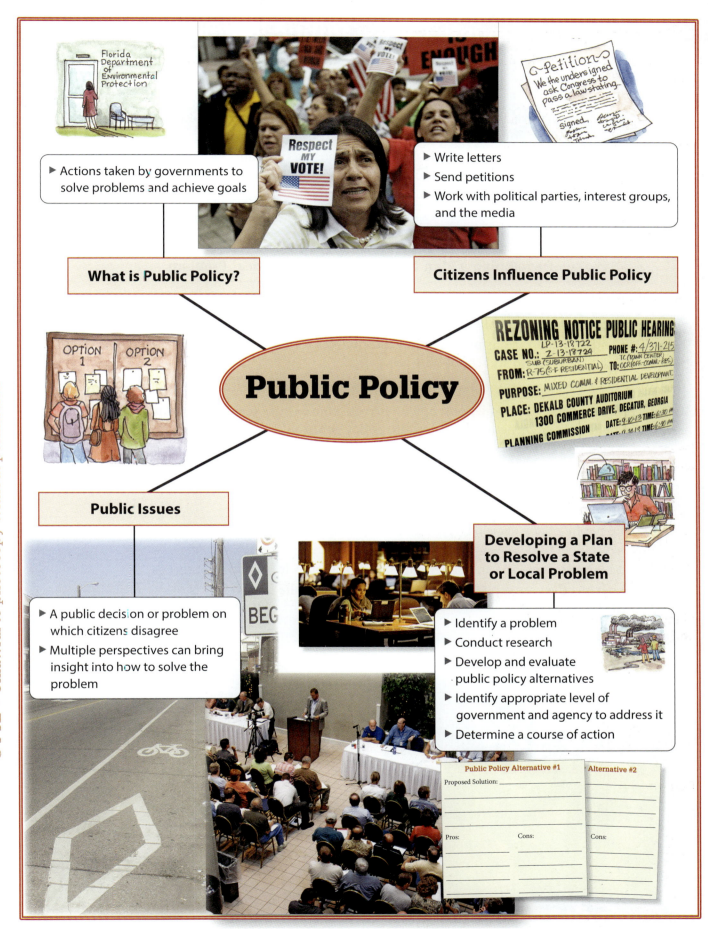

Chapter 15 | Public Policy

Review Cards: Public Policy

Public Policy

- **Public policy** concerns actions taken by governments to solve problems and to achieve goals for the **common good/public good** (*the good of the community*).
- Individual citizens can influence public policy by proposing programs or policy alternatives, by speaking at a public hearing, by petitioning government officials, or by working through an interest group or political party.

Developing a Plan to Resolve a State or Local Problem

1. **Identify** the problem.
2. **Conduct research** about the problem.
3. Develop and evaluate various **public policy alternatives** (or "options"). Consider the "pros" and "cons" of each alternative and choose the best one.
4. Identify the level of government and appropriate agency to address the problem.
5. **Determine a course of action.** Sometimes a **private community service solution** (based on private volunteer efforts) can be better than a **public policy solution** (based on government action).

Understanding Multiple Perspectives

- In making public policy decisions, it helps to consider **multiple perspectives**—different points of view on a problem or issue.
- Different interests, concerns and experiences lead each of us to see different things.
- Multiple perspectives are especially helpful in resolving **public issues**—decisions or problems on which citizens disagree.

Chapter 15 | Public Policy

What Do You Know?

SS.7.C.2.12

1. Juan and Maria have noticed that all the frogs in their local pond have been very quiet recently. When they went to the pond, they could no longer hear any of them. Then they saw a few of them were dead. To which agency should they report this problem?

   A. Florida Department of Education
   B. Florida Department of Elder Affairs
   C. Florida Department of Veterans Affairs
   D. Florida Department of Environmental Protection

SS.7.C.2.12

2. The local library has reduced its opening hours in order to save the community money. Many students and parents are upset at this change. Many students liked to go to the library after school. Which proposed solution would be fair and not overburden the community?

   A. charge borrowers triple fines for overdue books
   B. charge everyone in the community for their library card
   C. use community volunteers to extend the library's opening hours
   D. sell some of the books in the library to have more money for opening times

SS.7.C.2.12

3. John Smith lives in the downtown area. He is upset that local motorcycle riders sometimes come through his town in the early evening and make loud noises with their motorcycles. Which of the following should be John's first step in attempting to resolve this issue?

   A. speak to some of the motorcycle riders and ask them to ride more quietly
   B. write a letter to the local newspaper demanding a town ban on motorcycles
   C. propose a total ban on motorcycle use at the next town council meeting
   D. ask local police officers to arrest any motorcyclists who appear in the town again

SS.7.C.2.12

4. Which of the following is an example of a private community service solution to a local problem?

   A. A town raises its sales tax to pay for a new fire engine.
   B. A community increases its property taxes to build a homeless shelter.
   C. Retired teachers volunteer to help students in an after-school program.
   D. A local hospital increases its fees for some treatments in order to stay in business.

SS.7.C.2.13

5. Below are views for and against a town ban on motorcycle traffic.

1	2
Motorcycles are extremely dangerous and noisy. People can drive much more safely in cars. Motorcycles zoom in and out of traffic and may even lead automobile drivers to cause an accident. Motorcycles are dangerous, noisy and totally unnecessary. They should be banned.	Motorcyclists are individuals with rights just like everyone else. So long as they respect others' rights, motorcyclists are entitled to enjoy the sport of motorcycling. We have no more reason to stop motorcyclists than any other sport. Skiing and sky-diving may be dangerous but we permit those. Automobile drivers cause more accidents then motorcyclists. Should we ban automobiles?

Which conclusion can be drawn from these views?

A. Most people enjoy riding motorcycles.
B. There are multiple perspectives on public issues.
C. Motorcyclists generally fail to respect other people.
D. Motorcycles are safer than most other forms of transportation.

SS.7.C.2.13

6. In the 1950s and 1960s, one of the most important public issues facing Americans was the policy of racial segregation in Southern states.

Civil rights groups conducted sit-ins, marches, boycotts, and acts of civil disobedience. What was their perspective on this issue?

A. They believed Southern supporters of segregation should be threatened with acts of violence.
B. They felt it would be better to be patient and accept segregation in the South.
C. They believed it was time to move all African Americans to the North.
D. They felt it was necessary to take peaceful action against segregation.

SS.7.C.2.12

7. John and Maria have become concerned about the large number of stray pets that are often lost in their community. What is the next step they should take?

A. lobby local lawmakers for support
B. implement a plan for their community
C. run for public office in the next election
D. conduct research on the problem of stray pets

SS.7.C.2.12

8. What is one way that citizens can directly influence public policy?

A. by becoming better informed about issues
B. by watching more news programs on television
C. by sending petitions signed by citizens to local officials
D. by expressing their views to their closest friends and relatives

CHAPTER 16

Types of Government

SS.7.C.3.1 Compare different forms of government (direct democracy, representative democracy, socialism, communism, monarchy, oligarchy, autocracy).

SS.7.C.3.2 Compare parliamentary, federal, confederal, and unitary systems of government.

Names and Terms You Should Know

Government	Absolute monarchy	Governor
Democracy	Limited monarchy	President
Direct democracy	Autocracy	Prime minister
Representative democracy	Oligarchy	Parliamentary
Republic	Unitary	Socialism
Monarchy	Federal	Communism
	Confederal	

Florida "Keys" to Learning

1. There have been many theories on the origins of government. During the Enlightenment, many believed that people had once lived in a state of nature but then formed a social contract by banding together and creating a government. Social scientists today agree that a state of nature never existed. Humans have always needed some sort of government. Governments help people cooperate, enforce rules, provide public services, and protect the community.

2. There are many forms of government and different ways to classify them. One way to classify governments is by who holds power. A monarchy has a government ruled by one person, whose claim to rule is hereditary. In seventeenth- and eighteenth-century Europe, absolute monarchs enjoyed almost total power. They claimed their power came directly from God (*divine right*). In England, a limited monarchy emerged (*appeared; developed*). The monarch remained as head of state but political power was held by an elected assembly known as Parliament.

3. Democracy is rule by the people. In a direct democracy, citizens debate and decide public issues for themselves; in a representative democracy, citizens elect representatives to act on their behalf.

4. A representative democracy is also known as a republic. Unlike the government of a monarchy, the government of a republic is accountable to the public.

5. In an autocracy, one ruler holds all political power. The autocrat might be an absolute monarch or modern dictator.

6. In an oligarchy, the members of a small group, such as nobles (*wealthy hereditary landowners*) or army officers, hold power.

7. Systems of government can also be classified by the relationship between their central and local governments. In a unitary government, a central government holds all power. It creates local governments and delegates (*assigns; hands over*) certain powers to them, but can abolish them at any time.

8. In a federal government, the federal (central) and local governments exercise independent powers and cannot abolish each other. The United States has a federal government.

9. In a confederation—or confederal government—a group of independent states or nations form an association to cooperate. The majority of the power remains with the separate states, which are free to leave at any time. The United States under the Articles of Confederation had a confederal government.

10. Another way to classify systems of governments is by looking at the relationship between their legislative and executive branches. In the United States, the legislative and executive branches are separate. This system is based on the separation of powers.

11. In a parliamentary government, like Britain, the elected legislative branch (*Parliament*) actually controls the executive branch. The members of Parliament elect the chief executive, known as the Prime Minister. The Prime Minister and the entire Cabinet are all members of Parliament.

12. Socialism and communism were two forms of government that arose in reaction to the treatment of workers in the Industrial Revolution. Socialists favor peaceful reforms. They believe it is the government's job to improve conditions for its citizens. Socialist governments establish "welfare states" in which the government takes over some industries and increases taxes to provide more social services, like free health care.

13. Communists believe that a violent social revolution by workers is necessary to overthrow the rich and achieve genuine change. In theory, they wish to abolish private property. Everything would then be owned in common and government would eventually disappear. In practice, past communist governments became brutal dictatorships.

In previous chapters, you learned about the American system of government. This is the system of government you have probably known all of your life. But in fact, there are other forms of government. In this chapter, you will explore how some of these different forms of government are organized.

Enrichment: How Did Governments Develop?

Wherever you go in the world today, you will find some sort of government. But where did all these governments come from?

During the Enlightenment, people asked this very same question. Some writers came up with the idea that, once upon a time, there had been no governments at all. People had lived as separate individuals in a "state of nature." But people soon realized they could not protect themselves. They also could not do many of the things that they would be able to do in cooperation with others. So they banded together in small groups.

This was the thinking behind John Locke's social contract theory, which you learned about in Chapter 1. According to this theory, societies were formed by agreement. People also agreed to create an organization to make rules for their community, to organize work and land ownership, to settle disputes, and to provide for the community's defense. As you know, this organization is known as **government**. To make the government effective, members of the community agreed to give government leaders power over their lives.

Because people had formed their own government, Locke believed they also had the right to change it if it did not protect their rights and meet their needs.

Today, social scientists no longer believe there was once a time when people lived as isolated individuals without governments. They realize that people have lived together in groups for as long as they have existed on Earth. The first human groups may have been small bands of hunters and gatherers, but each group had its own leaders and rules. With the introduction of agriculture, humans were able to settle in one place. Their communities grew larger, and their forms of government became more complex.

The governments that ruled over the world's first civilizations were created by force and violence as much as by agreement. A ruler and his warriors forced others to obey. Then they conquered neighboring peoples to create vast empires.

In some places, religious beliefs gave rise to governments. A powerful priest, who claimed to communicate with the gods, took charge of the community. In Egypt, Persia and the city-states of Mesopotamia, powerful rulers were both military commanders and priests. Egyptian pharaohs, for example, combined both military and religious power.

These ancient civilizations developed vast government organizations to provide for the royal family, arrange public ceremonies, overlook public works projects, feed and command thousands of soldiers, and enforce laws over millions of people.

The world's first governments thus developed in many different ways: some from agreement, others out of religious belief, and still others from conflict and the use of force. Whatever their origin, all governments fulfill several essential roles. They help the people of a community to cooperate; they enable communities to develop rules that everyone should follow; and they enforce those rules. Governments provide public goods and services to community members, settle disputes and protect the community from outsiders.

In the United States, the purposes for our federal government are clear. They are stated in the Preamble to our Constitution: to establish justice, to insure tranquility (*peace and calm*), to promote the general welfare, to protect individual liberties, and to defend the community. In fact, these are the goals of any good national government.

Chapter 16 | Types of Government

Who Holds the Power? Monarchy, Democracy, Autocracy and Oligarchy

As you look around the world today, you will quickly see that there are many types of governments. There are also several ways in which these governments can be classified. One of the most useful ways to compare forms of government is by looking at who holds power.

Monarchy

In the earliest civilizations, one leader often arose as the most powerful member of society. This ruler then passed power on to one of his or her children, or to another member of the family. This form of government is known as a monarchy. A monarch inherits political power. The monarch might be known as a king, queen, emperor, or empress. A monarch rules by hereditary right.

In many ancient civilizations, monarchs combined political, military and religious power. In Rome, China, and Japan, all-powerful emperors claimed that their families had divine origins. There were no limits to their power.

In the Middle Ages, European monarchs were not all-powerful. They were limited by tradition, law and the Catholic Church. Monarchs also had to respect the rights of their nobles. Even a monarch's sources of revenue (*income*) could be limited. If a monarch wanted additional income, he or she usually had to ask an assembly of nobles for help.

In an absolute monarchy, a king or queen inherits absolute power.

Absolute Monarchy

In the 1600s, a new type of monarchy emerged in Europe. It was known as an absolute monarchy. These rulers claimed *absolute*, or total, power. Each asserted control over their nobles and over religious life. They established large standing armies and sharply increased tax collection. Absolute rulers claimed to hold their power by "divine right." This meant they were chosen by God. Their will was law. "I am the state," proclaimed King Louis XIV of France. There were few limits on the authority of an absolute monarch, although each ruler still relied on the cooperation and friendship of other groups—such as the nobles and the army—to survive.

Limited Monarchy

English kings tried to imitate the example of France and Spain by establishing their own absolute monarchy. They attempted to rule and collect taxes without Parliament. This effort failed when Parliament and its supporters rose up in rebellion. King Charles was defeated and executed in 1649. Just over a decade later, his son was restored to the throne. Charles II made skillful compromises, but after his death his younger brother, James II, angered Parliament again. James was overthrown in the Glorious Revolution of 1688. The British Parliament established its supremacy over the King in

392   Chapter 16 | Types of Government

the English Bill of Rights of 1689. Great Britain became a **limited monarchy** (more commonly known as a "constitutional monarchy"). This is a form of government in which there is a hereditary king or queen who serves as the ceremonial head of state. Actual political power is held by an elected legislature, usually known as Parliament.

This form of government is called a limited monarchy because, unlike an absolute monarch, this type of monarch is limited by the nation's constitution and other laws.

In a limited monarchy, the monarch is often a ceremonial figurehead. Real power is held by the people, who elect Parliament.

Enrichment

The Active Citizen

- Make a chart or Venn diagram comparing absolute and limited monarchy.
- Conduct research on one of the following absolute monarchs: Philip II of Spain, Louis XIV of France, Peter the Great of Russia, or Catherine the Great of Russia. How "absolute" was their power?
- Imagine you are an absolute or limited monarch. Write a short letter or speech explaining the advantages of your form of government.

Democracy

Another form of government is **democracy**, a system that first arose in ancient Greece. Because of its mountainous geography, independent city-states arose in Greece. These city-states had contact with one another and with the great empires of Egypt and Persia.

In the fifth century B.C., one of these Greek city-states—Athens—became the world's first democracy. The word "democracy" itself comes from ancient Greek. It combines **demos**, the word for "people," with **kratos**, or "power." In a democracy, power is held by the people.

In the Athenian form of democracy, all the adult male citizens were divided into groups. Each group selected members by lot to serve on a governing council. At the same time, all adult male citizens also had the right to participate in the assembly, which served as both a legislature and a court.

Although women, children, slaves and foreigners made up a majority of Athens' population, they were not considered citizens. They did not participate in either the governing council or the assembly.

Direct Democracy

The form of government established in ancient Athens, in which citizens directly debate and decide important public issues, is known as a **direct democracy**. In a direct democracy, all eligible citizens participate **directly** in making government decisions. Most experts believe that direct democracy works

Chapter 16 | Types of Government

Direct Democracy

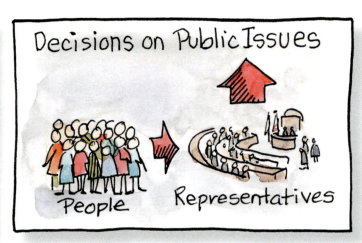
Representative Democracy

best for small communities. Not only Athens, but New England towns and the cantons (districts) of Switzerland also once practiced direct democracy.

Representative Democracy (also known as a Republic)

In larger communities, direct democracy does not work as well. There is no single place for all citizens to assemble, and it becomes impossible for so many people to discuss proposals and to make decisions together effectively. In these larger communities, citizens elect representatives. These elected representatives debate proposals and make decisions for the rest of the community. All the members of the community are bound by these decisions. This form of government, first developed by the ancient Romans, is known as a **representative democracy** or a **republic**.

The United States is a representative democracy. Ordinary citizens elect representatives to the House of Representatives. Since 1913, voters also elect U.S. Senators. Finally, ordinary citizens elect the members of the Electoral College, who choose our President. Our elected officials in turn make important decisions on the public issues we face. They act on our behalf. In a republic, government leaders are responsible to the public—not to a king or queen. If citizens disagree with the decisions of their representatives, they vote them out of office in the next election.

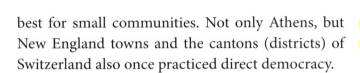

Autocracy and Oligarchy

Autocracy and oligarchy refer to the number of people in control of a government.

An **autocracy** is a form of government in which **one person** enjoys absolute power. An absolute monarchy is one type of autocracy. So is a modern dictatorship—a system in which one political leader, like Hitler or Stalin, has total power.

Benito Mussolini and Adolf Hitler

Oligarchy means rule by a few. In this form of government, a small group rules over a country. There are many types of oligarchies. In a plutocracy, a group of rich people rule over society. In other oligarchies, an aristocracy (nobles who inherit their wealth and status) controls the government. In still another type of oligarchy, power is held by leading members of the military or of a political party.

394   Chapter 16 | Types of Government

The Active Citizen

- Create your own slide show, PowerPoint presentation, or video on the development of democracy.
- Based on the chart below, write a letter to a friend on which of these four choices is the best form of government.
- Make a Venn diagram comparing autocracy and monarchy or oligarchy and democracy.

Comparing Different Forms of Monarchy and Democracy

Absolute Monarchy	Limited Monarchy	Direct Democracy	Representative Democracy
A king or queen (or emperor or empress) inherits power.	A king or queen (or emperor or empress) inherits power.	Ordinary citizens meet together or vote to decide public issues directly.	Citizens elect their representatives. These representatives in turn make political decisions for the community.
The monarch claims to rule by divine right—the will of God.	The monarch is chosen based on heredity and the support of the people.	The people themselves are the source of all political power.	The people are the source of all political power, but give their power to elected representatives.
The monarch is the supreme authority in all matters. The monarch's will is law.	The monarch is simply a figurehead. Real power is exercised by Parliament.	Citizens exercise their power directly by deciding public issues for themselves.	Elected representatives are the supreme authority during their terms of office, but they are subject to the rule of law.
The monarch has control over the nobles and the Church. The monarch can tax at will. The monarch controls a standing army.	The monarch is subject to the rule of law and the decisions of Parliament. The system is similar to a representative democracy.	Citizens make their own decisions, but they may be limited by the rule of law. Direct democracy is generally best only in cities or very small states.	Elected representatives decide public issues. If voters agree with their representatives' actions, they will re-elect them. If not, they will replace them at the next election.

The Nation and its Regions: Unitary, Federal and Confederal Systems of Government

Another way to classify governments is by the relationship between their central authority and local governments. You may remember that the relationship of the states to the central government was an important issue when our nation was founded.

Unitary Governments

In a **unitary** state, the central government is all-powerful. Local areas (which may be called provinces, departments, or counties) may have their own governments, but these local governments only exercise those powers given to them by the central government. The central government has the power to abolish (*eliminate*) these local units at any time.

This system of government is known as **unitary** because the whole government of the nation exists as a single unit. Local governments are mere extensions of the central government. The central government delegates (*assigns*) various tasks and responsibilities to the local governments to carry out.

Chapter 16 | Types of Government

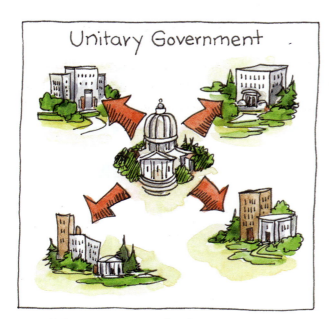

Unitary government: local governments are extensions of the central government.

> You won't need to know the names of specific countries with particular systems of government for the EOC test. But you will need to be able to identify a system of government from its characteristics.

> **Memory Hint:** To remember unitary government, remember that this system of government is based on a single unit.

has 21 counties, managed by administrators appointed by the central government. Other examples of unitary states include Algeria, China, Colombia, Cuba, Ghana, Egypt, Ireland, Israel, Italy, Japan, Poland, Saudi Arabia, South Korea, Thailand and Turkey.

Most states in the world today have unitary governments. For example, the United Kingdom (Great Britain and Northern Ireland), France and Sweden all have unitary governments.

In the United Kingdom, Parliament rules over the entire nation. The United Kingdom actually consists of four historic kingdoms—England, Wales, Scotland and Northern Ireland. Each of these areas has its own local institutions, but these are all subject to Parliament. England, for example, is divided into "regions," which in turn are divided into county councils, borough councils, and unitary authority councils. But Parliament has the power to change or even to abolish these local authorities at any time. When Parliament passes a law, it often delegates (*assigns*) enforcement of that law to these local authorities.

Similarly, France is a unitary state. Its national government has separate legislative, executive and judicial branches. Its local government units—called "regions" and "departments"—were created by the national government and remain under its control. Sweden

Federal Governments

In some countries, the central government and local governments each have their own powers. Local areas—often known as states or provinces—have an independent basis of authority. The central government has no right to abolish them. This is known as the **federal** system of government. Often a **federation** arises when several sovereign states join together to make a separate "federal" government with its own independent power.

In a federation, individual states do not have the right to leave the federation without the agreement of the other member states. At the same time, the central government of the federation does not have the right to take away the powers of the state governments. These powers are sometimes known as **states' rights**.

As you learned in earlier chapters, the United States has a federal government. Power is shared between the federal government and the states. Each state has its own government with an elected state legislature and an elected **governor**. The Supremacy Clause

Central government

Regional (state) governments

Federal government: a division of power between the central government and regional (state) governments. Each level has its own powers and responsibilities.

396   Chapter 16 | Types of Government

guarantees the supremacy of the federal government over the state governments, but the powers of the federal government are limited. The Tenth Amendment reserves for the states all those powers not granted to the federal government.

Germany also has a federal government. Germany has a powerful central government, but its *Länder* (lands or provinces) also have historic traditions and their own independent powers. Other examples of modern federal governments include Mexico, Brazil, Nigeria, and India.

Enrichment

The Active Citizen

By its very name and based on its constitution, the Russian Federation is a federation with 22 republics and several provinces and territories. However, since 2004, the President of Russia appoints all the governors and presidents of Russia's local regions. Is Russia still a federation, or has it become a unitary state? Members of your class should conduct a debate on the following resolution:

"Resolved: That Russia, despite its name, is no longer a federation but has become a unitary state."

Confederal Governments

A number of independent states or countries may decide to form an association in order to act together. Most often, such countries wish to cooperate over trade or foreign policy. At the same time, the independent states or countries joining the association do not wish to give up their sovereign (*supreme*) power. Such associations usually have very little power of their own. They depend on the cooperation of their members. Each member of the association is usually free to leave at any time.

This kind of association is known as a **confederation**. The central government of a confederation is far weaker than the central government of a federation. Most power remains with the member states that joined together to create the confederation.

As you learned in earlier chapters, the thirteen new American states joined together to form a confederation in 1781. However, the type of government established by the Articles of Confederation proved to be too weak. By adopting the Constitution, Americans moved from a confederal to a federal system.

Some political scientists consider the European Union an example of a confederal system. The European Union consists of member states that continue to have their own governments. These member states cooperate in a number of common European institutions, such as the European Parliament. They have created a large free trade area across Europe where goods, services, money, and people can move freely. All members also agree to follow certain European regulations. But many decisions remain with the members' national governments. German courts define the European Union as "an association of sovereign national states."

In a confederal government, several member states agree to cooperate in a central association with limited powers.

Chapter 16 | Types of Government   397

The Active Citizen

▶ Other experts consider the European Union to be a federation rather than a confederation. Conduct your own research on the organization of the European Union. Then state your opinion on whether the EU is a confederation or federation in a brief written paper or oral presentation.

◄ Most centralized   Least centralized ►

Unitary	Federal	Confederal
The central government is all-powerful. The entire government exists as a single unit.	The central government shares power with regional governments. (In the United States, these regional governments are the states.)	Several independent regions create an association, known as a confederation, for limited cooperation and common action.
Regional (local) governments are simply extensions of the central government. The central government may delegate some tasks and responsibilities to regional governments.	A constitution usually defines which powers and tasks are given to the central government and which powers are given to the regional governments.	Primary power remains with the members of the confederation. However, they may assign some tasks, such as managing trade and foreign policy, to the confederal government.
Regional governments owe their very existence to the central government. They can be abolished (eliminated) by the central government at any time.	Regional governments exist independently of the central government. The central government does not have the right or the power to abolish these regional governments.	The members of the confederation have the right to withdraw at almost any time.

▶ Imagine you are a member of a constitutional convention for a new country. Prepare a speech on whether or not this country should adopt a unitary, federal or confederal system of government.

The Executive and the Legislature: A Separation of Powers or a Parliamentary System?

Another way to compare governments, especially representative democracies and limited monarchies, is to look at how their executive and legislative branches are related. In some governments, the legislature and executive are separate branches. In others, members of the executive are also members of the legislature.

The Separation of Powers

The United States has a system of government based on a **separation of powers**. In this system, the executive branch of government is kept completely separate from the legislative branch. This system is sometimes known as the "presidential system" of government. The President is elected by voters. The members of the legislature are elected separately. Usually both the President and legislators are elected for fixed terms. The President and all government officials appointed by the President are prohibited from serving in the legislature while serving in the executive branch.

> You do not have to know the term "presidential government" for the EOC test, but you do have to know the **separation of powers**. This system of government is the very opposite of parliamentary government.

Chapter 16 | Types of Government

The separation of powers: in this system of government, the President is not a member of the legislature.

In addition to the United States, other countries with a separation of powers include Argentina, Brazil, Chile, Mexico and South Korea.

Parliamentary Government

In a parliamentary government, there is no direct election of the executive branch by voters. Voters simply elect the members of **Parliament** (the legislature). Then the members of Parliament elect the head of the executive branch—known as the "Prime Minister." The Prime Minister in turn selects other members of Parliament to head executive departments and to serve on the cabinet. In this system of government, leaders of the majority party in the legislature are placed in charge of the executive branch. Since they also remain in the legislature, these ministers are available to explain their policies and to answer questions from other legislators at any time.

A Prime Minister does not usually serve for a fixed term of office. A Prime Minister serves for as long as he or she has the confidence (*trust*) of Parliament. If a member of Parliament believes the Prime Minister no longer has the support of Parliament, the member calls for a "vote of no confidence." If the Prime Minister loses the vote, the Prime Minister and all the Cabinet officers must resign their offices.

The United Kingdom has a parliamentary form of government. During a general election, voters elect the members of the House of Commons (the lower house of Parliament). These members then choose the leader of the majority party in the House of Commons as Prime Minister. If no party has a majority, then several parties will act together in a coalition government.

The British Prime Minister then chooses other members to act as Cabinet ministers. The Prime Minister and Cabinet remain in office until they resign, lose "a vote of no confidence," or lose in a general election.

Members of Parliament hold their seats until the Prime Minister calls a general election. These are held at least once every five years, but can be more often. In a general election, every seat in the House of Commons is up for election at once.

Other countries with parliamentary systems include Bangladesh, Canada, Ethiopia, Germany, India, Ireland, Israel, Italy, Jamaica, Japan, South Africa, Thailand and Turkey.

A few countries have tried to combine the parliamentary system with a separation of powers. France, for example, has both an elected President and an appointed Prime Minister. The President serves for a period of five years. The President appoints the Prime Minister from the majority party in the French legislature—the National Assembly. The French President

In the parliamentary system of government, the head of the executive branch is also a member of the legislature.

Chapter 16 | Types of Government

and Prime Minister share the duties of government. If the Prime Minister loses control of the National Assembly, the French President appoints a new Prime Minister from the new majority party.

Other countries with both a President and Prime Minister include Cameroon, Côte d'Ivoire, Kazakhstan, Peru, Russia and Uganda.

How These Differences Arose

Enrichment

The British parliamentary form of government developed at a time when the monarch still held great political power. The king or queen was the head of the executive branch. The monarch appointed a member of the House of Commons to serve as Prime Minister, not only to assist in running the executive branch, but also to win the support of Parliament for royal policies.

In the United States, the authors of the Constitution were greatly influenced by Montesquieu. They wanted a complete separation of powers between the executive and legislative branches. They believed that the British parliamentary system had often led to corruption: the monarch and Prime Minister offered offices and other benefits to members of the Parliament to win their support. These officeholders then supported the government in Parliament on all issues. They acted to hold onto their offices rather than voting for the good of the country. To avoid this, the authors of the Constitution created a government with an elected President and a separation of powers.

Comparing the Parliamentary System with the Separation of Powers

	Parliamentary	Separation of Powers
Selection Process	The Prime Minister is not directly elected by the people. Instead, the Prime Minister is chosen by the members of Parliament.	The President is elected directly by voters.
Head of State	A monarch or elected President is usually the head of state rather than the Prime Minister.	The President acts as the head of state.
Separation of Powers	No separation of powers.	A separation of powers between different branches.
Term and Removal	The Prime Minister has no fixed term in office. The Prime Minister must have the confidence of Parliament. The Prime Minister can be removed by a vote of "no confidence." The Prime Minister can dissolve Parliament and call for a general election.	The President and the members of Congress all serve for fixed terms in office. Impeachment is the only legal way to remove the President from office. Impeachment is limited to cases of misconduct, not just political disagreement.
Cooperation between Branches	Because the Prime Minister is the leader of the majority party in Parliament, there is never any divided government in which the executive and legislative branches are controlled by different parties. Passage of legislation is easier because the Prime Minister is the leader of the majority party in Parliament.	If the President's party is not the majority party in Congress, a "divided government" occurs. The executive and legislative branches come under the control of opposing parties. This makes it hard to pass legislation or to take other actions. Each branch checks the other.

The Active Citizen

- Make a Venn diagram comparing the parliamentary system of government with the separation of powers in the United States.
- Based on the chart above, what are the advantages and disadvantages of each of these two forms of government?
- Imagine that you are either the President of the United States or the Prime Minister of the United Kingdom. One of your classmates should pretend to be the other leader. Then hold a discussion on which of these systems is superior and why.

Reactions to Industrial Society: Socialism and Communism

During the Industrial Revolution, most workers were very badly treated. They had to work long hours under unpleasant conditions for low wages. Reformers tried to reduce the suffering of factory workers, miners and other laborers. Their concerns gave birth to two new systems of thought—socialism and communism. The common goal of both of these systems was to improve conditions for workers.

Socialists believed that conditions for workers would gradually improve if the government took over some industries, imposed stricter regulations on employers, and provided more social services. Because a majority of citizens were workers, socialists believed that they could introduce these reforms gradually and peacefully by winning elections.

Communists believed that the rich would never give up their wealth and privileges peacefully. A violent revolution would therefore be needed to improve conditions for workers. After workers rose up, they could defeat the factory owners and other business owners who had amassed riches by taking unfair advantage of them. The workers would then abolish private property altogether. There would be no more rich and poor, no more bosses and workers. Everything would be owned in common, and all would work for the good of the community based on their abilities. Then the community would take care of the needs of every member of society. In this perfect society, government would not be needed and would gradually disappear.

Both socialist and communist beliefs led to the creation of new forms of government.

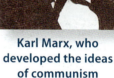

Karl Marx, who developed the ideas of communism

Socialist Government

In Europe, socialist political parties appeared in the mid-nineteenth century. They achieved temporary power in a few countries in the years after World War I (1914–1918). More socialist parties achieved power in Europe after World War II (1939–1945). Socialism also influenced political parties in Asia and Africa.

Socialists believed that conditions for workers and other citizens could be improved through government ownership of some industries and free public services. After World War II, socialist governments created "welfare states" in Britain, Sweden, Norway and several other countries. These governments increased taxes in order to provide free medical care, free higher education and other services to all their citizens. Socialist governments also took over

Chapter 16 | Types of Government

Features of Socialism and Communism

Characteristic	Socialism	Communism
Beliefs on obtaining power	Socialists believe that socialism can be introduced gradually by electing socialist candidates to public office.	Communists believe that communism can only be achieved through a violent revolution. Workers will overthrow the ruling classes.
Economic policies	Socialists favor government ownership of transportation, energy, and other key industries. However, they also believe in keeping private property and free enterprise.	Communists call for the abolition of private ownership. They want central planning to determine the use of all resources and to guide national production. The state takes over all industries, farms and businesses.
Actions in power	Socialist governments established state-owned industries and "welfare states" in Western Europe. These offered public services, such as free health care and education, but at the cost of high taxation.	In practice, communist parties established brutal dictatorships in the Soviet Union, Eastern Europe, China, North Korea, Vietnam and Cuba. Opponents were imprisoned or killed, and free thought was not allowed.

those businesses providing essential services, such as transportation, communication, and electric power. Socialist governments then provided cheap or free transportation, electricity and other services to their citizens.

In a few countries, such as Norway, socialist policies are still followed today. In other countries, however, socialism was considered to be only a partial success. In Britain and elsewhere, conservative parties defeated socialists in elections. Once in power, these conservatives sold off state-owned industries to private investors. They lowered taxes and raised tuition for attending university, but kept free health care.

Communist Government

The communist party was also first organized in Europe in the late nineteenth century. Communists seized power in Russia in November 1917. Russia—renamed as the Soviet Union—became the world's first communist state. After World War II, communism spread from the Soviet Union to the countries of Eastern Europe and to North Korea, China, North Vietnam, and Cuba.

According to communist theory, the government was meant to gradually disappear in a perfect society. In practice, communist leaders set up brutal dictatorships. They took away the property and wealth of landowners and business owners. The communist party took over the government, the newspapers, labor unions, and all other organizations. All other political parties were prohibited. Religious beliefs were ridiculed. Political opponents were arrested and sent to labor camps or murdered.

In most communist countries, a committee of the highest party officials, known as the Politburo, ran the government. They usually took their orders from the Chairman of the Communist Party. Joseph Stalin in the Soviet Union, Mao Zedong in China, and Fidel Castro in Cuba used this system to establish personal dictatorships.

Joseph Stalin

In these countries, the central government took control of all natural and human resources. All production was based on five-year plans set by government officials known as central planners. They established production quotas and decided how resources would be used. In the Soviet Union, farmland was taken away from farmers and given to state-owned collective farms.

Communism in the Soviet Union became less harsh after Stalin's death. There were not enough incentives to encourage hard work, investment or risk, and the Soviet economy stagnated (*stayed still; did not grow*). Communist parties fell from power in Eastern Europe in 1990. The following year, the Soviet Union itself divided into Russia, Ukraine, Kazakhstan and other states. North Korea officially rejected communism in 2009 in favor of a local philosophy started by the country's dictator. It remains a dictatorship today.

Forms of communism survive, however, in Cuba and China. In China, the Communist Party holds onto political power but has encouraged foreign investment, individual enterprise and economic competition. As a result, China now has one of the world's fastest economic growth rates. Nevertheless, political dissent is still severely punished. Dictator Fidel Castro resigned as President of Cuba in 2008. His brother Raúl was elected in his place. Although Cuba is taking steps to have a freer economy, it remains under the rule of the Communist Party.

The Comparative Government Game

Now you are ready to play a game based on what you have just learned about the different types of governments.

Rules of the Game

1. Your teacher should divide your class into small groups of 3–5 students.

2. Each group should research the governments of three countries.

3. The group should write a short description of the governments of each of these countries on a separate index card. Be sure to include characteristics that indicate whether that government is a monarchy or democracy, a unitary or federal system, an autocracy or oligarchy, has a parliamentary system or a separation of powers, or is communist or socialist. The same country's government might fit under several of these classifications. The summary of forms and systems of government on pages 404–405 can help you identify these governments.

4. On the bottom of the same card, include all those classifications that your group believes apply to that country. For example, the United States is a representative democracy, has a federal system, and has a separation of powers.

5. After all the groups are done, your teacher should collect the cards.

6. After mixing up the cards, your teacher should read aloud the description on each card. After hearing each description, you should write down on a separate sheet of paper all the classifications you have studied that fit that country's description (such as being representative democracy with a unitary system).

7. For every classification that you identify correctly, you will receive one point. After the cards are all read, the student with the most points wins the game!

Chapter 16 | Types of Government

A Summary of the Forms of Government

Who Holds the Power: One, Few or Many?

Monarchy: Government by a king, queen, emperor or empress who inherits power.

Absolute Monarchy: The monarch claims to rule by the will of God and enjoys absolute (*total*) power.

Limited Monarchy: The monarch is subject to law. Usually an elected Parliament holds the real power.

Autocracy: Rule by one person who claims total power. An absolute monarchy is one form of autocracy. Rule by a dictator is another example of an autocracy.

Oligarchy: Rule by a small group of people, such as a few very rich people, or the leaders of a political party.

Democracy: A form of government in which ordinary people hold the final power.

Direct Democracy: A form of democracy in which people participate in decision-making. Citizens decide public issues directly by attending meetings or voting.

Representative Democracy: A form of democratic government in which citizens elect representatives to make decisions for them. If citizens are unhappy with the decisions that their representatives make, they can vote them out of office in the next election.

Republic: Another name for a representative democracy. In a republic, there is no king or queen. The government belongs to the "public."

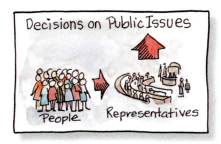

Responses to Industrial Society

Socialism: A form of government that arose in response to the Industrial Revolution. In the socialist form of government, the government owns some industries and provides many public services at no charge.

Communism: Another form of government that arose in response to the Industrial Revolution. Communists believe that workers will eventually overthrow owners and establish an ideal society. In the communist form of government, the government controls all farming and industry, and it owns all property. Central planners decide people's needs, and they tell farms and factories what to produce to meet those needs. In practice, communist governments became brutal dictatorships.

A Summary of the Systems of Government

Relationship between the Central Government and Regions

Unitary System: In this system, the central government holds all power. The central government can create or abolish local governments, and it tells those local governments what to do.

Federal System: In the federal system, the central government and local governments share power. States do not have the power to leave the federal government on their own authority, and the central government cannot abolish the states or take away their power.

Confederal System: This system of government is an association of independent states. The central government is weak and can only do what the states agree to let it do. Member states can leave the confederal government at any time. The United States had a confederal government under the Articles of Confederation.

Relationship between the Executive and Legislature

Parliamentary System: This system of government is the opposite of the system of separation of powers that we have in the United States. In the parliamentary system of government, members of the legislature, usually known as "Parliament," select the head of government, known as the "Prime Minister." The Prime Minister and all the members of the Cabinet also sit as members in the Parliament. There is no separation between the legislative and executive branches of government. There are no fixed terms to executive offices. A majority of Parliament can remove the Prime Minister at any time through a vote of "no confidence."

405

Here are three descriptions to help start the Comparative Government Game: What kind of government does each country have?

The government of Saudi Arabia is headed by a hereditary king with total power. The King is assisted by the Crown Prince and a Council of Ministers, or Cabinet. The King is also assisted by a legislative council, the Majlis Al-Shura, which recommends new laws. Its 150 members are appointed by the King. The country's judicial system is based on Islamic law. The king appoints the governors of 13 regional governments.

What kind of government does Saudi Arabia have? _____

The Constitution of the People's Republic of China guarantees the position of the Communist Party. The all-powerful Politburo, consisting of about ten individuals, makes the most important decisions. The Communist Party and the People's Liberation Army follow the orders of the Politburo. The Paramount (*supreme*) Leader is chosen by the Politburo. China's Paramount Leader acts as General Secretary of the Communist Party and as President of the People's Republic of China. China also has a State Council and National People's Congress with nearly 3,000 elected members. The central government appoints officials to run China's provinces and regions.

What kind of government does China have? _____

Norway adopted a written constitution in 1814. A hereditary king or queen acts as its head of state. The king or queen holds symbolic power and represents Norway in state ceremonies. Voters elect members of the legislature, known as the Storting. The leader of the parliamentary bloc holding a majority is appointed as Norway's Prime Minister. The Prime Minister appoints other ministers to form a government. When the Prime Minister loses the support of a majority of the Storting, the Prime Minister must resign from office. The government has an ownership share in oil, aluminum, telecommunications and other industries. Taxes are high but the government provides many social services to citizens, including retirement benefits, health care and higher education. Norway's county governments have some powers but are under the complete control of the national government.

What kind of government does Norway have? _____

Name _____

Fill in the charts below.

Monarchy	
Define this form of government:	How does this form of government differ from other forms?
An example of this form of government:	An example of a government that is **not** of this form:

Democracy	
Define this form of government:	How does this form of government differ from other forms?
An example of this form of government:	An example of a government that is **not** of this form:

Autocracy	
Define this form of government:	How does this form of government differ from other forms?
An example of this form of government:	An example of a government that is **not** of this form:

Name _____

Fill in the charts below.

Unitary System of Government	
Define this system of government:	How does this system of government differ from other systems?
An example of this system of government:	An example of a government that is **not** this type of system:

Federal System of Government	
Define this system of government:	How does this system of government differ from other systems?
An example of this system of government:	An example of a government that is **not** this type of system:

Confederal System of Government	
Define this system of government:	How does this system of government differ from other systems?
An example of this system of government:	An example of a government that is **not** this type of system:

Name _____

Fill in the charts below.

Parliamentary System of Government	
Define this system of government:	How does this system of government differ from other systems?
An example of this system of government:	An example of a government that is **not** this type of system:

Socialist Form of Government	
Define this form of government:	How does this form of government differ from other forms?
An example of this form of government:	An example of a government that is **not** of this form:

Communist Form of Government	
Define this form of government:	How does this form of government differ from other forms?
An example of this form of government:	An example of a government that is **not** of this form:

Chapter 16 | Types of Government

Name _____

Complete the following imaginary dialogue between Thomas Jefferson and King George III on the advantages and disadvantages of democracy and monarchy.

Thomas Jefferson: Governments are created to protect the rights of individual citizens. A democracy is the best form of government because it places power directly in the hands of its citizens.

King George III: There are many different groups in every society. Each of these groups tries to use the powers of government for its own benefit. A hereditary king or queen is the only person who stands above all these groups and represents society as a whole. A hereditary monarch is a neutral judge who will do what is best for all citizens.

Thomas Jefferson

_____
_____
_____
_____

King George III

_____
_____
_____
_____

Thomas Jefferson

_____
_____
_____
_____

King George III

_____
_____
_____
_____

Name _____

Fill in the chart below on the characteristics of the different forms of government.

Forms of Governments

Form	Description	Example
Monarchy		
Direct Democracy		
Representative Democracy		
Autocracy		
Oligarchy		
Socialist		
Communist		

Name _____

Fill in the chart below on the characteristics of the different systems of government.

Systems of Governments

System	Description	Example
Unitary		
Federal		
Confederal		
Parliamentary		

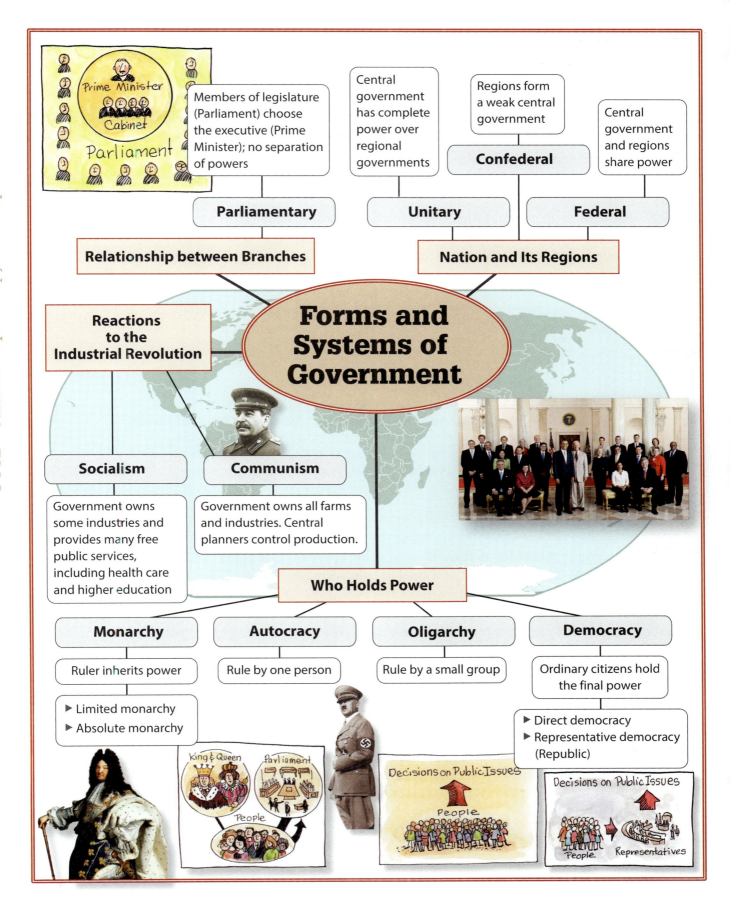

Chapter 16 | Types of Government

Review Cards: Types of Government

Theories of Government

- During the Enlightenment, writers developed different theories about the origins of government. One theory was that people had once lived in a **state of nature** with no rules or rulers, but then formed a **social contract** by banding together and forming a **government**.
- Social scientists today agree that a state of nature never existed, as humans have always needed some sort of government.
- All governments help communities to cooperate and to develop and enforce rules. They also provide public services and protect the community. The purposes of our own federal government are stated in the Preamble of our Constitution.
- In addition to our own type of government, there are several other types of government. These include forms and systems of government. Seven forms of government are monarchy, direct democracy, representative democracy, autocracy, oligarchy, socialism, and communism. Four systems of government are unitary, federal, confederal, and parliamentary.

Who Holds Power? Monarchy, Democracy, Autocracy and Oligarchy

To **classify** items is to arrange them into groups of related items (known as "classes"). One way to classify governments is by identifying who holds power in that form of government.

Monarchy
- A monarchy is a government ruled by one person, who holds hereditary power. Power passes down from one family member to the next—usually the monarch's oldest son or daughter.
- In the 17th century, **absolute monarchs** arose in Europe, like King Louis XIV of France. There was almost no limit to their power. They claimed to rule by divine right and their will was law.
- In Great Britain a **limited monarchy** arose when two kings, Charles I and later his son James II, tried to take too much power and were opposed by Parliament. The English Bill of Rights of 1689 kept the monarch as the head of state but gave most political power to Parliament.

Democracy
- The first **democracy** (*rule by the people*) arose in Athens, Greece. All male citizens could participate in government, but women, children, slaves, and foreigners were excluded (*kept out*) from political life.
- **Direct democracy** existed in Athens: citizens directly debated and decided public issues.
- In larger communities, a **representative democracy (a republic)** is best: citizens elect representatives to vote on their behalf. The United States is a representative democracy. Our elected representatives decide public issues for us but if a majority of citizens disagrees with their representatives' actions, they will be voted out of office at the next election.

Autocracy and Oligarchy
- In an **autocracy** (like an absolute monarchy or a dictatorship) one ruler holds all political power.
- In an **oligarchy**, a small group, such as a group of noblemen or the military, holds power.

414   Chapter 16 | Types of Government

The Nation and its Regions: Unitary, Federal and Confederal Systems of Government

Governments can also be classified based on the relationship between their central and local governments. There are three systems of government based on this relationship: unitary, federal, and confederal.

Unitary System

- A central government holds complete power in a **unitary** state. The central government gives certain powers to local governments, but can take back these powers at any time. It can change or even abolish those local governments if it likes. Most nations in the world today have unitary governments.

Federal System

- In a **federal government**, the central and local governments exercise independent powers and cannot abolish each other.
- States can join together to form a federal government, but a state cannot leave a federal government without the agreement of the other states.
- In the United States, the federal (central) and state governments share power. The central government has limited powers and other powers are reserved for the states. Wherever the federal government can lawfully exercise power, its power is supreme.

Confederal System

- In a **confederation**, a group of independent states or nations form an association to cooperate. The majority of power remains with the separate states, which are free to leave at any time.
- The Articles of Confederation created this type of government in the United States in 1781. The U.S. Constitution then changed the United States from a confederal to a federal system. Another example of a confederation is today's European Union, which consists of various sovereign European governments cooperating with one another. Each has a right to leave the European Union.

How the Branches of Government Relate: Separation of Powers vs. Parliamentary System

Another way to classify types of governments is by looking at the relationship between their legislative and executive branches. This creates two different systems of elected government. The United States has a separation of powers. Countries like Great Britain have a parliamentary system.

Separation of Powers

- In the United States, the legislative and executive branches are separate. The members of both branches are elected separately by voters for fixed terms. Members of the executive branch cannot also be members of Congress.

Parliamentary Government

- In a **parliamentary government**, like Great Britain, the elected legislative branch (Parliament) actually controls the executive branch. The members of Parliament elect the head of the executive, the **Prime Minister**, from their own members. The Prime Minister and the entire Cabinet are all members of Parliament. Voters do not separately elect members of the executive branch.
- There are no fixed terms in office, but Parliament can remove the Prime Minister with a "vote of no confidence." Parliament is re-elected when the Prime Minister calls a general election.

Some governments have aspects of both systems. In France, the President is elected separately but appoints the Prime Minister from the majority party in the National Assembly.

Responses to Industrialism: Socialism and Communism

Socialism and communism were two forms of governments that arose in reaction to the harsh treatment of workers during the Industrial Revolution. Socialists favor peaceful reforms, while communists believe a social revolution is necessary to achieve genuine change.

Socialism
- **Socialists** believe that it is the government's job to improve conditions for citizens. Socialist governments establish "welfare states" in which the government takes over some industries and increases taxes in order to provide more public services, like free health care, free higher education, and inexpensive public transportation.
- Socialist parties gained power in Europe after World War II, but today many socialist policies have been overturned by conservative parties.
- In the **socialist form of government**, the government owns some industries and provides many public services at no charge.

Communism
- **Communists** believe that a violent social revolution is necessary in which workers overthrow the rich and abolish private property. Everything will then be owned in common and the government will eventually disappear.
- In practice, actual communist revolutions, like the Russian Revolution in 1917, resulted in brutal dictatorships. In these countries, the communist party took over everything and suppressed opposition. A party leader, like Joseph Stalin in Russia and Mao Zedong in China, became dictator. The central government took control of all human and natural resources and owned all property.
- The Communist Soviet Union collapsed in 1991, but communism still survives in some countries like China and Cuba. Most members of the Communist Party USA, which you read about in Chapter 13, believe the best policy is to cooperate with other liberal parties that favor increased social services. They no longer believe a violent revolution is necessary.
- In the communist form of government, the government controls all farming and industry, and owns almost all property. Central planners decide people's needs, and they tell farms and factories what to produce to meet those needs. In socialism, the government owns some industries; in communism, it owns all industries.

What Do You Know?

SS.7.C.3.1

1. What do an absolute monarchy, autocracy, and oligarchy have in common?
   A. The head of state is chosen by Parliament.
   B. Their citizens decide public issues for themselves.
   C. Political power is exercised by representatives elected by the people.
   D. A single individual or small group exercises control over government.

SS.7.C.3.2

2. Which system of government selects its executive leadership from the majority party in the legislature?

   A. unitary
   B. federal
   C. confederal
   D. parliamentary

SS.7.C.3.1

3. The Venn diagram below compares two forms of monarchy.

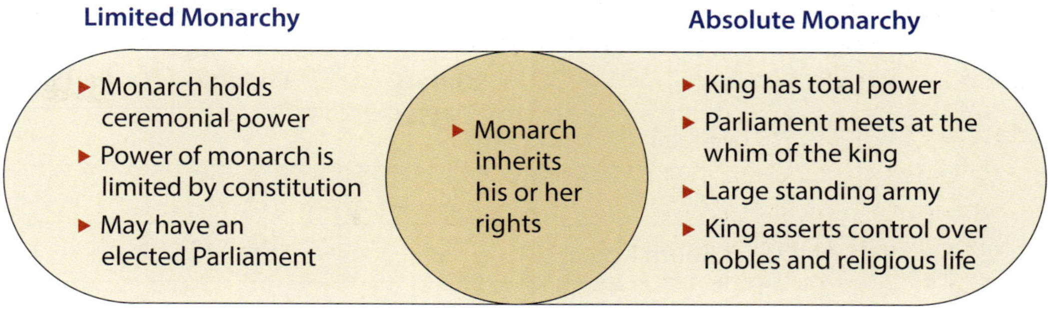

Limited Monarchy
- Monarch holds ceremonial power
- Power of monarch is limited by constitution
- May have an elected Parliament

(Both)
- Monarch inherits his or her rights

Absolute Monarchy
- King has total power
- Parliament meets at the whim of the king
- Large standing army
- King asserts control over nobles and religious life

Which might be considered an advantage of the type of monarchy shown on the right?

A. It can negotiate peace treaties.
B. It can act more quickly in a crisis.
C. It provides stronger guarantees of individual rights.
D. Its representatives can meet with foreign dignitaries.

SS.7.C.3.2

4. Which statement is true of a federal but not of a unitary system of government?

A. Its local governments are extensions of the central government.
B. Its local governments cannot be abolished by the central government.
C. Its central government usually appoints the leaders of local governments.
D. Its central government delegates responsibilities to local governments to carry out.

SS.7.C.3.2

5. The table below compares the parliamentary system with the government of the United States.

	Parliamentary System	Government of the United States
Selection of head of government	?	Elected by voters
Separation of powers	No separation of powers	A separation of powers among different branches
Term and removal of the head of government	Removed by a vote of "no confidence"	Fixed term

Which statement completes the table?

A. The Prime Minister is chosen by the monarch.
B. The Prime Minister is chosen by the President.
C. The Prime Minister is directly elected by voters.
D. The Prime Minister is chosen by the members of Parliament.

Chapter 16 | Types of Government

Use the table below to answer Questions 6 and 7.

SYSTEMS OF GOVERNMENT				
	Unitary	Federal	Parliamentary	Separation of Powers
Brazil		✔		✔
Mexico		✔		✔
South Korea	✔		✔	
Germany		✔	✔	
India		✔	✔	
Syria	✔			✔
United States		✔		✔
Cuba	✔		✔	

SS.7.C.3.2

6. Based on the table, in which country is the head of the government chosen by the legislature?

   A. Syria
   B. India
   C. Brazil
   D. Mexico

SS.7.C.3.2

7. Based on the table, how are the governments of Syria, Mexico, and Brazil similar?

   A. All three central governments are weak associations of separate states.
   B. All three governments guarantee certain rights to state governments.
   C. All three governments have separate executive and legislative branches.
   D. All three central governments exercise complete power over local government.

SS.7.C.3.2

8. Why did the authors of the Constitution create a federal system of government rather than a unitary system?

   A. They did not trust the state governments.
   B. They feared a central government that was too powerful.
   C. They wanted to limit the role of the people in government.
   D. They had seen how inefficient a weak central government was under the Articles of Confederation.

Chapter 16 | Types of Government

SS.7.C.3.2

9. The diagram below represents three systems of government.

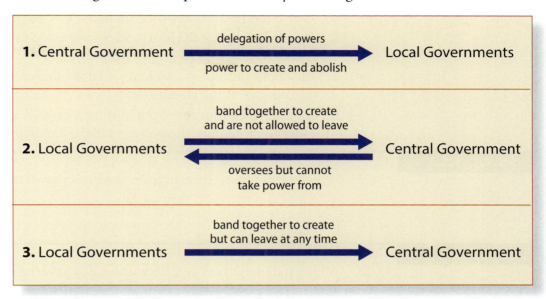

Which list correctly identifies the three types of governments in the diagram?

A. 1. Unitary; 2. Federal; 3. Confederal
B. 1. Federal; 2. Presidential; 3. Unitary
C. 1. Monarchical; 2. Parliamentary; 3. Communist
D. 1. Communist; 2. Democratic; 3. Monarchical

SS.7.C.3.2

10. The photographs below show one British and one American leader. One was a Prime Minister and the other was a President.

Prime Minister
Winston Churchill

President
Abraham Lincoln

What was a major difference between their governments?

A. Churchill sat in the legislature as well as leading the executive branch.
B. Churchill's power was checked by the executive branch.
C. Lincoln was chosen to lead the executive by Congress.
D. Lincoln did not serve for a fixed term in office.

Chapter 16 | Types of Government

SS.7.C.3.1

11. What did socialist and communist forms of government have in common?
    A. They often resulted in brutal dictatorships and economic stagnation.
    B. They believed that the ideal society was one in which the government abolished all forms of private property.
    C. They both promoted a violent social revolution in which workers would take control of the government.
    D. They believed that government should provide services to the community to raise the average standard of living.

SS.7.C.3.1

12. Which form of government gives the most power to ordinary citizens?
    A. autocracy
    B. oligarchy
    C. absolute monarchy
    D. representative democracy

SS.7.C.3.1

13. Which statement best describes a socialist government?
    A. Primary political power rests with local governments.
    B. Taxes are low, but government services are extremely limited.
    C. The government owns several basic industries and provides many services at no cost.
    D. Private property is abolished and all goods and services are provided to citizens by the government.

SS.7.C.3.1

14. The excerpt below comes from the writings of Jacques Bénigne Bossuet, a French bishop in the early 1700s.

    > Rulers act as the ministers of God and as his lieutenants on earth. It is through them that God exercises his empire. . . . It appears from all this that the person of the king is sacred, and that to attack him in any way is sacrilege. . . .

    Based on this excerpt, which form of government would Bishop Bossuet most likely favor?
    A. oligarchy
    B. direct democracy
    C. absolute monarchy
    D. representative democracy

Chapter 16 | Types of Government

CHAPTER **17**

American Foreign Policy

SS.7.C.4.1 Differentiate concepts related to U.S. domestic and foreign policy.

SS.7.C.4.2 Recognize government and citizen participation in international organizations.

SS.7.C.4.3 Describe examples of how the United States has dealt with international conflicts.

Names and Terms You Should Know

- Alliance
- Ally
- Ambassador
- Diplomacy
- Diplomat
- Doctrine
- Domestic policy
- Domestic affairs
- Embassy
- Foreign policy
- Foreign affairs
- International relations
- Secretary of State
- U.S. State Department
- Treaty
- World War I
- World War II
- Korean War
- Bay of Pigs
- Cuban Missile Crisis
- Vietnam War
- Gulf Wars I and II
- Iran Hostage Crisis
- Terrorism
- Non-Governmental Organizations (NGO)
- International Non-Governmental Organizations (INGO)
- North American Free Trade Agreement (NAFTA)
- North Atlantic Treaty Organization (NATO)
- International Red Cross/Red Crescent
- United Nations (UN)
- United Nations Children's Fund (UNICEF)
- World Court
- World Trade Organization (WTO)

Florida "Keys" to Learning

1. Domestic policy is any government policy that concerns affairs at home. Foreign policy is any government policy that deals with foreign affairs.

2. The Constitution gives both the President and Congress some control over U.S. foreign policy. The President has the power to appoint and receive ambassadors, to negotiate treaties, and to act as Commander in Chief. Congress has the power to declare war and to approve funding for federal programs. The Senate confirms (*approves*) Presidential appointments and ratifies U.S. treaties.

3. The Secretary of State is the member of the Cabinet entrusted with the day-to-day running of U.S. foreign policy. The Secretary of State heads the State Department. Ambassadors are diplomats who act as representatives between nations.

4. U.S. foreign policy pursues our national interests: the security of the United States; the protection of U.S. citizens and their property and investments abroad; the promotion of trade with the United States; the encouragement of democracy and free enterprise; protecting the environment; the humanitarian goals of world peace and improving global living standards; and the prevention of armed conflicts and genocide (*murder of an entire people*).

5. U.S. leaders have several foreign-policy tools they can use, including military force/intervention, economic sanctions (*penalties*) or assistance, negotiations, treaties, alliances, membership in international organizations, negotiations, influencing media and public opinion, and cultural exchanges.

6. Americans have entered a number of international conflicts. In 1917, the United States entered World War I and helped lead Allied forces to victory.

7. In December 1941, Japan attacked the U.S. fleet at Pearl Harbor. Americans joined World War II, helped defeat Germany and Japan, and developed the first atomic bomb.

8. The Cold War began when the Soviet Union turned the nations of Eastern Europe into communist satellites. Americans feared the spread of communism and adopted a policy of "containment."

9. When communist North Korea invaded South Korea in 1950, Americans became involved in the Korean War. The war ended in 1953 with an armistice (*truce*) that left Korea divided as it had been before the war.

10. When Castro established a communist dictatorship in Cuba, America cut off trade and diplomatic relations. In 1961, Cuban exiles landed at the Bay of Pigs but were defeated. In 1962, American spy planes discovered Cuban bases for Soviet nuclear missiles, triggering the Cuban Missile Crisis.

11. Americans sent troops to South Vietnam but proved unable to win the Vietnam War. In 1973, President Nixon withdrew U.S. forces.

12. In the 1980s, Soviet leaders introduced reforms into Soviet society. The Berlin Wall fell in 1989 and the Soviet Union itself dissolved at the end of 1991. The Cold War was over.

13. In 1990, Iraqi dictator Saddam Hussein invaded Kuwait. U.S. and coalition forces drove Iraqi forces out of Kuwait in the First Gulf War.

14. On September 11, 2001, the terrorist group al-Qaeda attacked the World Trade Center. President Bush declared a global "War on Terror" and sent U.S. forces to Afghanistan.

15. President Bush feared Saddam Hussein might be hiding weapons of mass destruction. In 2003, U.S. forces invaded Iraq in the Second Gulf War.

16. The U.S. participates in several international organizations such as the United Nations, the World Court, NATO, NAFTA, the World Trade Organization, and UNICEF.

17. There are also International Non-Governmental Organizations ("INGOs") that private citizens can join, such as the International Red Cross/Red Crescent.

In this chapter, you will learn how the United States conducts its relations with other countries.

What is Foreign Policy?

There are two types of government policies: domestic and foreign.

Domestic policy is any government policy that concerns affairs "at home"—such as setting tax rates, regulating safety in factories, or determining the academic requirements for students in middle school. **Domestic affairs** refers to things happening in the United States.

Foreign policy is any government policy that concerns foreign countries and events taking place outside the United States: for example, making an alliance with a foreign country, fighting a war overseas, or entering into a trade agreement with another country. **Foreign affairs** refers to things happening in other countries, outside the United States.

The Active Citizen

▶ Which of these are examples of domestic policy and which are examples of foreign policy?

Activity	Domestic Policy	Foreign Policy	Your Explanation:
Adopting health care reform	☐	☐	
Reducing carbon emissions in the United States	☐	☐	
Signing a treaty with the country of Jordan in the Middle East	☐	☐	
Attending a conference with leaders of the European Union	☐	☐	
Participating in negotiations between Israelis and Palestinians	☐	☐	
Increasing funding to public schools to reduce class sizes	☐	☐	
Negotiating with Russian leaders to reduce the number of nuclear warheads	☐	☐	
Investing in computer-science research in American universities	☐	☐	
Increasing the budget of the National Institutes of Health	☐	☐	

What's So Special about International Relations?

Foreign policy deals with "international relations." This phrase refers to relations between independent countries all around the world.

International relations is special because international law is not as powerful as the rule of law within a single country. To some extent, independent, sovereign nations still live in a "Wild West" atmosphere. They could be attacked, invaded or destroyed at any time. They might be able to defend themselves or to find allies, but they could just as easily be conquered and wiped off the map. Therefore, nation-states are constantly worried about their own security.

Who Makes Foreign Policy?

The U.S. Constitution gives authority over foreign relations to the federal government rather than to the states. Control over foreign policy is actually exercised by two branches of our federal government: the Presidency and Congress. This sharing of power illustrates both the separation of powers and the system of checks and balances.

Powers of the President
- The President appoints and receives ambassadors.
- The President acts as Commander in Chief of the armed forces.
- The President negotiates treaties.
- The President appoints the heads of executive departments, including the Secretary of State and the Secretary of Defense.

Powers of Congress
- The Senate confirms the President's appointments.
- The Senate ratifies U.S. treaties by a two-thirds vote.
- Congress has the power to declare war.
- Congress approves funding for all federal programs, including defense, foreign aid and the State Department budget.

The Secretary of State and the State Department

The Secretary of State is the member of the Cabinet entrusted with the day-to-day running of our nation's foreign policy.

The Secretary of State is the head of the State Department. This department manages our nation's foreign policy. The Secretary of State is assisted by two Deputy Secretaries of State and several Under Secretaries of State. Each Under Secretary specializes in some aspect of our nation's foreign relations, such as political affairs, economic growth, arms control and international security, democracy and human rights, and public diplomacy.

The State Department keeps in contact with our ambassadors and other diplomats sent to foreign countries. An ambassador is the official representative of one country sent to reside in another. Ambassadors are appointed by the President with the consent of the Senate. Each ambassador represents the United States abroad. The ambassador also monitors events in the country to which he or she is sent, and sends reports back to the State Department. Each ambassador is also placed in charge of the U.S. Embassy in that foreign country.

The Active Citizen

▶ The chart below shows the organization of the U.S. State Department. Based on the chart, which State Department officials would become involved in the event of a new famine in Somalia?

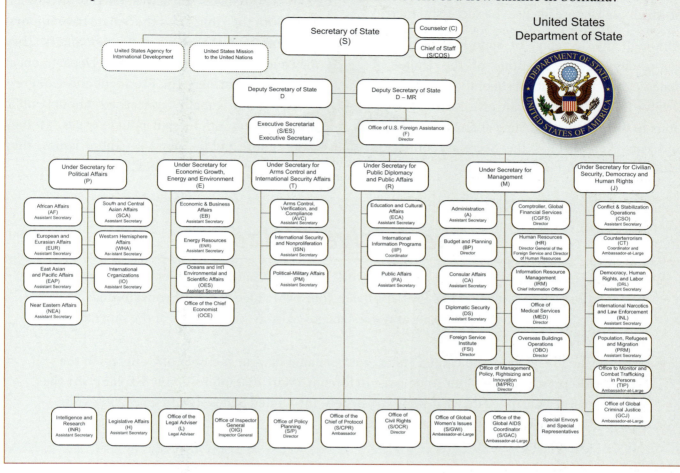

A consul general in each foreign country is placed just below the ambassador. The consul general looks after trade and commercial matters, including giving visas (*entry permits*) to those going to the United States. There may be more than one American consulate in a foreign country. Usually there is one consulate in each major commercial center.

There are also other members of the U.S. Foreign Service working inside each American embassy and consulate. The men and women of the U.S. Foreign Service are professional **diplomats**—officials who act as representatives between nations. They learn and practice **diplomacy**—the skill of handling relations between states.

The ambassador and other staff at the U.S. Embassy officially represent the United States. The ambassador will occasionally meet with the political leaders of the host country to exchange views. The ambassador will also attend and give speeches at many public and ceremonial occasions. At the same time, the ambassador and embassy staff gather information and send it back to the U.S. State Department in Washington, D.C. A member of staff at the State Department reviews this information and then reports to the Secretary of State, who in turn may report some of this information directly to the President.

If the President or Secretary of State has an official communication for a foreign country, it will often be sent to the ambassador to present to the leaders of the foreign government. Each ambassador also advises the Secretary of State—and the President—on foreign policy. Because the ambassador is living in the country, he or she develops a special understanding of which policies are likely to be successful there.

Although the Secretary of State manages the day-to-day foreign relations of the United States, the President frequently becomes involved. The President can give instructions to the Secretary of State at any time, and can even dismiss the Secretary of State in the event of disagreement.

Secretary of State Mike Pompeo

The President also meets with foreign leaders, and is regularly advised by U.S. military leaders, the National Security Advisor, and the Central Intelligence Agency (CIA), as well as by the Secretary of State.

Congress also takes an active interest in foreign affairs. Both the House and the Senate have important committees that focus on foreign affairs. They may question members of the State Department at committee hearings. The President and Congress are both equally concerned about public opinion on foreign-policy issues. If they ignore public views on these issues, they may easily lose the next election.

The Active Citizen

Enrichment

- Conduct research on the Internet about the work of the U.S. State Department and prepare an oral presentation using PowerPoint or Prezi, or make your own video to report your findings. Be sure to visit the State Department website at www.state.gov. Also be sure to look at the first tab on the menu on the top left, "About State."
- Write to the President of the United States, your Senator, or your member of Congress in the House of Representatives about some issue in foreign affairs that interests you. Explain why the issue concerns you and state what steps you believe the United States should take. After your parent or teacher reviews your letter, then send it.

The Goals and Objectives of United States Foreign Policy

The President, Congress, and the State Department generally agree that the basic aim of U.S. foreign policy should be to pursue the **national interests** of the United States and the American people.

U.S. National Interests: The Goals of American Foreign Policy

- Protect the security of the United States.
- Protect American citizens, their property, and investments abroad.
- Encourage other countries to trade with the United States.
- Spread the American system of democracy and free enterprise.
- Promote U.S. economic success and prosperity.
- Promote international peace and stability.
- Provide economic assistance to developing countries.
- Help prevent armed conflict or genocide (*mass murder*) around the world.
- Make humanitarian efforts to improve health, education, and living conditions around the world.

The Active Citizen

Compare these foreign policy goals with the goals of U.S. domestic policy. How are they similar? How are they different? Show your conclusions on a chart or Venn diagram.

The EOC test may ask you what steps to take in an international crisis. Remember that the use of armed force is usually the last step, not the first.

The Instruments of Foreign Policy

To achieve these goals, America leaders have several foreign-policy "tools" at their disposal. These include the use of American military and economic resources, participation in international organizations, attempts to persuade others through friendly negotiations, and cultural exchanges. In general, diplomats try to use friendly negotiations before turning to threats, economic sanctions or military intervention. The use of military force is only a last resort.

Military Resources

The United States spends more money on its armed forces than any other nation and has the most advanced military technology in the world.

▶ **Military Force/Intervention.** The President can use American air power, naval power, and/or troops to intervene overseas. The issue must be of extreme importance to the United States for the President to use armed force because of the high costs of any military action. Usually the United States will only go to war if its national security is at stake. The United States will also try to cooperate with its allies to obtain their assistance before employing military force. It will generally seek the help or at least the approval of the other members of the UN Security Council. Using air strikes generally has lower costs for the United States than sending in ground troops and may be tried first.

▶ **Deterrence.** The United States is defended by a large number of missiles with nuclear warheads. These were built to serve as a "deterrent" during the "Cold War" (see pp. 434–435). A deterrent is something that discourages others from acting. The leaders of every country know that if they attack the United States, we might strike back with nuclear weapons. Our military forces also act as a deterrent.

▶ **Making Threats.** A great power sometimes uses its military force to threaten other countries into taking some form of action. For example, suppose an aggressive country invades a weaker neighbor. The United States might threaten to intervene with military force *unless* the aggressor withdraws. Rather than face a war with the United States, the aggressor may retreat without fighting.

Economic Resources

The United States is the world's largest producer and consumer of goods and services. It sometimes uses its economic power to further its foreign policy goals. The use of economic power is often preferred to the use of military power.

▶ **Economic Sanctions.** The United States may boycott (*ban trade with*) any country that is violating international rules, committing acts of aggression or developing nuclear weapons in violation of international treaties. A ban on trade or travel to a country is a form of "economic sanction" or penalty. For example, the United States has had bans of trade with both Cuba and Iran. The threat of economic sanctions can be used to influence the behavior of foreign countries.

▶ **Economic Aid.** The United States provides economic assistance to many of its allies to help them develop their economies and to improve their standards of living. It also provides some

Chapter 17 | American Foreign Policy

of its allies with military assistance in the form of aircraft, missiles and other arms. This aid can be an important incentive for other countries to help the United States in meeting its foreign-policy objectives.

U.S. Foreign Aid

2008		2012	
Israel	$2.3 Billion	Israel	$3.0 Billion
Afghanistan	$1.9 Billion	Afghanistan	$2.3 Billion
Egypt	$1.7 Billion	Pakistan	$2.1 Billion
Jordan	$936 Million	Iraq	$1.6 Billion
Pakistan	$738 Million	Egypt	$1.6 Billion
Iraq	$605 Million	Jordan	$676 Million
Kenya	$599 Million	Kenya	$652 Million
South Africa	$574 Million	Nigeria	$625 Million
Colombia	$541 Million	Ethiopia	$560 Million
Nigeria	$485 Million	Tanzania	$531 Million

Other Foreign Policy "Tools"

▶ **Negotiations ("Diplomacy").** Negotiations are talks held between countries in order to reach an agreement. Whenever there is an international problem or dispute, the first step towards a settlement is usually for the countries concerned to enter into negotiations. This is also known as "**diplomacy**." Negotiations may be held at special conferences of top leaders, in secret peace negotiations, or on a simple day-to-day basis by ambassadors with government representatives in their host countries.

The aim of negotiation is to find a **compromise**, or middle ground, that all the parties to the dispute can somehow accept. Usually each side has to be willing to give up something for the negotiations to be successful.

Diplomats are trained negotiators. They recognize that it is usually better to compromise than it is to go to war. However, they do not want to appear too "weak" in negotiations and give up too much to obtain a compromise solution. Sometimes giving in to the demands of aggressors to avoid a conflict can be a mistake.

▶ **Treaties.** The United States enters into treaties with other countries. A **treaty** is a solemn agreement concluded between two or more countries, which is enforceable under international law. There are many kinds of treaties. These include a peace treaty ending a war, a treaty recognizing an exchange of territory, a treaty of alliance, a treaty creating an international organization, or a treaty of commerce laying down the terms of trade between countries.

▶ **Alliances.** An **alliance** is an agreement between two or more countries to act together. Usually, they agree to defend one another if attacked. An alliance is almost always created by a treaty.

The United States forms alliances to show its willingness to help defend other nations from attack. During the Cold War, the United States formed an alliance with the countries of Western Europe, known as the **North Atlantic Treaty Organization**, or **NATO**. The United States pledged to defend these countries, with nuclear weapons if necessary, from attack by the Soviet Union.

Alliances can sometimes bring nations into war. World War I began when Germany, Russia, France and Britain felt compelled to intervene in a conflict between Austria-Hungary and Serbia because of their alliance commitments. France and Britain similarly entered World War II because they had an alliance with Poland.

▶ **Membership in International Organizations.** Another "tool" of U.S. foreign policy is membership in international organizations, such as the **United Nations**. The United States holds veto power as a permanent member of the United Nations Security Council. It can block proposed UN actions. The United States also participates in several regional international organizations, such as the Organization of American States (OAS). These international organizations provide a place for member nations to discuss issues and establish rules.

By joining such organizations, the United States shows its support for cooperation among nations and a peaceful world order. American diplomats use these international organizations as places where they can explain American foreign policy actions to the rest of the world. You will learn more about U.S. participation in international organizations at the end of this chapter.

▶ **Diplomatic Recognition.** The President of the United States has the power to receive the representatives of other nations. Sometimes the President uses this power to refuse to recognize new leaders or new states. For example, the United States refused to give diplomatic recognition to communist China for 30 years. Instead, it continued to recognize the nationalist Chinese government, which had fled to the island of Taiwan, as the official government of China. It only changed this policy in 1979. Similarly, in 1961 the United States withdrew its diplomatic recognition of Cuba.

In other cases, the United States has extended diplomatic recognition to further its foreign policy goals. In the 1820s, the United States was the first country to extend diplomatic recognition to the newly independent republics of South America. In 1903, President Theodore Roosevelt quickly gave diplomatic recognition to the new country of Panama, so that he could negotiate the lease of the Panama Canal Zone. In 1948, the United States was among the first countries to give diplomatic recognition to Israel.

▶ **Cultural Exchanges.** Another way that the United States promotes its foreign-policy goals is through cultural exchanges. These might be visits of ballet companies, art exhibits, or joint sporting events. The goal of such exchanges is to develop good will. For example, American ping-pong athletes were the first Americans to officially visit communist China in April 1971. Four months later, President Nixon announced that he would also be visiting communist China. President Bill Clinton authorized cultural exchanges between Cuba and the United States in 1999, including two baseball games between the Cuban national team and the Baltimore Orioles, in the hope of improving Cuban-American relations. Americans also use cultural exchanges to increase international awareness of the benefits of democracy and our free market economy.

▶ **Public Opinion and the Media.** American diplomacy attempts to create favorable public opinion towards the United States throughout the world. Favorable public opinion places pressure on foreign governments to support U.S. foreign-policy goals.

The United States makes special efforts to obtain favorable news coverage of American events and policies. The federal government produces its own international broadcasts on Voice of America, Radio Free Europe/Radio Liberty, Alhurra (a satellite television channel broadcast in Arabic in the Middle East), Radio y Televisión Martí (stations broadcast from Miami into Cuba), and other stations in order to promote the American way of life.

| Enrichment | # The Active Citizen |

Crisis Management

You have just been appointed as a special adviser to the President during a dangerous international crisis. A group of more than 100 terrorists have surrounded the U.S. Embassy in Nairobi, Kenya in Africa. The terrorists may belong to al-Qaeda. The U.S. Ambassador and his staff are all trapped inside the embassy building. The embassy is guarded by five U.S. Marines. It is not clear if the government of Kenya is going to take any action or will ignore the crisis.

Continues ▶

The President of the United States has called an emergency meeting with the Vice President, the U.S. Secretary of State, the National Security Advisor, the Director of National Intelligence, the Chairman of the Joint Chiefs of Staff, and several other close advisers. You have been invited to the meeting. The purpose of this special meeting is to review all the options available for responding to the crisis at the embassy. Some of the alternatives being considered are the following:

- The U.S. could demand a special meeting of the UN Security Council.
- The U.S. could airlift a force of paratroopers to the embassy in Nairobi.
- The U.S. could denounce the actions of the terrorists on Alhurra, the Voice of America, and its other radio and television stations.
- The U.S. could offer to assist the Kenyan military in defeating the terrorists.
- The U.S. could impose economic sanctions on any country shown to have links to the terrorists.
- The U.S. could enter into negotiations with the terrorists to find out what they want.
- The U.S. could threaten to invade Kenya if Kenyan authorities fail to take action against the terrorists.
- The U.S. could wait patiently to see how the government of Kenya reacts.

Form a small group with some of the President's other "special advisers" (your classmates). Then decide which of these options you should recommend to the President. Next, decide in what order these options should be used. Finally, are there any other alternatives your group would recommend besides those listed above? Either have a member of your group present your recommendations to the class during a "debriefing" session, or write down your recommendations in the form of a memorandum to the President.

China now has a very strong economic relationship with the United States. It exports a large number of goods to America, and it frequently purchases U.S. Treasury Notes. Imagine that the U.S. Ambassador to China has just informed the Secretary of State that a series of human rights violations have been reported in Tibet, once an independent country, which China annexed by force in the 1950s. Which tools of U.S. foreign policy would you recommend that the United States adopt? Which step should be taken first, which steps should follow, and what would be an appropriate last resort? Some possibilities to consider are: diplomatic talks, public protests, economic sanctions, condemnation by international organizations, and military intervention. Prepare a PowerPoint or Prezi presentation, or a written memorandum to the Secretary of State, presenting your ideas.

A Capsule History of American Foreign Policy

In this section, you will examine the actual record of American foreign policy—with a focus on how the United States has dealt with past international conflicts.

In the early years of our history, American leaders tried to separate our nation from wars in Europe and to focus our energies on opportunities in the Western Hemisphere. A major goal of U.S. foreign policy in these early years was to avoid conflicts involving Europe. In 1796, President George Washington warned Americans not to enter into entangling alliances with other countries in his "Farewell Address":

> "The great rule of conduct for us, in regard to foreign nations, is, in extending our commercial relations, to have with them as little political connection as possible. . . . It is our true policy to steer clear of permanent alliances with any portion of the foreign world."

Another important goal of American foreign policy in these early years was to prevent European powers from re-establishing their colonial empires in nearby Latin America. A **doctrine** is an important statement of principles of foreign policy by the President. In the "Monroe Doctrine" of 1823, President James Monroe stated that the United States would oppose any attempts by European powers to restore colonial rule to places in the Western Hemisphere that had established their independence.

A third major goal of early American foreign policy was westward expansion. After defeating Mexico in the Mexican-American War (1846–1848), the United States obtained California and the Southwest, stretching the nation's boundaries to the Pacific Ocean. Fifty years later, the United States defeated Spain in the Spanish-American War (1898), and gained overseas colonies in the Pacific and Caribbean.

By the beginning of the twentieth century, the United States—with its growing population, powerful economy, and strong navy—had emerged as one of the world's "great powers." These were leading nations with far greater military and economic resources than other countries.

World War I

Who fought: United States, Great Britain, France, Italy, Russia (Allies) vs. Germany, Austria-Hungary, Ottoman Turkey (Central Powers)

When: 1914–1918

U.S. Entry: April 1917

Reason for U.S. involvement: German submarine warfare; German telegram offer to Mexico

World War I broke out in Europe in the summer of 1914. A group of terrorists assassinated (*killed for political purposes*) Archduke Franz Ferdinand, heir to the Austro-Hungarian Empire, while he was visiting the small country of Serbia. Serbian officials were secretly involved in the murder.

Austria-Hungary, encouraged by Germany, attacked Serbia in revenge. Serbia's ally, Russia, rushed to its defense. Russia also called on its own allies, France and Great Britain, for support. By August 1914, all

Chapter 17 | American Foreign Policy 431

the "great powers" of Europe had become involved in the conflict.

Because of advances in warfare—such as the invention of the machine gun—the armies on both sides became tied down in trenches (*long, fortified ditches*), which spread the length of eastern France. Soldiers could not advance without being mowed down by machine gun fire or choked by poison gas.

The British set up a naval blockade of Germany and Austria-Hungary. The Germans, with a smaller navy, established a submarine blockade of Britain. A submarine is a ship that can travel underwater for long periods. Submarines carry explosive torpedoes that they fire at ships.

For the first three years of the war, Americans remained neutral. However, German submarine attacks on allied ships with American passengers, such as the *Lusitania*, turned American public opinion against Germany. Early in 1917, Germany announced unrestricted submarine warfare and began sinking American ships. A secret German note to the Mexican government was also discovered by the British and published. The note promised Mexico the return of its former lands if it would ally with Germany against the United States. This telegram further inflamed American public opinion.

In April 1917, President Woodrow Wilson finally asked Congress for a declaration of war against Germany. U.S. entry into the war broke the deadlock in Europe. In just over a year, the United States sent an expeditionary force of a million men to France, forcing the Germans to surrender.

Woodrow Wilson

President Wilson sailed to Paris, where he helped to negotiate the Treaty of Versailles—the peace treaty between the Allies and Germany. Wilson promised to re-organize Europe along national lines, to promote democracy, and to establish a new international peacekeeping organization known as the League of Nations. The final treaty was harsh towards Germany and greatly resented by the German people. It did, however, include creation of the League of Nations just as Wilson had promised.

In the United States, there was a strong reaction against the bloodshed of World War I. The U.S. Senate rejected membership in the League of Nations and refused to sign the peace treaty. Americans retreated into a policy of isolationism, in which they generally ignored the rest of the world and focused more on their own domestic affairs.

			End of "Cold War"	2001: Terrorists strike World Trade Center and Pentagon	2001: U.S.-led coalition forces deployed to Afghanistan
1961: Bay of Pigs Invasion	1964–1973: War in Vietnam	1979: Iran Hostage Crisis	1989: Berlin Wall removed		

1960 — 1980 — 1990 — 2000 — 2010

1962: Cuban Missle Crisis | 1990: First Gulf War | 2003–2011: Second Gulf War

World War II

> **Who fought:** United States, Great Britain, Soviet Union (three main Allies) vs. Germany, Italy, Japan (Axis Powers)
>
> **When:** 1939–1945
>
> **U.S. Entry:** December 1941
>
> **Reason for U.S. involvement:** Japanese attack on Pearl Harbor

In Germany, the Nazi Party, led by Adolf Hitler, obtained power in 1933. Hitler blamed Germany's troubles on the Treaty of Versailles, Germany's democratic government, and the Jewish people of Europe. He believed that different races were competing for world domination, and that Germans were a superior race. Hitler had ambitious plans for the German conquest of Europe.

In September 1939, Hitler attacked the neighboring country of Poland. Meanwhile, the Soviet Union attacked Poland from the east. Britain and France were allied to Poland and declared war on Germany. World War II began in Europe.

Adolf Hitler

This time, Germany had developed a new form of warfare, based on the use of airplanes, tanks, and troop carriers (*modified trucks*). Airplanes bombed positions from overhead; then tanks and motorized vehicles with troops advanced. German armies quickly overran Poland; next they conquered Belgium, Denmark and France.

Italy's dictator had already concluded an alliance with Hitler before the outbreak of the war. The ambitious military leaders of Imperial Japan also decided to ally with Nazi Germany. Together, Germany, Italy and Japan became known as the Axis powers.

Most Americans were determined to stay out of the war. President Franklin D. Roosevelt grew alarmed, however, at the successes of the anti-democratic powers. In 1940, Great Britain stood almost alone against Germany, Italy and Japan. In June 1941, Hitler suddenly launched an invasion of the Soviet Union, bringing the Soviets into the war.

Five months later, on December 7, 1941, Japan launched a surprise attack on the U.S. Pacific fleet at **Pearl Harbor** in Hawaii. Germany and Italy also declared war on the United States. These events brought the United States into the war on the side of Britain and the Soviet Union.

The U.S. Navy ended Japanese supremacy in the Pacific Ocean at the Battle of Midway, only six months after the attack on Pearl Harbor. But American and British troops were not strong enough to fight the German army in France. The two Western Allies sent their troops instead to North Africa, Sicily and Italy. Meanwhile, enormous Soviet and German armies fought each other inside the Soviet Union. Germans also organized the mass murder of Jews and other groups. Finally in June 1944, American and British

Chapter 17 | American Foreign Policy   433

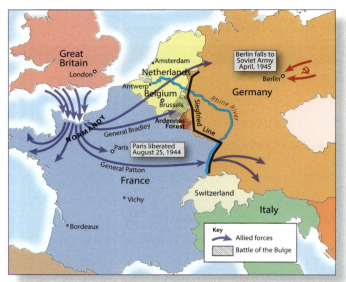

The Allied Advance, 1944–1945

forces landed on the beaches of Normandy, France, on "D-Day." They quickly moved westward, freeing Paris from Nazi rule by August 1944.

The American advance was temporarily halted in the cold winter of 1944–1945. Once German resistance collapsed, American troops resumed their advance. They entered Germany from the west, while Soviet troops came from the east. Hitler committed suicide at the end of April 1945, and Germany surrendered in May 1945.

In the Pacific, American troops fought a series of bloody battles against Japanese forces on a string of islands. After the surrender of Germany, U.S. forces planned a massive invasion of Japan, which would have cost more than a million lives. Instead, the United States dropped two atomic bombs on Japan, forcing its surrender in August 1945. World War II, the bloodiest conflict in human history, was finally over. More than 50 million people lost their lives in the war.

Unlike 1919, this time Americans welcomed the creation of a new peacekeeping organization, known as the **United Nations** (or UN). The UN replaced the unsuccessful League of Nations.

Outbreak of the Cold War — Enrichment

Who was involved: United States and Western allies vs. the Soviet Union and communist nations

When began: 1945–1948

Reason for U.S. involvement: To prevent the spread of communism

Almost as soon as World War II ended, Americans found themselves in the middle of a new contest, known as the "**Cold War.**"

Relations between the democratic United States and the communist Soviet Union had always been uneasy, even during World War II. The Soviet Union was under the control of Joseph Stalin, a brutal communist dictator. The United States was a representative democracy with a free market economy. Both countries looked at the other with suspicion.

After the heavy Soviet losses of World War II, Stalin demanded Soviet control of Poland and the rest of Eastern Europe. U.S. President Harry Truman believed, on the other hand, that Eastern Europeans wanted to establish democracies. Truman could do little because the Soviet army was still occupying the area. It established communist governments across Eastern Europe. An "Iron Curtain" fell on Eastern Europe, cutting off all contacts between it and the West.

When it seemed that communism might next spread to Greece and Turkey, President Truman offered to give these countries military and economic aid. He announced a new foreign policy doctrine—the "Truman Doctrine." Truman promised to give U.S. support to all free peoples resisting communism. American foreign policy now aimed at the "containment" of communism—preventing it from spreading any further.

The Korean War

Who fought: United States, South Korea, and other Allies (UN forces) vs. North Korea, China

When: 1950–1953

Reason for U.S. involvement: To contain communism in Asia and to stop an aggressor

President Truman's "containment" policy succeeded in stopping the spread of communism in Europe, but in 1949, communists seized power in China, the world's most populous nation.

Meanwhile, after World War II, the country of Korea was divided into North and South Korea. North Korea, with Soviet support, established a communist government. A Western-style government was established in the South. In 1950, North Korea invaded South Korea in an attempt to re-unite the country under communist rule.

When President Truman received news of the invasion, he immediately decided to send U.S. troops to South Korea to resist the North Koreans. Truman was able to get the support of the UN Security Council since the Soviet Union was boycotting it (*refusing to participate*) at the time. Congress, however, never officially declared war on North Korea.

UN forces, mainly consisting of U.S. troops, went to South Korea under the command of General Douglas MacArthur, former U.S. commander in the Pacific during World War II. MacArthur quickly defeated the North Koreans and advanced UN troops through North Korea. He took U.S. troops so close to the Chinese border with Korea that he actually brought Communist China into the war. The Korean War lasted two more years and only ended in an armistice (*truce*) in 1953. Korea remained divided just as it had been before the war.

The Bay of Pigs Invasion

Who fought: Cuban exiles aided by the United States (CIA) vs. Cuba

When: April 1961

Reason for U.S. involvement: The CIA hoped to overturn Castro in Cuba

The Cold War was far from over. By 1949, the Soviet Union had developed its own atomic weapons. By the early 1950s, both the United States and the

Chapter 17 | American Foreign Policy

In 1960, Democratic candidate John F. Kennedy was elected President. Kennedy was told of the secret plan to help the Cuban exiles invade Cuba. He decided to go ahead with the plan. In April 1961, only four months after Kennedy took office, 1,400 Cuban exiles landed at the Bay of Pigs. The night before the attack, CIA planes bombed Cuban airfields. Kennedy refused, however, to give air support to the exiles on the day of the invasion, and the exiles were defeated.

The Cuban Missile Crisis

Who was involved: United States vs. Cuba and the Soviet Union

When: October 1962

Reason for U.S. involvement: To stop placement of nuclear missiles on Cuba

Soviet Union had developed much more powerful and destructive hydrogen bombs.

In 1959, Fidel Castro and his force of guerilla fighters overthrew the dictator ruling in Cuba. Castro had raised money from supporters in the United States and had promised to establish a democracy in Cuba. Once in power, however, Castro imprisoned opponents and set up a communist dictatorship.

Castro next took over property belonging to American companies. U.S. President Dwight Eisenhower reacted by cutting off American trade and diplomatic relations with Cuba. Eisenhower also gave his approval to a secret plan to train an army of Cuban exiles (*people who leave their native country*). The exiles planned to invade Cuba and overthrow Castro. They were armed and given special training by the CIA (Central Intelligence Agency) in Guatemala and Florida.

After the Bay of Pigs invasion, Castro strengthened his ties with the communist Soviet Union. Soviet leader Nikita Khrushchev sent nuclear warheads to Cuba. These warheads were to be placed on missiles that could be fired at the United States.

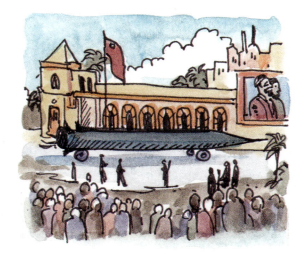

In October 1962, American spy planes discovered that Cubans were secretly building bases for these nuclear missiles, only 90 miles from Florida. This discovery triggered the Cuban Missile Crisis—the closest the world has ever come to a nuclear war. President Kennedy brought the matter before the UN Security Council. After consulting with his advisers, he also established a naval blockade of Cuba. The blockade prevented the Soviet Union from sending ships to Cuba. Next, Kennedy threatened to invade the island if the missiles were not immediately withdrawn. Khrushchev agreed to remove the missiles, and Kennedy promised that the United States would not invade Cuba. He also agreed to withdraw U.S. missiles from Turkey that had been aimed at the Soviet Union. After the crisis, the two leaders set up a special "hot line"—a direct telephone connection between their offices in Washington, D.C., and Moscow.

Indochina

The War in Vietnam

Who fought: United States, South Vietnam and allies vs. Viet Cong and North Vietnam
When: 1955–1975
U.S. Involvement: 1964–1973
Reason for U.S. involvement: To stop the spread of communism in Southeast Asia ("Domino Theory") and to help an ally

The Cold War also spread to Southeast Asia. Vietnam is a country in Indochina, a large peninsula on the southeastern edge of Asia. At one time, Vietnam was a French colony. After World War II, Vietnamese nationalists fought to drive the French out of their country. Vietnam was then divided, just as Korea had been, into two halves.

North Vietnam was placed under the control of a communist government. South Vietnam came under the rule of a dictator with ties to the West. The South Vietnamese government refused to hold elections to reunite the country. South Vietnamese communists—known as "Viet Cong"—reacted by launching a rebellion. The Viet Cong were helped by North Vietnam. President Kennedy sent advisers to help the South Vietnamese government. American leaders felt that they were aiding a friendly democracy. They also believed in the "Domino Theory"— that if communists took over South Vietnam, the other countries of Southeast Asia would quickly fall to communism like a row of dominoes.

In 1964, President Lyndon B. Johnson announced that North Vietnam had attacked U.S. ships in international waters. Congress passed a resolution giving the President authority to send U.S. ground troops to Vietnam. War was never officially declared, but by the end of 1965, almost 200,000 U.S. troops were in Vietnam; by 1968, there were half a million U.S. troops there. President Johnson also authorized

Chapter 17 | American Foreign Policy

bombing missions over North Vietnam. Americans used poisonous chemicals to bomb the Viet Cong and destroy their jungle cover.

Over the next eight years, American troops proved unable to win the war in Vietnam even though they had jet planes, helicopters, and superior weapons. American leaders had underestimated the determination of the leaders of North Vietnam to reunite Vietnam under their rule. The North Vietnamese continued to send supplies and troops to the South. The Viet Cong and North Vietnamese set booby traps and used guerrilla warfare (*a form of warfare in which they made attacks and then disappeared*) against American forces. Meanwhile, American soldiers were unfamiliar with the language, history and geography of South Vietnam. The South Vietnamese government became increasingly corrupt and unpopular. The war grew divisive in the United States.

American leaders began trying to find a way out of Vietnam. Richard Nixon won the Presidential election of 1968 by promising "peace with honor." Nixon started replacing U.S. troops with South Vietnamese soldiers. The United States conducted negotiations with the North Vietnamese in Paris while also increasing its bombing missions over North Vietnam. In 1973, the United States finally signed a treaty agreeing to withdraw its forces from South Vietnam. Two years later, North Vietnamese forces defeated the South Vietnamese and took over the country.

The Iran Hostage Crisis

Who was involved: United States vs. Islamic Republic of Iran
When: 1979–1981
Reason for U.S. involvement: Iranian protestors had seized staff of U.S. Embassy in Tehran

In 1979, popular demonstrations overthrew the Shah of Iran, one of America's strongest supporters in the Middle East. Religious leader Ayatollah Khomeini returned to Iran from exile, and Iranians created a new Islamic Republic. Laws were based on the *Qu'ran*, the Islamic holy book.

The Shah first fled to Egypt, and then went to the United States to seek medical treatment. When the Shah was admitted into the United States, the Iranian government let an angry mob seize the staff of the U.S. Embassy in their capital city of Tehran.

For more than a year, U.S. Embassy staff were held as hostages. President Jimmy Carter tried to negotiate their release without success. He even attempted a secret military operation to free them, which also failed. The hostages were not finally freed until January 1981, on the same day that Ronald Reagan took office as President.

The End of the Cold War
Enrichment

A strong anti-communist, President Reagan wanted to go beyond containment to "roll back" communism in countries where it already existed. He gave aid to anti-communist fighters in Afghanistan. Reagan built up the military resources of the United States and threatened to create a new anti-ballistic system against Soviet missiles.

The Soviet Union, in contrast, was facing severe economic difficulties. Soviet leader Mikhail Gor-

438 Chapter 17 | American Foreign Policy

bachev withdrew Soviet forces from Afghanistan and introduced greater "openness" in Soviet society. His efforts unleashed nationalist feelings in Eastern Europe and the Soviet Union. People demanded an end to Soviet rule. Rather than use force to put down popular demonstrations, Gorbachev permitted Eastern Europeans to enjoy greater freedom. In November 1989, the Berlin Wall, a hated symbol of the Cold War, came tumbling down. The Soviet Union itself dissolved at the end of 1991, and was replaced by the Commonwealth of Independent States, a loose confederation. The long and icy Cold War was finally over.

The First Gulf War

Who was involved: United States, Great Britain, Saudi Arabia, Egypt and allied coalition vs. Iraq

When: 1990–1991

Reason for U.S. involvement: Saddam Hussein, dictator in Iraq, had invaded neighboring Kuwait; the United States and its allies forced Iraqi forces out of Kuwait

At the end of the Cold War, the United States was the world's only "superpower." When Saddam Hussein, a dictator in Iraq, invaded neighboring Kuwait, President George H.W. Bush decided to act. He built up an impressive coalition of international forces to oppose Hussein's bold act of aggression (*unjustified attack*). Bush acted both for humanitarian reasons and to save Kuwait's oil. U.S. and coalition forces were first sent to Saudi Arabia to protect the Saudi kingdom from possible Iraqi attack. Then, when Hussein refused to withdraw from Kuwait, U.S. and coalition forces entered Kuwait. Iraqi forces were quickly defeated and retreated back to Iraq. As the Iraqis withdrew, they set Kuwaiti oil wells on fire. President George H.W. Bush refused, however, to topple Hussein from power in Iraq.

The Attacks of September 11, 2001 and the "War on Terror"

Who was involved: United States vs. al-Qaeda and Taliban

When: September 11, 2001

Reason for U.S. involvement: Al-Qaeda terrorists took control of commercial jet planes and crashed them into the World Trade Center and Pentagon; the United States invaded Afghanistan when the Taliban refused to hand over al-Qaeda leaders

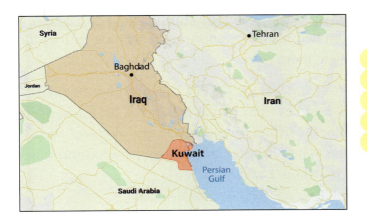

On September 11, 2001, Americans were shocked when commercial airplanes flew into the World Trade Center in New York City and the Pentagon building in Washington, D.C. Al-Qaeda, an Islamic Fundamentalist terrorist group, was responsible. Members of al-Qaeda had boarded several planes, taken their passengers as hostages, entered the cockpits, and flown each of the planes into their targets

Chapter 17 | American Foreign Policy

on a suicide mission. The two towers of the World Trade Center in New York City collapsed, leading to the deaths of almost three thousand people.

In response to the attacks, President George W. Bush (the son of President George H.W. Bush) declared a global "**War on Terror**." When the Taliban, the Islamic Fundamentalist government of Afghanistan, refused to turn over Osama bin Laden, the mastermind behind the attacks, President Bush sent U.S. forces to Afghanistan, where they overthrew the Taliban government.

The "War on Terror" also led to changes inside the United States. Americans introduced tighter security at U.S. airports, and Congress passed the USA PATRIOT Act, expanding the federal government's powers of surveillance (*ability to observe and spy on potential terrorists*).

The Second Gulf War

Who was involved: United States, Great Britain, Poland, Australia, Spain, and others vs. Iraq

When: 2003 (forces stayed until 2011)

Reason for U.S. involvement: To overthrow Iraqi dictator Saddam Hussein, who was suspected of having "weapons of mass destruction"

In Iraq, Saddam Hussein remained in power as a brutal dictator. President George W. Bush feared that Hussein might be hiding biological or chemical "weapons of mass destruction," which could be turned over to al-Qaeda terrorists. After presenting the U.S. position to the UN Security Council, President Bush warned Saddam Hussein to step down from power or face an attack from the United States. Bush then ordered the invasion of Iraq in March 2003.

The Iraqi army was quickly defeated. Saddam Hussein fled but was later captured, tried and executed by the new Iraqi government.

Although the American victory over Hussein was swift, a rebellion led by Hussein's former supporters and Fundamentalist Muslims broke out against moderate Iraqi leaders and the U.S. occupation force. This rebellion was much harder to defeat and resulted in American forces remaining in Iraq for eight more years.

President Barack Obama finally withdrew the last U.S. forces from Iraq at the end of 2011. Just a few months earlier, President Obama also sent special forces into Pakistan, where they captured and killed Osama bin Laden.

The Active Citizen

Complete the chart below.

How the United States Has Dealt with International Conflicts

Conflict	How/Why the United States Became Involved	Impact of U.S. Involvement
World War I		
World War II		
Korean War		
Bay of Pigs Invasion		
Cuban Missile Crisis		
War in Vietnam		
Iranian Hostage Crisis		
First Gulf War		
Second Gulf War		

- Select any one of the conflicts on the chart above and write a speech defending American policy. Be sure to mention one or more "tools" of American foreign policy that either were used or that might have been used to resolve the conflict.
- Make an illustrated timeline showing the history of American foreign policy from 1917 to the present with an emphasis on U.S. involvement in international conflicts.

U.S. Participation in International Organizations

Earlier in this chapter, you learned that one of the most important tools that American diplomats have to promote American foreign policy is participation in international organizations. Some of these organizations are alliances with other representative democracies for mutual defense; others are trade organizations; still others are peacekeeping or humanitarian organizations.

Many of these organizations have their headquarters (*central offices*) in New York City or some other city in the United States. Others have their headquarters in places such as Geneva, Switzerland.

In addition to official U.S. membership in these inter-governmental organizations, many individual American citizens participate directly in **international non-governmental organizations** (**INGO**) by giving money or volunteering service.

The United Nations (UN)

After the destruction of World War II, the United States and other nations created the United Nations. According to the **United Nations Charter**, the major aim of this organization is to maintain the peace of the world, while promoting friendship and cooperation among nations. The United Nations also seeks to eliminate hunger, disease, and ignorance in the world. The United Nations has its own peacekeeping forces, contributed by member nations.

All member nations belong to the **UN General Assembly**. This body provides a world forum for the discussion of important affairs.

Five nations serve as permanent members of the **UN Security Council**. These permanent members—the United States, Great Britain, Russia, China and France—enjoy special powers, including **veto power** over all UN peacekeeping operations. There are also

442   Chapter 17 | American Foreign Policy

ten elected non-permanent members on the Security Council.

Other important bodies in the United Nations are the International Court of Justice and the Economic and Social Council. Other institutions of the United Nations, such as UNESCO, support programs encouraging economic development and social reform. The UN Secretariat manages this complex organization. Its head, the **UN Secretary-General**, acts as spokesperson for the entire United Nations.

The UN Secretariat, Security Council and General Assembly are all located in New York City.

The Active Citizen

Enrichment

Article 1 The Purposes of the United Nations are:

1. "To maintain international peace and security, and to that end: to take effective collective measures for the prevention and removal of threats to the peace, and for the suppression (*ending*) of acts of aggression or other breaches (*breaks*) of the peace, and to bring about by peaceful means, and in conformity (*agreement*) with the principles of justice and international law, adjustment or settlement of international disputes or situations which might lead to a breach of the peace;

2. To develop friendly relations among nations based on respect for the principle of equal rights and self-determination of peoples, and to take other appropriate measures to strengthen universal peace;

3. To achieve international co-operation in solving international problems of an economic, social, cultural, or humanitarian character, and in promoting and encouraging respect for human rights and for fundamental freedoms for all without distinction as to race, sex, language, or religion; and

4. To be a center for harmonizing the actions of nations in the attainment of these common ends."

—*Charter of the United Nations* (1945)

▶ Which of these purposes do you think was most important to American leaders in 1945? Explain your answer.

▶ Which of these purposes is most important today? Explain your answer.

The "World Court" (International Court of Justice)

This is the judicial branch of the United Nations. It meets in The Hague in the Netherlands. The Court settles legal disputes between countries. It consists of fifteen international judges elected by the UN Security Council and General Assembly for nine-year terms. In 1986, the World Court ruled against the United States in the case of *Nicaragua v. United States*. The American government was accused of aiding opponents of the Nicaraguan government. Since 1986, the United States no longer automatically accepts the authority of the World Court, which it now accepts only on a case-by-case basis.

The North Atlantic Treaty Organization (NATO)

NATO was formed in 1949 at the height of the Cold War. Its purpose was to defend Western Europe against possible Soviet attack. It reassured Western Europeans that the United States would come to their defense, with nuclear weapons if necessary. NATO headquarters are in Brussels, Belgium.

Chapter 17 | American Foreign Policy

Since the end of the Cold War, NATO has expanded its functions and membership. Its focus remains on the defense of its member states, but it also acts to discourage militarism and to encourage a peaceful transition to democracy. Several Eastern European nations have joined NATO, including Poland, the Czech Republic, Hungary, Slovakia, Slovenia, Latvia, Estonia, Lithuania, Bulgaria, Albania, and Croatia.

Membership in NATO remains open to any European state that supports its principles and that can contribute to the security of the North Atlantic area.

The North American Free Trade Agreement (NAFTA)

NAFTA was negotiated by President George H.W. Bush and then successfully pushed through the Senate by President Bill Clinton. It created a giant trade zone in North America, consisting of the United States, Canada and Mexico. Although it did not abolish tariffs (*import taxes*) between members, each country pledged to lower its tariffs on other members' goods and to cooperate with its NAFTA partners.

President Donald Trump was critical of NAFTA. He negotiated new terms with Mexico and Canada. The new agreement has tougher protections for workers, the environment and intellectual property. It also encourages more car manufacturing in the United States. Once ratified by the three member countries, the new United States-Mexico-Canada Agreement (USMCA) will replace NAFTA.

The World Trade Organization (WTO)

The United States had signed the General Agreement on Tariffs and Trade, or GATT, in 1947. Its aim was to encourage international trade by eliminating tariffs. In 1995, GATT was replaced by the World Trade Organization, or WTO. Members of the WTO have agreed to a set of rules for world trade, including rules for settling disputes. WTO members have further agreed to take steps to reduce tariffs and to eliminate other obstacles to world trade. The WTO now has more than 150 member countries, covering 95% of world trade.

The WTO has a general council and several specific councils, such as the Council for Trade in Goods, the Council for Trade in Services, and the Trade Negotiations Committee. Its headquarters are in Geneva, Switzerland.

The International Red Cross/Red Crescent

The Red Cross was first proposed by a Swiss businessman after he saw the suffering of thousands of soldiers on a battlefield in 1859. After several international conferences at Geneva, the International Red Cross was born. Its original purpose was to help wounded soldiers and to monitor conditions in prisoner-of-war (POW) camps. According to its mission statement, the International Red Cross/Red Crescent remains "an impartial, neutral, and independent organization whose exclusively humanitarian mission is to protect the lives and dignity of victims of war and internal violence and to provide them with assistance." It coordinates international relief efforts, monitors the treatment of prisoners of war, cares for wounded on the battlefield, helps locate missing persons, and acts as a link between nations at war. Its fundamental principles are "humanity, impartiality, neutrality, independence, volunteerism, unity, and universality."

Unlike most of the agencies above, the International Red Cross/Red Crescent is an example of a non-governmental organization (NGO), an organization that is not part of a government. Its headquarters are in Geneva, Switzerland. National societies, like the American Red Cross, are associated with this international movement.

United Nations Children's Fund (UNICEF)

UNICEF was originally founded in 1946 to provide food and health care to children in countries that suffered destruction in World War II. In 1953, UNICEF became a permanent part of the United Nations. Its headquarters are in New York City, but

UNICEF has offices in more than 190 countries. In 1965, UNICEF won the Nobel Peace Prize.

UNICEF receives about two-thirds of its revenues from governments and one-third from private contributors (individuals and corporations). In the United States, children often collect money for UNICEF on Halloween. UNICEF distributes vaccines, medicines, nutritional supplies, and educational supplies. UNICEF promotes children's rights.

UNICEF is an intergovernmental organization (IGO), but it has independent national committees in 36 countries. These rely on private funding and are NGOs (non-governmental organizations).

International Non-Governmental Organizations (INGO)

There are now thousands of **international non-governmental organizations**, or "**INGOs**." These include such organizations as Doctors without Borders, Save the Children, OXFAM, the Ford Foundation, the Rockefeller Foundation and CARE. These INGOs often fund local NGOs that are implementing specific projects.

Governments cannot belong to NGOs or to INGOs. Individuals or corporations that are interested in supporting these NGOs can provide volunteer services or contribute funds.

How Individuals and Governments Participate in International Organizations

There are different ways that individuals and governments can participate in international organizations.

Many of the organizations you just learned about only permit countries to become members. These include:

- United Nations (UN)
- World Court
- North Atlantic Treaty Organization (NATO)
- NAFTA
- World Trade Organization (WTO)
- UNICEF

Governments join these international intergovernmental organizations ("IGOs") by signing a treaty or a charter. Member governments agree to follow the rules of the organization. Usually they also agree to pay dues to the organization to finance its operations.

Individuals cannot join these organizations but they can sometimes support them by joining separate, private associations that promote their work. For example, Friends of the United Nations is a private group that makes people aware of the activities of the United Nations. Its members work with educational groups, companies and the media. UNICEF also has private national committees in many countries. They raise money from individual contributors who wish to support UNICEF.

As you know, both individuals and companies can also join international non-governmental organizations (INGOs). These are private associations. Individuals can contribute money, volunteer their time, or enroll as members in these organizations.

Chapter 17 | American Foreign Policy

The Active Citizen

- Classify the international organizations you have just studied by placing them in the appropriate categories on the chart below.
- Then use your research skills to find one more example to add to each category.

Type of International Organization	Specific Examples
International organizations formed to promote trade	
International organizations formed as defensive alliances	
International organizations formed to maintain world peace	
International organizations formed for humanitarian purposes	

- To which of the following international organizations does the United States belong? You may need to search on the Internet to find the answers.

International Organization	Member	Non-member
European Union (EU)	☐	☐
Organization of Petroleum Exporting Countries (OPEC)	☐	☐
International Committee of the Red Cross (ICRC)	☐	☐
Amnesty International (AI)	☐	☐
Food and Agriculture Organization (FAO)	☐	☐
International Energy Agency (IEA)	☐	☐
World Customs Organization (WCO)	☐	☐
World Wildlife Fund (WWF)	☐	☐
Organization of American States (OAS)	☐	☐
Commonwealth of Nations	☐	☐

- Research additional INGOs on the Internet. Then decide which INGO you would most like to join. Write a paragraph explaining why you think this is the best INGO for individual citizens to belong to. Students should read their paragraphs to the entire class. Afterwards, the class should decide by vote which of these INGOs to join or support. After the decision is made, your class should take steps to join this group or to make a contribution.

Describe the relationships between the terms and phrases in the concept circles below and explain their significance.

Name _____

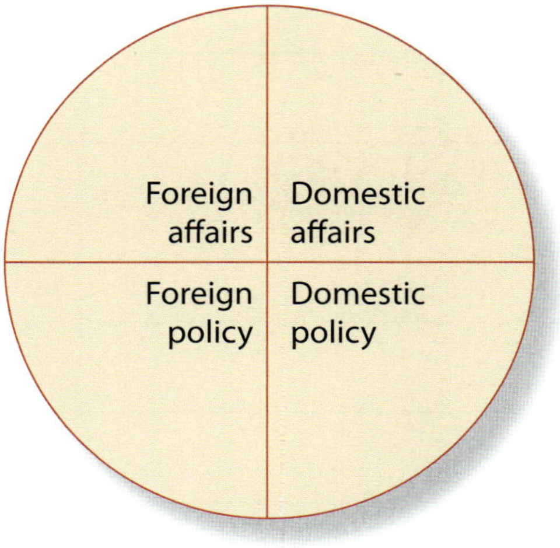

Circle 1:
- Foreign affairs
- Domestic affairs
- Foreign policy
- Domestic policy

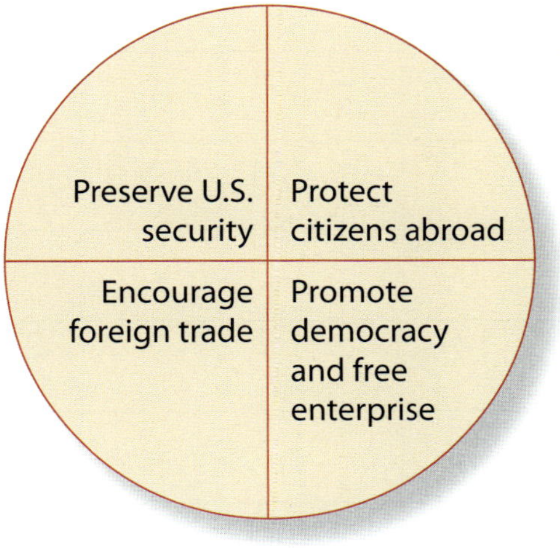

Circle 2:
- Preserve U.S. security
- Protect citizens abroad
- Encourage foreign trade
- Promote democracy and free enterprise

Circle 3:
- Negotiate treaties
- Commander in Chief
- Nominate ambassadors
- Receive ambassadors

Chapter 17 | American Foreign Policy

Describe the relationships between the terms and phrases in the concept circles below and explain their significance.

Name _____

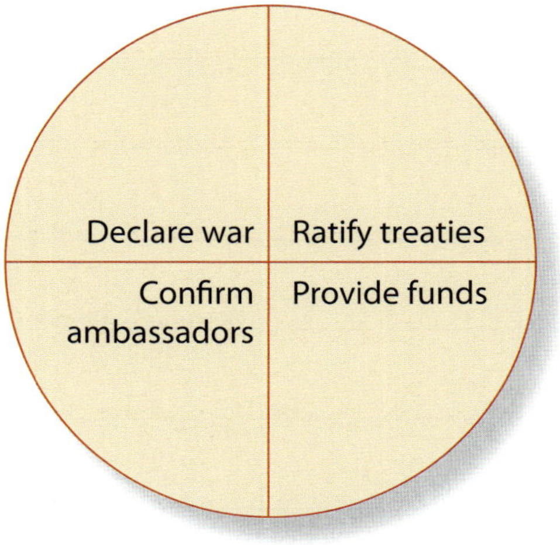

Circle 1:
- Declare war
- Ratify treaties
- Confirm ambassadors
- Provide funds

Circle 2:
- Negotiations
- Alliances
- Diplomatic recognition
- International organizations

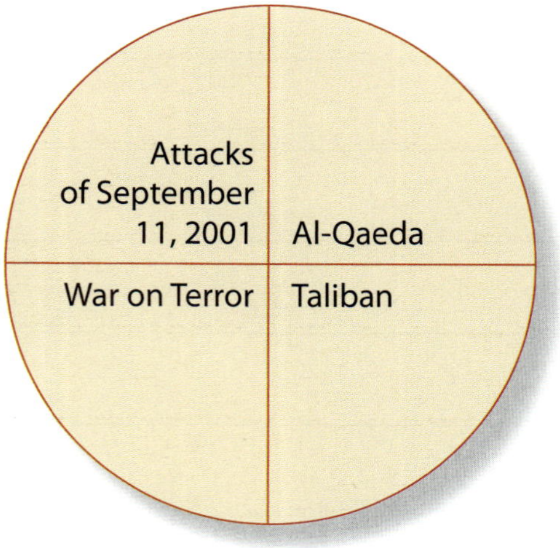

Circle 3:
- Attacks of September 11, 2001
- Al-Qaeda
- War on Terror
- Taliban

448   Chapter 17 | American Foreign Policy

Describe the relationships between the terms and phrases in the concept circles below and explain their significance.

Name _____

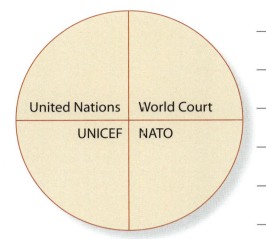

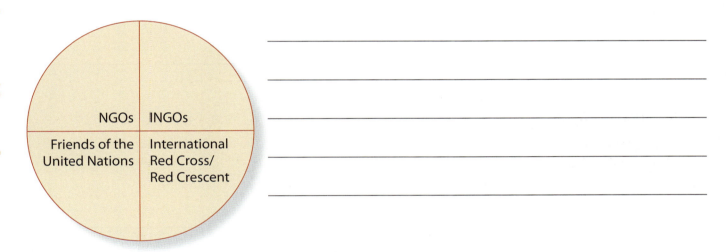

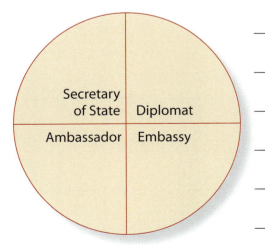

Chapter 17 | American Foreign Policy

Name _____

What were each of these important international conflicts about? Fill in the chart below.

Conflict	Description and Reason for U.S. Involvement
World War I (1917–1918) 	
World War II (1941–1945) 	
Korean War (1950–1953) 	
Bay of Pigs Landing (1961) 	
Cuban Missile Crisis (1962) 	

Chapter 17 | American Foreign Policy

Name _____

What were each of these important international conflicts about? Fill in the chart below.

Conflict	Description and Reason for U.S. Involvement
War in Vietnam (1964–1973) 	
Iran Hostage Crisis (1979) 	
First Gulf War (1990–1991) 	
September 11, 2001 Terrorist Attack on World Trade Center and Pentagon 	
Second Gulf War (2003–2011) 	

Chapter 17 | American Foreign Policy

Name _____

Do you agree with past U.S. policies abroad? Identify one of the conflicts you studied in this chapter. Then research that conflict in your school library or on the Internet. Decide if you agree with U.S. policy in that instance. Then complete an official "White Paper" (an official government report on a complex issue) presenting your findings and conclusions.

Office of the Historian, U.S. Department of State

Official White Paper on _____
(name of conflict)

Sources of information about the conflict:
_____
_____

How did this conflict arise?
_____
_____

Why did the United States become involved in this conflict?
_____
_____

What was the impact of U.S. involvement?
_____
_____

What was the final outcome of the conflict?
_____
_____

Would you have agreed with U.S. policy?   Yes [ ]   No [ ]

Explain your point of view.
_____
_____

Name _____

Fill in the chart below.

U.S. Participation in International Organizations

International Organization	What It Does
United Nations	
World Court	
NATO	
WTO	
NAFTA (USMCA)	

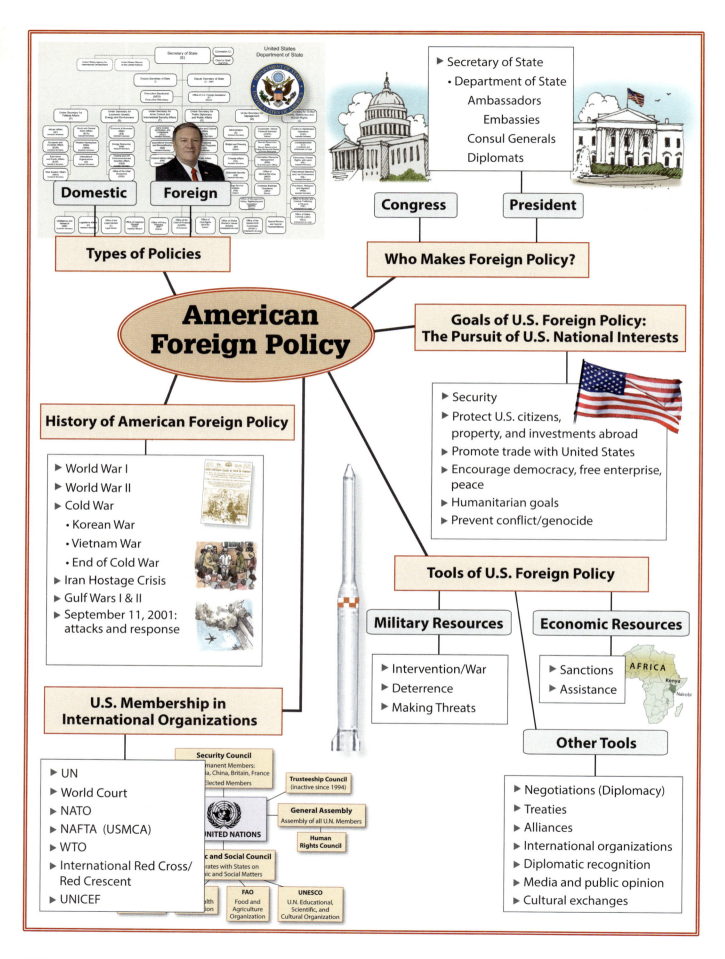

Review Cards: American Foreign Policy

American Foreign Policy

- **Domestic policy** is any government policy that concerns affairs "at home"—such as setting tax rates or regulating safety in factories.
- **Foreign policy** is any government policy that concerns foreign countries and events taking place outside the United States: for example, making an alliance with a foreign country, fighting a war overseas, or entering into a trade agreement with another country.
- Foreign policy thus deals with "**foreign affairs**," or "**international relations**." These terms refer to relations between independent countries all around the world.
- **International relations** are special because international law is not as powerful as the rule of law within a single country. Therefore nations are always concerned about their own security.

Who Makes Foreign Policy?

Control over foreign policy is actually exercised by two branches of our federal government: the Presidency and Congress.

Powers of the President
- The President appoints and receives ambassadors.
- The President negotiates treaties.
- The President acts as Commander in Chief of the armed forces.
- The President appoints the heads of executive departments, including the Secretary of State and the Secretary of Defense.

Powers of Congress
- The Senate confirms the President's appointments.
- The Senate ratifies U.S. treaties by a two-thirds vote.
- Congress has the power to declare war.
- Congress approves funding for all federal programs, including defense, foreign aid and the State Department.

The Secretary of State and the State Department
- The **Secretary of State** is the member of the Cabinet entrusted with the day-to-day running of our nation's foreign policy and heads the **State Department**.
- **Diplomats** are officials who practice **diplomacy**—the skill of handling relations between states. An **ambassador** is the official representative of one country sent to reside in another. Each ambassador is placed in charge of an **embassy**.

Chapter 17 | American Foreign Policy

The Objectives of U.S. Foreign Policy

The President, Congress, and the State Department generally agree on the fundamental objective of U.S. foreign policy: to pursue the **national interests** of the United States and the American people:

- Protect the security of the United States.
- Protect American citizens, their property and investments abroad.
- Encourage other countries to trade with the United States.
- Spread the American system of democracy and free enterprise.
- Promote U.S. economic success and prosperity.
- Promote international peace and stability.
- Provide economic assistance to developing countries.
- Help prevent armed conflict or genocide (*mass murder*) around the world.
- Make humanitarian efforts to improve health, education and living conditions around the world.

The Instruments of U.S. Foreign Policy

To achieve U.S. national interests, American leaders have several foreign-policy "tools" they can use, including American military and economic resources, and participation in international organizations. In general, diplomats try to use friendly negotiations before turning to threats, economic sanctions or military intervention. The use of military force is only a last resort.

- **Military Force/Intervention:** The President can use American air power, naval power, and troops to intervene overseas. Congress must approve any foreign intervention longer than 60 days.
- **Deterrence:** The United States is defended by a large arsenal of missiles with nuclear warheads. A **deterrent** is a threat that discourages others from doing something. Every country knows that if it attacks the United States, the United States could retaliate with nuclear weapons.
- **Making Threats:** A great power sometimes uses its military force to threaten countries into taking some form of positive action.
- **Economic Sanctions:** The United States sometimes uses its economic power to further its foreign policy goals. The United States may **boycott** (*ban trade with*) or penalize any country that is violating international rules, committing acts of aggression or developing nuclear weapons in violation of international treaties. These penalties are called "sanctions."
- **Economic Aid:** The United States provides assistance to some allies to develop their economies. It provides other allies with military assistance in the form of aircraft, missiles and other arms.
- **Negotiations:** Negotiations are talks held between countries. Whenever there is an international problem or dispute, the first step towards a settlement is usually for the countries concerned to enter into negotiations. The aim of diplomacy is to find a compromise, or middle ground, that all the parties to the dispute can somehow accept.
- **Alliances:** An **alliance** is an agreement between two or more countries to act together. Usually, they agree to defend one another if attacked.
- **Membership in International Organizations:** Another "tool" of U.S. foreign policy is membership in international organizations, such as the **United Nations.**

A Capsule History of American Conflicts

World War I (1914–1918: U.S. entry in 1917)

A great war broke out in Europe in the summer of 1914 between the Central Powers (Germany, Austria-Hungary, Ottoman Empire) and the Allies (Russia, France, Great Britain). At first, Americans tried to stay out of the war. Publication of a secret German offer to return U.S. lands to Mexico outraged American public opinion. When Germany announced **unrestricted submarine warfare** (sinking vessels without warning) and began sinking American ships in 1917, President Woodrow Wilson asked Congress for a declaration of war. The United States sent a million-man army to France. This broke the deadlock in Europe and forced Germany to surrender, bringing victory to the Allies.

World War II (1939–1945: U.S. entry in 1941)

In the 1930s, the **Nazi** (National Socialist) Party, led by Adolf Hitler, gained control in Germany. Hitler believed Germans were a superior race and planned to conquer the rest of Europe. Nazi Germany attacked Poland in 1939, beginning World War II. Americans were at first determined to stay out of the war, but in December 1941, Japan attacked the United States at **Pearl Harbor** in Hawaii. Germany and Italy also declared war on the United States. Americans became involved in the most bloody and destructive war in human history. The **Axis Powers** (Germany, Italy and Japan) were opposed by the **Allied Powers** (United States, Great Britain, and Soviet Union). Eventually, the Germans were defeated, Hitler committed suicide, and Germany surrendered in May 1945. In August 1945, Americans dropped atomic bombs on two Japanese cities. Japan then surrendered, ending World War II. More than 50 million people were killed in the war.

Korean War (1950–1953)

America wanted to contain communism, so that it would not spread to countries across Europe and beyond. Korea had been divided into North and South Korea after World War II. **North Korea** established a communist government and invaded **South Korea** in 1950. **President Harry Truman** sent U.S. troops to South Korea to prevent further communist expansion. The U.S. army quickly defeated the North Koreans in South Korea and advanced into North Korea. U.S. troops went so close to the Chinese border that **communist China** entered the war. The Korean War ended in 1953 and Korea remained divided the same way it had been before the war.

Bay of Pigs (1961)

In 1959, **Fidel Castro** and his force of guerilla (*rebel*) fighters overthrew the dictator Batista and took control of Cuba. Once in power, Castro imprisoned those speaking out against him and established a communist dictatorship. When Castro's government took control of property belonging to American companies, the United States cut off trade and diplomatic relations. President Eisenhower gave his approval to a secret plan to train **Cuban exiles** (*refugees*), who planned to invade Cuba and remove Castro. The exiles were armed and given special training by the CIA (Central Intelligence Agency). Newly elected President John F. Kennedy decided to continue with Eisenhower's plan. In April 1961, The Cuban exiles landed at the **Bay of Pigs**. When Kennedy refused to give air support on the day of the invasion, the exiles were defeated.

Cuban Missile Crisis (1962)

After the Bay of Pigs invasion in 1961, Castro increased his ties with the communist Soviet Union. In October 1962, **American spy planes discovered that Cubans were secretly building bases for Soviet nuclear missiles**, only 90 miles from Florida. **President Kennedy** established a **naval blockade of Cuba**, preventing any ships from passing through the area. Then President Kennedy threatened to attack the island of Cuba if the missiles were not immediately removed. **Soviet leader Khrushchev agreed to remove the missiles**, and Kennedy promised not to invade Cuba and to remove U.S. missiles from Turkey that were aimed at the Soviet Union. The world had come close to, but had avoided, a nuclear war.

Vietnam War (1964–1973)

After winning independence from France in 1954, **Vietnam** was divided. **North Vietnam** established a communist government. **South Vietnam** came under the control of a dictator with Western ties, who refused to hold elections to reunite the country. South Vietnamese communists (known as **Viet Cong**), with the help of the North, began a rebellion against the government of South Vietnam. American leaders believed that if communists took over South Vietnam, the rest of Southeast Asia would fall to communism like a row of dominoes ("Domino Theory"). **In 1964, Congress authorized the President to send ground troops to Vietnam.** Over the next eight years, American troops and bombing missions proved unable to win the war. The war became unpopular in the United States and President Nixon began removing U.S. troops while secretly negotiating with the North Vietnamese in Paris. In 1973, the United States signed the **Paris Peace Accords**, agreeing to leave Vietnam. Two years later, South Vietnam fell to the North Vietnamese army and the country was reunited under communist rule.

Iran Hostage Crisis (1979–1981)

In 1979, popular demonstrations overthrew the **Shah** (*ruler*) of Iran and installed an **Islamic Republic.** Iran began following Islamic law and was governed by religious leaders. The Shah first fled to Egypt, and then went to the United States to seek medical attention. The new Iranian government objected when U.S. leaders let the Shah enter the United States. They responded by allowing an angry mob to seize (*take*) the staff of the **U.S. Embassy** in the capital city of **Tehran** as hostages. For more than a year, U.S. Embassy staff were held as hostages until they were finally released in January 1981. President Jimmy Carter finally negotiated to their release, although they were not freed until his Presidency ended in January 1981.

The First Gulf War (1990–1991)

Saddam Hussein was a dictator who ruled over Iraq from 1979 to 2003. When Hussein invaded and occupied oil-rich **Kuwait** in 1990, President George H.W. Bush decided to act. He put together an **alliance** of countries to oppose Hussein's actions. At first, the U.S. and allied forces were sent to protect **Saudi Arabia** from attack. When Hussein refused to leave Kuwait they advanced into Kuwait. Iraqi forces were defeated and retreated (*went back*) to Iraq. However, President Bush refused to send U.S. forces into Iraq to overthrow Hussein.

Attacks of September 11, 2001 and the "War on Terror"

On **September 11, 2001**, commercial airplanes flew into the World Trade Center in New York City and the Pentagon in Washington, DC. **Al-Qaeda**, a terrorist group, was responsible for the attack. Members of al-Qaeda had boarded several planes, taken the passengers aboard as hostages, entered the cockpits, and flown each of the planes into their targets on a suicide mission. Almost 3,000 people died when the twin towers of the World Trade Center in New York City collapsed. Following the attacks, President George W. Bush declared a global **"War on Terror."** When the **Taliban**, the government of **Afghanistan**, refused to turn over **Osama bin Laden**, the mastermind behind the "9/11" attacks, President Bush sent U.S. forces to Afghanistan, where they overthrew Taliban rule.

Second Gulf War (2003)

Saddam Hussein remained in power as the dictator of Iraq. After the terrorist attack by al-Qaeda on September 11, 2001, President George W. Bush feared that Hussein might be hiding nuclear, biological, or chemical **"weapons of mass destruction,"** which could be turned over to al-Qaeda terrorists. Because of this, in March 2003, President Bush demanded that Hussein resign from office. When Hussein refused, Bush ordered the invasion of Iraq. The Iraqi army was quickly defeated by American forces. Hussein fled but was later captured and executed by the new Iraqi government. Despite their swift victory, American troops soon found they could not leave Iraq. They became involved fighting Hussein's supporters, Islamic Fundamentalists and other groups challenging the new Iraqi government. President Barack Obama finally withdrew the last U.S. forces from Iraq at the end of 2011.

Chapter 17 | American Foreign Policy

U.S. Participation in International Organizations

- **The United Nations (UN).** According to the **United Nations Charter,** the major aim of this organization is to maintain world peace, while trying to promote friendship and cooperation among nations. All member nations belong to the **UN General Assembly**. This organ provides a world forum for the discussion of important affairs. The United States and four other nations serve as permanent members on the **UN Security Council**. These permanent members enjoy special powers, including **veto power** over all UN peacekeeping operations.

- **The "World Court"** (International Court of Justice). This is the judicial branch of the United Nations. It meets in The Hague in the Netherlands, where it settles legal disputes between countries.

- **The North Atlantic Treaty Organization (NATO).** NATO was formed in 1949 to defend Western Europe against possible Soviet attack. It reassured Western Europeans that the United States would come to their defense, with nuclear weapons if necessary. Since the end of the Cold War, NATO has expanded its functions and membership. Its focus remains on the defense of its member states.

- **The North American Free Trade Agreement (NAFTA).** NAFTA created a giant trade zone in North America, consisting of the United States, Canada and Mexico. Each country pledged to lower its tariffs on other members' goods. In September 2018, it was announced that the United States, Mexico, and Canada had agreed to replace NAFTA with the United States–Mexico–Canada Agreement (USMCA).

- **The World Trade Organization (WTO).** Members of the WTO have agreed to a set of rules for world trade, including rules for settling disputes. WTO members have further agreed to take steps to reduce tariffs and to eliminate other obstacles to world trade. The WTO now has more than 150 member countries.

- **The International Red Cross/Red Crescent.** This organization coordinates international relief efforts, monitors the treatment of prisoners of war, cares for wounded on the battlefield, helps locate missing persons, and acts as a link between nations at war. The International Red Cross/Red Crescent is an example of a **non-governmental organization** (NGO), an organization that is not part of any government.

- **United Nations Children's Fund (UNICEF).** UNICEF was originally founded to provide food and health care to children in countries that suffered destruction in World War II. It is now part of the United Nations. UNICEF receives about two-thirds of its revenues from governments and one-third from private contributors. It distributes vaccines, medicines, nutritional supplies, and educational supplies, and promotes children's rights.

Hall of the UN General Assembly

What Do You Know?

SS.7.C.3.3

1. Which constitutional power helps the President in the conduct of U.S. foreign policy?
   A. the power to declare war on foreign nations
   B. the power to receive ambassadors from foreign countries
   C. the power to ratify treaties negotiated with foreign countries
   D. the power to make final appropriations for the U.S. State Department

SS.7.C.4.1

2. The diagram below shows details about the federal government.

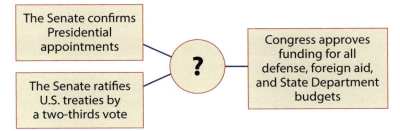

   Which phrase completes the diagram?
   A. How Congress influences U.S. domestic policy
   B. How Congress influences U.S. foreign policy
   C. How the State Department manages U.S. foreign policy
   D. How the House Committee on Foreign Affairs investigates issues

SS.7.C.4.3

3. The speech below was delivered to Congress by President Harry Truman in 1947.

   > *I believe that it must be the policy of the United States to support free peoples who are resisting attempted subjugation by armed minorities or by outside pressures... If we falter in our leadership, we may endanger the peace of the world and we shall surely endanger the welfare of our own nation.*

   Which foreign-policy goal did President Truman have in this speech?
   A. to prevent genocide around the world
   B. to protect the security of the United States
   C. to encourage foreign trade with the United States
   D. to achieve world peace through international organizations

SS.7.C.4.3

4. What was the primary reason for U.S. involvement in Korea and Vietnam?
   A. an imperialist longing to annex new colonies
   B. a fear of the international spread of communism
   C. the hope of expanding American frontiers westward
   D. a humanitarian desire to help these peoples improve their economies

Chapter 17 | American Foreign Policy

SS.7.C.4.1

5. Which action would be an example of a foreign-policy decision?

   A. Congress changes the naturalization rules for immigrants wishing to become citizens.
   B. The President signs an executive order modifying emissions standards for power plants burning coal.
   C. Congress passes a law providing tax benefits to companies manufacturing cars using electrical power.
   D. The President accepts an invitation to mediate between China and Japan over ownership of the Senkaku Islands.

SS.7.C.4.2

6. The two paragraphs below describe an international organization.

   > **NAFTA**
   >
   > The passage of (NAFTA) in November, 1993, was a stunning victory for President Clinton and a vivid illustration of how Presidents tend to get their way with Congress more often in foreign policy matters than in matters of domestic policy.
   >
   > Early in the NAFTA debate, Clinton argued that NAFTA was crucial to his economic program and a boon to the creation of high-skill, high-wage jobs.

   What was the main purpose behind this organization?

   A. to create a giant trade zone with Canada and Mexico
   B. to maintain peace and security while encouraging human rights
   C. to settle disputes between countries peacefully in the World Court
   D. to form a defensive alliance against attacks by potential aggressors

SS.7.C.4.1

7. President George Washington gave the advice below in his Farewell Address of 1796.

   > *The great rule of conduct for us in regard to foreign nations is in extending our commercial relations, to have with them as little political connection as possible. So far as we have already formed engagements, let them be fulfilled with perfect good faith. Here let us stop.*

   Which later event most closely followed President Washington's advice?

   A. The United States annexed the Philippines in 1898.
   B. Congress supplied ships to Britain for cash in 1940.
   C. Americans attempted to remain neutral at first during both World Wars I and II.
   D. Americans sent troops to Korea and Vietnam in order to prevent the spread of communism in Asia.

SS.7.C.4.2

8. Which organization has the U.S. government as a member?
   A. Doctors without Borders
   B. International Red Cross/Red Crescent
   C. North Atlantic Treaty Organization
   D. Organization of Petroleum Exporting Countries (OPEC)

SS.7.C.4.1

9. The two paragraphs below describe events during the Presidency of Bill Clinton.

"In response to the nuclear tests, people in New Delhi took to the streets lighting firecrackers, thanking Hindu gods and crying out 'Bharat Mata Jai!' (Victory to Mother India)."	"President Bill Clinton decided tonight to impose economic sanctions on India's government for detonating three underground nuclear explosions."

   What was President Clinton's reason for using "economic sanctions" in this example?
   A. to stop the spread of communism to India
   B. to prohibit Pakistan from testing nuclear weapons
   C. to discourage India from testing any more nuclear weapons
   D. to stop Indians from celebrating their successful nuclear program

SS.7.C.4.1

10. A country that has a military alliance with the United States faces a civil war from ethnic conflict. What would be an appropriate first response by the United States?
    A. threaten the parties to the conflict
    B. impose economic sanctions against the country
    C. send U.S. troops to that country to restore order
    D. encourage peaceful negotiations between the parties

SS.7.C.4.2

11. The list below identifies several organizations.

    - World Trade Organization (WTO)
    - United Nations Children's Fund (UNICEF)
    - United Nations (UN)
    - North Atlantic Treaty Organization (NATO)
    - North America Free Trade Agreement (NAFTA)

    What purpose is common to all of these organizations?
    A. military isolation
    B. collective security
    C. defensive alliances
    D. international cooperation

Chapter 17 | American Foreign Policy

SS.7.C.4.2

12. Which international organization gives both governments and private citizens an opportunity to provide food and healthcare?
    A. WTO
    B. NATO
    C. UNICEF
    D. The World Court

SS.7.C.4.2

13. The newspaper headline on the left describes an event that took place in the Middle East.

    Which course of action did the United States take in response to this international incident?
    A. It refused to give Iraq any additional humanitarian aid.
    B. It launched an invasion of Iraq to topple dictator Saddam Hussein.
    C. It organized a military alliance that forced the Iraqis out of Kuwait.
    D. It seized the staff of the Iraqi Embassy in Washington, D.C., as hostages.

SS.7.C.4.3

14. Why did President Roosevelt consider December 7, 1941, a "date which will live in infamy"?
    A. Japan attacked Pearl Harbor.
    B. Nazi Germany invaded Poland.
    C. North Korea attacked South Korea.
    D. Terrorists attacked the World Trade Center.

SS.7.C.4.3

15. The Joint Resolution below was passed by Congress on April 6, 1917.

    Therefore be it resolved by the Senate and the House of Representatives of the United States of America in Congress assembled, that the state of war between the United States and the Imperial German Government which has thus been thrust upon the United States is hereby formally declared; and that the President be, and he is hereby, authorized and directed to employ the entire naval and military forces of the United States and the resources of the Government to carry on war against the Imperial German Government.

    Which event led to this Joint Resolution?
    A. the German invasion of Poland
    B. a surprise attack on Pearl Harbor
    C. submarine attacks on American ships
    D. a terrorist attack on the World Trade Center and Pentagon

Chapter 18: A Practice End-of-Course Assessment in Civics

SS.7.C.1.3

1. How did the British government respond to the colonial concerns expressed during the Boston Tea Party?
   A. It passed the Intolerable Acts, closing Boston Harbor.
   B. It recognized colonial grievances and agreed not to pass any more taxes.
   C. It ordered troops to fire on colonial demonstrators in a public square of Boston.
   D. It declared the colonists to be in a state of open rebellion and outside the King's protection.

SS.7.C.1.4

2. According to the Declaration of Independence, when do people have the right to abolish their government and establish a new one?
   A. whenever a government passes a law that is disliked by some
   B. whenever their government becomes despotic and oppressive
   C. whenever the majority party in control of government changes
   D. whenever a king attempts to act without the approval of Parliament

SS.7.C.1.4

3. The photograph below shows Dr. Martin Luther King after giving his "I Have a Dream" speech during the Civil Rights Movement.

   Which part of the Declaration of Independence most influenced the events shown in this photograph?

   A. its list of colonial grievances
   B. its outrage at the British use of force
   C. its theory of government based on natural rights
   D. its claim of the right to overthrow a tyrannical government

SS.7.C.1.4

4. Based on the introduction to the Declaration of Independence, what was the main purpose of that document?
   A. to list all the injuries that the English King had committed against them
   B. to set forth a new American theory of government to help future nations
   C. to explain how the colonists had repeatedly tried to settle their differences peacefully
   D. to explain to the rest of the world why the colonists were ending their allegiance to Great Britain

SS.7.C.1.6

5. The passage below is from the Preamble to the U.S. Constitution.

We the People of the United States, in order to form a more perfect Union, establish justice, insure domestic tranquility, provide for the common defense, promote the general welfare, and secure the blessings of liberty, to ourselves and our posterity, do ordain and establish this Constitution for the United States of America.

In 1957, President Eisenhower sent the National Guard into Little Rock, Arkansas, in order to prevent racial violence. Which goal of government, listed in the Preamble, did this action illustrate?

   A. to insure domestic tranquility
   B. to form a more perfect Union
   C. to secure the blessings of liberty
   D. to provide for the common defense

SS.7.C.1.7

6. Suppose the following sequence of events occurs in our federal government:

   ▶ Congress passes a bill and sends it to the President.
   ▶ The President vetoes the bill and returns it to Congress.
   ▶ Both houses of Congress override the veto.
   ▶ The bill becomes a law.

   Which two constitutional principles do these events illustrate?

   A. federalism and limited government
   B. federalism and checks and balances
   C. individual rights and popular sovereignty
   D. separation of powers and checks and balances

SS.7.C.1.8

7. Below are views for and against ratification of the Constitution.

1	2
The Constitution will create a national government more tyrannical than the British government ever was. Our individual liberties will be under a constant threat. We need better safeguards than the assurances of the Constitution's supporters.	We must have a stronger national government to protect our interests against foreign powers and domestic unrest. The separation of powers and federalism will sufficiently curb the ambitions of the new national government.

Which conclusion can be drawn from these views?

   A. The proposed Constitution lacked a bill of rights.
   B. The proposed Constitution guaranteed free speech.
   C. The proposed Constitution had no national executive.
   D. The proposed Constitution strengthened state governments.

SS.7.C.1.8

8. During the ratification debates, Anti-Federalists demanded that the rights below be added to the Constitution in order for them to support it.

   ▶ Guarantee of a speedy trial
   ▶ Freedom from illegal searches and seizures
   ▶ Right not to have troops quartered in one's home

   Which document guaranteed these rights?
   A. The Bill of Rights
   B. The *Federalist Papers*
   C. The Articles of Confederation
   D. The Declaration of Independence

SS.7.C.3.3

9. Which example shows the exercise of implied powers by Congress based on the Elastic Clause?
   A. Approving changes to income tax rates
   B. Creating a national bank to hold federal funds
   C. Voting on annual appropriations for the U.S. Navy
   D. Passing legislation affecting the U.S. Postal Service

SS.7.C.3.9

10. The diagram below shows some of the steps involved in passing a federal law.

    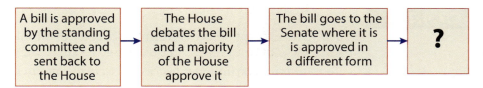

    Which step completes the diagram?
    A. The bill is sent to a conference committee.
    B. The bill is sent back to the House to be amended.
    C. The bill is pigeonholed until the next session of Congress.
    D. Both bills are sent to the President to choose which to sign.

SS.7.C.3.8

11. How does the Supreme Court decide which cases to review each year?
    A. It grants writs of certiorari to all cases that come before it on appeal.
    B. It grants writs of certiorari to some of the cases it believes to be of national importance.
    C. It grants writs of certiorari to all cases recommended to it by the President of the United States.
    D. It grants writs of certiorari to most of those cases on which the U.S. Circuit Courts are already in general agreement.

SS.7.C.3.11

12. Which statement identifies one way in which an appellate court differs from a trial court?

    A. An appellate court relies on a jury of impartial peers.
    B. An appellate court reviews the decisions of other courts.
    C. An appellate court is not subject to Constitutional limits.
    D. An appellate court decides questions of fact as well as law.

SS.7.C.3.8

13. In September 1957, President Dwight Eisenhower issued an Executive Order to protect nine African-American students facing racial violence at Central High School in Little Rock, Arkansas. President Eisenhower explained his actions to the nation in the televised address below.

Whenever normal agencies prove inadequate to the task and it becomes necessary for the executive branch of the federal government to use its powers and authority to uphold federal courts, the President's responsibility is inescapable. In accordance with that responsibility, I have today issued an Executive Order directing the use of troops under federal authority to aid in the execution of federal law at Little Rock, Arkansas. This became necessary when my proclamation of yesterday was not observed, and the obstruction of justice still continues.

What role was President Eisenhower exercising in issuing this Executive Order?

    A. Chief Diplomat   C. Party Chief
    B. Chief Legislator   D. Commander in Chief

SS.C.7.4.2

14. The excerpt below is from the charter of an international organization..

To maintain international peace and security, and to that end: to take effective collective measures for the prevention and removal of threats to the peace, and for the suppression (putting down) of acts of aggression or other breaches of the peace . . .

Which international organization has this purpose as its chief goal?

    A. United Nations (UN)
    B. World Trade Organization (WTO)
    C. International Red Cross/Red Crescent
    D. North Atlantic Treaty Organization (NATO)

SS.7.C.3.11

15. Which of these court decisions is an example of judicial review?

    A. The U.S. Supreme Court strikes down a state law as unconstitutional.
    B. The U.S. Supreme Court decides a dispute in which two states are parties.
    C. A trial court finds a defendant not guilty after barring illegally obtained evidence from the trial.
    D. The U.S. Court of Appeals for the 11th Circuit interprets an ambiguous phrase in the federal law.

SS.7.C.3.3

16. The newspaper headline on the left describes an event in U.S. history.

    Which parts of the national government cooperated to achieve the step announced in the headline?

    A. Cabinet and Senate
    B. Congress and President
    C. President and Supreme Court
    D. Congress and U.S. Chiefs of Staff

SS.7.C.3.3

17. The statement below was published in support of the Constitution.

    "Measures are too often decided, not according to the rules of justice and the rights of the minor party, but by the superior force of an interested and overbearing majority."
    —James Madison, *The Federalist, No. 10*

    Which feature of the Constitution was introduced to reduce the possible influence of an "overbearing majority"?

    A. having appointed rather than elected Supreme Court Justices
    B. the decision to place the executive branch in the hands of one person
    C. the requirement that the Senate confirm nominations by the President
    D. the establishment of a House of Representatives to represent the people

SS.7.C.3.8

18. How does an executive order differ from a federal statute?

    A. It is not approved by Congress.
    B. It is based on common-law principles.
    C. It is not subject to judicial review by the Supreme Court.
    D. It is not subject to limitations found in the U.S. Constitution.

SS.7.C.3.11

19. In which case would the U.S. Supreme Court have original jurisdiction?

    A. A dispute between a citizen of Florida and the Florida Department of Revenue.
    B. A dispute between a citizen of Florida and a hotel owner in California, over a civil rights issue.
    C. A dispute between the governments of Belgium and France over their boundaries.
    D. A dispute between North Dakota and South Dakota over diverting water from the Missouri River for irrigation and reservoirs.

SS.7.C.3.11

20. The diagram below provides details about the U.S. court system.

Which court completes the diagram?

A. Court martial
B. U.S. County Court
C. U.S. District Court
D. Florida Supreme Court

SS.7.C.3.8

21. How do Supreme Court decisions differ from laws passed by Congress?

A. Supreme Court decisions can be vetoed by the President.
B. Supreme Court decisions are not limited by the Constitution.
C. Supreme Court decisions can be "pigeonholed" in committee.
D. Supreme Court decisions are explained by a majority opinion.

SS.7.C.3.10

22. Naval Commander John Hart is accused of stealing $10,000 from the payroll purser during his tour of duty in the Arabian Sea near the Persian Gulf. Which type of law will he be subject to?

A. civil
B. criminal
C. military
D. constitutional

SS.7.C.3.6

23. The list below includes some of the rights of American citizens in legal proceedings.

- Right to have an attorney
- Right to be heard if accused
- Right not to have cruel or unusual punishment
- Right not to have double jeopardy

Which term is used to describe these rights?

A. Equal Protection rights
B. Arraignment rights
C. Due Process rights
D. Eminent domain rights

SS.7.C.3.10

24. Which statement identifies an important difference between civil and criminal trials?

　A. Juries only hear criminal cases.
　B. Only a criminal proceeding can be appealed.
　C. Lawyers only cross-examine witnesses in criminal trials.
　D. The defendant is presumed innocent only in criminal trials.

SS.7.C.3.11

25.

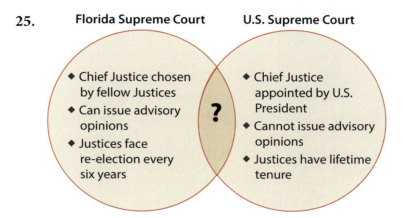

Which statement completes the Venn diagram?

　A. Consists of 9 Justices
　B. Exercises powers of judicial review
　C. Is the highest authority on federal law
　D. Is required to review all death penalty cases

SS.7.C.3.9

26. The diagram below shows some of the steps involved in passing a Florida state law.

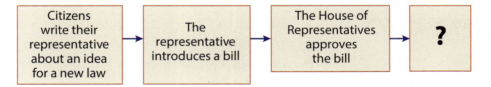

Which step comes next in the diagram?

　A. The Governor signs the bill into law
　B. The bill goes to the Senate for action
　C. The people vote on the bill in an election
　D. The bill goes to the Supreme Court for a hearing

SS.7.C.3.10

27. Which type of law protects our fundamental rights as individuals?

　A. civil law
　B. criminal law
　C. constitutional law
　D. military law

Chapter 18 | A Practice End-of-Course Assessment in Civics   471

SS.7.C.2.4

28. Which name is given to the first ten amendments to the U.S. Constitution?
    A. Bill of Rights
    B. Reserved Powers
    C. Civil War Amendments
    D. Articles of Confederation

SS.7.C.2.4

29. The passage below is from the Sixth Amendment to the U.S. Constitution.

    In all criminal prosecutions, the accused shall enjoy the right to a speedy and public trial, by an impartial jury . . . and to be informed of the nature and cause of the accusation; to be confronted with the witnesses against him; to have compulsory process for obtaining witnesses in his favor, and to have the assistance of counsel for his defen[s]e.

    How do the rights provided in this amendment help to protect democracy?
    A. They make it difficult for police officials to search citizens without just cause.
    B. They make it difficult for government officials to imprison political opponents.
    C. They protect the rights of citizens to publish remarks criticizing the government.
    D. They prevent government officials from taking private property without fair compensation.

SS.7.C.3.12

30. Which statement summarizes the outcome of the 1954 U.S. Supreme Court case *Brown v. Board of Education*?
    A. Students had the right to protest government policies by wearing armbands in school.
    B. Amish parents could not be forced to send their children to public high schools.
    C. Mexican-American children were entitled to protection from discrimination.
    D. States could not maintain segregated schools since racial segregation in public education is "inherently unequal."

SS.7.C.2.4

31. What has been a long-term effect of the First Amendment's guarantee of religious liberty?
    A. Americans have avoided divisive religious wars.
    B. Americans are less religious than people in most countries.
    C. Americans have established different official churches in each state.
    D. Americans with strong religious beliefs have generally left the United States.

SS.7.C.3.12

32. Which statement describes the outcome of the 1969 U.S. Supreme Court case *Tinker v. Des Moines*?
    A. Students were afforded the same "due process" rights as adults.
    B. Students had the right to wear armbands in school as an exercise of free speech.
    C. School authorities could censor school-sponsored student publications for legitimate educational purposes.
    D. States could not maintain racially segregated schools because segregation in public education was "inherently unequal."

SS.7.C.4.3

33. Which conflict did the United States enter after a surprise attack on the U.S. naval fleet in Pearl Harbor, Hawaii?
    A. World War II
    B. Vietnam War
    C. First Gulf War
    D. Spanish-American War

SS.7.C.2.8

34. The passage below is from the preamble to a political platform.

    > *[We] seek a society based on personal liberty and responsibility—a society in which all individuals are sovereign over their own lives. . . . People have the right to engage in any activity that is peaceful and honest, and pursue happiness in whatever manner they choose.*

    Which political party's views are represented in this platform?
    A. Socialist Party
    B. Communist Party
    C. Democratic Party
    D. Libertarian Party

SS.7.C.2.8

35. Which statement identifies a positive impact of political parties on American political life?
    A. Parties divide Americans into hostile groups.
    B. Parties encourage people to vote in elections.
    C. Parties often present voters with one-sided, biased information.
    D. Parties raise so much campaign money that they make it hard for independent candidates to compete.

Chapter 18 | A Practice End-of-Course Assessment in Civics

SS.7.C.2.8

36. What has been a negative impact of political parties on American government?

   A. Political parties offer alternatives and encourage debate.
   B. Political parties offer opportunities for civic participation.
   C. Divisions between parties often prevent government from getting things done.
   D. Political parties serve as useful bridges uniting members of the legislative and executive branches behind common goals.

SS.7.C.2.11

37. A U.S. government poster from World War II is shown at the left.

   Which media technique is used in this poster to encourage women to leave their homes and go to work?

   A. bias against foreigners
   B. demonizing opponents
   C. glittering generalities
   D. propagandized appeals to patriotism

SS.7.C.3.2

38. The passage below describes the government of Saudi Arabia.

   > The Kingdom of Saudi Arabia is divided politically into thirteen provinces. Each is headed by an emir who is appointed by the King and who answers to the Ministry of the Interior. These 13 provinces are further divided into 118 governorates headed by local mayors. The provinces are created by the King's authority and can be eliminated at any time.

   Based on this passage, which system of government does the Kingdom of Saudi Arabia have?

   A. unitary
   B. federal
   C. confederal
   D. parliamentary

SS.7.C.3.1

39. Which statement applies to all types of monarchies?

   A. Their ruler holds absolute power, unlimited by Parliaments or constitutions.
   B. The monarch inherits his or her power.
   C. They combine the executive and legislative branches.
   D. The monarch's power, whether total or limited, is established in a written constitution.

SS.7.C.4.3

40. The diagram below gives details about an important event.

Which completes the diagram?
A. The United States sends troops into Kuwait.
B. The United States attacks the Taliban in Afghanistan.
C. The United States places economic sanctions on Iran.
D. The United States overthrows Saddam Hussein in Iraq.

SS.7.C.4.3

41. How did President John F. Kennedy respond to the threat of nuclear missiles in Cuba?
A. He sent an army of exiles to invade Cuba at the Bay of Pigs.
B. He launched air strikes on Cuba to destroy the missile sites.
C. He placed economic sanctions on both Cuba and the Soviet Union.
D. He established a blockade around Cuba and threatened a U.S. invasion.

SS.7.C.2.2

42. Which action is a legal obligation of U.S. citizenship?
A. voting in all Presidential elections
B. serving on a jury when summoned
C. supporting one's parents in their old age
D. keeping informed about major public issues

SS.7.C.2.1

43. The diagram below shows some of the requirements for becoming a naturalized citizen.

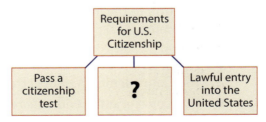

Which statement completes the diagram?
A. Be at least 21 years of age
B. Have served in the U.S. armed forces
C. Have a close relative who is a U.S. citizen
D. Have resided in the United States for five years

Chapter 18 | A Practice End-of-Course Assessment in Civics

SS.7.C.2.1

44. The passage below is from the Fourteenth Amendment.

"All persons born or naturalized in the United States, and subject to the jurisdiction thereof, are citizens of the United States and of the State wherein they reside."

What is an additional way for a person to have U.S. citizenship?

A. by treaty agreements
B. by purchasing citizenship
C. by having valuable work skills
D. by having U.S. citizens as parents

SS.7.C.3.12

45. What was the significance of the 1803 Supreme Court decision of *Marbury v. Madison*?

A. The Court defined free speech rights.
B. The Court upheld the existence of slavery.
C. The Court placed limits on the "Elastic" Clause.
D. The Court established the power of judicial review.

SS.7.C.3.12

46. What was the outcome of the 1974 Supreme Court decision *United States v. Nixon*?

A. Government surveillance of antiwar demonstrators during the Vietnam War was halted.
B. President Nixon was unable to block the publication of *The Pentagon Papers* in *The New York Times*.
C. A manual recount of votes in Florida was halted because of insufficient guidelines and inconsistent practices.
D. Executive privilege did not excuse President Nixon from handing over tapes of his conversations to investigators.

SS.7.C.3.12

47. The petition to the left was sent from prison by Clarence Earl Gideon to the U.S. Supreme Court.

What was the outcome of the petition?

A. The Court denied writ of certiarori to Gideon.
B. The Court granted Gideon's request for a writ of *Bill of Attainder*.
C. The Court ruled that minors have the same due process rights as adults.
D. The Court ruled that states must provide an attorney to those accused of a serious crime if they cannot afford one.

SS.7.C.2.4

48. Police entered Mr. Anderson's home without a warrant and without "probable cause." Which constitutional right of Mr. Anderson was violated?

    A. The Fifth Amendment right against double jeopardy.
    B. The Fifth Amendment right against self-incrimination.
    C. The Fourth Amendment right against unreasonable searches.
    D. The Sixth Amendment right against cruel and unusual punishments.

SS.7.C.2.5

49. Why did the authors of the Constitution prohibit *ex post facto* laws?

    A. Legislative bodies should not condemn individuals without a trial.
    B. It is unfair to penalize someone for behavior that was legal at the time.
    C. Judges with lifetime tenure might be tempted to use their power oppressively.
    D. Individuals should have the right to apply to a federal court against unjust imprisonment.

SS.7.C.3.7

50. How did passage of the Twenty-sixth Amendment affect the U.S. political process?

    A. Women were guaranteed the right to vote in all states.
    B. Poll taxes were no longer permitted for voting in federal elections.
    C. Citizens from 18 to 20 years old were given the right to vote.
    D. The federal government took over the regulation of statewide elections.

SS.7.C.2.10

51. What is one method that interest groups use to monitor government?

    A. They file lawsuits on special issues.
    B. They publish editorials in newspapers.
    C. They attend legislative committee hearings.
    D. They advise candidates on election strategies.

SS.7.C.4.1

52. Which action is an example of a foreign-policy decision?

    A. The President issued an Executive Order against cyber-bullying.
    B. Congress raised the residency requirement for naturalization to 7 years.
    C. The President signed an executive agreement with the President of Peru.
    D. The Supreme Court upheld the constitutionality of the Affordable Care Act.

SS.7.C.2.12

53. Maria is very upset that other students at her school are throwing litter on the school grounds. Which step should Maria probably take first to solve this problem?

    A. speak to her parents about changing her school
    B. write a letter to her Florida Representative and Senator
    C. speak to an attorney about filing a lawsuit against her school
    D. hold an after-school meeting with other concerned students

Chapter 18 | A Practice End-of-Course Assessment in Civics

SS.7.C.2.9

54. Monica and Max are running against each other for a seat on the county school board. Monica has been a teacher in another district for 15 years and has been elected twice to the school board. Max has no experience in educational administration but he owns a sporting goods store and would like to pay back his community for his success. Now that the county is doing better financially, Monica would like to bring back several student programs that were cut a few years ago. Max admits he is not familiar with the issues yet, but says he is a "quick learner." Why might Monica be considered more qualified than Max for the seat on the school board?

   A. She is less likely to spend money wastefully than Max.
   B. She has experience in the position and knows the issues.
   C. Teachers make better school board members than other professionals.
   D. People not in the education field should not try to help managing the schools.

SS.7.C.2.13

55. Review the statements below.

   Speaker 1: The Affordable Care Act creates too much government interference in our lives. We can handle our health insurance needs on our own.

   Speaker 2: We are the only major industrial nation that lacks national health care. This legislation can help to solve the problem by giving all Americans health care coverage.

   Which individual is most likely to share the perspective of the second speaker?

   A. a factory worker without health insurance
   B. a business owner with a small independent business
   C. a Tea Party member concerned about government expenditures
   D. a foreign visitor who has private health insurance in her home country

SS.7.C.1.2

56. How did Magna Carta influence the colonists' views of government?

   A. It encouraged them to declare their independence from Great Britain.
   B. It gave them the idea that everyone is entitled to certain natural rights.
   C. It led them to create a government based on a separation of powers among different branches.
   D. It granted them rights as English subjects, including the right to a trial by jury and not to be taxed without consent.

The Constitution of the United States

We the People of the United States, in Order to form a more perfect Union, establish Justice, insure domestic Tranquility, provide for the common defence, promote the general Welfare, and secure the Blessings of Liberty to ourselves and our Posterity, do ordain and establish this Constitution for the United States of America.

Article I

Section. 1. All legislative Powers herein granted shall be vested in a Congress of the United States, which shall consist of a Senate and House of Representatives.

Section. 2. The House of Representatives shall be composed of Members chosen every second Year by the People of the several States, and the Electors in each State shall have the Qualifications requisite for Electors of the most numerous Branch of the State Legislature.

No Person shall be a Representative who shall not have attained to the Age of twenty five Years, and been seven Years a Citizen of the United States, and who shall not, when elected, be an Inhabitant of that State in which he shall be chosen.

Representatives and direct Taxes shall be apportioned among the several States which may be included within this Union, according to their respective Numbers, which shall be determined by adding to the whole Number of free Persons, including those bound to Service for a Term of Years, and excluding Indians not taxed, three fifths of all other Persons. The actual Enumeration shall be made within three Years after the first Meeting of the Congress of the United States, and within every subsequent Term of ten Years, in such Manner as they shall by Law direct. The Number of Representatives shall not exceed one for every thirty Thousand, but each State shall have at Least one Representative; and until such enumeration shall be made, the State of New Hampshire shall be entitled to chuse three, Massachusetts eight, Rhode-Island and Providence Plantations one, Connecticut five, New-York six, New Jersey four, Pennsylvania eight, Delaware one, Maryland six, Virginia ten, North Carolina five, South Carolina five, and Georgia three.

When vacancies happen in the Representation from any State, the Executive Authority thereof shall issue Writs of Election to fill such Vacancies.

The House of Representatives shall chuse their Speaker and other Officers; and shall have the sole Power of Impeachment.

Section. 3. The Senate of the United States shall be composed of two Senators from each State, chosen by the Legislature thereof, for six Years; and each Senator shall have one Vote.

Immediately after they shall be assembled in Consequence of the first Election, they shall be divided as equally as may be into three Classes. The Seats of the Senators of the first Class shall be vacated at the Expiration of the second Year, of the second Class at the Expiration of the fourth Year, and of the third Class at the Expiration of the sixth Year, so that one third may be chosen every second Year; and if Vacancies happen by Resignation, or otherwise, during the Recess of the Legislature of any State, the Executive thereof may make temporary Appointments until the next Meeting of the Legislature, which shall then fill such Vacancies.

No Person shall be a Senator who shall not have attained to the Age of thirty Years, and been nine Years a Citizen of the United States, and who shall not, when elected, be an Inhabitant of that State for which he shall be chosen.

The Vice President of the United States shall be President of the Senate, but shall have no Vote, unless they be equally divided.

The Senate shall chuse their other Officers, and also a President pro tempore, in the Absence of the Vice President, or when he shall exercise the Office of President of the United States.

The Senate shall have the sole Power to try all Impeachments. When sitting for that Purpose, they shall be on Oath or Affirmation. When the President of the United States is tried, the Chief Justice shall preside: And no Person shall be convicted without the Concurrence of two thirds of the Members present.

Judgment in Cases of Impeachment shall not extend further than to removal from Office, and disqualification to hold and enjoy any Office of honor, Trust or Profit under the United States: but the Party convicted shall nevertheless be liable and subject to Indictment, Trial, Judgment and Punishment, according to Law.

Section. 4. The Times, Places and Manner of holding Elections for Senators and Representatives, shall be prescribed in each State by the Legislature thereof; but the Congress may at any time by Law make or alter such Regulations, except as to the Places of chusing Senators.

The Congress shall assemble at least once in every Year, and such Meeting shall be on the first Monday in December, unless they shall by Law appoint a different Day.

Section. 5. Each House shall be the Judge of the Elections, Returns and Qualifications of its own Members, and a Majority of each shall constitute a Quorum to do Business; but a smaller Number may adjourn from day to day, and may be authorized to compel the Attendance of absent Members, in such Manner, and under such Penalties as each House may provide.

Each House may determine the Rules of its Proceedings, punish its Members for disorderly Behaviour, and, with the Concurrence of two thirds, expel a Member.

Each House shall keep a Journal of its Proceedings, and from time to time publish the same, excepting such Parts as may in their Judgment require Secrecy; and the Yeas and Nays of the Members of either House on any question shall, at the Desire of one fifth of those Present, be entered on the Journal.

Neither House, during the Session of Congress, shall, without the Consent of the other, adjourn for more than three days, nor to any other Place than that in which the two Houses shall be sitting.

Section. 6. The Senators and Representatives shall receive a Compensation for their Services, to be ascertained by Law, and paid out of the Treasury of the United States. They shall in all Cases, except Treason, Felony and Breach of the Peace, be privileged from Arrest during their Attendance at the Session of their respective Houses, and in going to and returning from the same; and for any Speech or Debate in either House, they shall not be questioned in any other Place.

No Senator or Representative shall, during the Time for which he was elected, be appointed to any civil Office under the Authority of the United States, which shall have been created, or the Emoluments whereof shall have been encreased during such time; and no Person holding any Office under the United States, shall be a Member of either House during his Continuance in Office.

Section. 7. All Bills for raising Revenue shall originate in the House of Representatives; but the Senate may propose or concur with Amendments as on other Bills.

Every Bill which shall have passed the House of Representatives and the Senate, shall, before it become a Law, be presented to the President of the United States; If he approve he shall sign it, but if not he shall return it, with his Objections to that House in which it shall have originated, who shall enter the Objections at large on their Journal, and proceed to reconsider it. If after such Reconsideration two thirds of that House shall agree to pass the Bill, it shall be sent, together with the Objections, to the other House, by which it shall likewise be reconsidered, and if approved by two thirds of that House, it shall become a Law. But in all such Cases the Votes of both Houses shall be determined by yeas and Nays, and the Names of the Persons voting for and against the Bill shall be entered on the Journal of each House respectively. If any Bill shall not be returned by the President within ten Days (Sundays excepted) after it shall have been presented to him, the Same shall be a Law, in like Manner as if he had signed it, unless the Congress by their Adjournment prevent its Return, in which Case it shall not be a Law.

Every Order, Resolution, or Vote to which the Concurrence of the Senate and House of Representatives may be necessary (except on a question of Adjournment) shall be presented to the President of the United States; and before the Same shall take Effect, shall be approved by him, or being disapproved by him, shall be repassed by two thirds of the Senate and House of Representatives, according to the Rules and Limitations prescribed in the Case of a Bill.

Section. 8. The Congress shall have Power To lay and collect Taxes, Duties, Imposts and Excises, to pay the Debts and provide for the common Defence and general Welfare of the United States; but all Duties, Imposts and Excises shall be uniform throughout the United States;

To borrow Money on the credit of the United States;

To regulate Commerce with foreign Nations, and among the several States, and with the Indian Tribes;

To establish an uniform Rule of Naturalization, and uniform Laws on the subject of Bankruptcies throughout the United States;

To coin Money, regulate the Value thereof, and of foreign Coin, and fix the Standard of Weights and Measures;

To provide for the Punishment of counterfeiting the Securities and current Coin of the United States;

To establish Post Offices and post Roads;

To promote the Progress of Science and useful Arts, by securing for limited Times to Authors and Inventors the exclusive Right to their respective Writings and Discoveries;

To constitute Tribunals inferior to the supreme Court;

To define and punish Piracies and Felonies committed on the high Seas, and Offences against the Law of Nations;

To declare War, grant Letters of Marque and Reprisal, and make Rules concerning Captures on Land and Water;

To raise and support Armies, but no Appropriation of Money to that Use shall be for a longer Term than two Years;

To provide and maintain a Navy;

To make Rules for the Government and Regulation of the land and naval Forces;

To provide for calling forth the Militia to execute the Laws of the Union, suppress Insurrections and repel Invasions;

To provide for organizing, arming, and disciplining, the Militia, and for governing such Part of them as may be employed in the Service of the United States, reserving to the States respectively, the Appointment of the Officers, and the Authority of training the Militia according to the discipline prescribed by Congress;

To exercise exclusive Legislation in all Cases whatsoever, over such District (not exceeding ten Miles square) as may, by Cession of particular States, and the Acceptance of Congress, become the Seat of the Government of the United States, and to exercise like Authority over all Places purchased by the Consent of the Legislature of the State in which the Same shall be, for the Erection of Forts, Magazines, Arsenals, dock-Yards, and other needful Buildings;—And

To make all Laws which shall be necessary and proper for carrying into Execution the foregoing Powers, and all other Powers vested by this Constitution in the Government of the United States, or in any Department or Officer thereof.

Section. 9. The Migration or Importation of such Persons as any of the States now existing shall think proper to admit, shall not be prohibited by the Congress prior to the Year one thousand eight hundred and eight, but a Tax or duty may be imposed on such Importation, not exceeding ten dollars for each Person.

The Privilege of the Writ of Habeas Corpus shall not be suspended, unless when in Cases of Rebellion or Invasion the public Safety may require it.

No Bill of Attainder or ex post facto Law shall be passed.

No Capitation, or other direct, Tax shall be laid, unless in Proportion to the Census or enumeration herein before directed to be taken.

No Tax or Duty shall be laid on Articles exported from any State.

No Preference shall be given by any Regulation of Commerce or Revenue to the Ports of one State over those of another: nor shall Vessels bound to, or from, one State, be obliged to enter, clear, or pay Duties in another.

No Money shall be drawn from the Treasury, but in Consequence of Appropriations made by Law; and a regular Statement and Account of the Receipts and Expenditures of all public Money shall be published from time to time.

No Title of Nobility shall be granted by the United States: And no Person holding any Office of Profit or Trust under them, shall, without the Consent of the Congress, accept of any present, Emolument, Office, or Title, of any kind whatever, from any King, Prince, or foreign State.

Section. 10. No State shall enter into any Treaty, Alliance, or Confederation; grant Letters of Marque and Reprisal; coin Money; emit Bills of Credit; make any Thing but gold and silver Coin a Tender in Payment of Debts; pass any Bill of Attainder, ex post facto Law, or Law impairing the Obligation of Contracts, or grant any Title of Nobility.

No State shall, without the Consent of the Congress, lay any Imposts or Duties on Imports or Exports, except what may be absolutely necessary for executing it's inspection Laws: and the net Produce of all Duties and Imposts, laid by any State on Imports or Exports, shall be for the Use of the Treasury of the United States; and all such Laws shall be subject to the Revision and Controul of the Congress.

No State shall, without the Consent of Congress, lay any Duty of Tonnage, keep Troops, or Ships of War in time of Peace, enter into any Agreement or Compact with another State, or with a foreign Power, or engage in War, unless actually invaded, or in such imminent Danger as will not admit of delay.

Article II

Section. 1. The executive Power shall be vested in a President of the United States of America. He shall hold his Office during the Term of four Years, and, together with the Vice President, chosen for the same Term, be elected, as follows

Each State shall appoint, in such Manner as the Legislature thereof may direct, a Number of Electors, equal to the whole Number of Senators and Representatives to which the State may be entitled in the Congress: but no Senator or Representative, or Person holding an Office of Trust or Profit under the United States, shall be appointed an Elector.

The Electors shall meet in their respective States, and vote by Ballot for two Persons, of whom one at least shall not be an Inhabitant of the same State with themselves. And they shall make a List of all the Persons voted for, and of the Number of Votes for each; which List they shall sign and certify, and transmit sealed to the Seat of the Government of the United States, directed to the President of the Senate. The President of the Senate shall, in the Presence of the Senate and House of Representatives, open all the Certificates, and the Votes shall then be counted. The Person having the greatest Number of Votes shall be the President, if such Number be a Majority of the whole Number of Electors appointed; and if there be more than one who have such Majority, and have an equal Number of Votes, then the House of Representatives shall immediately chuse by Ballot one of them for President; and if no Person have a Majority, then from the five highest on the List the said House shall in like Manner chuse the President. But in chusing the President, the Votes shall be taken by States, the Representation from each State having one Vote; A quorum for this Purpose shall consist of a Member or Members from two thirds of the States, and a Majority of all the States shall be necessary to a Choice. In every Case, after the Choice of the President, the Person having the greatest Number of Votes of the Electors shall be the Vice President. But if there should remain two or more who have equal Votes, the Senate shall chuse from them by Ballot the Vice President.

The Congress may determine the Time of chusing the Electors, and the Day on which they shall give their Votes; which Day shall be the same throughout the United States.

No Person except a natural born Citizen, or a Citizen of the United States, at the time of the Adoption of this Constitution, shall be eligible to the Office of President; neither shall any Person be eligible to that Office who shall not have attained to the Age of thirty five Years, and been fourteen Years a Resident within the United States.

In Case of the Removal of the President from Office, or of his Death, Resignation, or Inability to discharge the Powers and Duties of the said Office, the Same shall devolve on the Vice President, and the Congress may by Law provide for the Case of Removal, Death, Resignation or Inability, both of the President and Vice President, declaring what Officer shall then act as President, and such Officer shall act accordingly, until the Disability be removed, or a President shall be elected.

The President shall, at stated Times, receive for his Services, a Compensation, which shall neither be encreased nor diminished during the Period for which he shall have been elected, and he shall not receive within that Period any other Emolument from the United States, or any of them.

Before he enter on the Execution of his Office, he shall take the following Oath or Affirmation:—"I do solemnly swear (or affirm) that I will faithfully execute the Office of President of the United States, and will to the best of my Ability, preserve, protect and defend the Constitution of the United States."

Section. 2. The President shall be Commander in Chief of the Army and Navy of the United States, and of the Militia of the several States, when called into the actual Service of the United States; he may require the Opinion, in writing, of the principal Officer in each of the executive Departments, upon any Subject relating to the Duties of their respective Offices, and he shall have Power to grant Reprieves and Pardons for Offences against the United States, except in Cases of Impeachment.

He shall have Power, by and with the Advice and Consent of the Senate, to make Treaties, provided two thirds of the Senators present concur; and he shall nominate, and by and with the Advice and Consent of the Senate, shall appoint Ambassadors, other public Ministers and Consuls, Judges of the supreme Court, and all other Officers of the United

States, whose Appointments are not herein otherwise provided for, and which shall be established by Law: but the Congress may by Law vest the Appointment of such inferior Officers, as they think proper, in the President alone, in the Courts of Law, or in the Heads of Departments.

The President shall have Power to fill up all Vacancies that may happen during the Recess of the Senate, by granting Commissions which shall expire at the End of their next Session.

Section. 3. He shall from time to time give to the Congress Information of the State of the Union, and recommend to their Consideration such Measures as he shall judge necessary and expedient; he may, on extraordinary Occasions, convene both Houses, or either of them, and in Case of Disagreement between them, with Respect to the Time of Adjournment, he may adjourn them to such Time as he shall think proper; he shall receive Ambassadors and other public Ministers; he shall take Care that the Laws be faithfully executed, and shall Commission all the Officers of the United States.

Section. 4. The President, Vice President and all civil Officers of the United States, shall be removed from Office on Impeachment for, and Conviction of, Treason, Bribery, or other high Crimes and Misdemeanors.

Article III

Section. 1. The judicial Power of the United States, shall be vested in one supreme Court, and in such inferior Courts as the Congress may from time to time ordain and establish. The Judges, both of the supreme and inferior Courts, shall hold their Offices during good Behaviour, and shall, at stated Times, receive for their Services, a Compensation, which shall not be diminished during their Continuance in Office.

Section. 2. The judicial Power shall extend to all Cases, in Law and Equity, arising under this Constitution, the Laws of the United States, and Treaties made, or which shall be made, under their Authority;—to all Cases affecting Ambassadors, other public Ministers and Consuls;—to all Cases of admiralty and maritime Jurisdiction;—to Controversies to which the United States shall be a Party;—to Controversies between two or more States;— between a State and Citizens of another State,—between Citizens of different States,—between Citizens of the same State claiming Lands under Grants of different States, and between a State, or the Citizens thereof, and foreign States, Citizens or Subjects.

In all Cases affecting Ambassadors, other public Ministers and Consuls, and those in which a State shall be Party, the supreme Court shall have original Jurisdiction. In all the other Cases before mentioned, the supreme Court shall have appellate Jurisdiction, both as to Law and Fact, with such Exceptions, and under such Regulations as the Congress shall make.

The Trial of all Crimes, except in Cases of Impeachment, shall be by Jury; and such Trial shall be held in the State where the said Crimes shall have been committed; but when not committed within any State, the Trial shall be at such Place or Places as the Congress may by Law have directed.

Section. 3. Treason against the United States, shall consist only in levying War against them, or in adhering to their Enemies, giving them Aid and Comfort. No Person shall be convicted of Treason unless on the Testimony of two Witnesses to the same overt Act, or on Confession in open Court.

The Congress shall have Power to declare the Punishment of Treason, but no Attainder of Treason shall work Corruption of Blood, or Forfeiture except during the Life of the Person attainted.

Article IV

Section. 1. Full Faith and Credit shall be given in each State to the public Acts, Records, and judicial Proceedings of every other State. And the Congress may by general Laws prescribe the Manner in which such Acts, Records and Proceedings shall be proved, and the Effect thereof.

Section. 2. The Citizens of each State shall be entitled to all Privileges and Immunities of Citizens in the several States.

A Person charged in any State with Treason, Felony, or other Crime, who shall flee from Justice, and be found in another State, shall on Demand of the executive Authority of the State from which he fled, be delivered up, to be removed to the State having Jurisdiction of the Crime.

erson held to Service or Labour in one State, under the Laws thereof, escaping into another, shall, in Consequence of any Law or Regulation therein, be discharged from such Service or Labour, but shall be delivered up on Claim of the Party to whom such Service or Labour may be due.

Section. 3. New States may be admitted by the Congress into this Union; but no new State shall be formed or erected within the Jurisdiction of any other State; nor any State be formed by the Junction of two or more States, or Parts of States, without the Consent of the Legislatures of the States concerned as well as of the Congress.

The Congress shall have Power to dispose of and make all needful Rules and Regulations respecting the Territory or other Property belonging to the United States; and nothing in this Constitution shall be so construed as to Prejudice any Claims of the United States, or of any particular State.

Section. 4. The United States shall guarantee to every State in this Union a Republican Form of Government, and shall protect each of them against Invasion; and on Application of the Legislature, or of the Executive (when the Legislature cannot be convened), against domestic Violence.

Article V

The Congress, whenever two thirds of both Houses shall deem it necessary, shall propose Amendments to this Constitution, or, on the Application of the Legislatures of two thirds of the several States, shall call a Convention for proposing Amendments, which, in either Case, shall be valid to all Intents and Purposes, as Part of this Constitution, when ratified by the Legislatures of three fourths of the several States, or by Conventions in three fourths thereof, as the one or the other Mode of Ratification may be proposed by the Congress; Provided that no Amendment which may be made prior to the Year One thousand eight hundred and eight shall in any Manner affect the first and fourth Clauses in the Ninth Section of the first Article; and that no State, without its Consent, shall be deprived of its equal Suffrage in the Senate.

Article VI

All Debts contracted and Engagements entered into, before the Adoption of this Constitution, shall be as valid against the United States under this Constitution, as under the Confederation.

This Constitution, and the Laws of the United States which shall be made in Pursuance thereof; and all Treaties made, or which shall be made, under the Authority of the United States, shall be the supreme Law of the Land; and the Judges in every State shall be bound thereby, any Thing in the Constitution or Laws of any State to the Contrary notwithstanding.

The Senators and Representatives before mentioned, and the Members of the several State Legislatures, and all executive and judicial Officers, both of the United States and of the several States, shall be bound by Oath or Affirmation, to support this Constitution; but no religious Test shall ever be required as a Qualification to any Office or public Trust under the United States.

Article VII

The Ratification of the Conventions of nine States, shall be sufficient for the Establishment of this Constitution between the States so ratifying the Same.

The Word, "the," being interlined between the seventh and eighth Lines of the first Page, The Word "Thirty" being partly written on an Erazure in the fifteenth Line of the first Page, The Words "is tried" being interlined between the thirty second and thirty third Lines of the first Page and the Word "the" being interlined between the forty third and forty fourth Lines of the second Page.

Attest William Jackson Secretary

done in Convention by the Unanimous Consent of the States present the Seventeenth Day of September in the Year of our Lord one thousand seven hundred and Eighty seven and of the Independance of the United States of America the Twelfth In witness whereof We have hereunto subscribed our Names.

The Bill of Rights
The First 10 Amendments to the Constitution

I

Congress shall make no law respecting an establishment of religion, or prohibiting the free exercise thereof; or abridging the freedom of speech, or of the press; or the right of the people peaceably to assemble, and to petition the Government for a redress of grievances.

II

A well regulated Militia, being necessary to the security of a free State, the right of the people to keep and bear Arms, shall not be infringed

III

No Soldier shall, in time of peace be quartered in any house, without the consent of the Owner, nor in time of war, but in a manner to be prescribed by law.

IV

The right of the people to be secure in their persons, houses, papers, and effects, against unreasonable searches and seizures, shall not be violated, and no Warrants shall issue, but upon probable cause, supported by Oath or affirmation, and particularly describing the place to be searched, and the persons or things to be seized.

V

No person shall be held to answer for a capital, or otherwise infamous crime, unless on a presentment or indictment of a Grand Jury, except in cases arising in the land or naval forces, or in the Militia, when in actual service in time of War or public danger; nor shall any person be subject for the same offence to be twice put in jeopardy of life or limb; nor shall be compelled in any criminal case to be a witness against himself, nor be deprived of life, liberty, or property, without due process of law; nor shall private property be taken for public use, without just compensation.

VI

In all criminal prosecutions, the accused shall enjoy the right to a speedy and public trial, by an impartial jury of the State and district wherein the crime shall have been committed, which district shall have been previously ascertained by law, and to be informed of the nature and cause of the accusation; to be confronted with the witnesses against him; to have compulsory process for obtaining witnesses in his favor, and to have the Assistance of Counsel for his defence.

VII

In Suits at common law, where the value in controversy shall exceed twenty dollars, the right of trial by jury shall be preserved, and no fact tried by a jury, shall be otherwise re-examined in any Court of the United States, than according to the rules of the common law.

VIII

Excessive bail shall not be required, nor excessive fines imposed, nor cruel and unusual punishments inflicted.

IX

The enumeration in the Constitution, of certain rights, shall not be construed to deny or disparage others retained by the people.

X

The powers not delegated to the United States by the Constitution, nor prohibited by it to the States, are reserved to the States respectively, or to the people.

INDEX

absolute monarchy, 87, 392, 394–395
Adams, John, 30, 227, 230
alien, 294
alliance, 30–32, 42–43, 57, 84, 423, 428, 431, 433, 442
ambassador, 83, 86, 111, 134, 424–426, 428
amendment, 84, 90, 111, 201–207, 209, 211–213, 232–237, 240–242, 265, 268–270, 274–275
appeal, 83, 154, 156–157, 178–180, 182, 185, 236–238, 242
appellate court, 154, 156–157, 159, 169, 178–179, 182
arms, right to bear, 10, 203, 207, 209, 235, 270
Articles of Confederation, 57–60, 67, 108, 133, 151, 405
assembly, right of, 202, 207
autocracy, 394

Bay of Pigs landing, 435–436
bias, 181, 205, 297, 327, 347, 350, 353–355
bill (lawmaking process), U.S., 117–118; Florida, 275–276
Bill of Rights, U.S., 90, 202–207, 209, 232–237, 265, 301–302
Bill of Rights, English 10, 12, 27, 90, 393
Boston Tea Party, 28
boycott, 27, 29, 213, 427, 435
Brown v. Board of Education, 242–243
Bush v. Gore, 246–247

Cabinet, U.S., 111, 135, 141, 424; Florida, 271–272; Parliamentary, 399
campaign finance, 331, 349
case law, 154, 174, 176
caucus (congressional), 114
checks and balances, 85, 87, 89, 95 (chart), 99, 113, 118, 133, 136, 151, 209, 424
Chief Justice, Florida Supreme Court, 179, 275
Chief Justice, U.S. Supreme Court, 140, 151, 154, 179
circuit courts, Florida, 178–180, 272
citizen, vi-vii, 293–300, 302
citizenship obligations, 295–297
citizenship responsibilities, 297–299

citizenship rights, 300–302; see also Bill of Rights
city/county commissioner: *see* commissioner
civic meetings, 298–299
civic participation, 297, 299
civil disobedience, 207, 212–213
civil law, 175, 180–183
Civil Rights Act of 1964, 213
colonial grievances, 29, 31–32, 39
Commander in Chief, 83, 88, 133, 135–136, 141, 424
commissioner, city/county, 276–277
common law, 173–174, 176
Common Sense, 3, 10–12, 29
communism, 324–325, 401–403, 434–439
Communist Party USA, 324–325
community service: see private community service solution
concurrent powers, 265–266
confederal system, 397–398
confederation, 397–398; see also Articles of Confederation
Confederation Congress, 57–59, 109
conference committee, U.S. Congress, 115–118
confession, 184, 204, 237
confirmation, 111, 136, 151, 227
Congress, U.S. 63–65, 82–83, 107–118, 424
constitution, 60, 268; see also Florida Constitution; U.S. Constitution
Constitutional Convention, 60–65, 79, 81, 85–86, 90, 107, 155
constitutional government, 61, 86
constitutional law, 174–176
constitutional monarchy: see limited monarchy
Continental Congress, 29, 30, 32, 46, 57–58, 108
council members, 277
counsel, right to legal, 231, 236; see also *Gideon v. Wainwright*
county commissioners: *see* commissioner
county courts, Florida, 178
court 151–152, 178; see also Supreme Court

court order, 152, 178, 227–228, 301
court summons: *see* summons
criminal law, 175, 184–185
cruel and unusual punishments, 12, 205
Cuban Missile Crisis, 436–437

debates, 89, 330–333
decisions based on the law, 171
Declaration of Independence, 12, 31, 43–44, 57, 60, 85, 203, 268
delegated powers, 112
democracy, 211–213, 297–298, 328, 393–395
Democratic Party, 321–322, 360–361
diplomacy, 425, 428–429
diplomats, 153, 424–425, 427–429, 442
direct democracy, 393–394
District of Columbia v. Heller, 203, 235
doctrine, 431, 435
domestic affairs, 423, 432
domestic policy, 423
double jeopardy, 204, 207
due process, 170–171, 204, 211–212, 238–240

economic freedom, 209
Elastic Clause, 109–110, 112
Electoral College, 65, 83, 111, 139, 246, 394
embassy, 424–425, 438
eminent domain, 204, 207
English Bill of Rights, see Bill of Rights
Enlightenment, 3, 6, 11–12, 391
enumerated powers, 82, 107, 109–110, 112, 265
Equal Protection Clause, 212, 240–242, 246
equal protection under the law, *see* Equal Protection Clause
Equal Rights Amendment, 212
ex post facto law, 301
executive order, 88, 135–136, 157

fair procedures, 170–171, 204, 212; see also due process
federal courts, 83, 108–109, 151–157, 159, 174–175, 301
federal system, 179, 265, 396–397, 405

486 Index

federalism, 206, 265–268, 396–397
Federalist Papers, 89–90
Fifteenth Amendment, 212
Fifth Amendment, 204, 237, 302
First Amendment, 90, 202, 207, 231–234, 302, 347
Florida Constitution, 268–275
Florida Declaration of Rights, 270
Florida Legislature, 271, 275
Florida Supreme Court, 178–180, 272
forced internment, 136, 205, 209
foreign affairs, 57, 423, 426
foreign policy, 88, 135, 137, 423–429, 431–440, 442–444
foreign relations, 135, 141, 424, 426
Founding Fathers, 11–12
Fourteenth Amendment, 211–212, 231, 236, 240–242, 246, 293–294
freedom of religion: *see* religion
freedom of the press: *see* press
freedom of speech, 202, 207, 231–232, 302, 325

George III, King, 29, 31, 41, 151
Gideon v. Wainwright, 236
government, v, 3–4, 31, 35, 391; forms and systems of, 392–403
government agency, 375, 380
Governor, 271–273, 397
grievances: *see* colonial grievances
Gulf War I, 439
Gulf War II, 440

habeas corpus, writ of, 238, 270, 300–301
Hazelwood v. Kuhlmeier, 233–234
House of Representatives, Florida, 270, 275–276
House of Representatives, U.S., 63–65, 82, 107, 110–111, 113–115, 117–118
immigrant, 108, 294–295
impeachment, 83, 110, 134, 139–141, 151–152, 231, 400
implied powers, 109–113, 135–136

In re Gault, 231, 238–239
interest group, 347–355, 358
international conflicts, 431–440
International Non-Governmental Organizations (NGO/INGO), 442, 444–445

international organizations, 428–429, 442–445
International Red Cross/Red Crescent, 444
international relations, 424
Intolerable Acts, 28
Iran Hostage Crisis, 438

Jefferson, Thomas, 30, 44, 135, 227, 230, 321
judge, 151–152, 178, 181–182, 184–185, 237–238
judicial branch, 6, 83, 151–157, 178, 272, 443
judicial review, 157, 179, 227–228, 230
jurisdiction, 152–154, 228, 230, 293
jury, 8, 11, 156, 173, 178, 181–182, 184–185, 204–205, 207, 296–297, 302
jury summons: *see* summons
justice, 79; for Supreme Court Justice, *see* U.S. Supreme Court
juvenile law, 175, 231, 238–240
juvenile rights, 240

Kennedy, John F., 351, 436–437
Korean War, 435

law, 169; *see also* rule of law
Law of Blood, 293
Law of Soil, 293
lawmaking process: *see* bill
Libertarian Party 325–326
limited monarchy, 9–10, 392–393
lobbying, 349–350
lobbyist, 349
Locke, John, 3, 10, 12, 31, 391
Madison, James, 59, 65, 87, 89–90, 202, 227, 230
Magna Carta, 8–11, 173
majority leader, 114, 116
majority vote, 111, 118, 151, 271, 276

Marbury v. Madison, 157, 227–230
Marshall, John, 157, 227–230
Marshall, Thurgood, 242
Mayflower Compact 9, 11–13
mayor, 277
media, 329–330, 351–353
military law, 175, 178
minority leader, 114, 116
Miranda v. Arizona, 237

monarchy, 9–11, 87, 90, 392–395
monitor (government), 347–349, 353
Montesquieu, Baron de, 6–7, 12, 63, 87, 107
multiple perspectives, 382

natural law, 3–4, 17, 31
natural rights, 3, 17, 31
naturalization, vi, 108, 293–295
naturalized citizen, 295
Nineteenth Amendment, 212
Ninth Amendment, 206
Nixon, Richard M., 244, 352, 429, 438
nomination, 111, 139, 329–330
Non-Governmental Organizations (NGO), 442, 444–445
North American Free Trade Agreement (NAFTA), 444–445
North Atlantic Treaty Organization (NATO), 428, 443

oligarchy, 394

Paine, Thomas, 11, 29–30, 46
pardon 88, 95, 134–135, 141, 271
Parliament, 4, 6, 9–12, 27–29, 173, 392–393, 395–400
parliamentary system, 398–400, 403
peacekeeping operations, of UN, 435, 442
permanent resident, of U.S., vi, 294, 301
petition, 10, 27, 29, 41, 90, 202–203, 299, 347, 375, 381
platform, 139, 321, 325, 327, 329, 333, 348
pleading the Fifth, 204
Plessy v. Ferguson, 240–242
policy, 27, 375–381, 423
political action committee (PAC), 331, 349
political advertisement, 330, 333, 358
political communication, 353–354, 358
political party, 114, 139, 298, 321–328, 348, 394
poll tax, 211–213, 265
Preamble, Florida Constitution, 268
Preamble, U.S. Constitution, 79–81
precedent, 174
President, U. S., 63, 65, 83, 110–111, 133–140, 244–247, 424–426, 429, 431–440

...sident pro tempore of the Senate, 114
press, freedom of, 202, 207, 209
Prime Minister, 399–400
privacy, 204, 207, 244
private community service solution, 375, 381
propaganda, 353–355, 358
property rights, 59, 204, 209
public good, 299, 381
public issue, 382–383, 393–394
public perspective, 382
public policy alternative, 375, 378
public policy solution, 380–381

quartering soldiers, 28, 32, 203

ratification, of amendments, 201
ratification, of U.S. Constitution, 84, 88–90, 202
ratification, of treaties, 111
Reagan, Ronald, 323, 352, 359–360, 438
religion, freedom of, 59, 90, 202, 211, 325
representative democracy, 328, 394–395
republic, 84, 394
Republican Party, 321–323, 326, 359–360
reserved powers, 265–266
right to bear arms: see arms
right to legal counsel: see counsel
rule of law, 169–171, 244–245

school board, 242, 277, 298–299
search and seizure, 203–204
Second Amendment, 203, 235
Secretary of State, U.S., 424–426
segregation, 240–243, 350
Selective Service, 296
self-government, 9, 11, 27
self-incrimination, 204, 237, 239, 270
Senate, Florida, 270–271, 275–276, 332
Senate, U.S., 107, 110–111, 113–115, 117–118, 424, 432

separation of powers, 6–7, 12, 63, 86–87, 89, 152, 209, 398–400, 424
Sharpton, Rev. Al, 359–361
Shays, Daniel: see Shays' Rebellion
Shays' Rebellion, 59
Sixth Amendment, 204–205, 236–237, 297
social contract, 3–5, 12, 17, 31, 85, 239, 268
socialism, 324, 401–402
Socialist Party, 324
sources of law, 173–176, 178
Speaker of the House, 114, 117
special committee, U.S. Congress, 28, 30, 115
special interest group, 117, 298, 347, 360
Stamp Act, 27
standing committee, U.S. Congress, 114–117
states' rights, 206, 325, 396
statutory law, 173–174, 176
suffrage, 212, 321
summary judgment, 152, 181
summons, 297
Supremacy Clause, 84, 265, 396–397
Supreme Court: see Florida or U.S. Supreme Court
symbolism, 354–355, 358

tax (taxation), 8, 10–12, 27–28, 30–31, 39, 57–58, 82, 107, 265, 296; see also poll tax
Tenth Amendment, 206, 265, 302, 397
Terrorism 431, 439–440
Thirteenth Amendment, 209, 211
Tinker v. Des Moines, 232
transparency of institutions, 170–171
treaty 111, 133, 428
trial by jury, 8, 11, 32, 39, 173, 205, 207, 302–303
trial court, 153, 156–157, 159, 179, 181–182, 272
Twenty-fourth Amendment, 212–213
Twenty-sixth Amendment, 213

unalienable rights, 31, 34, 44, 268
unenumerated rights, 206
unitary system, 403, 405
United Nations (UN), 428, 434, 442–445
United Nations Children's Fund (UNICEF), 444–445
United States v. Nixon, 244
U.S. Courts of Appeals, 156–157, 159
U.S. Constitution, 60–65, 79–90, 201; compared to Articles of Confederation, 67; interpretation of, 227–228; compared to Florida Constitution, 269
U.S. District Courts, 156, 159, 179
U.S. Supreme Court, 108–109, 134, 141, 151–157, 159, 170, 179, 227–228, 230, 231, 271

veto power: in U.S., 63, 83, 87, 95, 113, 118, 134, 136–137; in Florida, 271, 276; in UN, 428, 442
Vice President, 67, 83, 114, 116, 135, 138–140, 212, 271
Vietnam War, 135–136, 213, 296, 352, 437–438
voting, 44, 176, 213, 297–298, 300, 327, 329, 331, 358, 404
Voting Rights Act of 1965, 213

Washington, George, 29, 59–60, 135, 138, 321, 431
Watergate scandal, 244, 352
watchdog, 87, 107, 328, 352–353
World Court, 443, 445
World Trade Organization (WTO), 444–445
World War I, 135, 296, 428, 431–432
World War II, 135–136, 138, 296, 351, 355, 428, 432–435, 442
writ of certiorari, 154, 157
writ of *habeas corpus*: see *habeas corpus*